THE END OF "ISMS"?
Reflections on the Fate of Ideological Politics
after Communism's Collapse

THE END OF "ISMS"?
Reflections on the Fate of Ideological Politics after Communism's Collapse

Edited by Aleksandras Shtromas

BLACKWELL
Oxford UK & Cambridge USA

ISBN 0-631-19055-4

First published 1994

Blackwell Publishers
108 Cowley Road, Oxford, OX4 1JF, UK.

and

238 Main Street,
Cambridge, MA 02142, USA.

British Library Cataloguing in Publication Data
Applied for

Library of Congress Cataloguing in Publication Data
Applied for

Printed in Great Britain by Page Bros, Norwich

This book is printed on acid-free paper

CONTENTS

Introduction

The August 1991 collapse of Communist rule in Russia and the dissolution later in the same year of the Soviet Union, brought to inglorious end the historically unique seventy odd years long extraordinary experiment in construing a socio-political system according to an ideologically preconceived abstract blueprint and, then, in trying to make – by hook or by crook but still, as it now has been clearly proved, in vain – this system functional. The breakdown of communist totalitarianism in its Soviet cradle and the gradual coming apart of the remnant communist regimes in such places as China, Cuba, North Korea, etc., in the view of some social analysts, marked the conclusion of an entire era – an era in which ideology largely inspired and determined politics. According to these social analysts, the fall of communism has not merely fulfilled Daniel Bell's – at the time of his writing perhaps yet a premature – vision of the end of ideology; it, quoting the by now almost proverbial (and almost setting one's teeth on edge) Francis Fukuyama, brought to end history itself. Is it really so? Have we indeed seen the last of ideological politics? This book which is an enlarged and partly revised version of a special issue of *Political Studies* published in November 1993 is devoted to an in-depth discussion of those questions.

As editor, I tried to bring together for this discussion a group of authors who could cover the topic more or less comprehensively and, at the same time, expose the widest possible spectrum of views on the issues involved. Some difficult choices about the selection of particular topics had to be made, however, before an acceptably coherent structure of the contents of such an endeavour could be evolved. What I definitely wanted to include as first priority, was a general review and assessment of the state of ideological politics in the post-communist or post-Soviet world, done from at least two different, and preferably opposite, perspectives. Then, after such a general review and assessment have been made, I thought it necessary to present an analysis of the state of, and prospects for, Marxism and also non-Marxist socialism, given, again, from at least two, i.e. 'pro' and 'con', positions. Nor was there a way to avoid the discussion of the problem of the ideological potential of nationalism which, especially after the disappearance of communism and the end of Cold War, turned out to be in politics the major, if not the main, motivating force, promising to retain this role well into the 21st century. The fourth area I felt duty bound to include was the discussion of the situation with ideological politics in different regions of the world. Being unable to cover all or even most of them in the special issue of the journal, I decided to select only two, namely Russia and America, that is the very superpowers who waged and fought the forty years long Cold War on no other but ideological grounds. For the book, however, I could afford space also to cover the so called Third World which I have invited Professor Bhikhu Parekh to do. I also amended the book by my own piece in which I tried to summarize the discussion and also present my own assessment of the state of ideological politics in the contemporary world and the prospects for ideologies' shaping, or at least making a substantive impact on, politics in the foreseeable future.

It is for the reader to judge how well the ten authors writing for the book accomplished this plan. I personally think that the plan has been implemented quite adequately. Indeed, Kenneth Minogue and Noel O'Sullivan, dealing with the world's overall ideological situation, using for this purpose similar data and referring very often to the same phenomena, have come to pretty opposite assessments and conclusions. If Minogue sees an ominous ideological threat in what he calls the morality of egalitarian humanism; if, according to him, in a democracy this morality increasingly brings in the state to redress the balance of civil society and forcefully to menage it with the view of creating maximum happiness for the maximum number of people, O'Sullivan sees these same tendencies as rather positive and non-ideological trends representing 'the politics... of "inclusion" [of] the hitherto excluded sexual, racial, and ecological issues'; quoting Agness Heller, O'Sullivan states that with this politics of 'inclusion', 'we may be entering an era of "settling in"', following upon the era of ideology'. In the concluding paragraphs of my contribution, I try to take a stance on this controversy, too, and show that to a large extent the positions of Minogue and O'Sullivan are rather more complementary to one another than mutually exclusive.

The fate of socialism is the topic of David Marquand's essay. Recognizing that at present socialism is in a fatal crisis, Marquand however believes in its eventual resurrection, albeit most likely in a different conceptual structure and may be even under a different name. Socialism for him has an eternal dimension, as it ideally expresses the basic human need for communion and collective cooperation which, in his view, the capitalist market system is in principle unable to satisfy. Alex Callinicos is, however, much more radical. He bluntly denies the crisis of socialism which, according to him, has never been tested, and maintains that Marxism has suffered only an imaginary setback. To Callinicos, 'as long as capitalism continues on its unjust and destructive path, it is likely to find Marxism, in some form or other, confronting it'. And it was not socialism that has collapsed in the Soviet Union and Eastern Europe, but the Stalinist state which in its essence was not socialist but peculiarly capitalist. In Callinicos's own words, 'On this interpretation, the West triumphed not over 'existing socialism', but over a particularly antiquated form of capitalism'.

In contrast to both Marquand and Callinicos, Richard Ebeling treats socialism in every variety and form – from Marxist to mercantilist – as an ideological aberration and grave social disease. Socialism, as every other collectivist ideology, is to him a blunt denial of individual liberty, a system of ideas which, if implemented into practice, is capable only of creating a police state. Ebeling produces a staunch and powerful defence of classical liberalism, of its modern interpretations by such thinkers and scholars as Ludwig von Mises and Friedrich von Hayek, and concludes his essay by expressing hope that at the threshold of the 21st century a new generation, clearly seeing the preposterous absurdity of any shape of socialist collectivism and therefore naturally adherent to the constitution of liberty, may finally arise and triumph. Ebeling has enlarged his contribution to the book by devoting more attention to the critique of the social-democratic perspective and especially of its representation by Marquand in the special issue and this volume. A substantial part of my chapter of the book is devoted to the summing up of, and making positive conclusions from, this 'Marquand-Callinicos-Ebeling' debate, as well as to discussing the present and the potential future standing of both Marxist and non-Marxist socialism/communism in the world of political ideas and practical politics.

Although meant chiefly to illuminate the ideological situation in the Third World, Parekh's two contributions to this volume did in fact much more than just that. His piece on 'Decolonizing Liberalism', despite of its almost exclusive concentration on the deficiencies and setbacks of Liberalism in India and other former British colonies, represents indeed a much more universally set discussion of the role and fate of liberal ideology in the contemporary world at large. His singling out of the Millian variety of Liberalism and his smashing critique of this abstract and dogmatic creed unacceptable to the Third World and therefore likely to be rejected by its mainstream social forces, makes Parekh's analysis highly relevant not only to the ideological situation in a specific region of the world but also, and mainly, to liberalism's position and place as one of the leading world ideologies. It aptly qualifies the undifferentiated praise of Liberalism by Ebeling and therefore, as a piece continuing the discussion of Liberalism, had to be put in the volume after Ebeling's chapter.

Parekh's chapter on Religious Fundamentalism is also dealing with a problem of a rather universal dimension. For religious fundamentalism is indeed not merely a Third World ideology but an ideologically conceived response to the challenges of modernization, and to the levelling which goes with it, by traditionalistically minded people all over the world. In a way, such fundamentalism could be seen as one of the more extreme (and really ideological) forms of nationalist self-assertion, which makes Parekh's work on that subject an apt introduction to the general discussion of nationalism and its ideological contents – that is to the essay contributed to the special issue of the journal by the recently deceased veteran researcher of this problem, Eugene Kamenka. Kamenka's chapter in the book is thus logically following Parekh's treatment of fundamentalism.

Although he does not say so directly, Kamenka seems to deny to nationalism the very quality of an ideology. To him it is rather a natural orientation of people in establishing their primary collective identity and in trying to get proper recognition for that identity from other such collective groups or nations. Kamenka acknowledges of course that nationalism provides a fertile ground for developing a proper ideology, as it did in the cases of Fascism and Nazism in the interwar period. He talks about it a great deal and devotes a large part of his essay to the exploration of the ideological potential of contemporary nationalisms. Kamenka is however quite sceptical about the present day nationalist ideologues being able to become new Mussolinis and Hitlers, that is such leaders of their respective nations who would be able to commit these nations to the pursuit of globally conceived ideological goals. According to him, present day nationalist rulers, however authoritarian, do not have either the power or the strength of conviction to become truly totalitarian, that is requiring and wanting a world in their ideas' own image. They are nation, not world, centred, and, as such, are pragmatic opportunists setting themselves practically realizable, limited goals and willing, in order to achieve these goals, to make deals without ideological prejudice.

Finally, Marc Raeff and Robert Faulkner deal, respectively, with the ideological situations in Russia and the USA. Faulkner's essay is truly encyclopaedic which explains its relative length. British and generally non-American readers will get from it a fairly comprehensive picture and an astute interpretation of the

4 ALEKSANDRAS SHTROMAS

ideologies and policy orientations, presenting themselves in the guise of one or another "ism", competing on the American political stage today. Raeff, on the contrary, engages into an historical analysis of Russia's political culture trying to draw from it informed conclusions about the role ideologies may play in post-Soviet Russian politics.

In my own rather extended piece which concludes the volume, I do not discuss any regional or country related issues and thus do not comment on either Faulkner's or Raeff's pieces. I draw, however, a lot from Parekh's and Kamenka's contributions in my own discussion of liberalism, religious fundamentalism and nationalism.

In conclusion, I would like to thank all authors for their cooperation. After all, this special issue is the product of their collective effort. I really appreciate the graciousness with which they bore my, no doubt sometimes irritating, urgings and naggings to meet one or another requirement or a deadline, etc. I hope they will be as magnanimous in reacting to the comments on their work made in my contribution to this volume. I would also like to thank the editorial board of *Political Studies* and personally Jack Hayward for their attentiveness to all my needs and all other invaluable help in producing this volume. My very special thanks go to Terry McNeill. Without his wise comments and suggestions, without his constant care and generous willingness to help with the work on this project at every single stage of its realization, the whole enterprise would have flopped. I am extremely grateful to the wonderful people at Blackwell, especially Sue Corbett and Helen Simmons, with whom it was so easy and such a pleasure to work and who showed such a remarkable patience in dealing with all my transgressions against the accepted procedures of doing the job, as well as with my constant timetable breaches. And, finally, I wish to thank Carol Kratzer who devotedly spent long hours during many a day creating an orderly manuscript out of my hasty and confusing notes, as well as my wife Violeta for so kindly putting up with me when I had for over two years to divert so much attention from her and our family life to the completion of this work.

ALEKSANDRAS SHTROMAS
Hillsdale College, Michigan

Ideology after the Collapse of Communism

KENNETH MINOGUE*

London School of Economics

The collapse of communism has not, as might be expected, led to the end of ideologies. Instead of the grand revolutionary projects of the past, however, we now have a set of overlapping fragments of revelation which cooperate with each other in social transformation. These fragments exhibit an 'identity monism' which can tell us something about the character of ideology in general. This form of monism is the necessary condition of turning a modern state into a managed enterprise for the satisfaction of human needs – a project which happens also to be adumbrated in much normative political philosophy. A managed civil state responds to opinion rather than interest, and the opinions on which the project rests commend themselves by some version of self-evidence.

I

That the collapse of communism marks the end of an epoch has been argued by (among others) Francis Fukuyama, and makes a useful starting point from which to consider the contemporary situation of ideology. Liberal democracy, Fukuyama believes, is the 'end of history' in the sense that it solves the problem of recognition which, on Kojeve's interpretation of Hegel, had been the motor of history. Henceforth, politics must be understood in liberal-democratic terms, and liberal democracy is the master political form of the future.

It would follow that the Soviet collapse is also the end of ideology, and many commentators have seen Fukuyama as a direct successor to Bell, Glazer, Lipset and others who in the 1960's thought that the encounter of grand systems of ideas with names like communism and fascism had come to an end. Instead, what one might call 'normal politics' would resume. Normal politics is here the politics of liberal democracy, in which an endless stream of proposals is advanced, criticized, and implemented within the argumentative conditions of parliamentary democracy.

Ideologies, by contrast, were theories purporting to expose the repressive character of the entire system of liberal democracy. They purported to unmask the generally accepted belief that the modern state was an achievement of freedom for all after the oppressions of feudalism and slave societies. The cunning of the modern system was thought to be its concealment of the way in which power was exercised. Ideologies, intellectually triadic in structure, saw everything in terms of present *oppression*, emerging *struggle* and ultimate

* Dr Kenneth Minogue is Professor of Political Science at the London School of Economics.

liberation. Within that evolution, struggle was the dynamic arising from contradictions, and gave to everything a simplifying duality: *every* utterance in a divided society reflected either a defence of the *status quo* or a progressive position. For example, Lenin:

> . . . there can be no 'impartial' social science in a society based on class struggle. In one way or another, *all* official and liberal science *defends* wage-slavery, whereas Marxism has declared relentless war on that slavery. To expect science to be impartial in a wage-slave society is as foolishly naive as to expect impartiality from manufacturers on the question of whether workers' wages ought not to be increased by decreasing the profits of capital.[1]

Everything on the Marxist view, indeed on any ideological view, was thus politics. Claims to neutrality, impartiality or disinterestedness were the bogus expressions of the repressive system itself.

There is no doubt that the most familiar name for this repressive system is 'capitalism' and Marxism is the archetypal ideology. Others, however, fishing for other frustrations, called it 'patriarchy', 'imperialism', 'heterosexualism' and much else. Marx was certainly the genius who explored most of the possibilities of what I would argue is a quite specific intellectual form.[2] The intellectual influence of Marxism merely reflected its superiority, and later ideologists paid it the tribute of plagiarism by taking over the idea of a proletariat, the preoccupation with laws of history, the centrality of struggle and the insistence that all of us in the modern world live within a total system which must be unmasked and destroyed on the path of liberation.

Marx had insisted, however, that practice and theory were intimately connected. Being an intellectual opportunist, he changed his doctrines as his situation changed, and he never spelled out the conditions under which it would be appropriate to conclude that he had got it wrong: to have done so would have quite destroyed his cultivated image as the spokesman of Reality itself. Nevertheless, after the slaughter of millions and the destruction of many states, with varying political cultures, constructed in the name of doctrines purporting to be his, it is hard for anyone with a straight face to take up the position satirized in *New Yorker* cartoons as, 'O.K. back to the drawing board'. Fukuyama might have got a lot wrong but on the death of Marxism it would be hard to fault him – though looking at contemporary universities, one must remember Cicero's saying that there is nothing so absurd that it cannot be found in the works of the philosophers.

It is thus plausible, though not necessarily conclusive, to argue that the failure of Marxist regimes in practice amounted to their refutation in theory, and most people have certainly taken that view. That is why the end of communism might plausibly be taken as the final proof of the end of ideology. Instead, however, ideologies of one kind and another seem to be thriving. It is this new situation whose contours I wish to discuss. But first we must clarify the confusing idea of ideology itself.

[1] V.I. Lenin, 'The three sources and three component parts of Marxism' in *On Culture and Cultural Revolution* (Moscow, Progress Publishers, 1966), p. 33.
[2] I have argued this thesis in *Alien Powers: The Pure Theory of Ideology* (London, Weidenfeld & Nicolson, 1985).

II

The term was first used, of course, by Destutt de Tracy in the 1790's to describe a science of mental clarification by way of analysing concepts into their empirical components. It rapidly became a term of abuse, however, and was canonically used by Marx and Engels in 1846 to refer to the false ideas in philosophy and economics generated by uncritical reflectors of bourgeois society. The same word thus confusingly came to be used first for the cure for a kind of mental disease and then for the disease itself. After Marx things got even worse: the word stood in different contexts for *both* the cure *and* the disease: bourgeois ideology being the disease of thought to be cured by Marxism as the science of social reality, itself coming to be recognized as also (in a different sense) an ideology – that of the proletariat whose social location allowed them direct access to reality. Such was, for example, the Leninist usage. Perhaps the best way to understand this confusing range of references is to report that Marxism claimed to be the direct representation of reality, or true consciousness, and as such, not really a set of 'ideas' at all; bourgeois ideology, by contrast, was essentially a set of *mere* ideas, and therefore not only socially determined but also false.

It would have been a happy outcome if academic political scientists had left this terminology alone but they could not resist it. As the term 'ideology' floated into the academic world, the sociologists took up the idea that what most people thought about their own societies was a function of their social location.[3] Political scientists popularized the term as signifying any political doctrine whatsoever (as well as some bodies of ideas, like democracy, which were not political doctrines in this sense at all).[4]

The basic situation is thus that the term 'ideology' incorporates the contradiction of referring both to truth and to falsity. So comprehensive a range of reference has the power of subjecting the entire domain of thought to its malevolent confusions, with the remarkable result that *everything* has often been claimed to be ideology (including science, mathematics, history etc.) and any attempt to stand back and analyse the concept of ideology has been regularly slapped down as being itself ideological. Indeed, much of the literature consists of little else but misguided attempts to elicit a satisfactory definition of the term.

The way out of this appalling maze is to recognize, I suggest, that ideology as the truth about everything, on the one hand, and ideology as the false ideas being analysed in terms of the truth on the other, are two parts of a single doctrine, and that any such doctrine has a logic of its own. Taking Marxism as our paradigm, we find an explanation of human development presented as a revelation only now becoming available to the human race. Marx speaks for nothing less than reality itself. In need of a location in the contemporary map of knowledge, he opportunistically presented his revelation as *scientific* socialism, rhetorically exploiting the form of knowledge then commonly identified with truth itself. Marx's revelation, however, is quite different from a scientific hypothesis, and Marx and his successors picked and chose in science for those of its con-temporary conclusions convenient to them in assembling their account of the world. Any ideology claims to be the revelation of a total knowledge superior to

[3] The most famous version of this line is, of course, Karl Mannheim's *Ideology and Utopia* (London, Routledge & Kegan Paul, 1960).

[4] See, for example, Lyman Tower Sargent, *Contemporary Political Ideologies: A Comparative Analysis* (Pacific Grove, California, Brooks/Cole, 8th edn, 1990). For a recent British version of the genre, see Andrew Vincent, *Modern Political Ideologies* (Oxford, Blackwell, 1992).

all competitors, including science, philosophy and history. It is in this sense that ideology shares important logical features with religion.

There is in fact nothing particularly scientific about Marx's method (and much that is very unscientific about the dogmatic way he carries on). The actual ground of ideological certainty is that old familiar philosophical recourse of self-evidence. It is all derived from propositions such as 'Man must eat' and 'all history is the history of class struggle' which commend themselves irresistibly as they become entangled with a mass of vaguely confirmatory material about contemporary life. And as with all revelations, its truth is not empirical but criteriological. Once established as a conviction, the revelation floats free of any evidence; on the contrary, it *determines* the evidence.

What immediately follows from this criteriological role is that most current competing beliefs are revealed as false. In fact *everything* is revealed as false to the extent that it fails to confirm the revelation. Since Marx got most of his ideas from Hegel, the logical type of falsity invoked is usually that of abstraction. Bourgeois economics may over a stretch correspond to realities, but is false in failing to understand the place of production within the system of capitalism. The doctrine of Marxism and the errors of bourgeois thought are thus logical correlates of each other, and that is why the term 'ideology' can be used to cover this entire spectrum of thought.

How, one might ask, does this argumentative minuet differ from the ordinary give and take of argument in which anyone who asserts that anything is the case makes an implicit claim to truth? The answer to this question is complicated by the fact that almost anything can be taken by some people as revelatory and therefore as a ground for dogmatism; contrariwise, the believer in an ideology can take on the manners and character of someone merely advancing a theory – as happens, for example, when ideologists adopt academic protective colouration. But the basic answer lies in the logic of ideology. Those who characterize ideologies as 'action-oriented' are no doubt correct but one striking feature of ideologies is that, at their core, they do not advocate, exhort, propose or concern themselves with policy except tactically. Marx and Engels do indeed call on the workers to arise but the core of the ideology consists in an argument about the logic of social systems leading inexorably to the conclusion that capitalism, as contradictory to the essence of man, must collapse and be replaced by a true community. What constitutes an ideology as an ideology is precisely this claim to truth, and to truth of a higher, criteriological kind. To someone who might object that it would be unwise for the workers to arise since it would lead to violence and bloodshed, the Marxist response would be in terms of the irrelevance of such a comment. For the issue between the Marxist and an opponent is never a matter of what we *ought* to do. It is rather a matter of *how* an oppressive system is in the process of being replaced by another form of life.

An ideology therefore radiates truth of a higher kind, and thus illuminates the darkness of that other sense of ideology as false belief. This is why the term 'correctness' springs easily to the lips of ideologists because at any moment there usually is an ideologically correct line. What this entails is a special kind of relationship between the believer on the one hand and the mass of people sunk in false consciousness on the other; it is a tutorial relationship, a relationship of correction. And this, as one would expect of people who spend so much time thinking about power, is unmistakably a power relationship.

Ideology is thus distinguished by a specific logic and it is this logic which determines the sociology of relations between insiders and outsiders; that relationship in turn shapes the regimes in which ideologists have come to power. An elite party, or vanguard, takes over all power and proceeds to tutor the population in how to think and to act. Ideology is, as Hannah Arendt remarked, the logic of an idea; an ideological regime is the following through of this idea. And as Marx himself remarked,

> Social life is essentially *practical*. All mysteries which mislead theory to mysticism find their rational solution in human practice and in the comprehension of this practice.[5]

This famous remark is powerful but never totally conclusive evidence even from within the Marxist canon that the collapse of communism is the collapse of its ideology. However that may be, it certainly would seem difficult to deny the difference between a so-called one-party state in which a single doctrine is imposed on a society, and a liberal democratic state whose theories are institutionalized in the give and take of party debate and discussion in the media and throughout the country. Can it really be denied that there is a logical difference between the sets of beliefs involved in these two basically different situations?

Admittedly, reality itself is complicated by the fact that political doctrines adapt to the circumstances in which they find themselves. Communists living in a liberal democracy have had little option but to enter the discussion as one party among others.

Marxism is thus a model ideology and its regimes supply abundant evidence of the connection between theory and practice. Any regime to the extent that it is totalitarian will be based on a revelation of an ideological kind. Hence Nazism and fascism have been linked with communism as totalitarian ideologies, but religions may well function in a similar way. They are, after all, paradigm revelations, and the ambitions of Islamic fundamentalism in the modern world are certainly politico-tutorial in the way we have described. Indeed, anyone looking for religious analogues of the logic of ideology need go no further than early Christianity. For St. Augustine, the Christian revelation is criteriological in precisely the same way as ideology is for the ideological believer. It is what makes sense of everything and St. Augustine attacks pagan philosophers as dealers in mere ideas – as men prostituting their wits to their own fancies, as *fantastica fornicatio*.[6] This is ideology *avant la lettre*.

In specifying other ideologies, one must remember the mixed and contingent character of actual human thought and argument, and thus not put our trust in names. Much feminism, for example, is purely ideological, especially as it develops in the protective colouring of universities; but the term 'feminism' also refers to a sequence of proposals for changing the law and conventions regulating relations between men and women. And proposals, backed by reasons, advanced against others recognized as rational beings rather than creatures sunk in false consciousness, are not the stuff of ideology. 'Anarchism', 'syndicalism' and 'libertarianism' are all names of a miscellany of doctrines sometimes presented in ideological form, and sometimes as a family of proposals and political principles.

---

[5] Theses on Feuerbach VIII, *Karl Marx, Friedrich Engels Complete Works*, vol. 3, (London, Lawrence & Wishart, 1976), p. 8.

[6] See the discussion of this argument in Charles Norris Cochrane, *Christianity and Classical Culture* (Oxford, Oxford University Press, 1944), Ch. XII.

The interests of a variety of groups ranging from ethnic minorities to homosexuals or the disabled have been turned into ideologies by some intellectuals.

III

There is, then, a basic difference in logic, sociology and political outcome between ideologies on the one hand, and political doctrines on the other. It is also a difference in the passions. Ideologists, persuaded that they are living within an evil system against which they are struggling, are alienated from their society and often characterized by hatred of it. In the past, communists often found an outlet for this hatred in illusions about the utopian character of achieved Marxist regimes, and some of them went so far as to betray their own countries.[7] Black power ideologists have sometimes dreamed of an African perfection but little plausibility is left in such dreams. The situation of most ideologists today – feminists or anarchists, for example – blocks any indulgence in these utopian fantasies. Where would women find a better place? And whereas one might well conceive of a workers' state, there are problems about an all-female society.

This is not at all to say that contemporary ideologists are not alienated from their own societies. Indeed, one of the more remarkable features of ideology in our century is that the more the practicality of these dreams of liberation declines, the more intense is the hatred felt by many ideologists for the world in which they are doomed to live and the human beings with whom they are doomed to share it. By contrast with ideology, those who engage in the actual politics of modern liberal democratic societies share with the populations they rule a unifying patriotism and a respect for the shared rituals of everything from parliamentary government to respect for those who died in war.

Now the basic distinction I am using, which makes a sharp separation in logic, sociology and political practice between ideology and politics, is subject to a basic ideological counter move. Let us meet it in the words of Alasdair MacIntyre quoted with approval in a recent work on ideology:

> . . . the end of ideology theorists 'failed to entertain one crucial alternative possibility: namely, that the end-of-ideology, far from marking the end-of-ideology, was itself a key expression of the ideology of the time and place where it arose.'[8]

It is, as we have seen in the quotation from Lenin, a cardinal tenet of ideological thinking that there is no escape from ideology; everyone either expresses the ideological revelation or the false consciousness of the current system. MacIntyre is an acute philosopher but he has a regrettable tendency to come down with ideologies the way some people catch colds.

The most obvious thing to say about this remark is its irrelevance. I am advancing a distinction in logic and politics not altogether dissimilar from one advanced by the 'end of ideology' theorists, who were much mocked for it. But the *academic* issue raised by such an argument is simple: Is it true? This question

---

[7] The classic account of this phenomenon is Paul Hollander, *Political Pilgrims* (New York, Oxford University Press, 1981).

[8] Vincent, *Modern Political Ideologies*, pp. 12–13. The remark is from McIntyre's, *Against the Self-Images of the Age* (London, Duckworth, 1971), p. 5.

no doubt ramifies into others about its range, usefulness, coherence and so on, but it is the issue of truth on which we may focus. If this is in fact the basic issue, then whether or not this supposed truth itself expresses an ideology (Vincent, who mounts this argument, calls it 'pragmatic liberalism') is at best a secondary question. If it is raised at all, this secondary question must also force us to ask whether certain truths ought not to be advanced because they have such and such an ideological character. If my argument is in fact ideological, what is it that follows? Does it follow that it is therefore false? And what prevents me from saying that the critic's characterization of *my* argument as itself ideology is, in its turn, also ideological, and therefore presumably non-academic. We are happily embarked on a regress, yet books on ideology are full of these pointless gyrations.

It is tiresome to have to go down these mean argumentative streets but it is necessary if we are to clarify academically what is so commonly fogged up by ideological mystification. I do not think there is anything actually very mysterious about what is happening. Once a believer has become convinced of the truth of the ideological revelation, he is led to judge any future proposition – truths, exhortations, bits of information – in terms of how they bear upon the practical success of whatever struggle he conceives himself to be involved in. Again, it is ideology in power which reveals most clearly the otherwise obscured logic of the theoretical system: Truth, as Lenin put it, is what the Party judges, just as proletarian thought, as Lukacs argued, is not what workers think but what the Party knows.[9]

Perhaps the only way to make progress would be to abandon the term altogether but it sits grinning grotesquely upon a mountain of nonsense, challenging everyone to come to terms with it. It tries to appropriate everything, yet its actual achievements are minimal. As converted into the sociology of knowledge by writers such as Karl Mannheim, it promised a scientific treatment of the social origins of beliefs, but like the Marxist theory of dialectic, which also promised to make the world transparent, it has as a theory remained little but a set of dogmatic assertions about the false consciousness of opponents. How can such an empty piece of intellectual rhodomontade have survived so long?

Let me suggest an answer. Certain intellectually feeble ideas nonetheless cut a dash in the world because of the institutional consequences they suggest. Whether religious beliefs are intellectually powerful is a complex question, but they do constitute a superior class of person called a 'priest' and this gives them, for some people, a certain usefulness quite distinct from their intellectual virtues. Rather similarly, ideology may be epistemologically feeble but it is ontologically interesting in constituting a distinction between a knowledge-possessing elite and a benighted mass. The ideology of Marxism was the theory on the basis of which commissars and vanguards of the proletariat distinguished themselves from the masses. It is now only in the protected academic playgrounds of the West that anyone takes the doctrine seriously as a doctrine. For the rest, the absurdity of the practice has doomed the theory.

IV

Our concern so far has been with clarifying the character of ideology as the underlying logic of a variety of salvationist doctrines which have flourished in the

---

[9] I have discussed this example in *Alien Powers*, p. 88. Marxists sometimes try to ward off criticism along these lines by consigning these remarkable options to 'the cold war' as if it were an epoch totally unrelated to anything else.

last two centuries. We have taken Marxism as the paradigm of this type of doctrine, and extended our range of exemplification into ideologies current in liberal democratic societies today, leaving to one side such ideologies as fascism and racialism which would require special treatment. One of the central points about all these doctrines is that they are much more intellectual than political doctrines like liberalism and conservatism. At their core lies not advocacy but some theory of the human condition. In this lies their claim to superiority, even to science. And each specific ideology has historical conditions in which it may flourish, or disappear, as Marxism and syndicalism have fallen on evil days, while feminism and environmental forms of salvation have in recent decades flourished mightily.

Now the continuing currency of a variety of ideologies suggests that there is something in our civilization to which ideological doctrines correspond; indeed, that we may talk of 'ideology' in the singular not merely as the generalized character of a set of doctrines sharing a similar pattern of thought but as a real and influential movement in itself. It clearly speaks to very powerful tendencies in the modern world.

I propose now to consider ideology in this sense, in order first to locate it within the current intellectual world, and then to consider some of its contemporary ramifications. Our orientation point here lies in the fact that ideology is characterized by an insistence that human beings have a single basic identity: generically, no doubt, they are human beings but specifically they are workers, women, Blacks, colonials, nationals, participatory citizens or some similar idea. In this guise, the chosen class are constituted as the heroes of a melodrama, and appropriate corresponding abstractions filled in as evil figures.

We might call this 'identity-monism', because it corresponds to that other kind of monism, familiar in political theory, which seeks to understand a society in terms of some basic ideal – justice, democracy, welfare, community or some similar idea. Both forms of monism are attractive for the same reason: the implementation of *one* idea or criterion makes conflict logically impossible. A society in which both freedom and justice are valued, or in which community and individual welfare must be balanced against each other, constantly runs up against problems of coherence. Normative political philosophers these days spend much energy in trying to work out a set of coherent principles which would constitute, for example, a just society. The closer one gets to the real world, however, the more conflicts between values multiply.

The essence of a modern state is, then, as the American motto has it *e pluribus unum*. Out of a plurality of individuals and endeavours emerges, for limited purposes, a civil unity in which the government is authorized to act for us all. And the *unum* is constituted by the individual members of a civil association in their capacity of subjects and citizens. They enjoy rights as subjects and they participate in public life as citizens. They are, however, *plures* in respect of their participation in what we now call (reviving Hegel) 'civil society', the arena of the family, the firm, the club and all the other emanations of private life. Not the least of the underlying changes in a modern state is the way in which 'civil society' understood as a social realm is insinuating itself massively between public and private life, demanding more and more public regulation on the one hand, and spreading itself down into the remoter reaches of privacy on the other.

A modern state is thus a set of human arrangements in which a vast plurality of individual endeavours cannot help but lead to conflicts which are resolved at the political level by a process generating laws and regulations. Such states have been immensely successful in the last two centuries at keeping the peace and indeed at facilitating increased prosperity along with the growth of things called 'rights'. Paradoxically, however, as the involvement of the state in every sphere of life has increased, it has also come to operate in terms of the redress of grievances, a process not unlike the way in which the enlightened despots of the past brought justice to their subjects. Perhaps the basic principle at work in this restless form of politics is equality. Civil society, as a vast complex of different occupations, intelligences, sexes, races, nationalities, enthusiasms, temperaments, opinions, religions etc. constantly produces inequalities from which grievances spring; out of these grievances emerge citizenly demands for redress; out of the resulting laws come new situations in which the same process is repeated.

Further, there are good reasons why this process should never culminate in a final solution and therefore why it is ceaseless. A population as varied as this will value justice, but not to the extent that it obliterates freedom; democracy but not so that it threatens order; welfare, but not so that it impedes prosperity, and so on. Politics is thus a continuing debate about diverse desirabilities which are largely incommensurable.

The essence of liberal democratic states is that they are associations of individuals in which each person is both a subject and citizen on the one hand, and a member of civil society on the other – worker, Catholic, female, mother, Black, football supporter etc. etc. on the other. The essence of ideology is to find the problem of politics precisely in this divergence. A so-called 'worker's state' is one in which everyone is a worker (alias 'comrade') and associated together in respect of one basic activity, namely membership of a community devoted to the satisfaction of needs. The *unum* of liberal democratic society, by contrast, is the limited and artificial role of subject and citizen, leaving a whole private realm in which individual initiative is at play and therefore free to cause unplanned and troublesome developments. The *unum* aspired to by an ideologicial community is of a *natural* not an artificial character – it is that of being a worker, a female, a needs bearing organism, a sexual desirer, a member of a race, or a nationality.

Ideology is thus an attempt to solve the problem of political conflict by a kind of amalgamation of the state and civil society in terms of a single, supposedly natural identity, and fights between ideologists (socialists vs. anarchist, communists vs. fascists etc.) are (when not about questions of which is to be master) intellectual disputes about *which* natural role is the proper candidate for this ultimate solution to the problem of politics. In all cases, a theory of humanity is involved. Marxists identified humanity with the sociable worker, feminists often see in women part of the human essence previously repressed and necessary for the flowering of a full community, and so on. Racists like Hitler have a rather classical view of humanity as a hierarchy of desirable qualities, and regard the lower parts of the hierarchy (Jews and suchlike) as dispensable. But in all cases, actual human beings are essentially the *matter* out of which a real community can be constructed. A lot of them prove unsuitable and must be liquidated.[10]

[10] Throughout this argument, I have assimilated the logic of ideologists on the one hand, and their practice in power on the other as pieces of evidence reinforcing each other. On this point, one might well cite what I think is Marx's only recorded reference to death. It is, he tells us in the *Economic and Philosophical Manuscripts* merely a 'biological event'. (*Karl Marx, Frederick Engels Complete Works* (London, Lawrence & Wishart, 1976), vol. III, p. 299). I take it that this means that an individual human being is simply a physical organism plus his 'social being', ie. his participation in society. There would thus seem to be no real value in any particular human individual, and wiping out quite a lot of them for a desirable social purpose would present no serious problem.

It is clear that things would be a great deal simpler (and there would be much less conflict and breakdown) if society could indeed be organized according to a single principle and many accounts of needs, rights, utilities, etc. have been provided to suggest what such a principle ought to be. If it could ever be discovered, its implementation would certainly (as Engels promised) abolish politics, because it would transform the problem of order into the technical issue of implementing the single principle. The only problem is that it could only really work if modern peoples were basically homogeneous. They are not and attempts to create societies of this kind have thus led to hideous slaughter and repression.

The history of the twentieth century does for this reason seem to have taught one widely accepted political lesson: that the more ambitious the social transformation a government embarks upon (and such governments are usually of recent origin through revolution) the more likely is the body count to rise. Western liberal governments, which have kept ideological ambitions at bay, have by contrast allowed most of their subjects to get through their lives without finding it necessary to kill many of them. Our question now becomes one of trying to formulate the basic difference between these two modes of government and of considering whether this distinction remains central to contemporary politics.

V

The essential activity of a liberal democratic government is ruling, which is the generation of order by the authority of law. Individuals as subjects must accommodate their conduct to laws as they pursue *their own* projects. The unfettered pursuit of such projects, in families, clubs, firms, churches and all the rest, is precisely what we mean by freedom. It is what we describe as the 'rule of law' and it is also the exercise of discretion by moral beings, subject to the rules and conventions of law and manners. Needless to say, some of these projects, and many of the ways people find of pursuing them, are profoundly unattractive, hence crime, poverty and vulgarity are inseparable from liberal democratic societies. Some people, especially among the educated middle classes find in these unlovely aspects of modern societies a reason for embracing ideological projects of social perfection. Our problem becomes: how are we to characterize the activity which promises such perfection?

We already know that it is an activity uniting individuals all of whom have a *single* natural character. As usual, the quickest route to seeing what is at stake lies in following through Marxist doctrine, specifically, that a real community must emerge from a proletariat, conceived of as those whose character is less determined by the society in which they live.[11] What does one do with those who are nothing else but workers? The obvious answer is that they are to be managed as engaging in some single project – perhaps the production of steel or motor cars – but at the highest level of society, the production of happiness, or the

---

[11] See for example Marx's characterization of the proletariat in the 'Contribution to critique of Hegel's Philosophy of Law: introduction' in *Karl Marx Friedrich Engels Collected Works* vol III, p. 183. Here the proletariat 'can no longer invoke a *historical* but only a *human* title; . . . is the *complete loss* of man and hence can win itself only through the *complete rewinning of man* . . .'. This presentation of the proletariat as matter awaiting the new stamp of form corresponds to the ventriloquial character of ideology. It presents itself as representing abstract classes of people who are essentially inarticulate and must accept the characterization presented on their behalf by ideological activists.

satisfaction of needs. Ideology is thus a project for converting a state into a managed enterprise.

Management belongs, of course, in civil society. It is the activity of organizing and arranging resources in order to get the maximum desired benefit. It is a word that comes most directly from the Italian *manecchio* which referred to the control of horses. More remotely, it comes from *manus*, the Latin for hand, from which we appropriately derive the idea of manipulation. Management and control are descriptions of a relationship a person might have with anything from a tool or a few pounds in a bank account on the one hand, to a vast industrial enterprise spreading across many frontiers on the other. What is managed is an instrument; management reifies. This is to say that the manager of an enterprise resembles a despot in the kind of control he exercises. An industrial enterprise is, of course, bound by law, but an employer uses employees for some enterprise of his own – that is why he must pay them to work. They have, of course, freedom in the times when they are not working, and freedom also to resign and go elsewhere. Most people, of course, must make some accommodation to the conditions of earning a living, which means that they must up to a point submit to be managed, and that is why the Marxist description of them as 'wage slaves' is not entirely wide of the mark.

What mitigates the instrumental character of being managed is that modern employment relations have the character of a contract, and the freedom of the employee to move (often with his acquired skills) gives him bargaining power over an employer in whose interest it is to create a pleasant environment in which a person's working life takes place. The ideal situation is when the employee takes an active interest in the manager's project – when the project becomes, in other words, *his* project also. This is only possible, however, because employees have the freedom to influence management, to move to another employer and to enjoy their own time. If the citizen were to turn into nothing else but an employee of the state, those conditions would not apply. There would only be one employer and one enterprise.

In exploring the character of ideology, then, we must develop a distinction between ruling a state and managing it. Ruling is done with laws, management by commands. Laws, being abstract, are cumbersome and unsatisfactory instruments of management. Any project for social perfection must thus move away from law towards other instruments of control.

It is important to recognize, of course, that our distinction is a purely ideal one, and that modern liberal democratic governments engage both in ruling and managing their states. We do, of course, have in the twentieth century, a dramatic exemplification of the contrast I am sketching in the difference between totalitarian states and liberal democratic ones. But even in democratic states, governments devote an increasing amount of their energies to managing us.[12]

Some reasons for this are entirely familiar. In wartime, for example, governments understandably construe both their subjects and the property of those subjects as resources to be used in attaining the overwhelming objective of victory. Energies are conscripted and a great deal of attention is devoted to morale or persuading people that the government's project is their project. Again, democratic politics have led governments to claim increasing efficacity in

---

[12] A small example: Britain apparently has a 'Health of Nation' strategy; it has just ordered a survey to discover how miserable, anxious and neurotic people are and (as I discover in *The Times* of 30 Jan. 1993) one aim of government is to achieve a cut of 15% in the suicide rate by the year 2000.

promoting the happiness of their subjects, especially their economic prosperity. Making people prosperous has led to increased managerialism, ranging from vast increases in taxation to attempts to fine-tune the economy.

Other reasons are perhaps less obvious. One is the incessant focus of public attention on the problems of the poor. Poverty has been recognized as a central problem of modern states ever since the decline of feudalism in which everybody was somebody's responsibility. Dependence on the trade cycle and the labour market was a precarious existence for many people, and the state has sought popularity by taking on increasing responsibilities for the welfare of those who could not help themselves. In doing so, the state has often destroyed voluntary activities which previously catered to the same need. The argument is that the state performs these tasks more regularly and more efficiently. It is also true that it often performs them badly. It is certainly true that the habits acquired in looking after people who could not look after themselves have spread into broader areas of government. Governments now manage our sexual, social, dietary and other forms of conduct on the basis of what their experts tell them. It is all, of course, benevolent, but no one has ever claimed that despotism was always malevolent.

VI

What we find, then, is a striking tension between justice and freedom. Justice, and especially its recent offspring called 'social justice', drives us towards a perfected society, one which has overcome such evils as war, poverty, crime and conflict between races. On the other hand a free society of individuals living under law is necessarily imperfect. Laws are rules to which we must subscribe as we pursue our purposes, but those purposes may in some cases be deplorable, and there is no set of rules compendious enough to guarantee, even if all individuals were to subscribe to them, that evil would be banished and replaced by good. If man is a moral being, then many bad things will happen, because morality necessarily allows the freedom to act immorally. The sundry vices and sins to which human nature is subject are adept at finding outlets whatever the social or political circumstances, and it has always been recognized that any government which seeks to abolish vice will culminate in the most ferocious kind of despotism. Lest anyone doubt this ancient truth, the experience of Roundhead, Jacobin and Bolshevik severity would seem to make it inescapable. Hard cases make bad law, the lawyers say, but in politics that is not quite accurate: a focus on hard cases cannot but lead to the end of law altogether and its replacement by management, in which vast discretion must be given to the managers.

The constitutive problem of modern societies, then, is that freedom is the condition of morality and that moral beings are necessarily imperfect. Imperfection in turn inspires a demand for justice and justice in this sense is conceived as the abolition of imperfection. This new thing has therefore acquired the new name of 'social justice'; and the adjective signifies that the project goes beyond moral rules to the achievement of social conditions. The dream is to have *both* freedom *and* justice but often we must choose between them. Ideology pops out of this dilemma with the promise of realizing that dream. This was what Lenin and his analogues promised and whole generations of Western communists actually thought he had delivered. The more realistic, however, recognized that the dream had a price – the broken eggs of the omelette. We now know that that particular set of eggs were broken to no purpose. But so powerful a dream is not likely to disappear after even several nightmares.

It is impossible to traverse once more the sad story of these aspirations without falling into metaphorical confusions about omelettes and dreams. The metaphor of omelettes reminds us that one of the attractions of ideology, by contrast with utopianism, was always realism. Part of this realism was a fake. When earlier we reported Lenin's *obiter dictum* about the absurdity of expecting capitalists to agree to raising wages at the expense of profits, we were invoking the grimly set jaw of the ideological realist as he pretends to a superior insight about the wicked ways of the oppressive system. But realism is often not particularly realistic and the upper classes of the West are frequently the creatures of reasoning and persuasion rather than the selfish logic of a narrow self-interest. Such, indeed, is the reason why Marxism has turned out to be a false prophecy in liberal democratic societies.

Ideological realism is a delusion in a much more profound sense. It is not just that ideological policies will inevitably produce death and suffering. It is that they will produce something far more significant and something actively embraced by some late flowering descendents of ideology among French intellectuals: the death of man, or, more specifically, the death of human beings as moral creatures. It is part of the promise of ideology that the liberation of human beings will be the end of the alienation between human essence and the human situation. To be part of a true community will be to have transcended the agonies of human self-consciousness with its familiar moral problems. The withering away of the state that Engels describes is not only an end of history but also an end of man as a moral entity.

Man as a moral entity was to be replaced, in the most famous version, by the new Soviet Man. This was a creature who can best be described as 'single minded'. He was everything his master in the Kremlin would want him to be. In being an exponent of what was called 'socialist morality' he would face no serious moral problems. Both his ends and his means would be transparent for him and their moral quality would simply be their notional devotion to the common good. Unlike the inhabitants of a liberal democratic state, in which moral problems arise not in terms of ends but in terms of identities, he would have but one identity, that of comrade-worker. The only moral defect he could possibly have would be a falling away from the appropriate norm. Such a defect is not, of course, at all moral. It is a technical deficiency and the appropriate response to it would be therapeutic.

In the classic ideologies, transformation of the human condition depended upon a revolutionary seizure of power by a knowledge-possessing elite who would use their power first to smash the state and then to guide humanity towards the forms of communal life. That classic version seems now to be dead. No one now takes seriously the dream of a triumphant vanguard transforming the world. The great-party theory of history has gone the way of the great man. No doubt it finally collapsed with the end of the Berlin Wall but it had been long in decline. Its decline has seen a most remarkable revival: that of utopian socialism.

This revival has not come in an explicitly utopian form. Rather, it has taken over political philosophy, where the perennial conflict between justice and freedom has taken on a new utopian form. A positivist *Zeitgeist* which dominated the mid-century has been replaced by a form of idealism in which the dominant concern has been with what we ought to do. Ideology in the old sense had come to be associated with totalitarianism and concentration camps. The Hegelian world historical realism which was careless of life has given way to admiration for those who stand for conscience, human rights and social justice.

This admiration was no doubt fuelled by reflection on the resistance to Hitler and on the moral heroism of anti-Soviet dissidents.

The revived interest in a kind of moral discussion was fully established by the publication of *A Theory of Justice* by John Rawls[13] in 1971, since when political theory, for example, has abandoned its analytic and positivist inclinations in favour of absorption in the normative. Just such a moral preoccupation frees concern with transforming the social system from its fatal association with revolution and totalitarianism. It also fits in better with the programme of the 'long march through the institutions' which some revolutionaries adopted in the 1960's. Whereas in the earlier period, moral indignation and talk about justice were forms of rhetorical protective coloration for basically unscrupulous power-seeking ideologists bent on transformation of the system, these things now became sincerely central to the concerns of political activism. As with the ideologies of the past, this activism had the effect of turning most people into components in a system. It was done by the simple expedient of construing society as the process of allocating goods. The normative political philosopher became the notional adviser to an allocatory prince, whose principles of allocation would implement the justice which the contingencies of civil society could never provide.

In this new situation, the collapse of Communism was in many ways immensely beneficial to the project of socially managed perfection. The collapse of the Soviet Union liberated ideologists from a standing reproach about the real consequences of their enthusiasms. They were once more free to follow their fancies wherever inclination should beckon.

VII

Ideology, we have argued, is a direct attack on the modern liberal democratic state, with its entrenched distinction between the state on the one hand and the liberties of civil society on the other. States incorporate the distinction – understood by ideologies as a form of alienation – between the citizen and subject on the one hand and the private individual on the other. The immense expansion of the range of 'the social' in the twentieth century is a measure of success in breaking down this distinction. Soviet communism was a brutish solution to this problem in which the Party took over the state and the state took over society. But there are many ways of skinning a cat. Let us now consider the ways in which the amalgamation of the state and civil society is facilitated without the crudities of revolution.

The first point to notice is that ideology arose from recognition of a basic distinction in modern society between those whose general attitude was consonant with their economic and social interest, and those on the other hand whose conduct showed that some opinion had detached them from what might otherwise seem to be their interest. This is another aspect of the dual logical structure of the concept of ideology. Farmers and peasants are pre-eminent among those who tend to vote in terms of their interests. Intellectuals, by contrast, are creatures of ideas and their allegiances are, as it were, up for grabs. Already in Burke we find a sense of alarm that political outcomes might be tending to respond rather to the flightiness of opinion rather than the stability of

---

[13] J. Rawls, *A Theory of Justice* (Oxford, Oxford University Press, 1971).

interest. Marx and Engels attributed communist opinions to an interest – that of the industrial working class – but they did not find it doctrinally embarrassing that many of the most prominent supporters of communism were opinionated bourgeois, such as themselves. In this as in much else, they had detected one of the emerging conditions of modern society, and education has had the effect of increasing vastly the numbers of those whose political engagements responded to their opinions rather than to their interests. Mannheim was attacked for the inconsistency of thinking that free floating intellectuals could escape from the universality of social determination. He had, indeed, committed inconsistency; but in an important sense, he was merely making explicit exactly what is involved in the practice of communism and other ideologies. Ideologists are people who have detached themselves from an interest and hitched their wagon to an idea.

But not quite purely, of course, to an idea. In following their ideological inclinations, ideologists were affirming a certain kind of moral identity as superior beings and laying claim to a superiority which could make itself effective in a great variety of ways, especially if united to some already superior position on the rostrum, the pulpit or the administrative office. To abandon interest in favour of an idea was thus by no means the same as taking a vow of poverty, chastity and humility. It was a choice which paid its way not only in abundant psychological righteousness but also in the promise of future power.

The opinion or idea was no ordinary opinion; it had, as we have seen, the character of a revelation. Our second concern must therefore be with its source. In the Marxist case, the source was originally science, though it was tied up with elements of philosophy, and powerfully reinforced negatively by a form of realism dramatized by anti-religious derision. These elements enriched the elementary self-evidences of man's utter dependency upon society and its material base. Much in this package now looks outmoded and some of it is tainted by association with communism. What in the new ideological context has come to replace these elements?

The basic intellectual structure on which the ideological edifice was constructed was the dialectic of scepticism and dogmatism, an intellectual version of the game of soft cop/hard cop. In Marx, it is the scepticism about religion which reinforces the dogmatism about materiality; and that scepticism about truth has continued to be a central constituent of modern intellectuality. History has been dissolved into competing political stories, science, where not pernicious, is seen as merely an expression of Western technological culture and philosophy is thought to culminate in a relativism of frameworks and perspectives. Such scepticism operates here, as it did in earlier versions of ideology, to force to the forefront the issue of *cui bono?* or (in the versions we have earlier seen) of the ideological character of *any* argument advanced, whether academic or not. The question to be asked, in these new times, is again not: is it true? but still, as before, what interest does it serve? Any answer to this question is essentially indeterminate.

Scepticism of this kind merely softens the mind up for the dogmatism to follow and that responds to a sense of self-evidence. On what can that be based? The answer, it seems to me, is morality. The one basis on which absolutely dogmatic judgements are made in the contemporary world is a morality of egalitarian humanism. Any superiority in civil society – whether it be wealth, position, the advantages of skin colour, sex or inherited ability – is subject to the corrosion of a dogmatic morality.

The way in which such an ideology operates in the modern world brings us to our third consideration: the project of destroying the distinction between the state and civil society. That distinction marks off private from public life; it separates the citizen from the individual and it is individuality which is the focus of attack. For individuality is identified with self-interest, and self-interest with the vice of selfishness, and selfishness discovered to lie at the root of everything from inherited wealth to the current admirations in art and literature. These connections are used to diagnose a modern state as a system of oppression in a sense similar to that of earlier ideological indictments. But whereas the solution in earlier times was revolution, the current solution is bringing in the state to redress the balance of civil society. In a *real* community, all the abstract classes which have sought public visibility as aggrieved – women, coloured minorities, the handicapped, homosexuals etc. – would be respected as generating all the kinds of success admired in a nation: poetry, scientific achievement, a language of their own and a full range of successful people prospering in all the admired professions of a modern society. The movement of modern society would be away from ability towards collective self-expression. The more collectively people would think, the more we would achieve one of the basic ambitions of ideology in the past: the abolition of failure.

The remarkable novelty of the new situation is that this ambition, recognizably continuous with what went before it, is now being sought in terms of ideas precisely the opposite of earlier ideological endeavour. Communism in the past, for example, was hostile to the idea of rights (and sometimes even of justice) because they expressed the supposedly individualistic ideology of the bour-geoisie. No doubt some concessions were made to individuality, along the line that only in the true community could the individual find fulfilment. But this was merely the rhetorical opportunism by which communists in the past claimed that all ideas were patchily achieved in the modern state and that only communism could realise *true* rights, *true* individuality, *true* freedom, *true* justice and all the rest.

Now however, ideology generates an ever expanding set of rights which it is the duty of the state to implement, and with every implementation, the subject becomes a pensioner ever more dependent upon the state. The more dependent the subject becomes on the state, the less is he capable of operating as an independent citizen. In order to enjoy the benefits of a health service, for example, his attitudes must be corrected so that he no longer smokes cigarettes. In order to use the roads which the state provides, he must comply with the law about seat belts and much else. The old ambition of ideologies was to replace the market by a system of administrative allocation of goods and duties. The new ideology is enthusiastic about the market but insistent that the market must be thoroughly regulated so as to guarantee a set of desired outcomes.

The philosophical basis of this development is a rational choice theory of man as a bundle of needs, utilities, satisfactions and preferences. In a sense, this is the natural man of civil society, for political man as an independent citizen has lost his place at the centre of political philosophy. Utilitarianism has converted human beings into organisms suitable for management in terms of their happiness.

VIII

Let me now sum up the argument. Ideology, I have suggested, is the project of creating social perfection by managing society. In its earlier versions, that outcome was first in theory projected onto humanity as a potential which merely needed to be released from current repression in order to actualize itself. In current versions, self-evident moral principles dictate norms for transforming society into something socially just. Both versions assume that human beings are homogeneous and malleable.

Political Integration, the Limited State, and the Philosophy of Postmodernism

Noel O'Sullivan*†

University of Hull

The subject of this paper is the contemporary -ism which has done more than any other to cause temperatures to rise in discussions of who we are, where we are, and where we may be going. For devotees, postmodernism is an all-illuminating concept; for their critics, by contrast, it is a term which should be abandoned as soon as possible, being no more than a passing fad of French intellectuals who have lost their revolutionary faith and taken refuge in a destructive scepticism, rather than come to amicable terms with the bourgeois world in which they live.[1]

There are of course no knock-down arguments which would resolve this debate one way or the other; and to offer yet another definition would just create one more source of confusion. It will be best, therefore, to begin by ignoring the details of the debate for a moment, and also the various definitions, in order to fix upon the issue that is at stake. This is that postmodernism has lit a massive bonfire, comparable to the bonfires lit by the sophists in the ancient world; by Lucretius in the Hellenistic period; by St. Augustine at the beginning of the medieval period; by Pascal and Hume in more recent centuries; and by Nietzsche at the end of the last century. To recall these earlier bonfires at the outset is useful because it reminds us that every age has its own form of postmodernism, when it comes face to face with its own equivalent of deconstruction, and finds its intellectual and moral resources challenged to their core. The present concern, however, is not to dwell on parallels with earlier times, but to focus on the contemporary challenge and, in particular, to consider sympathetically the postmodern claim that it is a constructive bonfire, rather than a harbinger of nihilism.

What, then, has inspired the contemporary postmodern bonfire? The short answer is comprehensive dissatisfaction with the western humanist tradition, in the optimistic secular form it has assumed in the past two or three centuries. That

* Noel O'Sullivan is Professor of Political Philosophy at the University of Hull.

† I am grateful to Dr Roger Luckhurst, Alison Kelly and Rana Kurian for comments and advice on the draft version of this paper.

[1] Roger Scruton, *Times Literary Supplement*, December 18, 1992, p. 3.

tradition, on the postmodern interpretation of it, is now in an advanced state of intellectual disintegration. All the main answers which have been given by it to the most basic question of western philosophy – the question, What is man? – are regarded by postmodernism as inadmissible. To use the best known word in the postmodern vocabulary, those answers have been deconstructed. Indeed, the very concept of man is called into question, and the prospect of the end of man greeted with relish. So far as politics is concerned, the result is that the dream of emancipation which has inspired western progressive thought since the time of the French Revolution is now left without any intellectual underpinnings. The disturbing prospect thus emerges, more generally, of a complete relativism which leaves no defence against any manner of atrocity.

This paper is concerned to assess the nature and implications of the postmodern challenge, at both the intellectual and the political levels. In order to do this, it will be necessary to construct a composite portrait of postmodernism, based on the writings of the various thinkers associated with it. For this purpose, it is necessary to identify the specific interpretations of the modern period to which it stands opposed, and then consider the alternative interpretations postmodernism has to offer. Constructed in this way, the portrait has three elements. The first is the postmodern view of our cultural and social situation. The second is the postmodern view of philosophy. The third is the postmodern view of politics.

The Postmodern View of Culture and Society

It must immediately be acknowledged that even those who have promoted the concept of postmodernism do not agree on its implications for the interpretation of our cultural situation. As Fredric Jameson, one of its more ardent defenders, readily acknowledges, the concept itself 'is not merely contested, [but] is internally conflicted and contradictory'.[2] To make things worse, Richard Rorty, who once favoured the term postmodernism, now regrets ever using it at all, complaining that it 'has been so over-used that it is causing more trouble than it is worth'.[3] And to complicate matters still further, the concept has been a confluence point for two different intellectual traditions. One is the post-Nietzschean tradition of continental philosophy associated in particular with Heidegger and Derrida; the other is the Anglo-American tradition of analytic and pragmatist philosophy drawn upon by, for example, Richard Rorty. The nearest thing to agreement amongst postmodern thinkers is about the fact that they do not intend the term to refer to a completely new era: two of the most thoughtful protagonists of postmodernism have emphasized that 'Postmodernity is in every respect "parasitic" on modernity; it lives and feeds on its achievements and on its dilemmas'.[4] Postmodernist writers of this kind are therefore not perturbed to be told by Habermas, for example, that the framework of postmodern thought continues, rather than abandons, the debate with the Enlightenment.[5]

---

[2] F. Jameson, *Postmodernism, or, The Cultural Logic of Late Capitalism* (London, Verso, 1991), p. xxii.
[3] R. Rorty, *Essays on Heidegger and Others* (Cambridge, Cambridge University Press, 1991), p. 1.
[4] Agnes Heller and Ferenc Fehér, *The Postmodern Political Condition* (Cambridge, Polity Press, 1988), pp. 10–1.
[5] J. Habermas, *The Philosophical Discourse of Modernity* (Oxford, Blackwell, 1990).

Despite the absence of an agreed meaning, it is nevertheless possible to identify three features of our time which have become sufficiently marked for them to have been described, with varying degrees of plausibility, as postmodern. These features concern the changing character of our relationship to nature, space, and time. Consider first our relationship to nature. At the beginning of his book on *Postmodernism*, Fredric Jameson observes that modernity took for granted the existence of 'some residual zones of "nature" or "being" '. There was, in other words, still something 'out there', quite independent of us. Modernism[6] also assumed that man, through culture, 'can still do something to . . . nature'. The modernist debate was accordingly about the ways in which man should, or should not, seek to control and transform nature. Postmodernism, by contrast, 'is what you have when the modernization process is complete and nature is gone for good'. The postmodern world is therefore a purely man-made, artificial one in which we henceforth never encounter nature but only "culture". What has happened in postmodernity, in short, is that culture has undergone 'an immense dilation of its sphere', involving 'an immense and historically original acculturation of the Real'.[7]

It is the insistence that there can now be no such thing as nature, Jameson remarks, which distinguishes the postmodern critique of modernity from that of earlier radical theorists such as Adorno and Horkheimer.[8] In spite of themselves, thinkers like these remained squarely modern in so far as they took for granted a concept of nature as the key to the stand-point which they believed themselves to be representing. The same is true of Freud, who also remains inextricably tied to the modern culture he criticized because he assumed that there is an objective order to which we must try to adapt ourselves. To spell out the defects of Freud's modernism is the special concern of Deleuze and Guattari, who maintain that what is needed is a new postmodern discipline, which they call schizoanalysis, with which to replace the essentially modern discipline of psychoanalysis.[9] This will refuse to brand some forms of desire as neurotic, and hence illegitimate. It will seek, instead, to save man from the dehumanizing feature of modernity with which Freud and the psychoanalytic movement completely failed to grapple. This is its tendency to foster a fundamentally passive ideal of life which does not take issue with the instrumental concept of rationality by which modernity is dominated. To enthusiastic advocates of postmodernism like Jameson, Deleuze and Guattari, writers such as Henry Miller, Artaud, R. D. Laing, Foucault and Lacan, all of whom protest against a culture of passivity, are therefore more relevant and inspiring than the two most influential offspring of the Enlightenment, Marx and Freud. Jameson acknowledges in particular the influence of two other thinkers to whom he considers himself especially indebted, Baudrillard and McLuhan.

The end of nature theme is closely connected with the second feature of postmodernism. This is a new attitude towards space, or, more precisely, towards public space. From Rousseau down to Arendt, the great aim of modern radical thought was to find a means of constructing a public space which would secure

[6] I take it that Jameson is here using the term modernism loosely, to mean 'modern consciousness', in symmetry with his use of postmodernism to refer to postmodern consciousness. Jameson, *Postmodernism*, p. ix.

[7] Jameson, *Postmodernism*, pp. ix–x.

[8] T. Adorno and M. Horkheimer, *The Dialectic of Enlightenment* (London, Verso, 1979).

[9] G. Deleuze and Felix Guattari, *Anti-Oedipus: Capitalism and Schizophrenia*, (London, Athlone Press, 1984) (first published, 1972).

human rights and provide scope for freedom. Postmodernism, however, regards the prospect of constructing such a space with varying degrees of scepticism. This scepticism finds its most extreme expression in the writings of Foucault. Modernity, Foucault argues, defined the public realm in juridical terms. It therefore lost sight of the ever expanding network of bodies, such as prisons, mental homes and hospitals, which he calls the disciplines, that was being constructed alongside the juridical order. The power of the disciplines to produce submission is so great that the public space of postmodernity is permeated by what Foucault terms an 'infinitely minute web of panoptic techniques' of control.[10] The modern dream of freedom is thus an illusion, and every attempt to defend it merely reinforces the triumphant discourse of power. On this view, there is therefore no public space in postmodernity, and for Foucault there never will be: the postmodern condition is, rather, an inescapable cage whose bars he portrays in a monotonous monochrome.[11] It will be seen later, however, that other postmodern thinkers are more optimistic, and hold out the prospect of a new politics of inclusion.

We may turn, finally, to the third feature of postmodernity. This is described by Heller and Fehér as a novel sense of time or, as they put it, a 'novel historical consciousness'.[12] What characterizes this new sense of time is a feeling of powerlessness akin to that just noticed in connection with the postmodern idea of space: to shape either the present or the future in any grand fashion is dismissed as impossible. The modern sense of time, by contrast, was shaped by an enormous optimism about the power of human will to take history by the neck, so to speak, and make it conform to human hopes and aspirations. At a mundane political level, this optimism was expressed until very recently in the widespread faith in government planning which began to evaporate during the Thatcher decade, and finally disappeared with the collapse of communism.

The change in historical consciousness which constitutes the third feature of postmodernism is illuminated by a striking formulation used by Anthony Giddens. 'The transition from modernity to post modernity', Giddens remarks, is 'bound up with the discovery that reason does not create rationality'. By this he means that scientific knowledge, whether in its natural or social scientific form, does not allow us to 'project [the world] along a pre-given path'. Ironically, as we come to understand the world better, we find that 'the world remains erratic, . . . remains outside our control in fundamental ways'. The problem of the postmodern[13] world is therefore not that it has become tightly organized and bureaucratically controlled, in the way forecast by Max Weber, but that it is 'a world which is out of control in substantial ways through our attempts to control it'.[14] Lyotard characterizes modernism in a similar way when he distinguishes it from the postmodern attitude by saying that the moderns continued to believe in the possibility of meta-narratives.[15] These consist of discourses which claim to

[10] M. Foucault, *Discipline and Punish* (Middlesex, Peregrine, 1979), p. 224.

[11] Marshall Berman's remark is relevant here. 'The mystery', he writes, 'is why so many of today's intellectuals seem to want to choke in [the cage] with him. The answer, I suspect, is that Foucault offers a generation of refugees from the 1960s a world-historical alibi for the sense of passivity that gripped so many of us in the 1970s . . . once we grasp the total futility of it all, at least we can relax.' *All that is Solid Melts into Air* (London, Verso, 1983), pp. 34–5.

[12] Heller and Fehér, *The Postmodern Political Condition*, p. 11.

[13] Giddens prefers the term late or high modernity to postmodernity. See his *Modernity and Self-identity* (Cambridge, Polity Press, 1991).

[14] Bill Bourne, Udi Eichler and David Herman (eds), *Modernity and its Discontents* (Nottingham, Spokesman, 1987), pp. 112–14.

[15] J.-F. Lyotard, *The Postmodern Condition* (Manchester, Manchester University Press, 1989).

represent absolute truth, and take for granted man's ability to impose all-embracing projects, such as the Marxist one, on society. The postmodern world, by contrast with the modern, has no sympathy for meta-narratives.

It is now necessary to reflect for a moment on the response of postmodern thinkers to the changes in our relation to nature, space and time that have just been sketched. The characteristic response is not so much one of alienation as of varying degrees of disillusion, hope and resignation. For Anthony Giddens, the postmodern sensation is of what he graphically calls 'lurching', in a 'careering, tumbleweed kind of process'.[16] Still more graphically, Marshall Berman invokes Marx's vision of a world in which 'all that is solid melts into air', in order to express the experience of perpetual disintegration, and concomitant unending anguish, characteristic of high modernity or postmodernism.[17] Against this background, Heller and Fehér explain that what is definitely excluded from the postmodern setting is a radical response, in the form of 'redemptive politics of any kind'.[18] What the new sense of *post-histoire* intimates is, to that extent, 'a surprising vindication of Hegel's political philosophy, his celebrated thesis of the reconciliation with reality'. If the Hegelian idea of reconciliation seems too ambitious, it can at least be said that the postmodern time sense is marked by 'self-limitation to the present as our one and only eternity'. In political terms, then, the postmodern response is ambivalent. On the one hand, postmodernity views with suspicion even the milder, non-messianic types of utopianism; but on the other, it is susceptible to ' "doomsday myths" and collective fears stemming from the loss of future'.[19]

Alienation, then, has no place in the response of postmodern thinkers to what they take to be the contemporary situation. Their response can be more precisely described in terms of an overwhelming sense of the contingency of existence. But what does that mean? The postmodern reply is that in earlier conditions of society, myths or religions give everything a certain necessity, and thereby render everything in life in some degree acceptable. Men, in other words, are protected against the sense of contingency. In the postmodern condition, however, the world into which people are born 'is no longer seen as having been decreed by fate but as an agglomerate of possibilities'.[20] Everything is therefore constantly questioned, everything is provisional, and every individual is haunted by the great postmodern fear, which is the fear of having missed out on what might have been. It is hardly necessary to say that postmodern thinkers are sceptical about how much can be achieved in this respect by the goals which preoccupied the modern period – the goals, that is, of economic prosperity, welfare measures, and social and political reform. None of these alleviates the sense of contingency.

It is, indeed, the experience of contingency above all else that creates the problem which lies at the heart of postmodernism. This is the problem of identity in its most radical form. Heller and Fehér formulate that problem as follows: 'How can we transform our contingency into our destiny without resigning freedom, without holding on to the banister of necessity or fate? How can we translate the social context into our own context without relapsing into experiments which have proved futile or fatal, into the experiments of social

---

[16] Giddens, *Modernity and Self-identity*, p. 107.
[17] Berman, *All that is Solid Melts into Air*, p. 15.
[18] Heller and Fehér, *The Postmodern Political Condition*, p. 4.
[19] Heller and Fehér, *The Postmodern Political Condition*, pp. 3–4.
[20] Heller and Fehér, *The Postmodern Political Condition*, p. 17.

engineering or of redemptive politics?'.[21] Unless contemporary culture can solve this problem, they hold, it will inevitably be threatened by religious and secular fundamentalist movements of various kinds. In fact, the new fundamentalism may be seen as 'the voice of the bad conscience of the postmodern condition flagellating itself for its excessive indulgence in relativism'.[22] Ernest Gellner, it may be noted in passing, has similarly argued that the fundamentalist emphasis on truth is a direct response to what is taken to be the relativism of postmodernity.[23]

Such, then, is the postmodern interpretation of our cultural and social condition, in outline at least. It is clearly open to many objections, especially on the grounds of exaggeration and oversimplification; and some will no doubt continue to wonder whether it really adds all that much to what they had heard from the Frankfurt School at an earlier stage, despite postmodern protestations of novelty. In this context, however, the objections will be passed over in order to focus attention on the central problem raised by postmodernism, which is how we are to respond constructively to the sense of contingency. To find the answer, it is necessary to turn now to postmodern philosophy.

Postmodern Philosophy

Turning to the literature of the last decade, the most interesting response to the problem of contingency comes from critics of postmodernism who maintain that postmodernism itself is in no position to offer a constructive solution because it fails to recognize that what is really required is a massive recovery exercise, aimed at rediscovering spiritual resources within modernity which sheer illiteracy has led postmodernism to ignore. In one form, this is the argument imaginatively developed by Marshall Berman, who has maintained that if we will but return to great modernists such as Goethe, Dostoevsky, Marx, Nietzsche and Baudelaire, we will find a means of looking at ourselves and our situation with fresh eyes, and 'will see that there is more depth in our lives than we thought'.[24] A similar argument is developed by Stephen Toulmin in *Cosmopolis, The Hidden Agenda of Modernity*, except that Toulmin goes a step further and maintains that we must go right back to the early humanists, whose rich and open response to an emerging modernity was rapidly stifled and lost in subsequent centuries, mainly due to the cultural impoverishment caused by the obsessive search for a new form of certainty with which to make good the decline of belief in revelation.[25]

What will now be argued is that the judicious message of these scholars needs to be reinforced by something more than a recovery exercise. To be precise, the recovery exercise they have in mind will not succeed unless it is underpinned by a new perspective, involving a more modest way of thinking about man and his place in the world than has been usual during the past two centuries or so. If we can achieve this more modest perspective, it will be very much easier to come to terms with the sense of contingency. But how is this to be done? Strange as it may sound at first, the postmodern bonfire itself may prove to be the best means of achieving the revised humanism which is most suited to our situation.

---

[21] Heller and Fehér, *The Postmodern Political Condition*, p. 19.
[22] Heller and Fehér, *The Postmodern Political Condition*, p. 7.
[23] E. Gellner, 'Squaring the ménage à trois,' *Times Literary Supplement* 21.7.92.
[24] Berman, *All that is Solid Melts into Air*, p. 36.
[25] S. Toulmin, *Cosmopolis: The Hidden Agenda of Modernity* (New York, The Free Press, 1990).

In order to give substance to this contention, it is necessary to expand the brief cultural and social portrait of postmodernism already given by considering the philosophical critique of modernity to be found in postmodern literature. The essence of this critique is to the effect that the Western world has been dominated for at least the past two centuries by three untenable ideas. One concerns the nature of reason; the second concerns the nature of the self; the third concerns the nature of power.

It is the writings of Richard Rorty and Jacques Derrida that have done most to give philosophic depth to the postmodern critique of reason. Consider Rorty first, as the more immediately accessible of the two. Since at least the seventeenth century, Rorty maintains, our way of thinking about our relation to the world has been moulded by a completely misleading mental image.[26] This image consists of regarding reason as a mirror in which we can accurately reflect the external world. In Rorty's view, the western philosophic tradition is held together, not so much by propositions or ideas, as by this image.[27]

By thinking of knowledge as the mirror of reality, Rorty holds, we have created a series of pseudo-problems: problems, that is, which simply disappear, as soon as we realize that the mirror image is totally misleading. For example, one such pseudo-problem created by the mirror image is a tendency to think of our relation to reality in terms of a subject confronting an object. The image leads us, that is, into a fundamentally dualistic way of thinking, in which we begin by opening up a gap between ourselves and the external world which philosophers then try, with boundless ingenuity, to close again, by trying to find a type of knowledge which will guarantee that the image we see in the mirror is not deceiving us.

A second pseudo-problem is a demand for an unattainable ideal of objectivity, which requires that we must somehow perform the impossible task of occupying the position traditionally assigned to God. Anything short of this divine detachment is assumed to distort what appears in the mirror, by allowing bias to creep in. In practice, what this has meant is a tendency to favour the model of knowledge offered by the natural sciences, and a corresponding tendency to regard every other kind of knowledge as merely subjective, and therefore defective. The mirror metaphor has meant, finally, that the nature of moral and political value judgements has been misunderstood. Since they do not reflect an external reality, they have been regarded as merely subjective expressions of human desire, and the social sciences have therefore attempted to find a value-free method of study which would restore the objectivity which our moral and political life is believed to lack. The result has been not just inevitable failure, but also impoverishment of the scope of social science.[28]

From a different direction, more directly indebted to Heidegger in particular, Derrida has launched a full-scale attack on the 'logocentric' character of the Western intellectual tradition. By this he means its tendency to privilege reason as

[26] Whether Rorty is right to trace the origins of representational thought back as far as the Greeks, and to argue that the Western tradition was therefore prone to disaster from the moment when Plato opened up a gap between appearance and reality by introducing the analogy of the cave, is not a matter which need be pursued here, simply because it goes beyond what his critique of modernity requires him to establish. Cf. N. J. Rengger, 'No time like the present? Postmodernism and political theory', *Political Studies*, XL (1992), 561–70.

[27] R. Rorty, *Philosophy and the Mirror of Nature* (Oxford, Blackwell, 1980), p.12.

[28] R. Rorty, 'Method, social science and social hope', in M. T. Gibbins (ed.), *Interpreting Politics* (Oxford, Blackwell, 1987), pp. 241–59.

the key to achieving '*présence*' – that is, a direct, literal encounter with reality. If one looks more closely at the various attempts to achieve this literal knowledge, Derrida maintains, they themselves always turn out to rely, without realizing it, on images or metaphors. From this arises the need for deconstruction: what it does, in the first instance at least, is expose the imagery or metaphors underlying the claim to literal or absolute knowledge.

Descartes, for example, believed that he had found a literal, or completely rational, foundation for certainty in the form of clear and distinct ideas, but what he considered to be clear and distinct turns out to have been shaped by the powerful visual metaphor of natural light. As Derrida puts it, 'Natural light, and all the axioms it brings into our field of vision, is never subjected to the most radical doubt . . . . In escaping from the logical circle that has so occupied him, Descartes all the while inscribes the chain of reason in the circle of the natural light that proceeds from God and returns to God'.[29] In Heidegger's philosophy, likewise, discussion of Being is deeply coloured by what Derrida calls 'an entire metaphorics of proximity'. Heidegger, that is, constantly speaks in a way which associates the proximity of Being with the sensuous images of neighbouring, shelter, house, service, guard, voice, and listening. Once again, the desire for direct presence 'metaphorizes' the reality it set out to capture in literal terms. Heidegger's error thus becomes clear: he was right to criticize philosophy for using metaphors, and he deconstructed them in a pioneering fashion; but he was mistaken to believe that his own philosophy could encounter Being through an escape from metaphor.[30]

Once this inescapability is accepted, a mortal blow is struck at logocentrism. Deconstruction, however, also performs a second task. Not only does it undermine reason's claim to achieve absolute knowledge, in the form of *présence*, but in the course of doing so, it simultaneously brings back into focus aspects of the self and of reality which had been downgraded or marginalized in relation to the privileged area of *présence*. This does not mean, however, that deconstruction brings with it the end of philosophy. What it ends is only philosophy as the traditional Western search for a completely transparent, non-metaphorical language of *présence*, with all the arbitrary dualisms (such as the distinction between literal and metaphorical knowledge just referred to) which that search creates. On the postmodern interpretation, philosophy *is* deconstruction, and there can never be an end to the need for that. Deconstruction, it must be added, is not to be mistaken for one more version of the modern quest for a magical method which will guarantee objectivity. It is simply a close scrutiny of claims to objectivity that exposes the untenability of the privilege upon which they rely.

The postmodernist deconstruction of rationality is intimately connected with a second theme, which is a critique of the concept of the self that has dominated the modern period. The main feature of this concept of the self, postmodernist thought holds, has been the assumption that it has a fixed core which exists independently of social relations. Since this core stands outside space and time, it is thought of as the object of universally valid generalizations about the nature of man as such. The most important of these generalizations is that the good for man lies in achieving autonomy.

The postmodernist attack on this concept of the self has come from several directions. One stems from the revisionist psychoanalysis of Lacan. Freud is

[29] Jacques Derrida, *Margins of Philosophy* (Hemel Hempstead, Harvester, 1982), pp. 266–7.
[30] Derrida, *Margins of Philosophy*, pp.130–1.

typical of Western thinkers in the modern period, Lacan maintains, in taking for granted that a rational life is one which aims at creating, so far as possible, a unified, autonomous self. According to Lacan, however, the idea that we can ever have a unified self is absurd. Precisely why it is absurd becomes clear once we realize that our idea of selfhood is built upon quicksands from the outset. Its origin is a crucial moment in infancy when the child first sees a reflection of himself or herself. This moment, Lacan believes, is a vital and inescapable one in the development of everyone's idea of selfhood. Unfortunately, the moment is one which effectively ruins our chances of happiness for good, since it brings with it 'the armour of an alienating identity, which will mark with its rigid structure the subject's entire mental development'.[31]

The ingredients of this alienating identity are to be found in three consequences which follow upon the recognition of one's reflection. The first is the creation of a conception of the I which is prior to social relations and to the acquisition of language. The second is the identification of the aim of this I as the achievement of an inner unity akin to the exterior unity of the body reflected in the mirror. The third is a sense of lack, or incompleteness, caused by awareness that the actually experienced self does not possess the ideal, seemingly self-contained unity witnessed in the mirror. Since this unity exists only in the mirror, and is in fact impossible to achieve in the real world, modern individualism amounts to a wild-goose chase, in so far as it is based upon the quest for an I which is an illusion. Sanity therefore lies in deconstructing the modern image of the self as a potentially complete and absolute subject.

The subversion of the subject associated with Lacan is extended by Foucault into the process of 'decentring' the self which was touched upon earlier. What Foucault means by this is that the modern world has been dominated by ways of thinking which have taken it for granted that the self is sovereign, in the sense of being capable of moulding history in accordance with human aims. This concept of the sovereign individual is dismissed by Foucault as a piece of fantasy which cannot possibly provide a foundation for the social sciences. All it has ever produced, he observes, is specious 'teleologies and totalizations'. What is therefore necessary is a new mode of study which reveals how the supposedly sovereign self is in reality 'decentred' in the course of history, through 'endless processes of causality'. In works on madness, the history of the prison, and sexuality, he has traced specific ways in which the decentring occurs in different periods. This new study he calls archaeological description. Its aim, he explains, is to free the history of thought from its subjection to dogmatic preconceptions about where history is or ought to be going, opening it up instead 'to a temporality that would not promise the return of any dawn'.[32] Unfortunately, however, Foucault never makes quite clear how we can be sure that the new study of history is as free from distorting influences as he insists it is. He writes, as he puts it, 'in order to have no face', and adds sternly, 'Do not ask me who I am . . .'.[33] Well, we won't; but he cannot avoid being asked to give a clearer account than he does of the criteria of relevance by which the new study is to be conducted.

What happens to this deconstructed self, in postmodern thought? Or, more precisely, what constitutes its good? Here, the postmodern answer shades over

[31] Jacques Lacan (trans. by Alan Sheridan), *Ecrits, a Selection* (London, Tavistock, 1977), p.4.

[32] Foucault, *The Archaeology of Knowledge* (London, Routledge, 1991), p.203.

[33] Foucault, *The Archaeology of Knowledge*, p.17.

into the body of political theory known as communitarianism.[34] Rorty, for example, straddles the divide when he explains what happens once we have abandoned the age-old idea that we have a 'true self'. We can finally recognize, he writes, that we are 'centerless, random assemblages of contingent and idiosyncratic needs rather than . . . more or less adequate exemplifications of a common human essence . . . '.[35] Having grasped this, we can appreciate that morality is a matter of self-creation, rather than of self-knowledge, as the Greeks thought.

For those who appreciate this, the experience of deconstruction is profoundly liberating. By destroying the idea of a true self – a self, that is, with a fixed core or substance – it opens up new possibilities, helping us to become 'increasingly ironic, playful, free, and inventive in our choice of self-descriptions'.[36] The specifically communitarian dimension comes in when Rorty adds that we should 'tinker with ourselves' in order to create a deeper and broader sense of our historical identity. We can do this by creating historical narratives that 'help one to identify oneself with communal movements [which] engender a sense of being a machine geared into a larger machine'. This, Rorty insists, 'is a sense worth having', since it helps us realize that the best way of tinkering with ourselves is to tinker with something else.[37] All such tinkering is, no doubt, a delicate matter.

Moving on from the deconstructed self, the third and last general theme of postmodern thought to be considered may be described as the rehabilitation of power. During the early modern period, thinkers like Hobbes and Spinoza took it for granted that power is an ubiquitous and inescapable feature of the human condition, being built into the structure of existence itself, so to speak. The optimistic ideologies of our own time, however, have all defined the ideal society as one in which power would in principle be abolished, being used, so far as it survived, solely for benign administrative purposes. Since the Enlightenment, in consequence, power has been marginalized as an issue in progressive politics, being treated as a hangover from an undemocratic past. In a democratic age, it was assumed, self-government will automatically ensure good government: the abuse of power need no longer be a matter for concern, for what interest could any people have in governing itself badly? It is the merit of Foucault in particular to have restored the basis for a more realistic view of power. Power, for him as for the classical thinkers of the early modern period, is both ubiquitous and inescapable. From the postmodern standpoint, therefore, politics can only seek to canalize power and use it constructively; to aim at abolishing power is futile and potentially destructive.

These then are the central themes of postmodern philosophy. A hostile commentator would find it easy to maintain that the most obvious conclusion to be drawn from them is that postmodernism has in fact brought about the end of man, in the form of an extreme relativism which, although not openly nihilistic, nevertheless reduces modern Western culture to a mass of deconstructed débris. In what follows, the postmodern themes just outlined will be briefly re-examined from a more sympathetic point of view, in order to illustrate the sense in which they may be said to provide three fundamental manifestations of a philosophy of

[34] The most useful short discussion of communitarianism is Simon Caney, 'Liberalism and communitarianism: a misconceived debate,' *Political Studies*, XL (1992), 273–90.

[35] R. Rorty, 'Freud and moral reflection,' in *Essays on Heidegger and Others* (Cambridge, Cambridge University Press, 1991), p.155.

[36] Rorty, 'Freud and moral reflection'.

[37] Rorty, 'Freud and moral reflection', p.163.

modesty. After that, the implications of the new politics of difference associated with postmodernism will be explored.

Towards a Postmodern Philosophy of Modesty?

Consider first the postmodernist view of the self. The main feature of this deconstructed creature is, as has been noticed, its sense of contingency. Disconcerting as this experience may be, it also gives the postmodern self a wholly unpretentious character. The older classical and Christian view of the self, it will be recalled, taught that human beings occupy a privileged position at the centre of a meaningful universe. In spite of the rise of modern science and the concomitant Galilean revolution, which decentred man's position in the scheme of things, the old view of the privileged nature of the human self for long survived into the modern period in a secularized form, finding supreme expression in ideologies which found the meaning of history in a movement towards the realization of man's dreams. Even those who overtly rejected the notion of cosmic privilege, like the Existentialists, still suffered from nostalgia for a time when human beings could see themselves as part of a larger order of things, and felt nausea, or absurdity, as a result of not having any such sense of location. As the second half of the century ends, however, postmodernism marks the final abandonment of the yearning for a cosmic setting, and the contingency of existence is accepted as part of the natural order of human life. If melancholy is still discernible, a major change of mood is nevertheless evident in the fact that there is no longer a demand for spiritual heroics, of the kind formerly associated with the quest for authenticity – the ordinary may not catch the imagination, but postmodernism has rehabilitated it, as part of the general upgrading of what was once liable to be seen as the realm of *mauvaise foi.*

If this more modest sense of self is to have any real depth, however, it requires to be underpinned by something less precarious than the ironic detachment which is currently fashionable in some postmodern literature. Tentative suggestions may be found in two directions explored in postmodern writings. One is in postmodern theology, which indicates that the deconstructed self need not be a self without religion. The religion relevant to it, however, would reject the anthropocentric concepts of God and the world found in the Christian tradition, and would, in addition, be a religion – or, better, a path – of enlightenment, rather than a religion of revelation. To that extent, a postmodern religion would be sympathetic to oriental traditions. The other, related alternative to ironism is to be found in the inspiration which postmodern scholarship derives from Nietzsche. One of the merits of postmodern literature is to have grasped very clearly that the will to power is not a will to dominate, but an ideal of self-possession. There are, it is true, postmodern writers like MacIntyre who still misunderstand Nietzsche in this respect, but their misgivings, as well as those of readers for whom the name of Nietzsche still conjures up the blond beast, would be removed if they noticed that Nietzsche found one of the supreme exemplars of his ethic in the modest, unheroic and unpretentious concept of selfhood worked out by Montaigne at the beginning of the modern period.[38]

---

[38] 'The joy of living on this earth,' Nietzsche wrote of Montaigne, 'is increased by the existence of such a man . . . If I had the task of making myself at home on the Earth, I would choose him as my companion.' What Nietzsche admired in Montaigne was what he admired in Schopenhauer: the ability to confront an indifferent universe honestly, and in a spirit of joy and affirmation. Whereas

In the first instance, then, the modesty of the postmodern self lies in its acceptance of a de-centred cosmic existence. It is also modest, however, in its rejection of absolute knowledge. Rorty speaks for postmodern thinkers at large when he insists that this does not entail relativism, and asserts, more generally, that 'To accuse postmodernism of relativism is to try to put a metanarrative in the postmodernist's mouth'.[39] Relativism, that is to say, only makes sense in terms of the philosophic tradition from which postmodernism is trying to escape. If there is a single term which conveys the alternative position postmodernism is concerned to explore, it is the one Nietzsche used, which is perspectivism. What perspectivism connotes is not the relative character of rationality, but its unavoidable conditionality. For perspectivism, all experience is conditional, not merely in the subjective sense that it always belongs to somebody in particular, but in the objective sense that it has implicit in it impersonal criteria of relevance upon which its own claim to significance relies. The difficulty, of course, is to specify the precise nature of these impersonal criteria. Three different ways of interpreting them are to be found within postmodern thought.

One interpretation stresses the pragmatic basis of the criteria. This view has a degree of plausibility when the criteria in question are ethical ones, but has great difficulty in accounting for scientific truth, which may be felt to 'work' only because it corresponds to the way things actually are. Even in ethics, Rorty – a leading defender of pragmatism – introduces ideals, such as solidarity, which seem incapable of a purely pragmatic justification.

A second interpretation stresses the historicity of the criteria, maintaining that the meaning of moral rationality is necessarily tied to different intellectual traditions, and can therefore never, of course, yield a universally valid concept of justification. Thus in the case of Greek ethical thought, for example, 'There is no standard external to the *polis* by which a *polis* can be rationally evaluated in respect of justice of any other good. To apprehend what a *polis* is, what the good is which it is its function to achieve, and to what extent one's own *polis* has successfully achieved that good, all require membership in a *polis*'.[40] This stress on historicity does not amount to relativism, MacIntyre has argued, because it does not exclude rational choice between different traditions. The question of how one tradition can claim superior rationality to another, however, is complicated by the fact that MacIntyre regards Thomism as offering the best example of such superiority. The trouble is that he goes to great lengths to stress that this superiority owes as much to the place Thomism assigns to authority in the moral and political sphere, as to the place it gives to reason.

The third interpretation stresses, not so much pragmatism or historicity, as the impersonal linguistic conventions which govern signification independently of individual consciousness. Although associated with Derrida, whose main debt for his theory of language is to Saussure, this position has an obvious kinship with the philosophy of Wittgenstein. From this standpoint, a problem of relativism only arises for those committed to the modern philosophy of the subject. For Derrida, that philosophy is an abstract, reflective construct which is

Schopenhauer disappointed him, however, by turning to what he regarded as a quasi-Christian asceticism, Montaigne maintained an ideal of balance and moderation to the end. The hostile interpretation of Nietzsche given by MacIntyre in *After Virtue* is a misunderstanding which prevents him from recognizing that Nietzsche's enterprise is close to his own.

[39] R. Rorty, 'The social responsibility of intellectuals,' *The Journal of Philosophy*, 80 (1983), p. 589.

[40] A. MacIntyre, *Whose Justice? Which Rationality?* (London, Duckworth, 1988).

defective because it takes no account of a prereflective relation with the world upon which it is in fact parasitic. This prereflective relation is one of engagement with the world, and necessarily brings with it the experience of otherness as irreducible difference. In the philosophy of the subject, by contrast, otherness is grasped only in instrumental terms.

To explore these three interpretations in detail, however, is not the present concern. The relevant point is that, regardless of the difficulties the three interpretations may create, none can usefully be described as relativist, in any sense which denies to reason a critical function. In particular, the indignant claim that deconstruction blurs the 'genre-distinction' between literature and philosophy cannot be put forward as decisive evidence of such a denial. As one able defender of Derrida against Habermas has remarked, that criticism presupposes a dogmatic and compartmentalized way of thinking about philosophy which ignores the 'argumentative' capacity of literature, on the one hand, while confining philosophy to a realm of meta-theory, on the other.[41]

To stress the modesty of the postmodern 'conditional' or perspectivist view of knowledge, however, and to distinguish it from relativism, is not to claim that it is without dangers. The greatest of these is evident in Foucault's tendency to let deconstruction degenerate into something worse than relativism, which is his own version of the Marxist obsession with 'unmasking'. In Marxism, the unmasking consists of revealing that everything is a form of class interest. In Foucault, the class emphasis disappears, but the conviction still survives that seemingly benign practices and institutions must be exposed as mere disguises of an underlying exploitative system of power. In particular, he systematically dismisses the forms of civil society as a mask for the 'disciplines'. Historically, he writes, 'the process by which the bourgeoisie became . . . the politically dominant class was masked by the establishment of an explicit, coded and formally egalitarian juridical framework, made possible by the organization of a parliamentary, representative regime . . . [But] the real, corporeal disciplines constituted the foundation of the formal, juridical liberties'.[42] It is when one looks at the alternative which Foucault proposed to these formal liberties that they rapidly begin to look less oppressive than he implies. Thus on one occasion, he explained that the revolution 'can only take place via the radical elimination of the judicial apparatus, and anything which could reintroduce its ideology and enable this ideology surreptitiously to creep back into popular practices, must be banished'.[43] In place of the despised juridical forms he would put a new form of 'proletarian' justice, which would need no judge. But this, of course, would not in practice mean liberation; it would simply mean the exercise of arbitrary power.

Finally, the modesty of postmodernism emerges in its rejection of the Eurocentric tendency which has characterized Western political thought since at least the time of the French Revolution. On this view, the values of the Western self have a universal significance, reflected above all in Hegel's conviction that history begins in the East and ends in the West. Although postmodernism rejects the idea of a universal, a-historical self, it is important to emphasize that it does not conclude that this entails the rejection, or even the undermining, of liberal values and institutions. In its more moderate form at least, all it rejects is the

[41] C. Norris, 'Deconstruction, postmodernism and philosophy', in D. Wood (ed.), *Derrida: a Critical Reader* (Oxford, Blackwell, 1992), p.188.
[42] Foucault, *Discipline and Punish*, p. 222.
[43] Colin Gordon (ed.), *Power/Knowledge. Selected Interviews and other Writings, 1972–77* (Brighton, Harvester, 1980), p.16.

ambitious attempts of a long line of thinkers from Locke onwards to provide those values with absolute foundations.

The nature of postmodern intellectual modesty is especially evident in the alternative, revised form of liberalism which Rorty opposes to the rationalist version. This takes the form of what he calls 'postmodern bourgeois liberalism'. The ultimate basis of this revised liberalism is not reason but imagination, for only imagination enables men to transcend their tendency towards narrow, exclusive group identities by re-identifying outsiders as 'one of us'.[44] This is not irrationalism, Rorty maintains, because holders of radically different moral positions can nevertheless have discussions about who should be brought within the fold. Replying to Charles Taylor's fear that a moral position is 'subjectivist' unless it is grounded in reason or the nature of things, Rorty remarked that he was unperturbed by such charges. This, he explained, 'is because our moral positions, like all the other parts of our selves, are grounded in dialogue: they are not Sartrean 'choices', not acts of resolute will, but the products of discussion.' If "reason" just means "lots of conversation", he adds, 'then *of course* reason can adjudicate moral disputes. What else could?'[45] As Rorty notes, the fact that this meaning of reason may be, in effect, too modest for others does not make it a form of irrationalism.

The modesty of postmodern political thought, then, lies in the attempt to disengage liberal democratic theory from the more grandiose attempts to locate it within a foundationalist philosophy which have dominated the last three centuries. In this respect, it does no more than acknowledge that the only solid basis for moral and political thought now available is one which rests on a concept of self-limitation, and simultaneously acknowledges that the self in question is a specifically *Western* self, rather than man as such.

If postmodern philosophy must be taken seriously when it rejects the charge of relativism, what are far more problematic are the political implications of deconstruction. It is these that must now be considered.

Postmodern Politics: the Civil and the Administrative
Models of Postmodern Integration

The political problem posed in an acute form by postmodern philosophy is the problem of legitimacy. The problem, as it emerges from postmodern philosophy in its most general form, is easy to state: If deconstruction validates any and every difference, how is it possible to prevent the new politics of inclusion from either disintegrating into anarchy, or else giving rise to despotism as the only means of holding postmodern society together? Three different responses to this problem are discernible in postmodern literature. Unfortunately, two of them are so unsatisfactory that they must be set aside almost immediately.

The first response in effect simply ducks the problem, by enthusiastically assuming that the universal validation of difference is not likely to be a serious problem, in principle at least. It is taken for granted that removal of the obstacles to liberation will automatically mean the end of the problem of integration itself. This appears to be the response favoured by Toril Moi, for example, when she

[44] See e.g., Rorty's essay on 'Method, social science and social hope'; also *Contingency, Irony and Solidarity* (Cambridge, Cambridge University Press, 1989).
[45] Richard Rorty, review of Taylor's 'The Ethics of Authenticity,' *London Review of Books*, 15, 8 April (1993).

ends an excellent survey of the feminist authors Kristeva, Cixous and Irigaray, amongst others, by quoting with approval a passage in which Derrida tries to envisage what a society would look like in which all sexual discrimination had been eliminated and full sexual emancipation achieved. Here is the passage in which Derrida describes it:

> The relationship [to the other] would not be a-sexual, far from it, but would be sexual otherwise: beyond the binary difference that governs the decorum of all codes, beyond the opposition feminine/masculine, beyond homosexuality and heterosexuality which come to the same thing. As I dream of saving the chance that this question offers, I would like to believe in the multiplicity of sexually marked voices. I would like to believe in the masses, this indeterminate number of blended voices, this mobile of non-identified sexual marks whose choreography can carry, divide, multiply the body of each "individual", whether he be classified as 'man' or 'woman' according to the criteria of usage.[46]

In postmodern social thought of this kind, then, politics disappears from sight, being replaced by a naive, almost mystical faith in the natural harmony which, it is assumed, will automatically be brought about by deconstruction. Turning now to the second answer, we encounter the more sceptical solution proposed by Rorty. He solves the problem of legitimacy by simply dismissing the idea that we should respect difference as such – that is, 'every human being, and every human culture, no matter how vicious or stupid' – as merely 'the degeneration of fellow-feeling into self-indulgent cant and political frivolity'. What lurks beneath the uncritical celebration of difference is the same deadly complacency that characterizes the New Age movement, inspired as it is by the belief that 'all you need to do is . . . recognise how wonderful, how luminous, you already are'. For Rorty, then, the so-called new politics – the 'politics of difference' – amounts to nothing more than the absurd idea 'that both morality and politics can be reduced to niceness', and thus ignores the fact that moral choice 'is sometimes a matter of deciding who is going to get hurt'.[47]

The trouble is that none of this tells us who is entitled to decide the limits of toleration, or on what grounds. Even more crucially, Rorty does not so much as touch on the central question of how power is to be distinguished from authority, which is the precondition for anyone being entitled to do any hurting in the first place. As in the case of Derrida's response, Rorty merely ducks the problem of legitimacy, although by a different strategy: he assumes that an authoritative moral and social consensus will keep the problem of diversity under control and thereby obviate any need to theorize the nature of legitimacy at all.

What must now be considered is whether there is any other way of coming to terms politically with the postmodern vision of a pluralist social order in which all the old hierarchies have been destroyed and all differences given a certificate of validity. It will be suggested that there is, although it is a way that has tended to be ignored, largely because the debate between liberals and their postmodern critics has revolved around the issue of foundationalism. It is to the nature of this answer that we must now turn.

In a recent essay, John Gray posed the question: What are the political forms best suited to a condition marked by substantial cultural diversity? It is this

---

[46] Toril Moi, *Sexual Textual Politics* (London, Routledge, 1991), p.173.
[47] Richard Rorty, review of Taylor's 'The Ethics of Authenticity'.

question, he observed, which ought to be at the top of the agenda of modern states, in view of the fact that contemporary Western societies 'encompass a kaleidoscopic diversity of attitudes to sexuality and gender, death and the human condition, even as they harbour a prodigious diversity of ethnic inheritance and styles of life'.[48] Historically, Gray notes, political orders which have successfully accommodated extreme cultural diversity have either been empires (as with the Romans and the Habsburgs), religious institutions (such as those of medieval Christendom and Islam in their periods of greatest toleration), 'or else monarchies, as in the splendidly anachronistic case of the United Kingdom'. We may, Gray adds, go further, and reflect on the lesson to be derived from the historical experience of the liberal democracies. This is that:

> Allegiance to liberal orders, where it has not had its roots in religious faith, has typically been imposed by secular myths [or ideologies] which suffuse modernity and underpin the modern project of giving moral and political life a secular foundation. When we cease to subscribe to them, we acquire that paradoxical character of postmoderns, heirs to all the achievements of modernity but not its seminal myths.[49]

This, then, is the problem. What is unusual about Gray's tentative solution is that it arises from an awareness that in order to construct a model of postmodern liberal democracy, we do not need to look forward, but backwards. More precisely, what Gray recognizes is that Hobbes was in effect the first postmodern political theorist. Admittedly, to describe Hobbes in these terms may at first seem strange, for he is normally thought of simply as the defender of strong government, based on a pessimistic view of man. To approach Hobbes in that way, however, is inevitably to miss his contemporary relevance. It is to forget, in particular, that his state of nature is, in effect, a 'deconstructed' condition, in which no individual or perspective is privileged, and all differences are validated. His is the first serious attempt, in a word, to construct the state on the basis of radical diversity. The resultant problem is that of reconciling absolute freedom with authority – it is the postmodern problem, in short, of legitimacy.

The solution to this problem proposed by Hobbes is the model of civil association, and it is in this, Gray writes, that we may possibly find a means of political integration appropriate to postmodernity, since Hobbes constructed it for an age of religious wars and barbarous movements much like our own. It is a matter of more than academic interest, then, to recall what the civil model involves. Its first and most important feature embodies the greatest discovery of modern European politics. This is that men do not have to achieve a consensus on common aims and purposes in order to live in harmony, but need only acknowledge a common political authority or sovereign. The function of this sovereign is not to impose an ideology, religion, overall economic plan, or comprehensive ideal of social justice, but to provide an impersonal and formal framework of law. It is this formal characteristic which enables the rule of law to accommodate maximum social and cultural diversity. If we now take into account the additional features which were incorporated into the civil model in the course of the following century, then the second is an independent judiciary; the third is a set of institutions for ensuring the accountability of those who

---

[48] J. Gray, 'The politics of cultural diversity', *The Salisbury Review*, 7 (1988), 38.
[49] Gray, 'The politics of cultural diversity', p.44.

exercise power; and the fourth, which is associated in particular with Montesquieu, is acceptance of the plurality of spontaneous groups which constitute the tissue of society. A fifth, which is largely a twentieth century addition, is the supplementation of the formal civil model by a welfare system, without which it would of course lose contact with the realities of industrial society.

Now, John Gray's appreciation of the contemporary relevance of civil association is only one instance of a widespread revival of interest in civil association in recent decades, during which the model has been enthusiastically taken up and revised by a variety of political thinkers on both the Right and the Left.[50] In the course of this revival, however, a number of serious confusions have arisen which must be removed before the relevance of the civil model for the postmodern politics of difference can be established. Six of these confusions may be singled out for special consideration.

The first comes from feminism, and consists of the claim that the civil model is not an appropriate response to the postmodern politics of difference because it is in fact a gendered model. More specifically, Carol Pateman, one of the most scholarly exponents of this criticism, has argued that from the time of the early contract theorists down to John Rawls, the civil model has always been an exclusionist model, in the sense that it has pushed women outside the public realm and taken patriarchal domination for granted, thereby treating women as at best second class citizens. The model has skilfully done this by a spurious claim to universality based on a disembodied concept of the individual which finds its most extreme expression in Rawls. A moment's scrutiny will always reveal, Pateman maintains, that the supposedly disembodied individual of liberal theory is not really disembodied at all, but turns out to have very masculine values.

Presented in these terms, the overall cogency of Pateman's case may be granted straightaway; there can be no doubt about the fact that the traditional interpretation of civil association has been biased towards men. What is problematic, however, is Pateman's tendency to assume that civil association is inseparable from the (untenable) concept of a disembodied individual. If we take the most subtle interpretation of the civil model to have appeared in recent years, which is that given by Michael Oakeshott in *On Human Conduct* (1976), then it is clear that what the civil model entails is not the concept of a disembodied, non-gendered individual, but only the concept of citizenship as resting on a formal legal relationship. If that distinction is accepted, it becomes possible to recognize that although the historic interpretation of citizenship has in fact had exclusionary implications for women, the civil model itself does not *have* to be interpreted in that unfortunate way: what is required now is to put things right by reinterpreting it in a way which women find acceptable. What that means in practice is of course a matter for political debate by and with women, and not something philosophy can pronounce on.

The kind of feminist criticism which the civil model *cannot* accommodate comes not from a relatively moderate thinker like Pateman, but from a more extreme one like Luce Irigaray. Irigaray has taken the concept of patriarchy, immersed it in Heidegger, and extended it so far in the process that it becomes a synonym for total alienation from every aspect of Western history. The result, however, is not the devastating and definitive critique of the Western political

---

[50] Notable amongst them are R. G. Collingwood, Hayek, and Oakeshott, on the liberal and conservative side, and Charles Taylor, John Keane, Perry Anderson, Arato and Cohen, and Agnes Heller, on the more radical side.

tradition, including the civil model, which one might at first expect; it is rather, a counterproductive overshoot. Irigaray's all-embracing concept of patriarchy, that is to say, not only denies women moral status by presenting them as the uniformly passive victims of history, but also threatens to make the concept of citizenship unintelligible in *any* form. For feminism of this extreme kind, then, the problem lies not so much with the civil model itself, as with a concept of patriarchy that has been expanded so far that it loses all analytic value.

The second confusion comes from the radical tradition, and reveals in particular the influence of Gramsci and, more recently, of Habermas. It consists in the belief that civil association is to be interpreted as a purely voluntary ideal of community, in contrast with the coercive state order. The most subtle and ambitious version of this interpretation has been put forward by two of the most suggestive postmodern thinkers, Arato and Cohen, who develop a concept of civil association inspired by the discourse ethics of Habermas' later work.[51] According to their interpretation, what the postmodern world requires is a completely new concept of civil society which can overcome the principal defect of all earlier versions. This defect, they maintain, is that the earlier versions always presuppose a division between the political and the economic order, or between the state and the market, and always end by subordinating one to the other, thereby creating an unacceptable framework of domination.

Their own concern is to replace the traditional dualism of state and economy with a tripartite analysis of modern society. The third term introduced by this analysis is, they maintain, one which is peculiar to the democratic societies of the advanced industrial world. It consists of a fluid and critical body of public opinion that transcends the relatively rigid institutions of both state and economy, in an on-going process of public debate about the nature of the good society. This is what they term civil society. In other words, civil society becomes on this view a process of democratic will formation, which is continuously seeking to give rational embodiment to an on-going discourse ethic in communicative action. Only this new ideal of civil society, the authors claim, can provide the basis for a postmodern concept of democracy, because only this ideal can create a politics of self-limitation with which to replace the coercive and exclusionist elements in the traditional democratic order. The fact that their concept of civil society is inseparable from what they think of as a politics of self-limitation is, however, precisely the problem since the increasingly diverse order of the contemporary world shows no propensity towards the kind of self-limitation which the authors hope for. Even if such a propensity were discernible, it hardly seems realistic to expect governments to leave the formation of the discourse ethic uninterrupted and to behave, more generally, as if politics is a sort of unending seminar on the nature of the public good, from which the reality of power is to be scrupulously excluded. On this view, civil association is not so much a response to postmodern diversity, as a flight into a highly rationalist version of utopia.

More generally, the conception of civil association invoked here has become particularly influential in Eastern Europe in recent years. There, it has been associated above all with opposition movements such as Solidarity, and it is especially on developments such as this that Arato and Cohen have based their attempt to construct a new model of civil association. As Pelczynski has shown, however, the Solidarity movement did not in fact offer an example (as it claimed

---

[51] J. L. Cohen and A. Arato, *Civil Society and Political Theory* (Cambridge, Mass, MIT Press, 1992).

to do) of an independent civil society composed of voluntary, non-state institutions threatening to replace the state order with an alternative model of spontaneous republican association.[52] It was rather the case that Solidarity enjoyed the benefit of toleration by the regime, partly through the regime's incompetence, and partly through the survival in post-war Poland of a tradition of non-state association.

What mainly matters at present, however, is that the Gramscian and Eastern European interpretation of civil association has tended to subordinate the formal or procedural dimension which was fundamental to the classical meaning of the rule of law to a radical dream of community. In fact, the civil model can only accommodate and protect diversity so long as the rule of law is assigned an intrinsic or non-instrumental value. When its would-be friends turn to it as a means of doing more, they are likely to become its unwitting enemies instead. Why that should be so is dramatically illustrated by Václav Havel, for example, in a well-known essay he wrote in 1984 on the incompatibility of totalitarianism with what he termed 'meaningful human community'. What is problematic is the 'totalizing' impact of the quest for meaningful community on Havel's conception of civil association. What he advocates is an 'antipolitical politics' which is opposed to everything impersonal, and is at once a 'practical morality' and 'a service to truth'.[53] The trouble is that, like Rousseau's politics, this is to be a politics 'growing from the heart, not from a thesis',[54] and as such must end, as Rousseau ends, by politicizing everything. If diversity happens to be accommodated in this kind of politics, it exists only on sufferance, since an ideal of community conceived in these terms has at best only an incidental place for the impersonality which is fundamental to the classical ideal of civil society.

The third confusion which now attaches to the model of civil association owes much to one of the most determined liberal defenders of the ideal. This is Sir Isaiah Berlin's identification of civil association with negative liberty. The civil ideal is not, however, a negative one: it is a formal one, and there is nothing at all negative about it on that account. A fourth misunderstanding arose during the 1980s, due largely to the influence of the New Right. It is that the defence of civil society is synonymous with the defence of capitalism. Ironically, this equation – found at times in Hayek, for example – simply takes over and perpetuates the criticism which Marx made of Hegel. According to Marx, Hegel had failed to appreciate that civil society is the sphere of bourgeois egoism and material enterprise. The failure of communism, however, has made it easier to see that the Marxist critique is one-sided, and that civil society is also, and above all, the sphere of individual self-expression and political education. It is this latter emphasis, rather than the economic interpretation, which characterizes the more persuasive liberal and conservative conceptions of the civil ideal.

A fifth source of confusion has been created by the nationalist sympathies of the New Right, in so far as these have led some conservative thinkers to diminish the integrating capacity of the civil model by their insistence that civil society is only viable when it expresses the cultural identity of a group that possesses a precivil national unity. Roger Scruton, the best known defender of this view, has

---

[52] See Z. A. Pelczynski, 'Solidarity and "The Rebirth of Civil Society" in Poland 1976–81', in J. Keane (ed.), *Civil Society and the State: New European Perspectives*, (London, Verso, 1988), pp. 361–80.

[53] Václav Havel, 'Politics and conscience', in Roger Scruton, (ed.), *Conservative Thoughts: Essays from The Salisbury Review* (London, Claridge Press, 1988), p. 201.

[54] Havel, 'Politics and conscience'.

had to be reminded that the naturalistic interpretation of prepolitical unity which it involves does not conform to the reality of European history, the lesson of which in this respect was succinctly formulated by the Hungarian philosopher Aurel Kolnai as follows: 'There can be neither an order of states nor of frontiers in which there does not enter to a large extent the factor of arbitrariness, contingency and historical accident'.[55] Supposedly prepolitical unity, in short, itself turns out to be a political creation.

There is, finally, a sixth misunderstanding which has caused confusion about the implications of the civil model for limited politics. This is the view, nurtured by Nozick in particular, that the civil state means the minimal state. In response to this view, it may be replied that what Nozick forgets is that *the civil model has two dimensions, neither of which can give an adequate account of the nature of the state, when taken apart from the other*. One – the dimension upon which Nozick concentrates – is concerned with legitimacy. This first dimension is confined to the formal side of civil association, and it therefore bakes no bread: it has no remedy, that is, for problems such as the underclass, unemployment, or ethnic conflict. This is not because it is blind to them, however; it is because it is about something else, which may be restated as the distinction between power and authority, and the institutional conditions necessary to secure the basic condition for human dignity, which is protection against arbitrary power.

Although concern with legitimacy is the moral foundation of the Western ideal of limited politics, a complete account of the civil model must of course go beyond the formal conditions of legitimacy and consider the second dimension, which is the substantive area of welfare policy. The civil model does not require that this area should be minimal; what it requires is that policy should not be pursued in ways which threaten the rule of law, make power unaccountable, or confer on the state a monopoly of the services provided.

Such, then, are the confusions and misunderstandings which have to be removed, in order to refurbish the model of civil association for application to the postmodern interpretation of our political condition. Only the application of this model, it would seem, can ensure the survival of limited politics in the postmodern state. If that is so, then it follows that the main task of contemporary political science is to examine how the balance is to be struck between the two dimensions of the civil state – the formal and the substantive – in full awareness of the ineliminable tension between them, and of the need to ensure that the freedom only secured by forms is not sacrificed to intransigent demands for particular policies.

What gives this task a degree of urgency is a danger which has so far been allowed to hover on the horizon, but must now be brought more sharply into focus. This is the possibility that the very nature of postmodern politics may make it increasingly difficult to strike the balance required for the preservation of the limited state. One radical scholar, indeed, is convinced at the outset that what are called 'the new social movements' – movements such as ecology, feminism, and the peace movement – are by their very nature incompatible with the civil model. These new social movements, Slavoj Zizek writes,

> are reluctant to enter the routine political struggle, they continually emphasize their unwillingness to become political parties like the others, they exempt themselves from the sphere of the struggle for power. At the same time, however, they make clear that their aim is much more radical than that

[55] Quoted by John Gray in 'The politics of cultural diversity', *The Salisbury Review*, p. 42.

of the ordinary political parties: what they are striving after is a fundamental transformation of the entire mode of action and belief, a change in the "life paradigm" affecting our most intimate attitudes. They offer, for example, a new attitude toward nature, which would no longer be that of domination but rather that of a dialogic interplay; against aggressive "masculine" reason, they stand for a pluralistic "soft", "feminine" rationality, etc. In other words, it is not possible to be an ecologist or feminist in quite the same way as one can be a conservative or a social democrat in a Western formal democracy. What is at stake in the former case is not just a political belief but an entire life attitude. And such a project of radical change in the "life paradigm", once formulated as a political program, necessarily undermines the very foundations of formal democracy.[56]

Faced by a new politics of this kind, in which there is no room for compromise and no regard for civil forms, the danger is that the postmodern state will predominantly concern itself with policy issues, and ignore the conditions of legitimacy which are the foundation of limited politics. Such a development would merely intensify the indifference to legitimacy that has been an increasingly marked feature of Western politics since the second world war. The reason for that indifference is familiar: it is that postwar governments have tended to put questions of welfare and economic policy above constitutional ones. Even when constitutional issues seem to have resurfaced, as in the Citizens' Charter, the real concern is with securing more efficiency and accountability in the provision of services. Other factors, such as terrorism, the need to respond to population movements, the emergence of an underclass, problems of law and order, and an ideal of European unity that is generally conceived of in instrumental terms, are already creating pressures which lead to the formulation of policy solely in the light of administrative considerations. Unless moral primacy is assigned to the civil perspective, however, the link between human welfare and human dignity is severed.

Once that link is broken, the political fate of postmodernity is not hard to foresee. It is that the new politics of inclusion and difference may eventually be accommodated, but within an administrative rather than a civil framework. Ironically, this would mean that the dream of a more genuine and more open democracy which inspires the optimistic version of postmodern politics would end by unintentionally completing a very different revolution from the one at which it actually aims. This is the final replacement of the Western tradition of limited politics – the politics of dignity – by a postmodern politics of security. Since the danger of this other revolution was of course foreseen long ago by Tocqueville in one way, and by Dostoevsky (in the parable of the Grand Inquisitor) in another, it is unnecessary to elaborate on it any further here.

Conclusion

Drawing this review of postmodernism together, three tentative conclusions emerge. The first is that the central problem of advanced Western societies is one which cannot be solved by external programmes of social and political reform of the kind which have hitherto dominated modernity. This problem is defined as

---

[56] Slavoj Zizek, *Looking Awry: An Introduction to Jacques Lacan through Popular Culture* (Cambridge, Mass. MIT Press, 1991), p. 164. I am indebted to Dr. Roger Luckhurst for drawing Zizek's work to my attention.

the experience of contingency. Some thinkers will no doubt smile at the fact that what was taught long ago by Augustine, through his vision of man as a creature in a condition of eternal tension between membership of two cities, should be so long in being rediscovered. Since the secular orthodoxy of our age has been inspired by the vision of finding the human good in a single city identity, however, the rediscovery of the limits of social and political existence may be seen as a positive achievement. The second conclusion is that postmodern philosophy may have something more substantial to offer than the ironic posture which has come to be associated with it. It may, instead, be a step towards a more modest form of humanism than has been fashionable in the past two centuries. And finally, postmodernism may help to encourage and intensify the renewed intellectual interest in the classical model of civil association as the most appropriate mode of integration for a democratic politics of radical difference provided that it can extricate itself from the confusions which were identified. The result would not be a world beyond -isms; not the least merit of postmodernism is that it knows there isn't one; it would, however, be a world in which the -isms could be mutually accommodated – provided, of course, that the formal or civil model of postmodernity is adopted. As an eloquent radical political theorist recently observed, 'By its very nature . . . the modern state is a formal institution: its unity lies in its form, not in any substantive identity of race or unity of beliefs'.[57] How far postmodernism will go in appreciating the difference between the civil and administrative modes of implementing the new politics remains, of course, to be seen.

[57] Bhikhu Parekh, 'The New Right and the politics of nationhood', in *The New Right: Image and Reality* (London, Runnymede Trust, 1986), p. 40.

After Socialism

DAVID MARQUAND*

University of Sheffield

Believers in American-style private enterprise, declared the historian A. J. P. Taylor in November 1945, were 'a defeated party . . . which seems to have no more future than the Jacobites in England after 1688'.[1] Most of Taylor's fellow-socialists shared his triumphalism, if not his delight in titillating historical analogies. In striking contrast to the mood after the first world war, virtually no one dreamed of returning to a pre-war 'normalcy': this time, memories of pre-war were of destructive abnormality. The question was how *not* to return; how to construct a just and productive economic order in place of the inhumane and wasteful chaos of the recent past. Coerced by the Red Army, eastern Europe was to find the answer in the command economy patented by the Soviet Union. In most of western Europe, wholly or partially left or centre-left governments – some of them with Communist participation – sought it in a combination of nationalization, economic planning and improved social welfare. The swing to the right which took place as the cold war intensified in the late-1940s did not produce a significantly different answer. The governments of Adenauer, de Gasperi and Winston Churchill were not remotely socialist, but they were as comfortable with the 'second-best compromises'[2] which created the characteristic west European mix of market allocation, social welfare and state intervention as were their rivals on the left.

For non-socialists had increasingly come to share the primordial socialist assumption that the age of the individual, of the unorganized, of the classical entrepreneur and the classical free market was giving way to the age of the collective, of the bureaucratic, of the regulated and hence of an economy much closer to socialism than to capitalism as traditionally understood. Not long before, Joseph Schumpeter had famously argued that capitalism was making itself superfluous: that the giant firm was ousting the entrepreneur, the linchpin of the system, and 'expropriating' the bourgeoisie, which was losing both its income and its function. In the end, he had concluded, capitalism would give way to centralized socialism.[3] One of the pivotal assumptions underlying the ingenious

* David Marquand is Professor of Politics and Director of the Political Economy Research Centre at the University of Sheffield.

[1] A. J. P. Taylor, 'The European revolution', *The Listener*, 22 November, 1945, p. 576, quoted in Charles S. Maier, *In Search of Stability, Explorations in Historical Political Economy* (Cambridge, Cambridge University Press, 1987), p. 153.

[2] For these second-best compromises see Philippe Schmitter, 'Neo-corporatism and the state' in Wyn Grant (ed.), *The Political Economy of Corporatism* (London, Macmillan, 1985), p. 37.

[3] Joseph Schumpeter, *Capitalism, Socialism and Democracy* (London, George Allen and Unwin,

defence of the British tradition of autonomous executive power which the British Tory imperialist, L. S. Amery, offered in the mid-1940s was that an increasingly collectivist age needed 'more governmental action and more definite leadership'.[4] In modern conditions, argued his younger colleague, Harold Macmillan, the invisible hand of free competition led to 'discordance, disharmony and confusion'. To remedy these, private industry had already started to plan its own activities. But piecemeal, *ad hoc* planning of this sort was not enough; it was time to supplement it with comprehensive planning on the national level.[5] Even Hayek's dithyrambic anti-collectivist *cri de coeur*, *The Road to Serfdom*, reads more like a lament for a dying order than a celebration of an order waiting to be born.

Plainly, the boot is now on the other foot. The collapse of the Communist regimes of eastern Europe and the former Soviet Union in the late-1980s and early-1990s has destroyed the only rival to the capitalist market economy that the industrial world has ever known. Alternative models of economic organization may still exist in the minds of men and women but it is no longer possible to point to a living alternative in the real world – or not, at any rate, in industrial societies. On a deeper level, the extraordinary series of popular upheavals that caused the Communist regimes to collapse discredited the tradition of thought and action which those regimes claimed to embody. The crowds that thronged the squares of eastern Europe in the final months of 1989, like the crowd that tore down Dzherzhinksy's statue in the heart of Moscow two years later, consisted of citizens or would-be citizens, not proletarians. They were acting in the spirit of 1776 or 1789, not of October 1917. They were protesting *against* the October Revolution, against the proletarian dictatorship, against the vanguard party, against the foundation myths of the Soviet state and all the states modelled upon it. In doing so, they called into question the fundamental postulates, not just of Stalinism – Stalinism was discredited long ago – but of Marxist-Leninism itself. For if Marxist-Leninism had been true, nothing of the sort could have happened.[6]

Of course, it does not follow that the Marxist tradition – or even the Marxist-Leninist tradition – have nothing more to say. The 'endist' notion that liberal democracy and market economics have won a final and irreversible victory over all actual or possible ideological rivals[7] should be taken with a pinch of salt. As the Counter-Reformation showed, traditions of thought and practice can sometimes reconstitute themselves, after the most terrible blows. But if the Marxist or Marxist-Leninist traditions do reconstitute themselves – and on that question the jury will be out for some time – they are likely to take a very different form from the ones we have been used to for the last 70 years.

That is only the beginning of the story. The collapse of Communism in the east has been accompanied, indeed preceded, by an extraordinary renaissance of economic liberalism in the west. In country after country, markets have been de-regulated, state planning dismantled or down-graded, full-employment policies

---

1976), especially pp. 131–42.

[4] L. S. Amery, *Thoughts on the Constitution* (Oxford, Oxford University Press, 1947), pp. 14–8.

[5] Harold Macmillan, *The Middle Way: A study of Economic and Social Progress in a Free and Democratic Society* (London, Macmillan, 1966) p. 190.

[6] For a powerful alternative reading, arguing that the upheavals in eastern Europe should be seen as proletarian revolutions against state capitalism, see Alex Callinicos, *The Revenge of History, Marxism and the East European Revolutions* (Cambridge, Polity Press, 1991).

[7] Francis Fukuyama, *The End of History and the Last Man* (London, Penguin, 1993).

abandoned, welfare budgets reined back and nationalized industries privatized. To take only one example, in the world as a whole, state enterprises worth an estimated $185 billion were sold to the private sector in the course of the 1980s. [8] Just as conservative and christian democratic parties accommodated themselves to the collectivism and *dirigisme* of the 1940s, so social-democratic and even Communist parties have struggled, with varying degrees of success, to accommodate themselves to the reborn economic liberalism of the last twenty years.

Three examples stand out, each emblematic of a particularly striking aspect of the theme. The Italian Communist Party was once the flagship of western Eurocommunism, with an authentic national tradition to draw upon. Now it has dissolved itself, to be reborn as the Democratic Party of the Left, with a programme placing equal emphasis on the values of liberty and equality, and explicitly designed to appeal to all 'progressive' Italian traditions, democratic catholicism and social liberalism as well as communism.[9] In the 1970s, the reborn French Socialists sloughed off the compromising centrism of the old SFIO and emerged as the *pur et dur* champions of a total break with the existing system. Two years after Mitterrand's election as president in 1981, they abandoned the mixture of nationalization, state planning and *autogestion* on which he had campaigned. The centre-piece of their economic policy became the undeviating defence of the *franc fort* by means of high interest rates and budgetary rigour, supplemented by privatizations expected to yield FF10bn, while their rhetoric focused on that traditional stand-by of French Republicanism, the rights of man.[10] In the early-1980s, the British Labour Party was the most radical of the traditional, mass working-class parties of northern Europe. It fought the 1983 election on a platform of nationalization, import controls and withdrawal from the European Community. In 1992, it proposed only trivial modifications to the privatization programme carried out by the Conservatives, and campaigned on a combination of 'supply-side socialism' – market allocation, tempered by state intervention to promote national competitiveness – monetary orthodoxy and slightly redistributive tax and welfare policies.[11] The re-orientation of Labour rhetoric was even more instructive than the re-shaping of Labour policy. Appeals to class solidarity and even to social equality were conspicuous by their absence. Instead, Labour tried, somewhat implausibly, to whistle the neo-liberal tunes of choice and freedom. 'At the core of our convictions', insisted the party leader in a personal message at the beginning of its election manifesto, 'is belief in individual liberty'[12] – a proposition which would have raised eyebrows among the most embattled revisionists of thirty years before.

[8] Geoff Mulgan, 'Reticulated organisations: the birth and death of the mixed economy', in Colin Crouch and David Marquand, *Ethics and Markets, Co-operation and Competition within Market Economies* (Oxford, Basil Blackwell, 1993) forthcoming.

[9] Martin J. Bull, 'Doing a Bad Godesberg: the Italian Communist Party and the Democratic Party of the Left', paper presented at the Political Studies Association Annual Conference, 7–9 April, 1992.

[10] Robert Elgie, 'Doing a 'Bad Godesberg': Radical transformations of parties of the Left in comparative and historical perspective. The French Socialist Party'. Paper presented to the Annual Conference of the Political Studies Association, 7–9 April, 1992; Edmund Dell, 'A World of Care', *Political Quarterly'*, 1992, 377.

[11] The Labour Party, *Meet the Challenge, Make the Change, a New Agenda for Britain* (London, the Labour Party, 1991).

[12] *Labour's Election Manifesto: It's time to get Britain working again* (London, Labour Party, 1992), p. 7.

Whose Corpse? How Dead?

So far, so Fukuyama. Before swallowing the 'endist' thesis whole, however, it would be wise to pause and take stock. What precisely do these changes amount to and what do they imply for the future? Do they all spring from the same causes and point unambiguously in the same direction? Whose corpse, exactly, should we hasten to bury? And are we sure that the corpse is dead? If it is, what follows?

Certain points are clear enough. It is beyond dispute that the Communist regimes of eastern Europe and the former Soviet Union have collapsed. Though this is less certain, there is not much doubt that one reason for their collapse is that those who ran them were no longer inwardly convinced of their own right, or perhaps even of their own capacity, to rule; that the ideology on which their claim to power was based had degenerated into a set of ritualistic incantations, which numbed the mind without stirring the spirit or kindling the imagination; and that, because of all this, they lacked the stomach for repression as well as the humility for repentance. Another reason is that, partly as cause and partly as consequence, it was plain to all that the economic race between the Soviet-style command economy and the managed capitalist economies of the west – a race which the Soviet leadership had itself announced it was running in the late-1950s and early-1960s – had ended in a decisive victory for the latter. A third is that it gradually became plain that the irrationalities and misallocations which lay behind the defeat of the former were *systemic*: that they did not spring from the personal deficiencies of particular leaders, or even from remediable corruption in high places or slack discipline in low ones, but from the inner logic of the command economy and the postulates of Marxist economics; and that it was not possible to correct them without dismantling the command economy, disrupting the nexus of vested interests which had grown up around it and repudiating the ideology which sustained it.[13] The velvet revolutions of 1989 and the failure of the attempted Soviet coup in 1991 all told the same story – elites which had lost faith in themselves; internal contradictions which could not be resolved within the terms of the system; alienated masses which regarded their rulers with outwardly compliant, but inwardly cynical, contempt.[14] In short, there was a classic revolutionary situation, eerily reminiscent of Trotsky's picture of the Russia of Nicholas II.[15]

It is also beyond dispute that, in western Europe no less than in the east, communism and socialism as doctrines, as well as the political parties that wear (or, in some cases, wore) communist or socialist labels, have made remarkably heavy weather of the economic, cultural and social transformation of the last fifteen or twenty years. The dissolution of the PCI has already been mentioned.

[13] For a masterly account of the irrationality of Soviet central planning and its relationship with Marxist theory, see Alec Nove, *The Economics of Feasible Socialism* (London, George Allen and Unwin, 1983); for a vigorous attack on Nove, see Callinicos *The Revenge of History, Marxism and the East European Revolutions*.

[14] Vaclav Havel has painted the most vivid picture of this mixture of compliance and cynicism known to me. See Vaclav Havel, *Living in Truth*, (essays edited by Jan Vladislav: London, Faber and Faber, 1989).

[15] See, in particular, his description of the aristocracy and the monarchy on the eve of revolution: 'the dynasty becomes isolated; the circle of people loyal to the death narrows down; their level sinks lower; meanwhile the dangers grow; new forces are pushing up; the monarchy loses its capacity for any kind of creative initiative; it defends itself, it strikes back, it retreats; its activities acquire the automatism of mere reflexes'. Leon Trotsky, *The History of the Russian Revolution* (London, Victor Gollancz, 1934), p. 118.

The fate of the PCF is equally instructive. In 1945 it won more votes than any of its rivals. Through all the ups and downs of the Fourth Republic, and the first decade of the Fifth, it remained the dominant working-class party, with a significantly larger popular vote than the socialists. Then, in a series of manoeuvres as audacious as they were guileful, Mitterrand allied the much weaker socialists to it, proceeded to overtake it and finally smothered it. Now it is weaker than it has been since the 1920s. But the virtual disappearance of western European communism as a serious political force has brought scant benefits to social democrats or socialists. Of the major, class-based social-democratic parties of northern Europe, the British Labour Party has been out of power since 1979, and the German Social Democrats since 1982. The Swedish Social Democrats have fared better – having lost power for the first time for forty years in 1976, they returned to it six years later – but in the last Swedish general election, their share of the vote was lower than for more than 60 years. For much of the 1980s, it looked as if the traditionally much weaker, but for that very reason less hidebound, socialist parties of southern Europe might adapt to the social changes of the period more successfully than their slower-moving, less ideologically agile, social-democratic sisters around the North Sea.[16] With the Italian Socialists mired in scandal, and the French Socialists crushingly defeated in the 1993 parliamentary elections, the contrast between the adaptable south and the sclerotic north no longer seems so telling.

More striking than any of this is the absence of a distinctively socialist or social-democratic project. For the best part of a century, the socialist vision of a world re-made haunted the imaginations of the idealistic and the dispossessed. It inspired passionate loyalties, mobilized extraordinary energies and survived innumerable betrayals and disappointments. As recently as fifteen years ago, it still flickered through the common programme of the French Left and the Alternative Strategy of the British Bennites. Revisionist social democracy, of the sort the SPD embraced at Bad Godesberg in 1959 and the British Labour Party half-embraced under Hugh Gaitskell and Harold Wilson, did not look forward to a world re-made, but it offered a different kind of inspiration: a slow, stubborn, inch-by-inch struggle to remedy tangible injustices, which would gradually make the existing world a better place. Both, moreover, could and did inspire collective projects, alternative paradigms of thought and action, combining analysis of the present with hope for the future and enabling potential constituencies to see themselves and their destinies in new ways.

The SPD's *Modell Deutschland* was such a project. At least in intention, so was the Swedish Meidner Plan. However banal it may seem in retrospect, so too was Harold Wilson's 1964 vision of a growth-promoting, welfare-enhancing economic plan, underpinned by a marriage between socialism and science.[17] But all these projects presupposed a community of interest, or at least of aspiration, extending right across a homogeneous and solidaristic working-class, and a state able to deliver the required combination of policies within its own frontiers. The technological and economic changes which have transformed the occupational structures of all advanced societies in the last 20 years have destroyed the first of these preconditions, while the remorseless growth of international economic

---

[16] For an optimistic recent assessment of their prospects see Perry Anderson, *English Questions* (London, Verso, 1992), pp. 314–23.
[17] For a sympathetic account of the Wilson project see Ben Pimlott, *Harold Wilson* (London, Harper Collins, 1992), ch. 13.

interdependence has destroyed the second. The socialism and social democracy of the post-war period cannot encompass these transformations; for the time being, at any rate, their adherents are intellectually becalmed, unable to make sense of a world which has suddenly become alien, and still less able to devise plausible projects for changing it. In a sombre conclusion to a comparative study of the 'crisis' of European social democracy, Fritz Scharpf has warned,

> The vision is bleak. Unlike the situation in the first three postwar decades, there is now no economically plausible Keynesian strategy that would permit the full realization of social democratic goals within a national context without violating the functional imperatives of the capitalist economy. Full employment, rising real wages, larger welfare transfers, and more and better public services can no longer all be had simultaneously. . . .
>
> But that need not be the end of social democratic strategies. On the contrary: when not all goals can be realised at the same time, the ability to set strategic priorities increases in importance. . . . [T]he attempt to pursue all goals at once will not lead to 'system-transforming' reforms or to the realization of other postulates of an anticapitalist rhetoric, but to a war of all against all within the Left. The most likely outcome in that case would be a deepening division between the majority of relatively privileged jobholders in the private and public sectors and a growing minority of persons in long-term unemployment, early retirement, or occasional employment, and of young people who never gain access to regular employment at all. . . .
>
> This, I believe, is the crucial question for the political future of social democracy. If Social Democrats are unwilling to face it, they will cease to shape the future, leaving the field to the Social Darwinism of the market liberals and conservatives.[18]

The warning is as pertinent today as it was when it was written.

Which Victors? What Spoils?

Yet there are ironies in all this, which triumphant conservatives and liberals are unwilling to confront. The renaissance of economic liberalism in the west coincided with the collapse of the command economy in the east, but it came too late to cause it. The extraordinary growth of living standards and productive power which forced the command economy onto the defensive began long after the capitalism of the nineteenth-century fathers of free-market economics left the stage, and well before the capitalism of today's New Right made its entrance. The credit for it belongs to the reformed, regulated, corporatist or quasicorporatist, Middle-Way capitalism to which Schumpeter and Harold Macmillan had both looked forward before and during the Second World War, and which then emerged, piecemeal, from the improvizations of post-war reconstruction. Like many false prophecies, A. J. P. Taylor's 1945 prediction that belief in private enterprise was about to go the way of Jacobitism was based on the common assumption that the future would resemble the past. Before the war, belief in private enterprise *had* been waning. It had waned because – except in Roosevelt's

---

[18] Fritz W. Scharpf, *Crisis and Choice in European Social Democracy* (Ithaca and London, Cornell University Press, 1991), pp. 274–5.

United States – the reformed capitalism of the post-war period had not yet appeared on the scene; and because unreformed capitalism was in manifest and chaotic disarray. It was the capitalism of the long post-war boom, the capitalism of *Mittbestimung* and the *Commissariat Général du Plan*, the capitalism of the paid holidays, the tight labour markets and the rising welfare expenditures that won the race with the regimes of eastern Europe, not the capitalism of the Great Depression. If the contest had been between Herbert Hoover and the command economy, the command economy might have won.

In short, capitalism triumphed because – by the criteria which its apologists shared with its opponents for most of its history – it was no longer capitalist. The reasons why it ceased being so are manifold. The symbiosis between public power and private ownership which used to be called the mixed economy, and which it is now fashionable to call the social-market economy, has a varied ancestry. The interests of big business, the teachings of the Church, the imperatives of national survival in a cut-throat world economy and the aspirations of the professional salariat, private and public, all helped to bring it into being.[19] But it is doubtful if these would have done the trick if two other factors had been absent from the equation. One was the moral and political challenge of socialism-as-doctrine: the fact that there was, in existence, a living tradition whose bearers possessed both a moral yardstick against which unreformed capitalism could be measured and found wanting, and a social vision behind which its victims could be mobilized. The other was the insistent, half-loaf pressure of social-democracy-as-practice: the fact that broadly social-democratic labour movements had the strength, discipline and political creativity to help negotiate the second-best compromises which made reformed capitalism possible. In a wry apologia for the socialist tradition, Leszek Kolakowski pointed out some time ago, 'Even if it is true that we cannot ever abolish human misery, it may at the same time be true that the world would be even worse than it is if there were no people who thought it could be better'.[20] Capitalism became better partly because socialists campaigned to replace it, and partly because social democrats could bargain on approximately equal terms with its defenders.

Good Servant: Bad Master

Now that the challengers are disarmed and the bargainers in disarray, what will happen to the challenged? The endist answer is that nothing much will happen. Victorious capitalism will march ever onwards, its progress disturbed only by occasional petty disputes over the details of the route. It would be unwise to take that for granted. Unreformed capitalism was not much good at marching. Reformed, welfare capitalism is a gift of history, as fragile as it is precious. No iron law decreed its birth or its survival. It emerged, by serendipity, from the compromises and contingencies of war and post-war reconstruction. It has been sustained by a subtle moral and political balance, in which the criticisms of socialists and the demands of social democrats were crucial ingredients. As these pressures have lost force, the balance has become unstable. There are at least two reasons for fearing that, if present trends continue, it may topple over, dragging reformed capitalism with it.

[19] For the critical role of the last see Harold Perkin, *The Rise of Professional Society, England since 1880* (London, Routledge, 1989).

[20] Leszek Kolakowski, 'Introduction' in Leszek Kolakowski and Stuart Hampshire (eds), *The Socialist Idea, A Reappraisal* (London, Quartet Books, 1977), p. 15.

The first is Michael Walzer's.

> One can conceive the market as a sphere without boundaries, an unzoned city
> – for money is insidious, and market relations are expansive. A radically
> laissez-faire economy would be like a totalitarian state, invading every other
> sphere, dominating every other distributive process. It would transfer every
> social good into a commodity. This is market imperialism.[21]

Fear of 'market imperialism' – of unreformed capitalism's relentless pressure to
commodify all social goods – has, of course, been central to socialism since the
beginning. State imperialism, the classical socialist cure applied in eastern
Europe, turned out to be worse than the disease. But, in a remarkable display of
social creativity and political skill, western Europe found a way to check the first
without surrendering to the second. The unzoned city of the market-place was
zoned after all; money, Walzer's 'universal pander,'[22] was denied entry to social
spheres where non-market principles of distribution were thought more
appropriate; at the same time, market principles were allowed free rein in other
spheres. That was the real meaning of the second-best compromises of the post-
war years. But the boundaries between market and non-market zones were
drawn where the pressures of market imperialism met countervailing pressures;
and the real meaning of today's rebirth of economic liberalism is that these
countervailing pressures are ceasing to operate. The predictable result is that the
universal pander has been set free: that a whole range of social goods which were
laboriously de-commodified a generation ago are now being re-commodified.
    That is only the beginning of the story. Walzer's fear of market imperialism
derives from his pluralist and egalitarian values. These are not universally shared
but his insight has a broader application. The technological and economic
transformations which have made it impossible to practice Keynesianism in one
country have not invalidated Keynes's central message – that, in a world of
uncertainty and insecurity, in which money is a store of value as well as a medium
of exchange, savers do not necessarily invest; and that, in an unregulated market
economy, in which uncertainty and insecurity are endemic, there is therefore an
inherent propensity for supply and demand to balance at less than full
employment. Now, as much as in the interwar years, uncertainty, insecurity and
fear of the future erode the confidence of consumers and investors with the results
that Keynes and his contemporaries knew all too well. But uncertainty and
insecurity are the hallmarks of unregulated capitalism. By the same token, they
are also the hallmarks of Walzer's market imperialism. The classical free market
works through sticks as well as carrots and insecurity is the biggest stick. It is no
accident that the central objective of renascent economic liberalism is to
dismantle the post-war nexus of social welfare, Keynesian employment policy
and corporatist or quasi-corporatist bargaining, which took the edge off the
insecurities of the past. On economic-liberal assumptions, these insecurities were
functional: without them, the market would not work properly. For economic
liberals, only Hirschman's Exit and the threat of Exit keep producers on their
toes;[23] and they do so only because, and to the extent that, they are feared. The

---

[21] Michael Walzer, *Spheres of Justice, A Defence of Pluralism and Equality* (New York, Basic
Books, 1983), pp. 119–20.

[22] Walzer, *Spheres of Justice*, p. 95.

[23] Albert O. Hirschman, *Exit, Voice and Loyalty, Responses to Decline in Firms, Organizations and
States* (Cambridge, Mass, Harvard University Press, 1970).

Keynesian-corporatist welfare state of the post-war period calmed producer fear. Market imperialism is busy re-awakening it. The trouble, of course, is that in doing so it is re-creating the Keynesian paradox of unsatisfied wants in the midst of unutilized resources.

The moral is plain. The capitalist free market is a marvellous servant but a disastrous master. In one of the greatest achievements of the second half of this century, a few favoured societies learned to convert it from master to servant. The danger now is that a smug and vainglorious capitalism will not remember the lesson.

The Five Dimensions of Socialism

Before consigning socialism to the tender mercies of the historians of political thought, it would therefore be as well to re-examine it. Granted that it can no longer generate persuasive answers, can it still ask worthwhile questions? Granted, above all, that capitalism is now in the ascendant, is there anything in socialism's legacy to help us to secure the achievements of the post-war period and save the victor from itself?

The first thing to notice is that it is a more complicated creature than the endist hypothesis allows. Socialism had at least five dimensions. It was, in the first place, an ethic. It was a difficult ethic to put into words and socialists disagreed among themselves about how best to do so. Central to almost all their gropings, however, were words like 'co-operation', 'commonwealth' and 'fellowship'. Classical socialism was not primarily about equality, as the Gaitskellite revisionists imagined in the 1950s. As Brian Barry has argued, it is possible for liberals and anarchists to be egalitarians, while the distinctive socialist belief that the distribution of rewards should be socially determined leaves open what the distribution ought to be.[24] Still less was socialism about liberty, as Roy Hattersley and Bryan Gould have insisted more recently.[25] The term in the revolutionary triad that mattered most to socialists, the term that encapsulated the essence of the socialist ideal, was fraternity. That was what William Morris meant when he said that fellowship was heaven and the lack of fellowship, hell.[26] It also lay behind Marx's gnomic (and inegalitarian) prophecy in the *Critique of the Gotha Programme* that, in the higher phase of communism, society would 'inscribe on its banners: From each according to his abilities, to each according to his needs!'[27] In non-sexist language, we might call it 'community'.

Secondly, socialism was an economic theory. Here too there were disputes, sometimes violent, within the socialist camp. Now that the fires have burned low, however, we can see that the differences were much less significant than the similarities. Socialists of all kinds, Fabians as well as Marxists, gradualists as well as revolutionaries, took it for granted that social ownership would be more efficient than private ownership, and a planned economy than the free market.

[24] Brian Barry, 'The continuing relevance of socialism', in Robert Skidelsky (ed.), *Thatcherism* (London, Chatto and Windus, 1988), p. 146.

[25] Roy Hattersley, *Choose Freedom* (Harmondsworth, Penguin, 1987); Bryan Gould, *A Future for Socialism* (London, Jonathan Cape, 1989).

[26] Quoted in Norman Denis and A. H. Halsey, *English Ethical Socialism, Thomas More to R. H. Tawney* (Oxford, Clarendon Press, 1988), p. 213.

[27] Karl Marx, 'Marginal notes to the Program of the German Workers' Party', Karl Marx and Frederick Engels, *Selected Works*, vol. II (Moscow, Foreign Languages Publishing House, 1951), p. 23.

The mighty productive powers of modern industry were held back by the chaos of private competition. Robert Blatchford's famous contrast between the efficient rationality of the state-owned post office and the wasteful irrationality of the competing private milkmen, unnecessarily duplicating their efforts with two or three carts to a street, was paradigmatic.[28] But in the socially-owned economy of the future, in which production would be for use, not profit and the blind fumblings of the capitalist entrepreneur replaced by conscious social direction, the contradiction between productive potential and the capitalist mode of production would no longer exist. The result would be a promethean upsurge of wealth creation – Engels's 'unbroken, constantly accelerated development of the productive forces'[29] – freeing mankind at last from the tyranny of want.

Not only was socialism an economic theory, it was also a science of society. Like their liberal adversaries, socialists were children of the enlightenment and suffused with its imperious rationalism. Society, they assumed, followed a determinate path towards a knowable goal. That goal was socialism. It was coming, not only or even mainly because it was right, but because it was inevitable. Socialism thus had two faces. Socialists were, of course, committed partisans, embattled advocates of human emancipation. But, in their own eyes at least, they were also dispassionate enquirers, teasing out the laws of social development as chemists and biologists teased out the laws of nature. So, for Engels, Marx was at one moment a second Lavoisier; at another, more famously, a second Darwin.[30] And so Sidney Webb saw nothing improper in founding the London School of Economics with the proceeds of a legacy intended to finance socialist propaganda: the facts were socialist and dispassionate study of the facts would automatically promote socialism.[31] These two faces reinforced each other. Socialists claimed a special moral authority by virtue of their special mastery of social dynamics. Of course, they did not all picture these dynamics in the same way. Marxist historical materialism and Fabian gradualism sprang from different philosophical roots and pointed to different practical conclusions. As on economics, however, these differences seem less significant in retrospect than the similarities. Webb was as confident as Marx that he had charted the course society was destined to follow and that his prescriptions for the future were uniquely compelling because he had done so. Once in power, Fabians were as apt as Marxists to treat society as a set of building blocks, to be rearranged in accordance with a scientific grand design. Although socialists like Rosa Luxembourg or even Keir Hardie put their faith in the spontaneous anger of the masses rather than in the laws of history, they were in a minority – icons rather than exemplars.

Fourthly, socialism was the vehicle of a social interest – the instrument, inspiration and mentor of the labour movement. To be sure, the relationship between vehicle and passenger was often ambivalent and always problematic. Socialist doctrine, again whether revolutionary or gradualist, allotted a unique, redemptive role to the proletariat. Unfortunately, real, live proletarians did not

[28] Robert Blatchford, *Merrie England* (London, Clarion Newspaper Company, 1895), p. 43.
[29] Frederick Engels, *Anti-Duhring, Herr Eugen Duhring's Revolution in Science* (Moscow, Foreign Languages Publishing House, 1954), p. 391.
[30] Preface to volume 2 of *Capital* (Moscow, Foreign Languages Publishing House, 1961), p. 15; 'Speech at the graveside of Karl Marx', Karl Marx and Frederick Engels, *Selected Works*, volume II (Moscow, Foreign Languages Publishing House, 1951), p. 153.
[31] For the details of this transaction see my *Ramsay MacDonald* (London, Jonathan Cape, 1977), pp. 41–3.

all want to be redeemers. They cheered the vision of a new society on high days and holidays, but on weekdays their aims were more prosaic – better wages, better conditions, a better future for their children. So the literature of socialism is full of complaints about the narrow horizons, limited ambitions, short-sighted materialism and dull-headed stodginess of the working class, ranging in severity from Ernest Bevin's complaints about 'the inferiority complex amongst our people'[32] to Lenin's contempt for trade-unionism as the 'ideological enslavement of the workers by the bourgeoisie'.[33] By the same token, the history of organized labour is full of tensions between the practical needs of working men and women and the pure flame of the socialist ideal.[34]

Yet it would be wrong to exaggerate these tensions. In spite of them, millions of working people came to view themselves and their destiny through the prism of socialist theory. For, in varying degrees, socialism shaped the political and economic culture of the working class in almost all industrial countries outside North America. It threw a glow of principle over the everyday struggles of the factory floor, and gave dignity and meaning to lives which market economics treated as commodities. It was a school for citizenship, a source of self-respect, a stimulus for self-discipline and personal growth: the Hardies and Bebels, Bevins and Neumanns who found, through socialism, a vocation for leadership had humbler equivalents in every working-class community. By a strange irony, the moral legacy of these achievements still helps to underpin the co-operative understandings on which reformed capitalism depends – not the least of the reasons why the Scandinavian and central European economies, where the working-class movement was most influenced by socialist teaching, have been the most successful in the Atlantic world.[35]

Finally, socialism was a secular religion. It had a heaven and a hell; saints and sinners; martyrs and persecutors; heretics and heresy-hunters; saved and damned; clergy and laity. Its language and iconography were particularly revealing. Socialists had 'faith'; they were engaged on a 'crusade'; their projects were 'New Jerusalems'; they marched to the 'Promised Land' across 'deserts' of tribulation; their leaders were 'prophets';[36] their songs were 'hymns'; their funeral processions were ceremonies of collective dedication.[37] Above all, they had an eschatology – a science of last things. One day, the expropriators would be expropriated, the humble would be exalted and a new society, free of exploitation and injustice, would arise from the ruins of the old. No one knew when that day would come but there was no doubt that it was coming. By the same token, the

---

[32] Alan Bullock, *The Life and Times of Ernest Bevin*, volume 2, *Minister of Labour 1940–1945* (London, Heinemann, 1967), p. 381.

[33] Quoted in Leszek Kolakowski, *Main Currents of Marxism*, vol. II *The Golden Age* (Oxford, Clarendon Press, 1978), p. 387.

[34] For their effect on the British Labour movement see Henry Drucker, *Doctrine and Ethos in the Labour Party* (London, George Allen and Unwin, 1979).

[35] For the importance of these co-operative understandings, see Johnathan Boswell, *Community and the Economy, the theory of public co-operation* (London, Routledge, 1990); for a German view of the relative weakness of socialist influence on the British Labour Movement see Egon Wertheimer, *Portrait of the Labour Party* (London and New York, Putnam, 1929).

[36] Sometimes more than prophets. After being howled down at an anti-war meeting in his constituency in August, 1914, Keir Hardie told a friend 'I now understand the sufferings of Christ at Gethsemane'. K. O. Morgan, *Keir Hardie, radical and socialist* (London, Weidenfeld and Nicolson, 1975), p. 226.

[37] For two vivid examples, see Caroline Benn, *Keir Hardie* (London, Hutchinson, 1992), pp. 351–2 and Jean Lacouture, *Léon Blum* (Paris, Seuil, 1977), pp. 556–7.

details of the new society were a little vague: like Christians, socialists were better at anathematizing vice than at describing virtue. But its vagueness was an asset. It shimmered in the distance, all the more glorious because no one knew what it would be like. And, as with Christianity, the force of that vision justified the most appalling crimes, as well as calling forth the most astounding displays of heroism and self-sacrifice.

Ethic and Insight

Now it is all – or nearly all – over. No one, not even the Chinese, still accepts the economic theory of socialism. A promethean upsurge of wealth creation has indeed taken place, but in the mixed or social-market economies of central Europe and the Pacific Rim. The ancient socialist assumption that public ownership and production for use were bound to be more efficient than private ownership and production for profit has turned out to be the reverse of the truth. The wave of privatizations which has swept across the globe in the last ten years has not been driven wholly, or even mainly, by ideology. At least as important has been the discovery by governments of all colours that publicly owned industries are extraordinarily difficult to discipline, to motivate and to manage; that the state can be as myopic and greedy as any private shareholder; that, in any case, it lacks the knowledge and capacity to control the undertakings it owns; and that efficiency can best be promoted by devolving responsibility to private owners, while retaining regulatory powers to ensure strategic oversight.[38] To be sure, the doctrinaire apologists for the free market are as mistaken as the doctrinaire socialists whom they mimic unintentionally. The economies which have succeeded most spectacularly have been those fostered by developmental states, where public power, acting in concert with private interest, has induced market forces to flow in the desired direction.[39] But the developmental state is as remote from the socialist state as from the Nightwatchman State of classical economics. Its purpose is to constrain the market and to allocate the costs and benefits of economic change in such a way as to enhance the capacity of a capitalist national economy to compete with other capitalist national economies, not to supersede market forces or to socialize the means of production.

The social science of socialism has fared no better. Imperious enlightenment rationalism and scientific social engineering are now discredited, on the Left even more than on the Right. We have learned that the social sciences are quite different in character and logical status from the natural sciences; that contingency and unpredictability are fundamental to social life; that the social sciences therefore cannot generate falsifiable laws with strong predictive power; that, as Alasdair MacIntyre puts it, their generalizations have the same logical status as 'the proverbs of folk societies, the generalizations of jurists, the maxims of Machiavelli';[40] and that the socialist theoreticians who thought they could uncover the dynamics of social progress were searching for fools' gold. We have also learned – perhaps even more disturbingly – that the search for this

---

[38] Mulgan in *Ethics and Markets*.

[39] For the notion of the developmental state see Ronald Dore, 'Industrial policy and how the Japanese do it', *Catalyst* (1986), 45–58.

[40] Alasdair MacIntyre, *After Virtue, a study in Moral Theory* (London, Duckworth, 2nd edn 1985), p. 105.

particular fools' gold was dangerous as well as pointless; that the steps from believing that it is possible to predict the future to believing that it is possible to shape it, and from believing that it is possible to shape it to believing that those with the appropriate knowledge have the right to shape it and to force their shape on others, are terrifyingly short. The first lesson implies that civil society cannot be re-made to fit a grand design – not just because it is apt to resist, but because the very notion of a grand design is an absurdity. The second implies that it is wrong to try.

To the extent that socialism is still the vehicle of the working class, that is now a handicap rather than an asset. The classical working class, the proletariat which Marx described and helped to form, has almost disappeared. Some of it – in most developed societies, the majority – has been absorbed, for all practical purposes, into a vast, almost boundaryless, middle class. The rest – the unskilled, the handicapped, the victims of racial prejudice – have become an under-class, effectively excluded from full citizenship and, in Ralf Dahrendorf's chilling phrase, 'split a hundred ways so that most of its members look for their own personal ways out. It does not care much either way about most issues of current concern. . . . The crucial fact about the underclass and the persistently unemployed is that they have no stake in society'.[41] As Dahrendorf's description implies, however, this under-class has little in common with the disciplined class warriors who were supposed to carry the future in their knapsacks. If anything, it is more reminiscent of the *lumpenproletariat* which the early socialists saw as recruiting material for militarists and strike breakers.

Partly because of all this, the secular religion seems to be losing its power as well. Vestiges of the old language and iconography remain, of course, but the emotional resonance is draining out of them. The agile, and until recently successful, socialist politicians of southern Europe – the Mitterrands, the Craxis, the Papandreous – have had about the same relationship with the socialism of the pioneers as Renaissance popes with the Christianity of the apostles. The heavier-footed, slower-moving social-democratic parties of the north still try to represent the victims of economic change but they long ago ceased to promise salvation to the elect or damnation to the unregenerate. They stand for reform, progress, amelioration, not for transformation. In the East, meanwhile, the very words 'socialism' and 'social democracy' have been discredited by their association with the old regimes.

Yet in this catalogue of decay, one item is conspicuous by its absence. Nothing has happened to invalidate the socialist ethic. The values of community and fellowship speak as loudly (or, of course, as faintly) to the late-twentieth century as to earlier periods. Indeed, in some respects they are more pertinent, if not necessarily more resonant, than they used to be. For with the ethic went an insight – the insight that all societies, even capitalist ones, depend on ties of mutual obligation; and that such ties are public goods, which have to be provided to everyone if they are to be provided to anyone, and which the competitive free market therefore cannot supply, although it may conceivably destroy them. Different socialists expressed that insight in different ways, but almost all of them believed that a society based on the acquisitive individualism of the market-place would be a contradiction in terms and feared that, if acquisitive individualism had free rein, if all social relationships were mediated through the cash nexus, the

---

[41] Ralf Dahrendorf, *The Modern Social Conflict, an Essay on the Politics of Liberty* (London, Weidenfeld and Nicholson, 1988), p. 161.

ties of mutual trust which hold society together would snap. 100 years ago, when the socialist critique of capitalism first developed political momentum, that danger was remote. Marx, Morris, even the young Tawney lived in societies saturated with the communal ethic of the pre-industrial past and shot through with institutions that embodied it. Churches, universities, municipalities, crafts, professions, armies all, in different ways and to differing degrees, expressed a collective morality of some kind. Indeed, the capitalist free market drew on the moral legacy of earlier centuries, even while depleting it. Now the danger has come close. The old communalism is fading and no one has yet found a new communalism to replace it.

Perhaps the central question for our time is whether insight and ethic can be brought together in a new project with some purchase on social reality. The only honest answer is that there is, as yet, no way of telling. The obstacles are formidable: the transformation of the world market which has made it impossible to practice even Keynesianism, let alone socialism or social democracy, in one country; the changing patterns of production and employment which are eroding the old solidarities of class and occupation; the simultaneous globalization and fragmentation of culture and identity which make it increasingly difficult to speak resonantly of public, as opposed to private, interests. One may detect the germs of a possible new paradigm – the communitarian critique of liberalism which has become a major theme of moral and political thought; the feminist critique of traditional conceptions of politics and the public sphere; the green emphasis on sustainability and stewardship; the growing realization that human capital and economic co-operation hold the key to high-quality production – but no one has yet succeeded in putting them together into a persuasive whole.

That said, it is hard to believe that Hirschman's cycle of 'involvement', from the private to the public sphere and back again,[42] has, for some mysterious reason, come to a halt at the end of the twentieth century. To be sure, it is equally hard to guess what form a new era of public involvement would take. Outwardly, at least, it is unlikely to bear much resemblance to the socialism or even to the social democracy discussed in this essay. Yet some of the pioneers would have been prepared for that. It was, after all, William Morris who dreamed of 'How men fight and lose the battle, and the thing they fought for comes about in spite of their defeat, and when it comes turns out not to be what they meant, and other men have to fight for what they meant under another name'.[43]

---

[42] Albert O. Hirschman, *Shifting Involvements, Private Interest and Public Action* (Oxford, Martin Robertson, 1982).

[43] Quoted in Peter Stansky, *William Morris* (Oxford, Oxford University Press, 1983), p. 64.

Premature Obituaries: A Comment on O'Sullivan,* Minogue,† and Marquand‡

ALEX CALLINICOS§

University of York

Legend has it that an official of the British Foreign Office declared after the Hitler-Stalin pact was signed in August 1939: 'All your 'isms are now wasms'. As the context makes clear, the 'isms in question were the two great ideological challenges to liberal democracy at mid-century, fascism and communism. These days, however, when there is talk of the end of ideology, it is the ideology of the Left – that is, the socialist critique of capitalism – whose death is being announced. Thus, in the most widely discussed recent variation on this theme, it was the triumph of liberal capitalism over 'existing socialism' which Francis Fukuyama took to mark the end of history – or rather, of 'History: that is, history understood as a single, coherent, evolutionary process'.[1]

The end of history is also, for Fukuyama, the end of ideology at least in the sense that those ideologies which claimed to offer a systemic alternative to liberal capitalism have collapsed: 'for a very large part of the world, there is now no ideology with pretensions to universality that is in a position to challenge liberal democracy'.[2] The advanced industrial countries have become, in effect, one-ideology societies, in that liberal democracy now provides the inescapable framework in which individual and collective projects must be pursued. Fukuyama's chief worry for the future concerns the adequacy of this framework to contain the demands for recognition which he believes to be the driving force of history.

The upshot is a far more ambivalent appraisal of the prospects for humankind than Fukuyama's reputation as a bourgeois triumphalist might suggest. A famous passage in his original article revealed Fukuyama's less than total enthusiasm for the capitalist eternity he predicted:

> The end of history will be a very sad time. The struggle for recognition, the willingness to risk one's life for a purely abstract goal, the worldwide

---

§ Dr Alex Callinicos is Reader in Politics at the University of York.

* Noel O'Sullivan, 'Political Integration, the limited state, and the philosophy of post-modernism', *Political Studies* XLI Special Issue (1993), 21–42.

† Kenneth Minogue, 'Ideology after the collapse of communism', *Political Studies*, XLI Special Issue (1993), 4–20.

‡ David Marquand, 'After socialism', *Political Studies*, XLI Special Issue (1993), 43–56.

[1] F. Fukuyama, *The End of History and the Last Man* (New York, The Free Press, 1992), p. xii.

[2] Fukuyama, *The End of History and the Last Man*, p. 45.

ideological struggle that called forth daring, courage, imagination and idealism, will be replaced by economic calculation, the endless solving of technical problems, environmental concerns, and the satisfaction of sophisticated consumer demands. In the post-historical period there will be neither art nor philosophy, just the perpetual caretaking of the museum of the human spirit.[3]

There are various ways in which one might respond to the picture painted by Fukuyama. I shall be concerned in this paper with two. One is to accept the general accuracy of Fukuyama's picture, but to argue that we should not feel as gloomy about it as he is at least occasionally disposed to be. This seems to me the path taken by Noel O'Sullivan. The other is to reject the picture, and to argue that liberal capitalism is likely to face powerful internally generated challenges in the future. This is the course followed by Kenneth Minogue and David Marquand, though their reasons for doing so are very different.

O'Sullivan does not make any sweeping claims to the effect that the end of history is now upon us. Indeed, his sympathetic discussion of postmodernism suggests that he might consign Fukuyama's world-historical speculations to the same bonfire into which Lyotard flung Hegel's and Marx's grand narratives. Nevertheless O'Sullivan's overall account of our present situation is remarkably similar to Fukuyama's description of 'the post-historical period'. After the great ideological and political storms of the past few centuries postmodernism's 'philosophy of modesty' offers a return to safer waters. No more attempts to found our theories on the very nature of reality or, on the basis of such purportedly objective knowledge, to carry out comprehensive socio-political transformations. But, rather than share the nostalgia Fukuyama sometimes betrays for 'the worldwide ideological struggle', we should welcome the end of the era of meta-narratives and revolutions as the recovery of an older wisdom, of 'the model of civil association' first developed by Hobbes. Only his sovereign (suitably hedged in by the institutions of liberal democracy) can provide the 'impersonal and formal framework of law' within which the 'social and cultural diversity' celebrated by postmodernists can flourish.

There is plenty one could find to quarrel with in O'Sullivan's account of postmodernism as intellectual history. Tedious though it is to say it yet again, it still seems necessary to insist that very few of the propositions associated with postmodernism are particularly new or original.[4] For example, the theme of 'the contingency of existence' of which O'Sullivan makes great play is explored in depth by Heidegger in *Being and Time*, where it provides the basis of a critique of the banality and conformity of everyday life which, far from displaying a 'yearning for a cosmic setting', points towards Heidegger's espousal of National Socialism as the expression of a collective will to power capable of reversing the decline of the West.[5] There have, of course, been attempts to claim a suitably denazified Heidegger for postmodernism, but this then points to a characteristic feature of the enterprise, namely the way in which thinkers who did not seek to locate their own theories by appeal to the contrast between modernity and

---

[3] F. Fukuyama, 'The end of history', *The National Interest*, Summer 1989, 3–18, p. 18.

[4] See A. Callinicos, *Against Postmodernism* (Cambridge, Polity, 1989), esp. Ch. 1.

[5] See especially M. Heidegger, *Being and Time* (Oxford, Blackwell, 1967), 'Division Two: *Dasein* and Temporality', pp. 274–488, and, on Heidegger's relationship to National Socialism, J. Herf, *Reactionary Modernism* (Cambridge, Cambridge University Press, 1984), and R. Wolin, *The Politics of Being* (New York, Columbia University Press, 1990).

postmodernity, and who even, like Foucault, may have expressed reservations about the distinction, are nonetheless now marketed under the postmodernist label.[6]

It is probably, however, now mere Quixotry to protest about the way in which the selling of postmodernism – one of the most remarkable pieces of cultural entrepreneurship of the past decade or so – has misrepresented the real lines of intellectual development. O'Sullivan undoubtedly gives an accurate rendering of how postmodernism is generally taken. And it is refreshing to find, instead of the apocalyptic rhetoric offered by Baudrillard and his camp-followers, an argument which seeks to show how postmodernism is best understood as one way of shoring up the old 'western ideal of limited politics'.

But have we really returned, after the distractions of 1789 and 1917, to safe waters? O'Sullivan confesses to the fear that we may not. He notes the tendencies in contemporary politics to 'ignore the conditions of legitimacy which are the foundation of limited politics' and to 'lead to the formulation of policy solely in administrative terms'. He warns of 'a silent and unnoticed revolution, in the course of which the Western tradition of limited politics – the politics of dignity – is replaced by a postmodern politics of security'. The existence of these tendencies is undeniable. But is there anything particularly postmodern about them? O'Sullivan tacitly replies in the negative when he invokes Tocqueville and Dostoevsky as earlier critics of the rising 'administrative state'.

To take the case of Tocqueville, his analysis of the 'irresistible revolution' brought about by '[t]he gradual development of the principle of equality', whose chief political consequence was likely to be 'an immense and tutelary power, which takes upon itself alone to secure their [i.e. citizens'] gratifications and to watch over their fate', was intended as a diagnosis of the condition of Western society in the era after the American and French Revolutions.[7] It is a major contribution to the debate over the nature of and the prospects for modernity in which Hegel, Marx, Nietzsche, and Weber can also be regarded as participants. The fact that O'Sullivan can with such ease take over Tocqueville's vocabulary in order to characterize the main political danger currently facing us (the very phrase 'politics of security' irresistibly recalls the discussion of 'What Sort of Despotism Democratic Nations Have to Fear' with which *Democracy in America* effectively concludes) suggests that we are still mired in modernity and its contradictions, still caught up in its characteristic dilemmas and debates.[8]

Neither Marquand nor Minogue will have any truck with the idea that we live in 'postmodern' or 'post-historical' times. Both seek to identify, beneath even such striking discontinuities as the East European revolutions and the collapse of the Soviet Union, certain fundamental continuities. Where they differ is in their account of the nature of these continuities.

Minogue's main preoccupation is with 'ideology'. This is the name which, rather confusingly, he gives to the class of theories which employ the concept of ideology. The primary characteristic of such theories is the bisection they effect between true and false beliefs. The theory itself is the paradigm of true belief, and consists (so it says) of 'the revelation of a total knowledge superior to all competitors'. By contrast, 'most current competing beliefs are revealed as false.

[6] See, for example, M. Foucault, 'Structuralism and post-structuralism', *Telos*, 55 (1983), 204.
[7] A. de Tocqueville, *Democracy in America* (2 vols., New York, Random House, n.d.), I, pp. 6–7; II, p. 336.
[8] See esp. J. Habermas, *The Philosophical Discourse of Modernity* (Cambridge, Polity, 1987).

In fact, *everything* is revealed as false to the extent that it fails to confirm the revelation'. Knowledge of the 'ideological' kind is power: it leads to 'a special kind of relationship between the believer on the one hand, and the mass of people sunk in false consciousness on the other: it is a tutorial relationship, a relationship of correction'. Naturally enough, when ideologists gain control of a state, '[a]n elite party, or vanguard, takes over all power and proceeds to tutor the population in how to think and to act'.

Surely we have heard this all before? Minogue's is a variation on a well-worn theme beloved of theorists of totalitarianism. And, like most such theorists, Minogue takes little trouble to conceal that the main example of 'ideology' in his terms is, of course, Marxism. But since he is pretty sure that Marxism is dead, should not Minogue's critique of 'ideology', after receiving suitable decoration for its services during the Cold War, be honourably retired? The answer is that 'ideology' has survived Marxism, and continues to be 'a real and influential movement'. It is to be found in certain forms of monism. One, 'identity monism', insists on conceiving human beings as the bearers of 'a single basic identity', as 'workers, women, Blacks, colonials, nationalisms, participatory citizens or some similar idea'. The other, typical of 'normative political philosophers', consists in demanding that society conform to a single ideal – Minogue mentions Rawls's *Theory of Justice* as an example. The effect of either monism is to seek to homogenize the irreducible diversity of civil society – a project which threatens 'hideous slaughter and repression' – and to transform the state from an institution which merely rules (providing the formal conditions of private life – the model of state espoused also by O'Sullivan) to 'a managed enterprise', which seeks, under the influence of some theory of justice, to attain the unattainable – social perfection.

What is there to be said about all this? The term 'ideology' has acquired so many meanings, some mutually incompatible, that it would be futile to seek to deny Minogue the right to his own, admittedly eccentric, use of it.[9] He expresses some annoyance at the idea that his own argument might be cited as an instance of ideology. But if we return to the concept's origins, we find that its emergence reflected the search for a social explanation of collective error.[10] Even the more naive Enlightenment accounts of religion as superstitions cooked up by greedy priests had begun to explore the connections between shared beliefs and social interests: in different ways Hegel and Feuerbach, Marx and Nietzsche, took this enterprise much further. Now Minogue seems to be following in their footsteps when he asks how 'such an empty piece of intellectual rhodomontade [as 'ideology'] could have survived so long'. The answer is that 'ideology may be epistemologically feeble but it is ontologically interesting in constituting a distinction between a knowledge-possessing elite and a benighted mass'. Just as, according to the *philosophes*, religion gave social power to the priests (Minogue indeed toys with such a claim in the sentence before the one just cited), so 'ideology' allows its exponents to dominate. Whether Minogue likes it or not, he seems to be engaged in the same kind of intellectual project as that undertaken by the classical theorists of ideology.

How good an example his argument is of this or indeed any other form of theoretical enquiry is another matter. His comments on Marx simply do not meet

[9] For a comprehensive list of these different usages, see T. Eagleton, *Ideology* (London, Verso, 1991), pp. 1–2.

[10] See H. Barth, *Truth and Ideology* (Berkeley and Los Angeles, University of California Press, 1976).

the standards of acquaintance with the texts set in contemporary discussion.[11] And what is one to make of the claim that 'ideology' continues to wage its war against liberty by other means – for example, in the shape of left-liberal theories of justice like Rawls's? It is hard to be sure how seriously one should take this idea. Were one to do so, there are a number of questions which one would need to put to Minogue. How, for example, can a theory be treated as an instance of 'ideology' (in Minogue's sense of the term) whose author has consistently denied any claim to epistemological privilege and indeed in recent years tended to present it as an articulation of the self-understanding of liberal democratic societies?[12] Again, Minogue charges the 'new ideology' with demanding that 'the market must be throughly regulated so as to guarantee a set of desired outcomes': does this mean that any attemt to regulate the market carries with it a proto-totalitarian logic, or only attempts at 'thorough regulation', and if the latter, how does one distinguish between acceptable and unacceptable forms of regulation? Until Minogue at least seeks to address questions of this nature it is tempting to dismiss his depiction of Rawls as Marx's heir as the philosophical counterpart of the right-wing Republican attacks during the 1992 US presidential elections on Hilary Clinton as 'the last Bolshevik' – that is, not to put too fine a point on it, as McCarthyite fantasy.

Minogue's target is essentially the social-democratic project of regulated capitalism. This forms the focus also of Marquand's paper, though here it is explored, not as the bearer of hidden totalitarian ambitions, but from a sympathetic viewpoint. Social democracy's triumph, Marquand contends, was to have tamed unbridled capitalism during the first half of the twentieth century. Today, however, it is becalmed, both because of the discredit caused to the idea of socialism by the collapse of the Eastern bloc and thanks to 'an extraordinary renaissance of economic liberalism in the West'. Nevertheless, there is still a role for social democracy. What Michael Walzer calls the 'market imperialism' favoured by the New Right is recreating the social strains and economic uncertainties which the postwar synthesis of Keynesian economics and high levels of welfare expenditure was called into existence to end forever. Marquand does not believe we can simply restore this synthesis; too much of the intellectual furniture shared by Marxists and social democrats is now obsolete for that. But the socialist ethic has lost none of its power in a world where 'acquisitive individualism' has been given free rein, and it may inform new, as yet unimagined attempts to pursue collective goals.

Marquand provides a lucid and judicious account of the current plight of the Left. It suffers, however, from one extremely serious weakness, namely that it greatly exaggerates the strength and stability of contemporary capitalism. The key Western industrial countries – the Group of Seven – did enjoy an extraordinary and largely unanticipated economic and political triumph at the end of the 1980s when the coalition of states constituting their main geopolitical rivals and claiming to embody a superior social system collapsed ingloriously. Whether this amounted to a victory for capitalism *tout court* is another matter altogether. For one thing, it is at least arguable that Stalinism represented, not

[11] One example must suffice. It was not, as Minogue claims, later '[r]ealists in the Marxist movement', but Marx himself, who distinguished between the dictatorship of the proletariat and communism: see, for example, his famous letter to Weydemeyer of 5 March 1852, in K. Marx and F. Engels, *Collected Works*, XXXIX (London, Lawrence & Wishart, 1983), pp. 60–6.

[12] See, for example, J. Rawls, 'Justice as fairness: political not metaphysical', *Philosophy and Public Affairs*, 14 (1985), 223–51.

any form of socialism, existing or otherwise, but an extreme and highly autarkic version of the kind of militarized state capitalism which was the norm throughout the global economy in the era of the two World Wars and the Great Depression. Insulated from the world market for a generation or more thanks to the strictures of the Cold War, the former Stalinist societies now find themselves seeking to make, in an abrupt and catastrophic form, the kinds of changes which the Western economies were able to make gradually in the course of several decades.[13]

On this interpretation, then, the West triumphed, not over 'existing socialism', but over a particularly antiquated form of capitalism. The ease with which large sections of the *nomenklatura* in both Eastern Europe and the former Soviet Union have been able to adapt themselves to the successor regimes' market-oriented policies, often dominating, for example, the privatization of state enterprises, suggests that the basic structures of social power in these countries have changed much less than their outward forms.[14] But, one might argue, the condition of the post-Stalinist states is of little moment to the world economy, since most have been reduced to the status of Third World countries and have joined the long queue of petitioners for Western aid and investment. Whatever the precise character of the socio-political upheavals of the former Eastern bloc, they underline the predominance of the dynamic Western economies (perhaps soon to be joined in world councils by the most powerful of the East Asian miracle economies).

Even here, however, the balance sheet is considerably more mixed than most commentators and analysts are prepared to acknowledge. The early 1990s have, after all, been marked by a major world recession which severely affected not merely the United States, lone superpower after the fall of the Soviet Union, but also Japan and Germany, often regarded as the real victors of the Cold War thanks to their pre-eminence as manufacturing exporters. This recession, whose length and severity were greatly underestimated by most official forecasters, was the third global economic slump since the early 1970s. It was notable in revealing *both* the main capitalist models in the West to be in crisis.[15]

The strains within the first of these models – perhaps best described as the Anglo-Saxon, *laissez faire* model – were obvious enough. Hit upon first by the Reagan administration and copied by governments of various political colours in Britain, Australia, Canada and New Zealand, this involved both highly regressive distributive measures which through cuts in taxation and welfare expenditure transferred wealth and income from poor to rich, and a resort to deregulation and easy credit to float the economy out of the last great recession of the early 1980s. The frenzied, largely speculative boom which followed led, predictably enough (though few predicted it), to a crash which left the economies which had gone furthest in this direction loaded down with private and public

---

[13] See A. Callinicos, *The Revenge of History* (Cambridge, Polity, 1991). Incidentally, Marquand misreads my argument, claiming that I see 'the upheavals in Eastern Europe . . . as proletarian revolutions against state capitalism'. In fact, I argue that the 1989 revolutions were much more limited changes, political revolutions which involved an alteration of political regime, rather than of social system: see *Revenge*, pp. 50–66.

[14] See M. Haynes, 'Class and crisis – the transition in Eastern Europe', *International Socialism*, 2:54 (1992), 45–104, and, for a theoretically confused but empirically revealing account of recent changes in Russia, S. Clarke, 'Privatization and the development of capitalism in Russia', *New Left Review*, 196 (1992), 3–27.

[15] See, for a comprehensive analysis of the early 1990s recession, C. Harman, 'Where is capitalism going?', *International Socialism*, 2:58 (1993), 3–57.

sector debt. The political fallout swept George Bush from the White House; though the other vanguard New Right government managed to hang onto office in Britain, it was at the price of an apparently permanent internal crisis within a deeply factionalized ruling party.

The irony is that it should be at precisely this point that many of the successor regimes in the former Eastern bloc sought to put into practice the *laissez faire* economic doctrines now discredited in the West. Often, these new Eastern liberals did so with a sincerity and enthusiasm which far exceeded anything seen in Washington and London in the heyday of Reagan and Thatcher. The lack of alignment of the theories they had learned from Hayek and Friedman, not only with the economies they were seeking to reform, but also with the realities of Western capitalism, would have been comic, were not the consequences of applying them so disastrous. The zeal, for example, of Yeltsin's young ministers recalled nothing more than the millenarian dreams with which Komsomolniks had poured into the Soviet countryside at the beginning of the 1930s to force the peasantry into collective farms. Indeed, since the new Russian political elite was drawn largely from the old *nomenklatura*, Yeltsin's Thatcherite advisers were also ex-Komsomolniks. Only now their slogans were not 'the construction of socialism' and 'class war', but 'civil society' and 'sound money'. It is to be hoped that this new experiment has a less catastrophic outcome than its predecessor.

But the tragicomic collapse of the New Right should not obscure the crisis of the other main Western model – that of social-market capitalism. This was most fully developed in West Germany and much of northwestern Europe. Here, relatively high levels of economic regulation and social expenditure provided the framework for a process of corporate bargaining involving the state, big business and organized labour. Japan can in certain respects be seen as a variant of this model, with a far weaker welfare system than in continental Europe, but a strong emphasis on state intervention in the economy and on social bargaining. The early 1990s have seen the social-market model crack as well. In Japan this was associated with the financial sector's participation in the speculative boom of the 1980s. The collapse of the 'bubble economy' has left the Japanese banks loaded down with debt, and thereby helped drastically to reduce world markets' main sources of capital in the 1980s. In the German case it was, of course, the destabilizing effects of reunification which marked the turning point. The huge financial flows required to rescue the eastern economy have created a fiscal and monetary crisis felt throughout Europe through the regime of high interest rates imposed by the Bundesbank. The resulting social strains can be seen not only in the growth of a far Right that has profited from the rise in unemployment in both east and west, but also in a series of labour disputes which may portend the collapse of the old corporatist structures.

It is the crisis of both the main Western economic models, as much as the political instability caused by the collapse of the Eastern bloc (most evident, of course, in the wars in the Balkans and parts of the former Soviet Union), which casts a shadow over liberal capitalism's hour of triumph. Moreover, the difficulties faced by the social-market as well as the *laissez faire* model suggest that the problems confronted by the social-democratic tradition are even deeper than Marquand admits. The plight of southern 'Eurosocialism', which in the early 1980s had seemed to represent a realistic adaptation of social democracy to the new, globalized capitalism, but now represents a panorama of scandal-ridden governments struggling to retain office in the face of the unpopularity of their conservative economic policies, implies that the regulators of the market can all too easily take on its most unattractive characteristics.

Maybe, in the light of all this, we should not be too eager to throw onto the dustheap those variants of socialism which have based themselves on root-and-branch opposition to capitalism, and have insisted that its very logic makes it resistant to any fundamental reform. Of these radical, even revolutionary socialisms, Marxism is undeniably the most intellectually consequent. Of course, it is essential to be clear about what is meant here by 'Marxism'. 'Marxism-Leninism', for two generations the official religion of the USSR, is unlikely to survive the regimes which imposed it by force. There may, of course, be some local conditions which would give it a bit of life. Harry Gwala, the most influential leader of the African National Congress in the war-ravaged townships and squatter settlements of Natal, is an unrepentant Stalinist and supporter of the August 1991 coup. The ideology may survive through transmutation: witness, for example, the sinister 'red-brown' coalition of Stalinists, monarchists and outright fascists which forms the extreme right wing of the opposition to the Yeltsin government. But it is unlikely that an ideology which views with regret the passing of 'existing socialism' will get much of a wider hearing.

The variant of Marxism most likely to have a future is what Isaac Deutscher called 'classical Marxism' – the tradition as it was first developed by Marx and Engels, which prevailed in the Russian revolutionary movement in 1917, and which Trotsky and the Left Opposition sought to defend against the emerging Stalinist *nomenklatura*. This tradition has three strengths which make it of contemporary relevance. First, it is based on a critique of capitalism which sees the inequality and instability it generates not as accidents or contingent flaws but as inherent features of a system based on exploitation and prone to crisis. Given the profound difficulties confronted by both the prevalent capitalist models, Marxism's *systemic* critique cannot simply be dismissed as obsolete dogma. Secondly, Trotsky and those influenced by him sought to marry this analysis to a critique of Stalinism which sought both to provide an explanation within the canons of historical materialism of the monster spawned by the October Revolution and to measure Stalinism's distance from an authentic socialist society. It is in no small measure thanks to this tradition of anti-Stalinist Marxism (and the price which many of its exponents paid for their beliefs in Stalin's heyday) that socialists can still hold up their heads today, when the full dimensions of the Soviet catastrophe are evident to all.[16] Finally, this rejection of capitalism and Stalinism presupposed a particular view of socialism perhaps best summed up by Marx's formula 'the self-emancipation of the working class'. Social transformation is not the achievement of an elite, whether it takes the form of a 'Marxist-Leninist' party or that of social-democratic parliamentarians, but is a process of self-liberation, driven from below by the mass of working people's aspiration to take control of their lives.

The difficulties confronting even this version of Marxism are well-known. Intellectually, they include the claim, advanced, for example, by Marquand, that the class structure of modern societies no longer provides a basis for the kind of project envisaged by classical Marxists, and the demand for a model of socialist planning not vulnerable to the dysfunctions of the Stalinist command economies.[17] Politically, anyone who still calls themselves a Marxist has to

---

[16] See esp. L. Trotsky, *The Revolution Betrayed* (New York, Pathfinder, 1970); T. Cliff, *State Capitalism in Russia* (London, Bookmarks, 1988); and, for a general survey of this tradition, A. Callinicos, *Trotskyism* (Milton Keynes, Open University Press, 1990).

[17] For attempts to confront these issues see, respectively, A. Callinicos and C. Harman, *The*

grapple with the embarrassment of association with the shipwreck of 'existing socialism'. But the defects of capitalism are of so comprehensive and traditional kind (even the more lucid conservative commentators have been prepared to acknowledge the extent to which social and economic inequalities have widened in recent years)[18] as to demand that the case made against it by its most powerful critic still be heard. It was as a critique of capitalism that Marxism took shape. Then as long as capitalism continues on its unjust and destructive path, it is likely to find Marxism, in some form or other, confronting it.

Changing Working Class (London, Bookmarks, 1987), and P. Devine, *Democracy and Economic Planning* (Cambridge, Polity, 1988).

[18] See, for example, K. Phillips, *The Politics of Rich and Poor* (New York, Harper Collins, 1991).

Liberalism and Collectivism in the 20th Century

RICHARD M. EBELING*

Hillsdale College, Michigan

Several times during our century, the Western world has passed through 'watershed' periods of crisis. The first occurred as a result of the First World War. It brought the Liberal Epoch to an end in August, 1914. How far away that Liberal era now seems to us. Governments hardly fleeced their citizens: total tax burdens in Great Britain and the United States were only in the range of ten or fifteen percent of national income; and the United States had had an income tax for only one year when the war began. The British government ran its world-encompassing empire as a vast free trade zone, open to all comers for trade and investment regardless of their nationality or citizenship. The United States, it is true, fluctuated between higher and lower tariffs, but within its three thousand mile span, the country contained no barriers to production, trade and exchange. And across the European continent, the tariff barriers were miniscule compared to what the rest of the 20th century has experienced.

Matching the free movement of goods was the free movement of people. Emigration restrictions and immigration barriers were in their infancy. It was still a world with neither passports nor visa requirements. For the price of a railway ticket or passage in steerage across the Atlantic, even the poorest could pick up and move wherever personal inclination or economic opportunity lead them to take up residence – and millions of people did so. Nor were there any barriers to the free movement of money and capital. Exchange controls, restrictions and limits on the transfer of investment capital between countries, and fluctuations in the exchange rates among currencies were unknown. The Western world was bound together by one monetary system – the gold standard. Each national currency was redeemable on demand for a fixed amount of gold, gold coins circulated as actual media of exchange and these gold coins jingled in most people's pockets.

The welfare state was unheard of. Help for the unfortunate and those in temporary financial need was considered primarily to be matters of community charity, individual philanthropy and church-related assistance. The degree to which voluntarism had succeeded was demonstrated by the comments of English

* Richard Ebeling is Ludwig von Mises Professor of Economics at Hillsdale College, Michigan, USA.

economist, William Stanley Jevons (who was not an advocate of *laissez-faire*), in his 1870 Presidential address to the British Association for the Advancement of Science, that 'Could we sum up the amount of aid which is, in one way or another, extended by the upper to the lower classes, it would be almost of incredible amount, and would probably far exceed the cost of poor law relief'. But Jevons believed that voluntary charity, in this period of supposed Victorian stone-heartedness, had become excessively generous: 'It is well known that those towns where charitable institutions and charitable people abound, are precisely those where the helpless poor are most numerous . . . [T]he casual paupers have their London season and their country season, following the movements of those on whom they feed. Mr. Goschen and the poor law authorities have of late begun to perceive that all their care in the administration of relief is frustrated by the over-abundant charity of private persons, or religious societies'. (It is worth recalling that this was before the charitable deduction could be made from one's income tax.)[1]

The Western nations were in their stated principles, if admittedly not always in their actual practice, committed to the ideal of individual liberty in practically all areas of life – social, economic and political.[2] This ideal has been explained by Wilhelm Röpke: 'It is the liberal principle that economic affairs should be free from political direction, the principle of a thorough separation between the spheres of the government and the economy . . . The economic process was thereby removed from the sphere of officialdom, of public and penal law, in short from the sphere of the "state" to that of the "market", of private law, of property, in short to the sphere of "society" . . .'[3]

Collectivist clouds, it is true, had already started to form over the Liberal terrain, even before the war. In 1913, German historian Hermann Levy pointed out that, 'The Manchester School of *laissez-faire* has of recent years been brought face to face with two very momentous phenomena – Socialism and Neo-Mercantilism. These two very different tendencies have a common element in their opposition to the individualist doctrines of political economy. Socialism is concerned with the division of the product according to certain principles of "justice", rather than with the development of potential production. Mercantilism is the most complete expression of an all-embracing regulation of industrial conditions by political wisdom and administrative practice. But both agree that industry should be organized by the State. Manchester Liberalism has been undermined bit by bit by the union of these two forces'.[4] But while the foundations of the old Classical Liberal order were being slowly chipped away in the years preceding the Great War, in the daily affairs of ordinary men, the political and economic environment in which people went about their business of living and earning a living was still one of widely respected civil liberty and economic freedom.

All of this changed with World War I. The transformation that the Great War produced was described by the German economist Gustav Stolper:

---

[1] William Stanley Jevons, *Methods of Social Reform* [1883] (New York, Augustus M. Kelley, 1965), p. 197.

[2] On the economic and political era before the First World War, see, John Maynard Keynes, *The Economic Consequences of the Peace* (New York, Harcourt, Brace and Howe, 1920), pp. 10–12; and Gustav Stolper, *This Age of Fable: The Political and Economic World We Live In* (New York, Reynal & Hitchcock, 1942), pp. 1, 7–8.

[3] Wilhelm Röpke, *International Order and Economic Integration* (Dordrecht-Holland, Reidel 1959), p. 75.

[4] Hermann Levy, *Economic Liberalism* (London, Macmillan, 1913), p. 1.

Just as the war for the first time in history established the principle of universal military service, so for the first time in history it brought national economic life in all its branches and activities to the support and service of state politics – made it effectively subordinate to the state . . . Not supply and demand, but the dictatorial fiat of the state determined economic relationships – production, consumption, wages, cost of living . . . [A]t the same time, and for the first time, the state made itself responsible for the physical welfare of its citizens; it guaranteed food and clothing not only to the army in the field but to the civilian population as well . . . Here is a fact pregnant with meaning; the state became for a time the absolute ruler of our economic life, and while subordinating the entire economic organization to its military purposes, also made itself responsible for the welfare of the humblest of its citizens, guaranteeing him a minimum of food, clothing, heating and housing.

And Professor Stolper pointed out that even after the war came to an end, 'The free movement of capital has ceased. So has the free movement of emigration. Men and money both lie shackled under the might of the state . . . The choking of free movement in manpower and capital is being intensified by the choking of free movement of commodities'.[5] The Classical Liberal world of individual rights, private property and civil liberty died on the battlefields of the war. Many of the cherished and hard-won freedoms of the 19th century were sacrificed on the altar of winning the war. And when the war was over, liberty, as it turned out, was the ultimate victim. Behind the war-time slogans of 'making the world safe for democracy', 'the right of national self-determination', and 'a league of nations for the securing of world peace', nation states had grown strong with power. Wartime controls had replaced free enterprise; exchange controls and import-export regulations had replaced free trade; confiscatory taxation and inflation had undermined the sanctity of private property and eaten up the accumulated wealth of millions. The individual and his freedom had shrunk . . . and the state and its power were now gigantic.

And the Collectivist demons had been set loose on the world. By the 1930s, there was not one major country devoted to the principles of Liberalism. Regardless of the particular variation on the Collectivist theme, practically every government in the world had or was implementing some form of economic planning and restricting the personal and commercial freedoms of its own citizenry. In the Soviet Union, the state owned and controlled all of the resources and means of production. Production and distribution was directed by the central planning agencies in Moscow. In Fascist Italy and Nazi Germany, property and resources remained nominally in private hands, but the use and disposal of that property and those resources were controlled and directed according to the dictates of the state. In Great Britain, free trade and the gold standard had been abandoned in the early 1930s during the depths of the Great Depression. Protectionism, interventionism, welfare-statism and monetary manipulation were the active policy-tools of the British government.

Throughout Europe and the rest of the world, the various nation-states had erected tariff barriers, regulated industry and agriculture, limited the free movement of their people and restricted civil liberties. The United States

---

[5] Gustav Stolper, 'Lessons of the world depression', *Foreign Affairs* 9, no. 2 (1931) 244–5; and G. Stolper, 'Politics versus economics', *Foreign Affairs*, 12, no. 3 (1934) 365.–6.

followed the same course. Franklin Roosevelt's New Deal was a conscious and active attempt to impose a fascist-type economic order on America, through the National Recovery Administration (NRA) and the Agricultural Adjustment Act (AAA). As Stuart Chase, one of the intellectual developers of the New Deal ideology, said, 'We propose then a National Planning Board [be] set up under the auspices of the Federal government . . . and manned by engineers, physical scientists, statisticians, economists, accountants and lawyers . . . Why should Russians have all the fun of remaking a world?'[6] And even after much of the New Deal had been declared unconstitutional in 1935, the Roosevelt administration continued on the Collectivist road with economic regulation, deficit-spending, public works projects, welfare-statism, and monetary central planning through a paper currency no longer backed by or bound to gold.[7]

World War II only re-enforced the Collectivist tendency. When the economists and political scientists in the West looked forward to the brave new world that would follow the destruction of Hitler, they all repeated in chorus that planning was inevitable in the postwar era. The only question open to dispute was whether it would be 'democratic' or 'totalitarian'. But either way planning was coming. And plan they did. There was Sweden's attempt at a democratic 'middle way'.[8] There was the British Labour Party, which implemented nationalization of industry and tried to introduce forms of state planning.[9] There was French indicative planning.[10] And the planning fever soon spread to the emerging countries of the Third World, which fell under the sway of the Soviet planning model. New political elites in Asia and Africa seized the reins of power as the flags of the colonial rulers were lowered. They saw themselves as 'nation-builders', and building a nation required an economic foundation. The battle cry became: from national liberation to national socialism. There was 'African Socialism', 'Indian Socialism', 'Islamic Socialism', 'Zionist Socialism', and even the 'Burmese Road to Socialism'.[11]

It is often forgotten the appeal that the Soviet planning model had for the Third World in the late 1950s and the 1960s. This appeal was re-enforced by the economists in the West. Soviet statistics were often accepted at more or less face value – statistics that were frequently extrapolated out into the future and which suggested that the Soviet Union might surpass the Western world in industrial production and standards of living as early as the 1980s and 1990s.[12] Maybe

[6] Stuart Chase, *A New Deal* (New York, Macmillan, 1932), pp. 219, 252.
[7] Cf., Francis Neilson, *Control from the Top* (New York, Putnams, 1933); Lewis W. Douglas, *The Liberal Tradition* (New York, Van Nostrand, 1935); and A. S. J. Baster, *The Twilight of American Capitalism: An Economic Interpretation of the New Deal* (London, King, 1937).
[8] Roland Huntford, *The New Totalitarians* (New York, Stein and Day, 1972).
[9] Cf. John Jewkes, *Ordeal by Planning* (London, Macmillan, 1948); Bertrand de Jouvenel, *Problems of Socialist England* (London, Batchworth, 1949); Ivor Thomas, *The Socialist Tragedy* (New York, Macmillan, 1949); R. Kelf-Cohen *Nationalization in Britain: The End of a Dogma* (London, Macmillan, 1959).
[10] Cf., Vera Lutz, *Central Planning for the Market Economy: An Analysis of the French Theory and Experience* (London, Longmans, Green, 1969).
[11] Cf., Arnold Rivkin, *Nations by Design: Institution-Building in Africa* (New York, Anchor Books, 1968); P. T. Bauer, *Indian Economic Policy and Development* (Bombay, Popular Prakashan, 1961); B. R. Shenoy *Indian Planning and Economic Development* (Bombay, Asia Publishing House, 1963); Roger A. Freeman, *Socialism and Private Enterprise in Equatorial Asia: The Case of Malaysia and Indonesia* (Stanford, Hoover Institute, 1968): Alex Rubner, *The Economy of Israel* (London, Frank Cass, 1960); Deepak Lal, *The Poverty of "Development Economics"* (Cambridge, Harvard University Press, 1985).
[12] Paul Samuelson, *Economics* (New York, MacGraw-Hill, 7th ed., 1967), pp. 790–2.

history *was* on the side of the communists? From the perspective of the mid-1990s this seems like pure fantasy, but in the 1960s many intellectuals in the West were not sure.

And now in the wake of the collapse of Soviet socialism, with the last of the totalitarian demons set loose by events of World War I buried in the rubble of its own contradictions and impossibilities, Europe, America and indeed the world faces another watershed of crisis. The crisis concerns whether the West will finally turn its back on the Collectivist experience and attempt to retrace its steps to the Liberal path that was left in 1914 – whether the Western world will return to the ideal of liberty over statism. For some the answer is already obvious. Has not the market economy shown its superiority over government planning, has not capitalism triumphed over economic collectivism? Is it not just a matter of the eastern European countries transforming themselves into economic and political systems similar to the ones in place in western Europe and the United States?

This view demonstrates just how successful the triumphs of Collectivism and socialism have been over the ideal of Liberalism and free market capitalism. The vast majority of people in the West believe that what they have is Liberalism and the market economy. This is as true for Americans as it is for the people of western Europe. What exactly is anti-Liberal and anti-capitalist in America?

In the new world of politically correct newspeak, Americans are free to say whatever they want – as long as it does not offend any ethnic, gender or racial group. They can pursue any career they choose – as long as they have been certified and licensed and have successfully passed inspection by an army of state regulators. They may come and go as they please – as long as they have been approved for a government-issued international passport, declared whether they are carrying more than $10,000 in currency, reported all taxable or forbidden items they wish to bring into the country, and not attempted to visit any foreign lands declared off limits by the state. They may buy whatever satisfies their fancy – as long as it has been manufactured, packaged and priced according to government standards of safety, quality and fairness, and as long as it has not been produced by a foreign supplier who exceeds his import quota or who offers to sell it below the state-mandated 'fair-market price'.

Americans are free to go about their own affairs – as long as they send their children to government schools or private schools approved by the state; as long as they do not attempt to employ in a business too many of a particular ethnic, gender or racial group; as long as they do not attempt to plan fully for their own old age rather than to pay into a mandatory government social-security system; as long as they do not pay an employee less than the governmentally imposed minimum wage; as long as they do not attempt to construct on their own property a home or a business in violation of zoning and building ordinances; that is, as long as they do not try to live their lives outside the permissible edicts of the state.

And Americans freely take responsibility for their own actions and pay their own way – except when they want the state to guarantee them a job or a 'living wage'; except when they want the state to protect their industry or profession from competition either at home or from abroad; except when they want the state to subsidize their children's education or their favourite art or the preservation of some wildlife area or the medical research into the cure of some hated disease or illness; or except when they want the state to ban some books, movies or peaceful acts between consenting adults rather than trying to change the behaviour of their fellow men through peaceful persuasion or by personal example.[13]

[13] Cf, David Boaz and Edward H. Crane, (eds), *Market Liberalism: A Paradigm for the 21st*

That most who have just read this list of lost freedoms in America will be shocked that anyone should suggest that the state should not be concerned with these matters shows more than anything else how far we have come and are continuing to go down the Collectivist road to serfdom. Whether the proponents of the Collectivist path called their programme socialism, social democracy, 'liberalism', progressivism, the Swedish 'third-way' or the welfare state, during the past three-quarters of century the end result has been the same: an increasing undermining of the sanctity of private property, an expanding compulsory redistribution of wealth, a growing spider's web of government regulations over private enterprise, and state direction of economic activity through either nationalized industries, government-business 'partnerships', or subsidies and tax-incentives to induce private business into those activities and locations desired by the State.

And regardless of the political label under which this gradual transformation of Western economic and social life has been brought about, the journey has lead to one end. As economist Melchior Palyi expressed it in his book, *Compulsory Medical Care and the Welfare State*, 'In democracies the Welfare State is the beginning and the Police State the end. The two emerge sooner or later . . .'[14] Why? Because, and inevitably, wherever the State superimposes itself on the affairs of men, compulsion and command replace the peaceful and voluntary relationships that are the hallmark of the truly free society. For if men do not obey, the State applies its police power to insist. If the reader considers the last statement an exaggeration, I suggest that he try to open and operate a business without proper government licenses; or that he publicly announce and undertake the hiring of people below the state-mandated minimum wage; or that he try to replace a trade union member with a non-union worker in his business where union membership is required by law for employment; or that he try to not pay his social security taxes; or that he try to construct a building outside of the state-mandated building codes or zoning ordinances; or that he try to enter or leave his country without a valid passport; or that he try to openly buy or sell chemical substances that the state has deemed the use of as 'socially undesirable'.

The French social philosopher, Alexis de Tocqueville, already understood in the first half of the 19th century the dangers from the incrementally-imposed form of the Collectivist ideal: The State, he explained in *Democracy in America*, 'covers the surface of society with a network of small complicated rules, minute and uniform, through which the most original minds and energetic characters cannot penetrate . . . [government] provides for [people's] security, foresees and supplies their necessities, facilitates their pleasures, manages their principle concerns, directs their industry, regulates the descent of property, and subdivides their inheritances . . . people . . . [are] reduced to nothing better than a flock of timid and industrious sheep, of which the government is the shepherd. I have always thought that servitude of the regular, quiet, and gentle kind which I have just described might be combined more easily than is commonly believed with some of the outward forms of freedom, and it might even establish itself under the wing of the sovereignty of the people'.[15]

Century (Washington, D.C., Cato Institute, 1993), p. 6.

[14] Melchior Palyi, *Compulsory Medical Care and the Welfare State* (Chicago, National Committee of Professional Services, 1949), pp. 13–14.

[15] Alexis de Tocqueville, *Democracy in America*, vol. II [1840] (New York, Vintage Books, 1945), pp. 336–7.

The extent to which the state now dominates, supervises, regulates, controls, manages and directs the social and economic order of the Western world frees Liberalism and the market economy from any of the responsibility for society's ills for which the Collectivists still attempt to blame capitalism. The market economy cannot be blamed for unemployment, when it is the state that long ago began the process of undermining a free, competitive labour market by imposing minimum wage laws, legalizing trade union monopolies and organized labour's strike threat, establishing unemployment benefits that subsidize the preferred choice of receiving income without the necessity of working, and imposing increasingly burdensome taxes connected with the private employer's hiring of workers in his firm or enterprise.[16]

The market economy cannot be blamed for pollution and environmental damage, when it is the state that has failed to fully specify or enforce private property rights, and therefore has prevented the market from 'internalizing' negative externalities connected with production and exchange.[17] The market economy cannot be blamed for inflations and recessions, when for practically the entire 20th century it has been the state's monetary and fiscal policies that have been responsible for causing macroeconomic fluctuations in employment, output and prices through the government's use of purely paper monies, central banking and deficit spending.[18]

The market economy cannot be blamed for international trade conflicts, when it has been the state that has prevented the freedom of trade, investment and exchange between the citizens of various countries through the introduction of tariff walls, import quotas, domestic content requirements, central bank

[16] See, W. H. Hutt, *The Theory of Collective Bargaining, 1930–1975* (London, Institute of Economic Affairs, 1975; W. H. Hutt, *The Strike Threat System: The Economic Consequences of Collective Bargaining* (New Rochelle, N.Y., Arlington House, 1973); Emerson P. Schmidt, *Union Power and the Public Interest* (Los Angeles, Nash Publishing, 1973); F. A. Hayek, *1980s Unemployment and the Unions* (London, Institute of Economic Affairs, 1980); Morgan O. Reynolds, *Power and Privilege: Labor Unions in America* (New York, Universe Books, 1984); Hans F. Sennholz, *The Politics of Unemployment* (Spring Mills, PA, Libertarian Press, 1987); Richard K. Vedder and Lowell E. Gallaway, *Out of Work: Unemployment and the Government in Twentieth-Century America* (New York/London, Holmes & Meier, 1993).

[17] See, John Baden and Richard L. Stroup (eds), *Bureaucracy vs. Environment* (Ann Arbor, University of Michigan Press, 1981); Bernard J. Frieden, *The Environmental Protection Hustle* (Cambridge, MIT Press, 1979); Richard L. Stroup and John A. Baden, *Natural Resources: Bureaucratic Myths and Environmental Management* (San Francisco, Pacific Institute for Public Policy Research. 1983); Walter E. Block. *Economics and the Environment: A Reconciliation* (Vancouver, B.C., Fraser Institute, 1990); Terry L. Anderson and Donald R. Leal, *Free Market Environmentalism* (San Francisco, Pacific Research Institute for Public Policy, 1991); Roy E. Cordato, *Welfare Economics and Externalities in an Open Ended Universe: A Modern Austrian Approach* (Boston, Kluwer, 1992).

[18] See, Melchior Palyi, *The Twilight of Gold, 1914–1936: Myths and Realities* (Chicago, Henry Regnery, 1972); Palyi, *Managed Money at the Crossroads* (Notre Dame, University of Notre Dame Press, 1958); Jacques Rueff, *The Age of Inflation* (Chicago, Henry Regnery, 1964): Rueff, *The Monetary Sin of the West* (New York, Macmillan, 1972); Henry Hazlitt, *The Inflation Crisis, and How to Resolve it* (New Rochelle, N.Y., Arlington House, 1978); F. A. Hayek, *Denationalization of Money* (London, Institute of Economic Affairs, 1976); H. Geoffrey Brennan and James Buchanan, *Monopoly in Money and Inflation* (London, Institute of Economic Affairs, 1981); Llewellyn H. Rockwell, Jr. (ed.), *The Gold Standard: An Austrian Perspective* (Lexington, Mass, Lexington Books, 1983); Barry Siegel (ed.), *Money in Crisis: The Federal Reserve, The Economy and Monetary Reform* (San Francisco, Pacific Institute for Public Policy, 1984); Hans F. Sennholz, *Money and Freedom* (Cedar Falls, Iowa, Center for Futures Education, 1985); Catherine England, *Banking and Monetary Reform* (Washington, D.C., The Heritage Foundation, 1985); Kevin Dowd, *The State and the Monetary System* (New York, St. Martin's Press, 1989).

intervention and manipulation of foreign exchange rates, and restrictions on the free movement of people from one part of the world to another.[19]

The market economy cannot be blamed for poverty, homelessness or the breakdown of the family, when it has been the state that has imposed tax and regulatory disincentives to capital formation, investment and job creation; when it has been the state that has retained rent controls in some urban areas and destroyed the profitability of low-income housing construction, and imposed zoning ordinances and building codes that raise the costs of apartment construction and maintenance; when it is the state that has undermined the nuclear family through its welfare rules for eligibility, created intergenerational welfare dependency among the poor, and weakened family values by the introduction of Collectivist indoctrination and cultural social engineering in the curriculum of public schools.[20]

Nor can the market economy be blamed for continuing and even worsening race relations in the society, when it has been the state that has imposed a new tribal Collectivism in both the public and private sectors, in which ethnic, racial and gender quota rules increasingly determine an individual's fate in terms of opportunities for higher education, employment and income earning; the politicizing of an individual's life-opportunities on the basis of the accident of birth has resulted in people increasingly viewing those of other ethnic, racial and gender groups as threats to their own advancement, and therefore enemies in the battle for political power and the financial disbursements from the state.[21]

---

[19] See, W. M. Curtiss, *The Tariff Idea* (New York, Foundation for Economic Education, 1953); Ryan C. Amacher, Gottfried Haberler and Thomas D. Willett, *Challenges to a Liberal International Economic Order* (Washington, D.C., American Enterprise Institute, 1979); Melvyn B. Krauss, *The New Protectionism; The Welfare State and International Trade* (New York, New York University Press, 1978); Jan Tumlir, *Protectionism: Trade Policy in Democratic Societies* (Washington, D.C., American Enterprise Institute, 1985); Jagdish Bhagwati, *The World Trading System at Risk* (Princeton, Princeton University Press, 1991); James Bovard, *The Fair Trade Fraud* (New York, St. Martin's Press, 1991); Julian L. Simon, *The Economic Consequences of Immigration* (Cambridge, Basil Blackwell, 1989); Richard M. Ebeling, 'Economic freedom and a new liberal international economic order' in Richard M. Ebeling (ed.), *Global Free Trade: Rhetoric or Reality?* (Hillsdale, Hillsdale College Press, 1993).

[20] See, Cecil Palmer, *The British Socialist Ill-Fare State* (Caldwell, Idaho, Caxton Press, 1952); Henry Hazlitt, *Man vs. The Welfare State* (New Rochelle, N.Y., Arlington House, 1969); Henry Hazlitt, *The Conquest of Poverty* (New Rochelle, N.Y., Arlington House, 1973): Martin Anderson, *Welfare: The Political Economy of Welfare Reform in the United States* (Stanford, Hoover Press, 1978); Terry L. Anderson and Peter J. Hill, *The Birth of the Transfer Society* (Stanford, Hoover Press, 1980); Roger A. Freeman, *The Wayward Welfare State* (Stanford, Hoover Press, 1981); Charles Murray, *Losing Ground: American Social Policy, 1950–1980* (New York, Basic Books, 1984); Ralph Harris and Arthur Seldon, *Welfare without the State* (London, Institute of Economic Affairs, 1987); Richard E. Wagner, *To Promote the General Welfare: Market Processes vs Political Transfers* (San Francisco, Pacific Research Institute for Public Policy, 1989): Jack D. Douglas, *The Myth of the Welfare State* (New Brunswick, N.J., Transactions Books, 1989); William Tucker, *The Excluded Americans: Homelessness and Housing Policies* (Washington, D.C. Regnery Gateway, 1990).

[21] See, Thomas Sowell, *Race and Economics* (New York, David McKay, 1975); T. Sowell, *Civil Rights: Rhetoric or Reality?* (New York, William Morrow, 1984); T. Sowell, *Preferential Policies: An International Perspective* (New York, William Morrow, 1990); Walter Williams, *The State Against Blacks* (New York, McGraw-Hill, 1982); Nathan Glazner, *Affirmative Discrimination* (New York, Basic Books, 1975); W. E. Block and M. A. Walker (eds), *Discrimination, Affirmative Action, and Equal Opportunity* (Vancouver, B.C., The Fraser Institute, 1981); Anne Worthham, *The Other Side of Race* (Ohio State University Press, 1981); Herman Belz, *Equality Transformed: A Quarter-Century of Affirmative Action* (New Brunswick, N.J., Transactions Books, 1991); Jarad Taylor, *Paved With Good Intentions: The Failure of Race Relations in Contemporary America* (New York, Carroll & Graf, 1992); Richard A. Epstein, *Forbidden Grounds: The Case Against Employment Discrimination Laws* (Cambridge, Harvard University Press, 1992); Ellen Frankel Paul, *Equity and Gender: The*

The crisis of the late 20th century, therefore, is the crisis of the failure of Collectivism in all of its forms, both its totalitarian type in the East and its democratic varieties in the West. But one would think that the experiences of the last half century had never occurred when listening to some of the intellectuals on the Left. Recently, philosopher Richard Rorty has told his fellow intellectuals that 'the word "socialism" has been drained of force' and that after the experience of 'our Eastern European friends . . . Marxist rhetoric is no more respectable than Nazi rhetoric'. But did this mean that he now accepted the fact that the belief in and the desire for social engineering should be given up, that there is no alternative to a truly free, unregulated market economy? No. 'Even now', Rorty said, 'I am unwilling to grant that Friedrich von Hayek was right in saying that you cannot have democracy without capitalism. All I will concede is that you need capitalism to ensure a reliable supply of goods and services, and to ensure that there will be enough taxable surplus left over to finance social welfare'.

Indeed, for Rorty, the only lesson learned from the Soviet experience is that comprehensive planning cannot work and that other less radical means must be pursued to attain the same end, i.e., social outcomes that he prefers to the ones that emerge spontaneously out of the choices and interactions of free men in the market economy. He is still searching for a 'kinder and gentler' socialism. 'American leftist intellectuals stand in need of a new political vocabulary', Rorty explained, '[and] I suggest that we start talking about greed and selfishness rather than about bourgeois ideology, about starvation wages and layoffs rather than about the commodification of labor, about differential per-pupil expenditure on schools and about differential access to health care rather than about the division of labor into classes.'[22] Rorty may be trying to change his vocabulary, but the ideological concepts behind the words remain the same. He may admit that the attempt to make a 'new socialist man' is impossible, but he still desires to manipulate men's lives and socially engineer the distribution of the fruits of their labour. He still wants to impose his own conception of egalitarian justice on society.

Professor Rorty is joined in this crusade to save some of the premises and foundations of the socialist critique of the market economy by others, e.g., by Professor David Marquand. In his contribution, "After Socialism?" included in this volume, Professor Marquand asks for some second thoughts before an unreserved conclusion that market liberalism has triumphed over the socialist ideal. While admitting that some of socialism's premises have been proven wrong with the passage of time—the belief that socialism was historically inevitable, that central planning by the state was more efficient than decentralized private enterprise; and that socialism was the vehicle for the progress of the working class in society—he believes that the ethics of socialism continues to stand the test of time. "Central to almost all [of the socialist] gropings, however, were words like 'co-operation', 'commonwealth' and 'fellowship'. . . [T]he term that encapsulated the essence of the socialist ideal was fraternity." The market economy, Professor Marquand argues, has always represented a "relentless pressure to commodify all social goods," i.e., to reduce all social relationships to a cold and calculating nexus of exchange in which the warmth of human intercourse and the sense of community was smothered by the "bottom line" of profit and loss.

Comparable Worth Debate (New Brunswick, Transactions Books, 1989), pp. 1–16.
[22] Richard Rorty, 'The Intellectuals at the end of socialism', *Yale Review* (Spring 1992).

But it may be asked, with the advantage of historical perspective, whether it was the market economy or socialism and the welfare state that has destroyed many of the networks of human relationships that have traditionally been among the defining characteristics of civil society. As University of Chicago sociologist, Edward Shils, has reminded us, "The idea of civil society is the idea of a part of society which has a life of its own, which is distinctly different from the state, which is largely in autonomy from it. . . The hallmark of a civil society is the autonomy of private associations and institutions as well that of private business firms. . . A market economy is the appropriate pattern of life of a civil society."[23]

In civil society there is no longer a single focal point in the social order, as in the politicized society in which the State designs, directs and imposes an agenda to which all must conform and within which all are confined. Rather, in civil society there are as many focal points as individuals, who all design, shape and direct their own lives guided by their own interests, ideals and passions.

But the society of free individuals is not a society of unconnected, isolated individuals—"atomistic man" as the critics of liberty will sometimes refer to him. As 18th and 19th century French Classical Liberal, Count Destutt de Tracy, concisely expressed it, "the social state . . . is our natural state . . . Society is . . . a continual series of exchanges . . . in which the two contrasting parties always both gain, consequently society is an uninterrupted succession of advantages, unceasingly renewed for all its members."[24]

The "exchange" relationships that emerge among free men in civil society, however, should not be viewed as meaning merely or only those involving the trading of what is narrowly thought of as "goods and services," within the institutions of the market place. The network of exchange relationships include community endeavors, religious and church activities, cultural associations and clubs, professional organizations and charitable callings. Indeed, any relationship in which men find that they have common interests, goals or shared beliefs becomes the foundation for the emergence of "exchange," involving agreed upon terms for association and collaboration for mutual benefit, and the enhancement of the quality, character and meaning of life for each and every participant.

Every free man belongs to numerous voluntary associations and institutions in the civil society. He forms or joins new ones as new interests and ideals develop during his life, and withdraws from others as his inclinations and circumstances change; and the associations and institutions to which individuals belong modify their goals and structures over time as the members revise their purposes and discover new rules more effective in achieving the ends of the organization.

Each individual, therefore, simultaneously participates in a variety of "social worlds" with different people, with each of these social relationships representing different purposes and needs in his life. And cumulatively these various social worlds of civil society, with all the relationships within each of them and between them, create what the Austrian economist, Friedrich Hayek, called the spontaneous social order. He called it a "spontaneous order" because the institutions, associations and activities among men that are the elements of this order are not the result of any prior central plan or regulated design, instead, they arise, evolve and maintain themselves as a result of the independent actions and interactions of the members of society.[25]

---

[23]Edward Shils, "The Virtue of Civil Society," *Government and Opposition* [Winter, 1991] pp. 3–20.
[24]Count Destutt Tracy. "Treatise on the Will and Its Effects" in *A Treatise on Political Economy* [1817] (New York: Augustus M. Kelley, Publishers, 1970) p. 6.
[25]Friedrich A. Hayek, *Order—With or Without Design? Selections from F. A. Hayek's Contribution*

But in the welfare state, all of these relationships of civil society are weakened and threatened with extinction as the state preempts the duties, responsibilities and obligations that traditionally have belonged to the family and the voluntary efforts of community members. And as David G. Green has demonstrated in his recent monograph, *Reinventing Civil Society: The Rediscovery of Welfare without Politics*, throughout the 19th century, during the heyday of "unbridled" capitalism and in an environment of "rugged individualism," voluntarism and community effort were the free society's *successful* answer and natural method for "cooperation" and "fellowship."[26]

The dehumanizing and anti-social consequences of the welfare state were understood even before the modern version was implemented in the 20th century. The older British welfare state—the Poor Laws system—came under heavy criticism by the classical liberals of the 19th century. Dr. Thomas Chalmers, Professor of Moral Philosophy at St. Andrews University in Scotland, in the 1820s and 1830s, for example, pointed out many of the unintended consequences that always seem to follow in the wake of dependency upon the state.[27]

Criticizing the British poor laws system, under which the status of "pauperism" was legalized and on the basis of which individuals and families could draw their financial support from the state, Dr. Chalmers saw four serious consequences: First, he said, it reduced the incentive for people to manifest the industriousness and frugality to care for themselves and their families, since now they knew that whether they worked and saved or not, the state could be relied upon to provide them with all the minimal necessities of life.

Second, he feared, it reduced if not eliminated the sense of family responsibility, knowing that the state would care for the old and the infirm, "there is a cruel abandonment of parents, by their offspring, to the cold and reluctant hand of public charity," as children develop the attitude that since they have paid their taxes it is now the government's duty to do what relatives have traditionally done for each other.

Third, it threatened to harden the hearts of men towards their fellows, and diminish the spirit of voluntary giving to others in the community. When assistance to others in society is voluntary, there usually is aroused in us "the compassion of our nature ... [which] inclines us to the free and willing movement of generosity." But when charity is made compulsory by the state, Dr. Chalmers argued, there is aroused in us, instead, "the jealousy of our nature ... [which] puts us upon the attitude of surly and determined resistance."

And, fourth, it weakened the spirit of community and assistance among those who were less well off. Dr. Chalmers noted that those who live in simple or poor conditions often show a support and sympathy for those around them who fall into even worse circumstances, and which creates a network of mutual help within those poorer portions of the wider community. But when each is made a ward of the state, the ties and connections between people in similar

---

to the Theory and Application of Spontaneous Order (London: The Centre for Research into Communist Economies, 1989).

[26]David G. Green, *Reinventing Civil Society: The Rediscovery of Welfare Without Politics* (London: Institute of Economic Affairs, 1993), also, Robert Sugden, *Who Cares? An Economic and Ethical Analysis of Private Charity and the Welfare State* (London: Institute of Economics Affairs, 1983), Stepen Macedo, *Liberal Virtues: Citizenship, Virtue, and Community in Liberal Constitutionalism* [Oxford: Clarendon Press, 1990]: and Marvin Olasky, *The Tragedy of American Compassion* (Washington, DC: Regnery Gateway, 1992).

[27]Thomas Chalmers, *Problems of Poverty* (London: Thomas Nelson & Sons, 1912) pp. 213–220.

circumstances are weakened, with each now connected by one thread: their own individual dependency upon the state for all they need and desire.

And it should be added that Dr. Chalmers, in the early decades of the nineteenth century, had already been confronted with all the types of arguments heard in the twentieth century as to why the welfare state could not be repealed. He was confronted, for example, with the counter-arguments that without the mandatory provision of the state, the poor would fall into even worse conditions. And an even more forceful impediment to the denationalization of the welfare state, he said, came from the resistance of those who administered the system, that is, when the proponent of voluntarism "comes into collision with the prejudices or partialities of those who at present have the right or power of management" of the welfare programs.

The negative effects of the welfare state were also pointed out by Henry Fawcett, one of the last great classical economists. In his book, *Pauperism: Its Causes and Cures*, published in 1871, he explained that pockets of severe poverty existed in England at the very time of a growing and expanding British economy in which many in the society were obtaining rising standards of living that had never been known before. A primary culprit for this poverty amongst plenty, Fawcett argued, was the poor laws. The incentives of the poor laws system and the consequences that followed from them were no different from what we have seen in, for example, modern America in our own times. In Fawcett's words of 1871:[28]

> ". . . [M]en were virtually told that no amount of recklessness, self-indulgence, or improvidence would in the slightest degree affect their claim to be maintained at other people's expense. If they married when they had no reasonable chance of being able to maintain a family, they were treated as if they had performed a meritorious act, for the more children they had the greater was the amount of relief obtained. All the most evident teachings of commonsense were completely set to nought. . . An artificial stimulus was then given to population. . . Population was also fostered by a still more immoral stimulus. A woman obtained from the parish [the local agency for the distribution of welfare] a larger allowance for an illegitimate than for a legitimate child. From one end of the kingdom to the other people were in fact told not only to marry with utter recklessness and let others bear the consequences, but it was also said, especially to the women of the country the greater is your immorality, the greater will be your pecuniary reward. Can it excite surprise that from such a system we have had handed down to us a vast inheritance of vice and poverty?"

And Fawcett pointed out to his readers that the welfare programs of his day had created dependency "by successive generations of the same family." He reported that a government commission investigating the effects of the poor laws found "three generations of the same family simultaneously receiving relief." And, he also pointed out, that after a time it was common for those on welfare to begin to believe that they were entitled to it: ". . . [T]he feeling soon became general that pauperism was no disgrace, and the allowance which was obtained from the parish was just as much the rightful property of those who receive it, as the wages of ordinary industry."

Can anyone deny that the problems and concerns raised by people like Dr. Chalmers and Professor Fawcett have been intensified many times over during

[28]Henry Fawcett, *Pauperism: Its Causes and Cures* [1871] (Clifton, N.J.: Augustus M. Kelley, Publishers, 1975) pp. 16–22.

our own century when socialist ethics have been put into action by the modern welfare state? Can anyone, with a straight face, say that the politicization of social life has made that life more human or more humane? This it has produced that greater sense of community and fraternity that socialists have longed for for almost two hundred years? Or that it has raised public spiritedness among the general population?

To the contrary, it can be argued that socialist ethics have destroyed the source for such communitarian endeavors. The welfare state has weakened man's sense of societal responsibility because it has stolen from him, through redistribution of income, much of the financial means of practicing it. What socialists never understood, and still do not understand, is that accumulated wealth is not merely a means for physical maintenance of oneself and one's family, plus additional sums of money for selfish leisure activities, but an expression of ourselves and what we wish and hope to be. And the way we use our wealth enables us to teach our children about those things which are considered worthwhile in life, as well. Accumulated wealth is also the way individuals have had the means to perform many activities "for free" that are considered the foundation of a free and good society—from community and church work to support for the arts and the humanities.

Deny an individual the honest income and wealth he has earned and you deny him the ability to formulate, and give expression to, his own purposes as a human being. And you deny him the capacity to make his voluntary contribution to the civilization and society in which he lives, as he sees best. Instead, these decisions and actions of responsible individuals are more and more concentrated in the hands of the state because, through taxation, the state denies individuals the capacity to do these things themselves and as they see fit. The state, thus, increasingly plans our lives, takes care of our children, and decides what "socially desirable" projects and activities should be given support, and to what extent. And as the state grows stronger, the individual grows weaker. Individuals become weaker, not only in relation to the state, but as human beings because they no longer exercise those qualities and habits of mind that only self-responsibility and a sense of voluntary social interaction teach and make possible.[29]

In spite of Professor Marquand's beliefs and deepest desires, socialist ethics have been shown to be as bankrupt as all the other premises of the socialist system. There is neither ethical behavior nor moral choice when the freedom to make both good and bad decisions are preempted by state monopolization of how resources and income are allocated along alternatives in the name of some higher societal good. And to the extent the state taxes incomes earned and wealth accumulated for redistributive purposes, to that degree the range of moral decision-making is narrowed for the citizens of the country. It is a measure of the amount of anti-ethics introduced into the society by the state in the name of a mythical collectivist social good.[30]

Only in the free society can the spirit of charity, community and social responsibility be fostered and developed in an ever increasing number of men.

[29]See, Bertrand de Jouvenel, *The Ethics of Redistribution* [1952] (Indianapolis: Liberty Press, 1990); also, David G. Green, *Equalizing People: Why Social Justice Threatens Liberty* (London: Institute of Economics Affairs, 1990); and Wilhelm Röpke, *Welfare, Freedom and Inflation* (University: University of Alabama Press, 1964),

[30]See, Ludwig von Mises, "The Economic Foundations of Freedom," in *Economics Freedom and Interventionism* (Irvington-on-Hudson, N.Y.: The Foundation for Economic Education, 1990) pp. 3–4.

Only in an environment in which individuals are required to learn to exercise such behavior, precisely because the state does not preempt or substitute itself for such conduct, can the ethical fiber of human beings be strengthened. And until we fully and completely give up the ethics of socialism, we will not have created the circumstances in which that desired voluntaristic and social ethic can mature and become habituated through intergenerational tradition.

But if the socialist variety of Collectivism remains alive under the cover of a new vocabulary of word manipulation and under the continuing rationale for a "socialist ethics," so too is neo-mercantilism. Herbert A. Henzler (Professor of International Management at Munich University) defends 'The New Era of Eurocapitalism'. 'The competitive battle senior [corporate] managers now face', Henzler says, 'is a deeper struggle among different capitalist systems, each with its own distinctive set of values, priorities, institutions, and goals'. Corporate managers in the United States, 'are most deeply committed to free markets and the effectiveness of individual action'. While 'capitalism in Japan is far less individualistic than its U.S. counterpart . . . Japanese managers are expected to use profits to fund high, sustained levels of corporate investment, not to distribute them to shareholders'.

On the other hand, in Europe, he says, under 'our form of capitalism', corporate managers 'are expected to balance the need for corporate growth with the health of the physical environment and with the broader social welfare of the countries in which they operate'. Thus, 'Eurocapitalism supports a social compact' between business, labour and government, because 'most Europeans would sacrifice the possibility of an unrestricted business environment that rewards a few with extreme wealth for the reality of many people with comfortable income'. Indeed, 'because of our mercantilist tradition, Europeans know that the interests of private companies and the state can run together in comfortable harness', with government serving as a 'potential source of managerial ideas and approaches'.[31]

At the same time, Thomas K. McCraw (Straus Professor of Business History at Harvard University) has recently told us what he sees as, 'The Trouble with Adam Smith'. McCraw admits that 'the battle between Adam Smith and Karl Marx is over . . . Smith and capitalism have won. But a second championship is under way, a contest between different kinds of capitalism. In one corner stands a relatively *laissez-faire* consumer variety represented by the United States. In the other corner is a more nationalistic, producer-oriented capitalism epitomized by Germany, Japan and the "Little Dragons" of East Asia'.

McCraw believes that in our corporate industrial world of mass and giant production, long-term investments crucial to a nation's well-being cannot be left 'to the whims of individuals, who usually act in their own short-run interest . . . It must be done through organizations, and it is best done with the positive assistance of wise public policy'. If the United States is to match its Japanese and German rivals, America must follow their lead and 'act from a premise that the key unit of analysis is not the individual but the nation-state'. There must be a concerted action by 'firms, industrial groups, and elite public-sector ministries . . . to deploy resources so as to achieve stronger economic performance'. The keys to America's future, in McCraw's prevision, are 'nationalism, technology, organization, and power'.[32]

[31] Herbert A. Henzler, 'The new era of eurocapitalism', *Harvard Business Review* July–August (1992), 57–68.

[32] Thomas K. McCraw, 'The trouble with Adam Smith', *The American Scholar*, Summer (1992),

Finally, Clyde V. Prestowitz, Jr (president of the Economic Strategy Institute and general-director of the Pacific Basin Economic Council) has recently told us that we must go 'beyond *laissez-faire*'. Like our two other authors, Prestowitz argues that 'the truth is that there are different forms of capitalism, each deeply rooted and in competition with the others'. America's traditional policy of fostering global free trade and a borderless world must be set aside if America is not to merely survive in the world economy, but continue to be industrially and technologically pre-eminent. America's trading partners, particularly the Europeans and the Japanese, 'pursue policies designed to foster a favourable mix of industries . . . All of them . . . have a producer rather than a consumer mentality'. Where industries are located 'can be influenced by policy, so that a clever country could raise its living standards by capturing a preponderance of [high-tech, high profits] industries'.

Prestowitz believes that agencies in the government should be assigned the task of targeting high-tech, high-wage industrial winners; transportation and communications infrastructures should be invested in by the government; a national health-care programme should be sponsored by the government; only those foreign investments should be allowed in the U.S. that benefit America's 'national interest'; and in trade negotiations with America's world partners, Americans must be ready to fight economic wars to protect their industries from foreign competition. 'Americans must reconcile themselves to a certain amount of trade management with Japan', he says. And 'to break old structures and overcome the effects of industrial policies [of other nations] it may be necessary to negotiate affirmative action for imports and foreign investments'.[33]

In the post-Soviet era, both 'socialism' and 'central planning' have lost their respectability as language used in polite (and intelligent) society. And 'fascism' has been a word banished from serious public-policy discussions for half a century. This has left advocates of Economic Collectivism without a vocabulary – a legitimized set of terms with which to categorize and defend their case for government control and management of economic activity. The Economic Collectivists, therefore, are resorting to the same tricks they have used in the past: adopt the labels of their opponents and then subvert and pervert their meaning. At the beginning of this century, this was the method that the socialists and neo-mercantilists used when they stole the word 'Liberalism'. They argued that they – the newer Liberals – wanted to complete the work the older Liberals had begun. Their new Liberalism wanted to add to the 'negative' protections of the older Liberalism a set of 'positive' protections to enhance human freedom in the form of government welfare guarantees and a regulated or nationalized economy for a better serving of the common good.

Now a similar process is at work with the terms 'capitalism' and 'market economy'. To manage trade between nations is no longer mercantilism; to foster government-business partnerships for targeted and directed industrial development is no longer economic fascism; to regulate and tax business for purposes of income redistribution is no longer the welfare state; to assign governmental agencies the task of guiding the investment decisions of private enterprises is no longer state planning. No, rather all such policies are now nothing more than different forms of 'competing capitalism'. Through this linguistic subversion, the Economic Collectivists hope to legitimize their statist

352–73.
[33] Clyde V. Prestowitz, 'Beyond *laissez-faire*', *Foreign Policy* Summer (1992), 67–87.

agendas by making it appear that arguing for socialism, planning, interventionism, state welfarism, and neo-mercantilism is merely a dispute over which kind of capitalism we want.

It also enables them to avoid all the questions that would have to be answered if things were called by their right names. For example, after the disaster of central planning, how do they propose to know how to efficiently allocate resources and labour into alternative investment paths better than a price-guided, profit-driven system of decentralized decision-making in a competitive market? Once they seriously start down the road of systematic national industrial policy to win against international competitors, what will be the outcome, in terms of international relations, when several national governments try at the same time to establish their respective economy's pre-eminence in the same 'high-tech' industries and supposed 'high-wage' occupations? With a further politicization of the allocation of resources, with intensified government-business 'partnerships' for targeting of investments, and with even more conscious 'producer-oriented' policies in the form of various tax-breaks and subsidies for business, how do the neo-mercantilist social engineers propose to prevent the increased incentives for 'producer-oriented' special interests to lobby and manipulate the political process for their own benefit at the expense of the general taxpaying and consuming public? As the ethnic and gender collectivism of educational, employment and income quotas and group privileges are extended even further, what will happen to the foundations of civil society as people view their neighbours less and less as individuals with whom they interact for peaceful, mutual benefit, and instead come to view each other more and more as members of antagonistic groups in political competition for power and control?

In the 19th century, the Liberals had offered solutions that not merely defused and minimized, but did away, with many of these problems. Their method was to de-politicize and privatize social and economic relationships, to make the interactions among people in society the private affairs of voluntary, mutual agreement and peaceful persuasion. But in spite of the failure of Italian fascism, German National Socialism and now Soviet socialism; even in the face of the political corruption and societal and economic failure of the welfare state; with total disregard for the contradictions and impossibilities inherent in all attempts to plan and direct the economic activities of millions, the Political and Economic Collectivists seem determined to continue their resistance to the only rational political-economic alternative: the Liberal society and the free market economy.

In 1932, the Austrian economist, Ludwig von Mises, admitted that, 'I know only too well how hopeless it seems to convince impassioned supporters of the Socialist Idea by logical demonstration that their views are preposterous and absurd. I know too well that they do not want to hear, to see, or above all to think, and they are open to no argument. But new generations grow up with clear eyes and open minds. And they will approach things from a disinterested, unprejudiced standpoint, they will weigh and examine, will think and act with forethought'.[34] At the threshold of the 21st century, we can only hope that such a new generation may finally arise and triumph. Another century of various experiments in attempting to apply variations on the Collectivist theme is too high a price for society to pay just so some can indulge their fantasies in trying to remake the political and economic orders in their preferred images.

---

[34] Ludwig von Mises, *Socialism, An Economic and Sociological Analysis* [1932] (New Haven, Yale University Press, 1951), p. 24.

Decolonizing Liberalism

BHIKHU PAREKH[1]

University of Hull

In nineteenth-century Europe liberalism and colonialism developed alongside each other.[2] With rare exceptions liberals approved of colonialism and provided it with a legitimizing ideology. Although the liberal and even the non-liberal accounts of the history of liberalism ignore the fact, the colonial experience deeply shaped the nineteenth-century liberal thought and introduced elements that are either absent in or at best marginal to its predecessors. Liberalism became missionary, ethnocentric and narrow, dismissing non-liberal ways of life and thought as primitive and in need of the liberal civilizing mission.

Although what I say applies to all imperial countries, I shall concentrate on Britain, which had the largest empire and was long regarded as the home of liberalism. In the first part I shall outline the liberal justification of colonialism as articulated by British liberal thinkers especially J.S. Mill, and in the second, spell out its general implications. In the third part I shall trace the continuing influence of what I call Millian liberalism on the thoughts of several contemporary liberals. In the last part of the paper I shall argue that liberalism stands to gain from a sympathetic dialogue with non-liberal ways of life and thought, and that such a dialogue is impossible unless it purges itself of the assumptions acquired during the colonial era. I shall conclude by tentatively suggesting how liberalism, traditionally predicated upon the assumption of cultural homogeneity, needs to be revised if it is to come to terms with multicultural societies, which most contemporary societies are.

---

[1] This paper was first presented at the ECPR workshop in Leiden. I am grateful to Andrew Mason, Richard Ashcraft and Geraint Parry for their helpful comments.
[2] One could go further and argue that from the very beginning, liberalism had a colonialist thrust and justified the domination and even the destruction of the so-called uncivilized ways of life. It had dogmatic ideas on what constituted a truly human way of life and how best to use time, space and natural resources. Several parts of America, Canada and Australia had long been occupied by the native people. Liberal writers of the seventeenth century argued that since they were not enclosed and owned and since their productive resources were not fully exploited, these lands were really 'empty', 'free', 'wasted', 'wild', '*vacuum domicilum*', '*terra nullius*'. In the Liberal view the Europeans, who knew how to enclose, appropriate and make fullest use of them, had a much stronger claim to these lands, including the right to 'constrain' the natives to live in limited areas or to turn them into workers. See Michael Oakeshott (ed.) *Hobbes' Leviathan* (Oxford, Blackwell, 1957), p. 227, and Locke's *Second Treatise*, sections 32, 33, 34, 36, 37, 41, 180, 182, and 184. Neither Hobbes nor Locke nor any of their followers could see why the natives should be allowed to lead their self-chosen but 'primitive' ways of life and why their lived spaces should not be deterritorialized and then reterritorialized on liberal terms. In this paper I am concerned to explore how liberals justified colonizing not the so-called empty lands but people living in settled societies. I therefore ignore the seventeenth-century liberals and concentrate on their eighteenth- and nineteenth-century successors.

I

By the beginning of the nineteenth century Britain had built up a large empire and India was its largest and much cherished possession. A majority of British liberals approved of British colonialism, and even the tiny minority who took a different view wanted Britain to hold on to India. Many prominent liberals of the time were in one way or another connected with, and some were even directly involved in, the administration of India. They included such men as James Mill, John Stuart Mill, Thomas Macaulay, William Wilberforce and Edward Strachey. The two Mills, who were their leaders, were at the centre of the British colonial policy on India. After twelve years of hard work James Mill published in 1818 his massive *History of British India*, which for decades shaped the British liberal attitude to India and other colonies. It ran into three editions in a period of ten years, and new editions continued to appear after his death in 1836. In 1819 on the strength of 'extraordinary talents' displayed in his book, James Mill was appointed an Assistant Examiner in the East India Company, and promoted in 1830 to the highly influential post of the Examiner. His son John Stuart Mill entered the Company's service in 1823, eventually succeeded to the Examinership, and remained in charge of India until 1858, the year the company was abolished.[3]

The liberal justification of colonialism showed a remarkable consensus. In order to justify the inherently unequal and exploitative colonial rule, liberals needed to show that the British had something to give to their colonies which the latter badly *needed*, were unable to acquire *unaided*, and which was so *precious* as to compensate for whatever economic and political price they were required to pay. The logic of colonial justification required a perfect match between British gifts and colonial needs, between British strength and native deficiency. Following the fashion of the time, the British wrapped their gifts in the language of civilization, which had latterly replaced Christianity as the dominant idiom in Europe and taken over its universalist and proselytizing mission. Since the liberal case was best represented by J.S. Mill (hereafter Mill), I shall concentrate on him.

For Mill man was a progressive being whose ultimate destiny was to secure the fullest development of his intellectual, moral, aesthetic and other faculties. 'Among the works of man, which human life is rightly employed in perfecting and beautifying, the first in importance surely is man himself.'[4] As a self-creating being, his 'comparative worth as a human being' consisted in becoming 'the best thing' it was possible for him to become. He was constantly to improve himself, develop new powers, cultivate a 'striving and go-ahead character', dominate his natural and social environment, experiment with different ways of life, and evolve one best suited to his 'natural constitution'.[5] For Mill only such an autonomous and self-determining person had 'character' or 'individuality'. 'One whose desires and impulses are not his own has no character, no more than a steam-engine has a character.'[6]

For Mill individuality, a product of self-conscious and autonomous choices,

---

[3] For an excellent discussion, see Eric Stokes. *The English Utilitarians and India* (Oxford, Clarendon Press, 1959).

[4] J.S. Mill, *Utilitarianism, Liberty and Representative Government* (London, Dent 1912), p. 117.

[5] Mill, *Utilitarianism, Liberty and Representative Government*, pp. 117, 118, and 125.

[6] Mill, *Utilitarianism, Liberty and Representative Government*, p. 118.

benefited both the agent and others.[7] It gave the agent the aesthetic pleasure of self-creation, evolved a form of life suited to his level of 'spiritual development', created inner harmony, was a source of deepest happiness, and made him a 'noble and beautiful object of contemplation'. Individuality also benefited society because it created a rich, diverse and stimulating environment, challenged dogmas and customs, encouraged a healthy moral competition between different ways of life, saved society from becoming stagnant, created a climate in which creative geniuses could grow, and led to progress. For Mill a civilized society was one in which individuality was widely cherished and developed and which was well-advanced 'in the road to perfection'.

For Mill, as for other nineteenth-century liberals, individuality was an extremely difficult and precarious achievement. It required the courage to be different, the willingness to make choices and to accept responsibility for their consequences, thinking for oneself, and so on, which most human beings found painful. In Mill's view human beings had both a natural and historically acquired tendency towards conformity, which only a few were able to fight successfully on their own.[8] The tendency was for obvious reasons reinforced by vested interests, including not only the rulers and the religious establishment but also corporate and self-reproducing institutional structures. For Mill as for most other liberals, individuality represented human *destiny*, but it was not underwritten by and even went against some of the deepest tendencies of human *nature*. There was a profound tension between human nature and human destiny, between what human beings tended to do and what they ought to do. The liberal way of life required them to rebel against themselves, and only a few, the 'salt of the earth' as Mill called them, were capable of it. The rest had to be educated into it and, until such time as they were ready, held in check.

For Mill and other liberals individuality was the 'delicate fruit of a mature civilization'.[9] Its 'natural enemies' as Lord Acton called them were 'legion', and its 'sincere friends' were 'rare.'[10] It was an uniquely European achievement and conspicuous by its absence in non-western societies. Even in Europe it was a 'novel invention', anticipated by such heroic figures as Socrates and Jesus but not fully developed and widely cherished until the Renaissance.[11] Being an unique achievement of the 'European race' it was inextricably tied up with the history and even the geography of the European people, and had only flourished where the latter had settled.[12]

Mill divided human societies into two. In some, which he called civilized, human beings were in the 'maturity of their faculties' and had 'attained the

---

[7] Mill, *Utilitarianism, Liberty and Representative Government*, pp. 125f.

[8] The habit of forming opinions and acting on them without evidence is 'one of the most immoral habits of the mind, the foundation of most of what is vicious and degraded in human character'. J.S. Mill, 'Formation of opinions', *Westminster Review*, July 1826, p. 134.

[9] The expression in quote is Lord Acton's, See E.K. Bramsted and K.J. Melhuish, (eds), *Western Liberalism: a History in Documents from Locke to Croce* (London, Longman, 1978), p. 669.

[10] Bransted and Melhuish, *Western Liberalism*, pp. 669, 670; see also, p. 737.

[11] For Lord Acton, the seeds of liberty were sown in Athens '2460 years ago', Bransted and Melhuish, *Western Liberalism*, p. 670. For Benjamin Constant, in all earlier societies save Athens men 'were, so to speak, merely machines whose gears and cog-wheels were regulated by the law', and who were subject 'to an almost total social jurisdiction', Bransted and Melhuish, *Western Liberalism*, pp. 103 and 312. Similar remarks are to found in many a liberal writer.

[12] This is a standard view among liberals in both the nineteenth and twentieth centuries. See Bransted and Melhuish, *Western Liberalism*, pp. 737, 738 and 745. The view is vigorously asserted by Michael Oakeshott in *On Human Conduct* (Oxford, Clarendon Press, 1974).

capacity of being guided to their own improvement by conviction or persuasion'.[13] In his view most European societies had 'long since reached' that stage. By contrast all non-European societies were 'backward', and human beings there were in a state of 'nonage' or 'infancy'. Mill did not think much of Africa, a 'continent without a history'. And although he thought that India, China and 'the whole East' had begun well, he was convinced that they had been 'stationary for thousands of years'.

Such backward societies were incapable of being improved by 'free and equal discussion' and lacked the resources for self-regeneration. Mill argued that 'if they are ever to be farther improved, it must be by foreigners'. He did not think much of the likely objection that all societies including the backward had a right to territorial integrity. The right to non-intervention, like the right to individual liberty, only belonged to those capable of making good use of it, that is, to those 'mature' enough to think and judge for themselves and to develop unaided. Since backward societies lacked that capacity and were basically like children, the right to non-intervention was 'either a certain evil or at best a questionable good for them' and only perpetuated their primitive and subhuman existence. For Mill the right to non-intervention only applied to the relations between civilized societies.

Mill repeatedly insisted that the vast masses of men and women in every society, including the European, were not much interested in individuality and other liberal values. But that did not prevent him from arguing that they were all capable of being improved by free and equal discussion. In saying that non-European societies lacked the means of self-improvement and needed foreign help, Mill implied that they did not possess even a small group of talented men capable of playing a catalytic educational role. In other words, for Mill all or almost all the members of non-European societies were backward, and all Europeans including the illiterate masses were civilized. From time to time Mill thus came pretty close to sharing the crude racism of his time, but by and large he managed to avoid it. Unlike the racist writers he insisted that the non-Europeans once had their glorious periods and were not inherently inferior, that the Europeans too had their dark ages and were not naturally superior, and that the differences between them had a non-biological explanation.

Mill's own explanation was muddled. Discussing why 'the whole East' had remained decadent for centuries, he observed:[14]

> the greater part of the world has, properly speaking, no history because the despotism of custom is complete. This is the case over the whole East . . . A people, it appears, may be progressive for a certain length of time and stop; when does it stop? When it ceases to possess individuality.

For Mill the East had become stationary because it lacked individuality. That was so because it had fallen under the sway of despotic customs, and that in turn was due to bad forms of government and social structures. As to why and how the latter came into existence, he had no answer. This is hardly surprising, for Mill's very question and manner of dealing with it were naive in the extreme. He generalized about 'the whole East' as if it only consisted of India and China, and treated these two vast societies as undifferentiated wholes. He talked of their

[13] Mill, *Utilitarianism, Liberty and Representative Government*, p. 73.
[14] Mill, *Utilitarianism, Liberty and Representative Government*, p. 128.

'thousands of years' of decline without bothering to inquire if they had really declined or only met a better equipped enemy, when exactly the decline began, whether it was limited to specific areas of life, why the Indians had for decades succeeded in putting up strong resistance to the British conquest and won important battles, and so on. He talked about despotic customs and absence of individuality without explaining what customs he had in mind, how vast societies could remain stationary so long, and how millions of human beings, unless they were assumed to be mindless morons, could blindly follow oppressive customs and practices. It is striking that not once did Mill consider it necessary to check his facts, let alone make a careful study of the history, cultures and social structures of the societies about which he glibly and indiscriminately generalized. When non-European societies were concerned, he apparently did not think that the truth about them needed to be carefully and sympathetically ascertained.

In the ultimate analysis Mill was not really interested in India, China and 'the East'. He was basically concerned to do two things. First, he aimed to show to the Europeans, especially the British, what they would become if they did not cultivate the spirit of individuality, and constructed the East with that objective in mind. Mill's East was the nineteenth-century counterpart of the seventeenth-century idea of the state of nature, and designed to perform a similar ideological function. As he repeatedly observed, if it did not cherish individuality 'Europe, notwithstanding its noble antecedents and its professed Christianity, will tend to become another China'.[15] Secondly, Mill intended to show that the hopelessly decadent Eastern societies needed external help, and that the British interference with them was fully justified.

Having disposed of thousands of years of the arbitrarily homogenized East, Mill went on to explain why Europe was able to come out of its backward past unaided.[16]

> What is it that hitherto preserved Europe from this lot? What has made the European family of nations an improving, instead of a stationary portion of mankind? Not any superior excellence in them, which, when it exists, exists as the effect not as the cause; but their remarkable diversity of character and culture. Individuals, classes, nations, have been extremely unlike one another; they have struck out a great variety of paths, each leading to something valuable; and although at every period those who travelled in different paths have been intolerant of one another, and each would have thought it an excellent thing if all the rest could have been completed to travel his road, their attempts to thwart each other's development have rarely had any permanent success, and each has in time endured to receive the good which the others have offered. Europe is, in my judgement, wholly indebted to this plurality of paths for its progressive and many-sided development.

For Mill the Europeans avoided the 'Chinese' fate because of their 'remarkable' diversity of character and culture.[17] In Europe individuals, classes and

---

[15] Mill, *Utilitarianism, Liberty and Representative Government*, p. 129.

[16] Mill, *Utilitarianism, Liberty and Representative Government*, pp. 129f.

[17] Among the Europeans, Mill did not think much of the 'bureaucracy-ridden nations of the continent', *Utilitarianism, Liberty and Representative Government* p. 226. In his view the English were the only people likely to 'do most to make the world better'. On them lies 'the best hope' for human progress. *Utilitarianism, Liberty and Representative Government*, p. 214.

states cherished their differences, struck out diverse paths of development, and resisted attempts at assimilation. As a result, they never entirely lost their vibrancy and creativity, so that a society passing through a bad period was able to draw inspiration and strength from the liveliness of the rest. Mill's explanation raised more questions than it answered. He did not explain why Europe declined for centuries and passed through the dark ages, and why and when its people began to develop the love of diversity. He did not explain either why the presence of different classes should by itself cultivate and sustain the love of diversity when similar social differences in India, China and elsewhere did not.

Mill's defence of colonialism was based on his theory of man and his 'analysis' of European and non-European history sketched above. Since, according to this theory, the non-Europeans were moral and political infants, and thus below the age of consent, a 'parental despotism' by a 'superior people' was perfectly 'legitimate' and in their own long-term interest.[18] It facilitated their transition to a 'higher stage of development' and trained them in 'what is specifically wanting to render them capable of a higher civilisation'.[19] As human beings such backward individuals had equal *moral* claims to the pursuit and protection of their interests with the members of civilized societies, but as collectivities they had no *political* claims to independence and self-determination.

Unlike the Canadians, Australians and other British dominions who were of 'European race' and of 'her own blood', the non-Europeans were only fit for a 'government of leading-strings'.[20] Their affairs were best run by a body of carefully selected, well-meaning and professionally trained bureaucrats free from the control of elected politicians who were all bound to be subject to the influence of shifting public opinion. Strange as it may seem in a man advocating the virtues of an open mind, Mill was convinced beyond a shadow of doubt that the colonial bureaucracy should not be accountable to the elected representatives either in Britain or in the colonies. That was why when the British parliament abolished the East India Company and brought India under direct British rule, Mill chose to take early retirement rather than co-operate with the new arrangement even on an experimental basis.[21] That was also why he kept resisting right until his last working days every parliamentary attempt to give the Indians a measure of self-rule. Even when Ceylon, which was directly under the colonial office, was granted considerable local autonomy with no apparent adverse results, Mill continued to argue against its extension to the Indians.[22]

Mill maintained that even as a civilized society had a right to rule over a primitive or semi-civilized society, a more civilized group or nationality within a civilized society had a right to 'absorb' and dominate inferior groups. He had no doubt that the Breton and the Basque stood to benefit greatly if absorbed into the French 'nation' and given the opportunity to share in the latter's dignity, power and civilization. The Scottish Highlanders and the Welsh would similarly gain if absorbed into the British, by which Mill meant the English, way of life. As he put it:

[18] Mill, *Utilitarianism, Liberty and Representative Government*, pp. 224 and 382.
[19] Mill, *Utilitarianism, Liberty and Representative Government*, pp. 199.
[20] Mill, *Utilitarianism, Liberty and Representative Government*, pp. 377, 378 and 199.
[21] Mill, *Utilitarianism, Liberty and Representative Government*, pp. 386f and 391f.
[22] See Stokes, *The English Utilitarians and India*, pp. 321, 255 and 251. Mill did, of course, want the Indians to be given power when they were ready but he did not think that they were ready even when others thought otherwise. Since his criteria of cultural improvement were vague, they could not protect him against his own prejudices.

Nobody can suppose that it is not more beneficial to a Breton, or a Basque of French Novarre, to be brought into the current of the ideas and feelings of a highly civilised and cultivated people – to be a member of the French nationality, admitted on equal terms to all the privileges of French citizenship, sharing the advantages of French protection, and the dignity and prestige of French power – than to sulk on his own rocks, the half-savage relic of past times, revolving in his own little mental orbit, without participation or interest in the general movement of the world. The same remark applies to Welshman or the Scottish Highlander as members of the British nation.[23]

Mill welcomed the 'blending' or 'admixture of nationalities' on the ground that like a 'crossed breed of animals', the new group was likely to 'inherit the special aptitudes and excellences' of the constituent groups.[24] However that was likely to happen only if the superior group remained the dominant partner. If there was any danger of the inferior group acquiring ascendancy by virtue of its greater numerical strength or power, that would constitute a 'sheer mischief to the human race and one which civilized humanity with one accord should rise *in arms* to prevent'. The cultural 'admixture' between the English and the Indians, and between the Europeans and the Russians, was desirable only if the former group in either pair dominated the relationship.

This view lay at the basis of Mill's approval of Lord Durham's Report on Canada. Lord Durham was hostile to the 'backward' French Canadians' 'vain endeavour' to preserve their cultural identity, and insisted that their true interests lay in being subjected to the 'vigorous rule of an English majority', that 'great race which must . . . be predominant over the whole' of North America.[25] Although Lord Durham advocated responsible government for Canada and was genuinely liberal in several respects, he had very little understanding of the strength of ethnic loyalties and even less sympathy for the desire to preserve ethnic identities. Not surprisingly many Canadian commentators have criticized his cultural 'chauvinism', and some have even accused him of racism.[26] Mill enthusiastically welcomed the Durham Report, calling it an 'imperishable memorial of that nobleman's courage, patriotism and enlightened liberty'.[27] Just as Lord Durham wanted the French Canadians to become English, Macaulay wanted to make the Indians English in all respects save the colour of their skin.[28] Liberals in other parts of the British empire felt the same way about the indigenous ways of life and thought. Drawing inspiration from Mill they wondered why people should 'blindly' adhere to their traditions and customs, and why the colonial rulers should not use a subtle mixture of education and coercion to get them to adopt the liberal ways of life and thought.

[23] Mill, *Utilitarianism, Liberty and Representative Government*, p. 363.

[24] Mill, *Utilitarianism, Liberty and Representative Government*, p. 304.

[25] Sir C.P. Lucas, *Lord Durham's Report on the Affairs of British North America*, (Oxford, Clarendon Press, 1912), vol. 11, pp. 285 ff. Following Locke and other liberals, Durham insisted that unlike the English, the natives and the French Canadians lacked the will and the talent to develop the unused land and to create a 'prosperous' and 'civilized' society. He was also convinced that the French Canadians represented a 'flawed' and 'inferior' race.

[26] Kenneth McNaught, *The Pelican History of Canada* (Harmondsworth, Penguin 1969), p. 94; and Mason Wade, *The French Canadians 1760: 1967*, (Toronto, Macmillan, 1968) Vol. 1, p. 197.

[27] Mill, *Utilitarianism, Liberty and Representative Government*, p. 377.

[28] For a detailed discussion see my *Gandhi's Political Philosophy*, (London, Macmillan, 1989), pp. 11 ff and *Colonialism, Tradition and Reform*, (Delhi, Sage, 1989), pp. 25 ff.

II

I have so far sketched the outlines of a dominant strand of nineteenth-century liberalism of which Mill was the ablest and most influential spokesman. What I might call Millian liberalism had several distinctive features which it would be useful to identify and analyse.

First, Millian liberalism was developed against the background of British colonialism. Mill not only approved of the latter but was also actively involved in its administration. And many colonial civil servants drew their inspiration from his ideas. Mill's liberalism aimed to show not only how British society and state should be constituted, but also why Britain was right to rule over a large part of the world. It was at once a theory of how civilized societies should be constituted and how they should relate to their uncivilized or semi-civilized counterparts. Its defence of colonialism was not incidental to but an integral part of its theoretical structure and cannot be explained away as a mere political prejudice. To be a Millian liberal is to take a condescending and paternalistic view of non-liberal societies. Millian liberalism is inherently bipolar: all societies for it are either liberal or non-liberal, and the latter are by definition illiberal and unworthy of human beings. It is also inherently restrictive in the sense that liberal values and principles are to apply only to civilized people. It is underpinned by what I might call a Manichean theory of two worlds, one is an area of light, the other that of darkness, one is perfect and without blemish, the other irredeemably evil, and each governed by radically different principles and norms.

Secondly, since the colonizing countries were all European and their subjects all non-European, the distinction between Europeans and non-Europeans became central to Millian liberalism. The Millian liberal is obsessively conscious of his European identity and sees liberalism as an exclusively European phenomenon. He cannot imagine that non-European societies might either have contributed to or possess their own distinct forms of liberalism.

The Europeanization of liberalism creates acute theoretical and practical difficulties for the liberal. Within the colonial context the Millian liberal is subject to two conflicting demands. He justifies colonialism on the ground that backward societies need to be civilized and that only the Europeans can do this. He must therefore argue *both* that the liberal principles are universally valid and that they are uniquely European in their origin and inspiration. In other words, he must both universalize and Europeanize them, and that is not easy. Since he Europeanizes the liberal principles, he is unable to show that they are teased out of universally shared human experiences and aspirations. On his own testimony the backward societies have managed to do without them for centuries and can continue to do so for several more. He has no moral basis and not even a shared language in terms of which to persuade them to accept the liberal principles. The abstract appeal to the excellence of the liberal conception of man has no meaning for those in whose experiences and ways of life it has no resonance. Furthermore, since the Millian liberal Europeanizes liberal principles, the 'backward' societies, which do have some self-respect and pride, find it psychologically difficult to accept a wholly 'alien' import backed up by little more than a self-serving ideological justification.

The Millian liberal has only one way to overcome the philosophical and psychological difficulties, namely to appeal to quasi-historicist utilitarianism. He argues that the Europeans have become rich, powerful and dominant because of their acceptance of individuality, rationality and other liberal principles, and that if the non-Europeans want to become as rich, powerful and dominant as the Europeans, they must do the same. As we saw this was how Mill often defended liberalism. That was also how the colonial rulers and later their native successors commended it to their humiliated subjects dazzled by and desperately anxious to 'catch up' with their imperial masters. Liberalism came to be associated with and was largely seen as a *means* to gaining power and prosperity, and was deprived of its moral basis and depth. In a colonial context it had no other way of harmonizing its contradictory Europeanist and universalist claims.[29]

Thirdly, since the Millian liberal developed liberalism against the background of colonialism and since he presented it as the major source of difference between the Europeans and the non-Europeans, he was led to define it in contrastive terms. Liberalism was seen as the opposite, the antithesis, of the allegedly tradition-bound non-European ways of life. Not surprisingly it became obsessively anti-tradition, anti-prejudice, anti-custom, anti-conformity, anti-community, and both defined extremely narrowly and exaggerated the importance of such values as autonomy, choice, individuality, liberty, rationality and progress. The process of thought at work here was complex and dialectical. The Millian liberal had a certain view of himself, in the light of which he conceptualized and judged non-European ways of life. Since he needed sharply to separate himself from the latter, he redefined himself in the light of the way he had defined them. Liberalism thus became the other of its other and gave itself an impoverished identity. In misreading the so-called East, it misread itself and became a victim of double distortion. The colonial experience was not marginal to Millian liberalism but penetrated its core and shaped its self-definition.

Fourthly, even as Mill Europeanized liberalism, he liberalized Europe. He asserted not only that liberalism was uniquely European in origin, but also that *only* liberalism expressed the true European identity. For him it *alone* represented the deepest desires and aspirations of the European people and was the sole source of their stability and progress. European history came to be seen as a struggle between traditions, customs and religion on the one hand and reason and critical thought on the other, and only the latter accounted for all that distinguished Europe and made it great. Mill's two theses, that liberalism was European in origin and that it alone expressed the European identity, were not necessarily related, although he thought otherwise, and neither was correct. Mill traced liberalism to Christianity, especially to its doctrine of the sacredness of each human being, and to classical Athens. But Christianity is not European in origin. As for classical Greece, it is neither Asian nor European or perhaps both, and the liberal is wrong to appropriate it for Europe. Mill's second thesis is even less persuasive. European civilization is made up of many strands of which liberalism is but one. Christianity, Judaism and Islam, as well as conservative, communitarian, socialist and many other intellectual currents have shaped

---

[29] It is striking that many nineteenth-century liberals and even their predecessors justified liberal values on the ground that they were a source of economic and political *power*. This happy coincidence between morality and worldly success had distinct Protestant, especially Calvinist, overtones, and offers an important clue to the religious basis and ethos of liberalism.

European identity. We may not go as far as many Catholic and Conservative historians who regard liberalism as a historical upstart, claiming credit for European achievements to which it has in fact contributed little and disclaiming responsibility for many of Europe's tragedies and disasters. However their criticism does contain important insights. By presenting liberalism as an unique expression of the European soul, the Millian liberal essentialized, homogenized and distorted European thought, marginalized and suppressed a large body of important ideas, and encouraged a dangerously misleading debate about who was a true or authentic European.

Fifthly, although Millian liberalism stressed the value of diversity, it defined its nature and permissible range in narrow terms. As we saw Mill linked diversity to individuality and choice, and valued the former only in so far as it was grounded in the individualist conception of man. This ruled out several forms of diversity. It ruled out traditional and customary ways of life, as well as those centred on the community. It also ruled out ethnically grounded ways of life as well as those limited to a 'narrow mental orbit' or 'not in tune' with the dominant trend of the age. Although it does not perhaps rule them out, Millian liberalism does take a low view of ways of life that stress contentment and weak ambition rather than a go-getting character, or are centred around religion, or place little value on worldly success and material abundance. As one would expect Millian liberalism cherishes not diversity *per se* but *liberal* diversity, that is diversity confined within the narrow limits of the individualist model of human excellence.

In his relation to non-liberal ways of life, the Millian liberal therefore displayed considerable intolerance. His intellectual tools were too blunt to allow him to make sense of them and he thought them inhuman and stifling. He dismissed them as illiberal and sought to dismantle them. If that required a vigorous policy of assimilation, he saw nothing wrong in it. And if some measure of coercion and violence was necessary, he accepted it as morally legitimate.[30] Given his view of life the Millian liberal could not avoid being a missionary, a stern pedagogue, a civilizer at large, a global guru. It is not at all surprising that Millian liberalism is suffused with educational metaphors.

Finally, Millian liberalism displayed a deep sense of diffidence and insecurity. It regarded individuality as the master key to human progress and the only protection against barbarism. However it was also convinced that individuality was a fragile plant constantly threatened by hostile forces, some of them rooted in human nature itself. Not surprisingly the Millian liberal was deeply apprehensive about the future of liberalism, and displayed extreme nervousness in the face of such things as the demands for universal franchise and a greater popular accountability of government, in both of which he saw mortal threats to 'civilization'. Decades later the liberal showed similar nervousness in the presence of communism and even socialism. Now that the latter have ceased to be threats, religious, especially Muslim fundamentalism, has become the new liberal nightmare. In the quasi-Manichean view of the Millian liberal, a world without enemies is inherently impossible, and lovers of liberty can never afford to relax their vigilance.

---

[30] Contrary to its self-understanding, liberalism has a deep-seated tendency towards violence, which it has extensively used in its relations to non-liberals both at home and abroad. The fact that violence is often justified in pedagogical terms makes it difficult for the liberal to acknowledge and regulate it.

III

In the previous section I highlighted some of the essential features of Millian liberalism. I argued that it is Eurocentric, narrow, missionary and dogmatic. Although liberalism has mellowed over the decades and become less self-righteous, it has not yet fully liberated itself from its Millian legacy. This is as true of those who derive their inspiration from him as of those claiming to depart from him. I shall take Joseph Raz and Brian Barry to illustrate the point. I take these two writers because they are two of the most distinguished liberal theorists, and because they deal, albeit too briefly, with the Third World especially Muslim immigrants settled in the West. The immigrants' ways of life are widely believed to be non-liberal, and they come from parts of the world the liberals once went out to civilize. They therefore provide a useful test of whether and how much liberal attitudes have changed in the aftermath of decolonization.

Joseph Raz consciously departs from Mill in several respects, yet some of the implications of his thought are distinctly Millian. Like Mill he regards autonomy as one of the central liberal values, and links it to 'self-creation'. As he puts it:

> The ruling idea behind the ideal of personal autonomy is that people should make their own lives. The autonomous person is a (part) author of his own life. The ideal of personal autonomy is the vision of people controlling, to some degree, their own destiny, fashioning it through successive decisions throughout their lives.[31]

For Raz an autonomous person shapes his life by making conscious choices from among an adequate range of valuable options available to him. A non-autonomous person is one who drifts through life, is determined by his tradition, or whose choices are made by others. Unlike Mill, Raz argues that it does not matter what an autonomous individual chooses to do or become as long as it is he who makes the choice. Not *what* but *how* a decision is made is central to autonomy. Although useful, the distinction does not amount to much, for Raz also talks about self-authorship and a life of continuing choices. For him it is not enough that an autonomous person makes choices; his choices must be such that they do not foreclose future choices and are significant enough to involve self-creation. Although Raz's notion of autonomy is less substantive than Mill's, it is not purely formal either.

Raz bases his case for autonomy on at least three different grounds. First, it is a necessary condition of human development and desirable for all men. Secondly, autonomy has struck 'deep roots . . . in our culture' and is the basis of the modern European society, so that 'we can prosper in it only if we can be successfully autonomous'.[32] Indeed, since autonomy is an inescapable necessity in such a society, 'there is no choice but to be autonomous'. Thirdly, Raz links autonomy to industrialization, and argues that no individual can cope with the constant social, economic, ideological and other changes characteristic of the industrialized society unless he or she is capable of autonomy.[33] While Raz's

[31] J. Raz, *The Morality of Freedom* (Oxford, Clarendon, 1986), p. 369. See also pp. 370 and 408.
[32] Raz, *The Morality of Freedom* p. 394.
[33] Raz, *The Morality of Freedom* p. 369.

second argument limits the value of autonomy to Europe, the third extends it to all industrialized societies.

Of the three arguments Raz says little about the first, and himself qualifies it.[34] He rightly argues that autonomy is central to the liberal conception of life. But since he does not show that non-liberal ways of life represent incoherent, deeply flawed or unviable conceptions of human excellence he cannot argue that autonomy is the precondition of all forms of human development. Raz's third argument is empirically dubious and does not ground autonomy as he has defined it. Industrialization can take many forms, of which that characteristic of the liberal West is but one. As the cases of Japan, South Korea, Singapore and other countries show, some forms of industrialization do not require and are even best achieved without autonomy. They do, of course, require mobility of capital, labour and so on, but that has little to do with self-creation and self-authorship. The willingness to follow the forces of the market and to go where the job is or to take up a career likely to land a worthwhile job falls far short of the kind of autonomy Raz cherishes.

Raz's second argument on which he generally relies is ambiguous and formulated in both essentialist and functionalist terms. Sometimes he argues that the modern European individual has come to be historically so constituted that autonomy is an integral part of his self-conception and is his deeply cherished value. On other occasions Raz argues that the modern European society is so structured that we can prosper in it only by becoming autonomous. Although the two formulations are related, they clearly point in different directions.

Neither formulation is persuasive. The essentialist argument is a partial and partisan reading of the contemporary European way of life. The Europeans do value autonomy, but they also value heteronomy as is amply evident in the popular support for Fascism, Nazism, Communism, Collectivism, fundamentalism and bizarre religious cults. And even the intellectuals who cherish autonomy in some areas are sometimes strong supporters of collectivist and even totalitarian movements. Since the European culture is composed of several different and at times conflicting elements, Raz is wrong to privilege one of them and to give it a pseudo-ontological foundation in the reified European character. Even if we accepted Raz's reading of the modern European character his conclusion would not follow, for we might regret the historically acquired desire for autonomy and decide to fight it. What the Europeans have acquired during the past three centuries, they surely have the power to undo over the next two. Like many contemporary liberals, Raz is guilty of a historicist version of the naturalistic fallacy.

The functionalist argument fares no better. It views autonomy as a functional requirement of the modern society, treats it as if it were no different from such socially necessary amoral skills as literacy and numeracy, and denies it the status of a moral value that Raz claims for it. The argument is also empirically false. Although he does not explain what he means by 'prosper', he has in mind both material success and a sense of well-being. For Raz the Asian immigrants to Britain do not value autonomy. Yet their material success is remarkable and widely acknowledged. Indeed they have prospered precisely because they do not set much store by autonomy and draw on the ample resources of a flourishing communal life and a readily available network of social support. As for personal well-being, the Asians do have their share of suffering and unhappi-

---

[34] Raz, *The Morality of Freedom* p. 189.

ness, but no more and some might say even less than their allegedly autonomous white fellow-citizens.

On the basis of his inadequately defended conception of autonomy, Raz goes on to classify and grade different ways of life. His argument proceeds by means of the five dubious steps characteristic of Millian liberalism.[35] First, like Mill he is worried about the presence of communities whose cultures do not value autonomy. He has in mind immigrant communities, indigenous people and religious sects. He lumps together very different groups with very different social structures and attitudes to the mainstream liberal society. Since they are not liberal, they are all the same! It is interesting too that Raz associates autonomy with the Western way of life, and its absence with immigrants and indigenous people, both black. He does talk of religious sects, but largely sees them as embarrassing relics of the past and marginal to the *essentially* liberal western way of life. Like Mill he westernizes liberalism and sees it as an uniquely western phenomenon.

Second, since the immigrants and others allegedly do not value autonomy, Raz calls them non-liberal. One would have thought that since autonomy is a matter of degree and since no human community can ever dispense with it altogether, different ways of life form a spectrum and cannot be neatly divided into liberal and non-liberal. Like Mill, Raz assumes that non-liberal ways of life do not value autonomy and choice, and fails to explore whether they may not define these values differently or locate them in different activities and areas of life. Although not always at liberty to marry whoever he likes, the Hindu, for example, enjoys the incredible freedom to choose his gods, to borrow without a sense of guilt the practices and imageries of other religious traditions, and to make up his own religion without ceasing to be a Hindu. At the social level the Hindu is less autonomous than the modern European; at the religious level he would seem to enjoy a much greater degree of choice and autonomy. Even in matters of marriage and choice of occupation, the situation is extremely complex. The average Hindu is not at liberty to choose his spouse. But if he were to exercise his choice, more often than not it would eventually be endorsed by his community and he would be readmitted into its fold. Choice is formally disallowed, but once it is made it is accommodated and sometimes even admired. Those involved know how to play the game and exploit the available space. Again, although Raz finds the Western way of life autonomous, like most non-Western people the Hindu sees it differently. He cannot see how it can be said to respect choice when it has rules about everything including what to wear at a funeral, at a wedding and at work, how to respond to different levels of friendship or social relations, how to conduct oneself in different contexts, and so on. Since his society leaves these matters to individual choice, he finds the Western society rigid and oppressive! This is not at all to say that all ways of life are equally autonomous, only that none is wholly devoid of it, that their comparison requires much sharper conceptual tools than Raz provides, and that the concepts of choice autonomy are too vague to bear the moral weight Raz and other liberals put upon them.

Raz's third step consists in equating non-liberal with illiberal. In a manner characteristic of the Millian form of thought, which Hegel had brilliantly

[35] Raz, *The Morality of Freedom*, p. 423 f. Raz's discussion is extremely brief and sketchy. But since it points to the 'direction in which the conclusions of this book lead', I use it to uncover and assess his central assumptions and arguments.

exposed in his *Logic*, Raz mistakenly turns difference into opposition and implies that those who are different from us are necessarily opposite of us, that those who are not liberal are necessarily illiberal, and that they pose a threat. As we saw, the immigrant way of life is, like any other, a mixture of different kinds of values and practices, some of which are liberal, some non-liberal, some others illiberal, and yet others not amenable to such categorization. To call it illiberal on the basis of its illiberal values and practices is to mistake the part for the whole.

Furthermore the concept of autonomy presupposes the concept of the self, and since different cultures individuate the self differently, they arrive at different conceptions of autonomy.[36] Although Raz lacks a clearly worked out theory of the self, his conception of autonomy presupposes a liberal ontology. Non-liberal societies rest on what I might call a theory of overlapping selves. Those bound together by familial, kinship, religious and other ties do not see themselves as independent and self-contained ontological units involved in specific kinds of relationship with 'others', but rather as bearers of overlapping selves whose identities are constituted by, and incapable of being defined in isolation from, these relationships. For them individual and self are distinct and their boundaries do not coincide, so that naturally distinct individuals may and do share their selves in common. Each individual is deeply implicated in the lives of those related to him, and their interests, lives and life plans are inextricably interlinked and incapable of individuation. They believe that they are therefore not only accountable to each other for their decisions but ought to take them in common. This is generally how matters relating to marriage, occupation, residence and so on are taken in many 'non-liberal' communities. The decision-making is less individualist and liberal than in the modern Western society, but it is more co-operative and *democratic*. It entails a different conception (concept?) of personal autonomy from Raz's, but to dismiss it on that score and to call these communities illiberal is to be dogmatic.

Having characterized non-liberal ways of life as illiberal with all its pejorative associations, Raz takes the fourth predictable step of calling them 'inferior'. Apparently he does not notice that his reasoning is circular. Since he judges non-liberal societies in liberal terms, they are bound to appear inferior. If we took the Indian, the Chinese or the Islamic views of man as our standard, it is the self-centric and even self-obsessed liberal societies that would appear inferior. Even if Raz were to avoid the charge of circularity by redefining his assumptions, he would still be open to the charge of taking the momentous and, in the light of colonial history, dangerous step of grading cultures in terms of a principle which he has neither defined nor defended with the kind of rigour its importance in his theory requires.

Raz is now set for his fifth and final step. Since 'illiberal' cultures are 'inferior', he asks the high-minded question whether we should 'tolerate' them and 'allow them to continue'.[37] Who this homogenized 'we' refers to is not clear. It excludes 'them', the illiberal cultures which evidently have no say in deciding how they should be treated. It also excludes a large body of non-liberal opinion within the West itself which cherishes the religiosity and the communal way of life of the immigrant and hopes that they will deepen and enrich the morally and

---

[36] For a further discussion see my 'The cultural particularity of liberal democracy' in David Held (ed.), *Prospects for Democracy* (Cambridge, Polity, 1993), especially pp. 168 f.

[37] Raz, *The Morality of Freedom*, p. 424.

spiritually shallow dominant way of life. Raz's 'we' largely refers to liberals, and shows that, like Mill, he regards liberalism as the sole authentic voice of Western history.

Since immigrant cultures are illiberal and inferior, Raz wonders what to do with them. Unwittingly using the very language Mill had used, he argues that they should be 'assimilated' or 'absorbed' into the dominant liberal culture, and either radically reformed or allowed to die. Following the long line of Millian liberals, he turns to schools for the necessary moral and cultural engineering. Raz appreciates that both prudence and compassion require us to bring about a 'gradual transformation' of immigrant cultures. But if that were to prove difficult or be obstructed by immigrant leaders, the state may use coercive measures, this being the 'only humane course' left to save the immigrant children allegedly condemned to 'an impoverished, unrewarding life'. It is depressing that the Millian missionary legacy continues to cast its dark shadow on the thought of an otherwise generous, broadminded and self-critical liberal.

Having discussed Raz at some length, we may be brief with the other contemporary liberals. Brian Barry defines liberalism in terms of such familiar Millian values as the spirit of critical and independent thought, personal choice and individuality. He is convinced that liberalism as he understands it is currently under threat and that 'we are headed for a new Dark Age', the old Millian nightmare. Although Barry thinks that 'the evidence is there for all to see', he does little more than point to Fascist and fundamentalist movements, none of which really threatens the fabric of Western civilization.[38] He insists that a liberal society cannot survive without 'a large proportion' of the population sharing a 'liberal outlook'. He therefore urges the liberals 'to go on the offensive and promote liberal activity', but does not specify the character and content of the activity. He is particularly worried about Islamic fundamentalism for more or less the same reasons that the earlier generations of liberals were worried about democracy and communism. He thinks that it will take 'centuries rather than decades' to liberalize Islam, and that even then there is no guarantee of success.[39] This is broadly what Mill and other liberals had said about India! Until such time as the Muslims are civilized, Western societies have to do something about those settled in their midst. Barry seems to think that the schools, the traditional site of aggressive liberal intervention, should actively cultivate liberal values and fight dogmatic and obscurantist beliefs.[40] He also wants the state to fund liberal Muslim groups and writers, to avoid contacts with the traditionalists, and to eschew 'unprincipled' compromises with Muslim values and practices.[41]

Barry's language, tone and basic message are distinctly Millian. His liberalism, like that of Mill, centres around a single and narrow view of the good life and has little patience with the religious and communal ways of life. Like Mill, he is deeply nervous about the stability of liberal institutions, and thinks that offence is the best form of defence. Like Mill, again, he makes little attempt to understand the nature and history of Islam, homogenizes a large array of Muslim societies and movements, and asserts on the basis of recent aberrations

[38] B. Barry, *Liberty and Justice, Essays in Political Theory 2* (Oxford, Clarendon, 1991), p. 39.

[39] Barry, *Liberty and Justice* p. 2.

[40] Barry, *Liberty and Justice* p. 26.

[41] Barry, *Liberty and Justice* p. 3.

that Islam is inherently illiberal and fundamentalist and perhaps beyond hope. Again, he wants to inculcate liberal virtues in Muslim children and to use the coercive authority of the state for that purpose. He even thinks that the state should interfere with the internal debates within Islam, and fund and encourage liberal as opposed to conservative writers. Barry does not think that Muslim parents might have a right to preserve and transmit their way of life to their children, and that although the right might sometimes be curtailed, it could not be completely overridden or ignored. Barry does not ask if liberalism may not learn something from a sympathetic dialogue with the Islamic, communal and other ways of life, and assumes that liberalism represents the last word in human wisdom.

Like Raz and Barry, John Rawls too in his *Theory of Justice* and subsequent writings advocates a narrowly based liberal society. He does not recognize cultural identity as a primary good and a source of legitimate claims on the state. In his society citizens may follow the religious, communal and other ways of life, but the basic thrust of the social structure is against them. Enjoying neither public recognition nor public support, they are on the defensive and at a disadvantage compared to the officially institutionalized liberal ways of life and thought. Rawls acknowledges that his principle of justice are biased against some ways of life, which therefore may not be able to reproduce themselves in his kind of society. He accepts this as inevitable, and neither explores a more broad-based liberalism nor asks if they might not legitimately complain of unequal and discriminatory treatment and question their obligation to obey the state.

Although Ronald Dworkin is more sensitive to these problems, he too assumes a culturally homogeneous society committed to individualism and autonomy. He says that we have inherited 'a cultural structure' which we have a duty to preserve.[42] He homogenizes the undefined 'we' and assumes that 'we' have a single cultural tradition, that it is essentially liberal, that it is integral to our self-conception, and that we have a duty to protect it against threats from illiberal ways of life. Like Mill, Raz and others he homogenizes the West, marginalizes its non-liberal traditions, presents liberalism as the only authentic expression of modern Western history and character, and is open to the objections we made against Mill and Raz. By a series of dubious steps, such as that justice requires a shared system of meanings and values, that the latter presupposes a homogeneous cultural community, and that such a community is inherently inhospitable to minority claims to cultural self-preservation, Michael Walzer too concludes that the cultural minorities must either get 'assimilated' or leave the country.[43]

The tendency to homogenize the West and to view liberalism as its sole authentic voice is also evident in the way many contemporary liberals ground their moral judgements. Take the frequently invoked and philosophically dubious concept of moral intuition. Although liberal philosophers admit that moral intuitions are fallible and often confused and contradictory, they assign them an ontologically privileged status and view them as more or less authentic indicators of our cultural identity and expressive of our deepest moral being.

---

[42] Ronald Dworkin, *A Matter of Principle* (London, Harvard University Press, 1985), pp. 230, 233.

[43] For an excellent discussion of Walzer, see Will Kymlicka, *Liberalism, Community and Culture* (Oxford, Clarendon Press, 1991), ch. 11.

When carefully examined, their intuitions turn out to be liberal in content. This is obvious in the case of Rawls' two principles which clearly do not conform to the moral intuitions of Conservatives, Marxists, deeply religious people, many ethnic minorities and others. It is also evident in Dworkin's reference to the 'intuitive appeal' of Rawls' principles to 'people of good will'. Whether he intended it or not, Dworkin's view implies that those who do not find Rawls' principles intuitively appealing are not people of good will! In claiming the monopoly of the Western soul, the liberal engages in the most illiberal form of moral blackmail.

IV

In spite of their emphasis on choice and diversity then, most contemporary liberals are hostile to non-individualist forms of life. They aspire to a culturally homogeneous world in which all alike are wedded to the narrowly defined values of autonomy and choice. If the tribals, the Eskimos, the American Indians, the Aborigines, the Maoris, the Amish community, the ethnic groups, the religious orders, and the traditional, the communal, and the religious ways of life were to disappear, many contemporary liberals would not regard that as a grievous and irreparable loss. For them, as for Mill, these non-liberal ways of life have contributed and are capable of contributing nothing to human civilization and 'history'. They are atavistic legacies of a pre-liberal past, a drag on progress, a moral embarrassment, and nurseries of obscurantist and fundamentalist forces. Some liberals are prepared to use force to eliminate them; some others prefer more humane methods; yet others leave it to 'history' to bring about their peaceful demise. But they are all convinced that these and other ways of life neither enrich nor deserve secure spaces of growth in a liberal society.

When confronted with multi-cultural societies such as ours, in which liberal and non-liberal ways of life assert their rights to exist and reproduce themselves, the intolerant, dogmatic and missionary Millian liberalism runs into difficult theoretical and practical problems, of which I might mention three by way of illustration. First, the liberal is committed to equal respect for persons. Since human beings are culturally embedded, respect for them entails respect for their cultures and ways of life. Not that we may not criticize the latter or condemn their specific practices, rather that we owe them an obligation of sympathetic understanding, cannot condemn them out of hand and resent them for being different, and must generally allow them to change at their own pace and in their own way. Being engaged in a cold or open war against non-liberal ways of life, the liberal is unable to offer them respect and violates his commitment to the principle of equal respect.

Second, the liberal is unable to solve the problem of political obligation. He rightly insists that all citizens have an equal obligation to obey the law, and rests the obligation on the ground that the liberal state treats all its citizens equally. As we saw, the liberal does not satisfy this basic precondition of equal obligation. Even when he does not suppress or persecute non-liberal ways of life or subject them to cultural engineering, he privatizes them and denies them public recognition, status and support. The institutions of the state embody and enforce liberal values, and devote the resources of the state to creating a climate conducive to them. Since non-liberal ways of life are unequally treated and discriminated against in areas that matter most to them, the liberal cannot show how they have an equal obligation to obey the law.

Third, the liberal values cultural diversity and pluralism on both moral and epistemological grounds. As he rightly argues, cultural diversity increases the range of available options, expands more imagination and sympathy, and enriches life; it also encourages a healthy competition between different ways of life and deepens our knowledge of the nature and possibilities of human existence. Since this is so, the liberal cannot consistently privilege the liberal way of life and conduct an assimilationist campaign against ways of life and thought that differ from his own, for to do so is to assume that the liberal way of life alone is 'true' and represents the last word in human wisdom.

No way of life, however rich, can express the full range of human potentiality. Since human capacities and aspirations conflict, to develop some of them is necessarily to neglect, suppress, or marginalize others. Every way of life cherishes and nurtures some human capacities and forms of excellence, and in so doing it necessarily marginalizes, ignores or suppresses others. Different ways of life therefore correct and balance each other and restrain each other's partialities. They should therefore be judged not only on the basis of what they are in themselves, but also in terms of their contribution to the overall richness of society. Even if a culture is 'poorer' than another, it may nevertheless play a vital role in preserving values and aspirations ignored by the latter. As Herder and other German Romantics argued, cultures are spiritual creations of their relevant communities, and products of their unique historical experiences as distilled and interpreted over centuries by their unique imaginations. They are like works of art or literature, and worthy of similar respect. If we are prepared to preserve rare botanical and zoological species even when we do not at present see their value, it makes no sense to destroy ways of life that do no obvious and identifiable harm to themselves or to others. Once the long-established ways of life are destroyed in the dogmatic belief that the autonomous way of life alone is valuable, they are lost for ever. If the liberal way of life were to run into unexpected difficulties, as it is beginning to do today, we would have no resources left from which to draw new inspiration and strength. Even if aesthetic, moral, spiritual and other considerations did not weigh with us, prudence would require that we do not dissipate the inherited cultural capital and invest all our hopes in one cultural enterprise.

Millian liberalism represents the British and European self-consciousness during the heyday of imperialism, and bears the deep imprint of an age in which the liberal way of life and thought exercised unchallenged intellectual and political hegemony over its defeated rivals. Since the victims of history are now feeling confident enough to assert their cultural identity in a decolonized world, and since we now appreciate better than before that no way of life including the liberal represents the last word in human wisdom, liberalism cannot afford to remain trapped within the arrogant colonial mode of thought. It needs to become more open-minded, more self-critical, more tolerant of its rivals, and far more sensitive to the diversity and complexity of human existence than it has been hitherto. It must reassess its Millian commitment to a single mode of human excellence and evolve a view of the world in which different ways of life, including the non-liberal, can converse as equals and enrich both individual and collective existence. A truly liberal *society* is characterized by diverse ways of life, both liberal and non-liberal, both secular and religious, both individualist and communitarian, and each in turn nurturing its own diverse forms. A truly liberal *state* cherishes and gives public recognition to this diversity, provides such resources and conditions of growth as they need, encourages a civil dialogue between them, and enforces norms that they have agreed upon and without which their peaceful coexistence is impossible.[44] To evolve such a rich, generous and self-limiting liberal doctrine, and to fashion an appropriate social and political structure, is one of the greatest challenges confronting the modern liberal.[45]

[44] For a tentative exploration of what this entails in a British context, see my 'British citizenship and cultural difference' in Geoffrey Andrews (ed.) *Citizenship* (London, Lawrence & Wishart, 1991). Whether and in what sense the kind of society and state I advocate can be called liberal is largely a semantic question.

[45] This challenge confronts not just liberalism but *all* modern ideologies, including Marxism and the different varieties of socialism. In one way or another, they are all deeply influenced by liberalism and share its missionary and ethnocentric ethos. If anything, they have been even more intolerant of ethnic, religious and the so-called pre-modern ways of life. Since every modern society is multi-cultural, *all* modern ideologies, predicated as they are on the assumption of a single conception of the good, need to be radically reassessed and *aufgehoben*.

The Concept of Fundamentalism

BHIKHU PAREKH[1]

University of Hull

The rise of what is called religious fundamentalism has caused and continues to cause enormous havoc in many societies. Hundreds of thousands of people have died as a result of it, the development of many societies has been deeply distorted by it, and there is no end in sight to this tragedy. The phenomenon is not confined to the developing, especially the Muslim, countries, although they have suffered the most from it. Even in the stable and secular West where they have no real chance of coming to power, the fundamentalists have sometimes exercised a considerable influence. In America, for example, they helped Presidents Reagan and Bush come to power and contributed to fostering a climate of intolerance toward secular humanist and liberal ideas. This paper examines the nature, logic and historical specificity of fundamentalism.

Since such characteristic features of fundamentalism as the fusion of religion and politics, mass mobilization, religious zeal and a gross over-simplification of social and political life fall outside the normal experience of the largely secular and rationalist west, especially the intellectuals, the study of fundamentalism has often suffered from several limitations. First, there is a tendency to demonize it, to see in it a denial of civilized values, and to present it as an expression of dark and atavistic forces. As a result we fail to explore fundamentalism with a measure of sympathy or even scholarly detachment, and to ask if legitimate fears, anxieties and aspirations might not perhaps be struggling to express themselves in these distorted and outrageous forms.

Second, there is a tendency to use the term fundamentalism as a kind of polemical hand-grenade to be thrown at whoever is not whole-heartedly committed to liberal values. Not surprisingly a large body of quite disparate movements get lumped together and their historical specificity is ignored. We talk of Hindu, Sikh, Buddhist, Jewish, Christian, and Islamic fundamentalism as if they were all of the same kind. We ignore the vital fact that since different religions have distinct structures, histories and traditions, they necessarily throw up distinct movements with their own unique modes of discourse, dissent and forms of self-assertion. Indeed we naively imagine that every religion has a fundamentalist impulse, and fail to ask if fundamentalism may not be peculiar to certain kinds of religion.

Third, Since the so called fundamentalists seem to share several features in common with such other groups as the conservatives, the orthodox, the ultra-orthodox and the revivalists, we make the further mistake of lumping them all together, as if all those who did not come up to our norms of critical rationality

---

[1] Several versions of this paper were tried out at senior seminars in the Universities of Warwick, Cambridge, Oxford, Delhi and Amsterdam. I am grateful to the participants for their searching comments.

or who refused to sail with the secularist tide were cast in the same mould. Saudi Arabia is declared fundamentalist just as much as and in the same sense as Khomeini's Iran. And there is believed to be no or little difference between the ultra-orthodox Jews largely anxious to be left alone and fighting back under provocation with nothing more lethal than stones, and the revolutionary *hezbullahs* seeking to transform their societies radically and delivering instant 'justice' to anyone appearing to challenge even a minor Koranic injunction. Not to distinguish between different kinds of religious movements is to display the very vices of dogmatism and insensitivity to truth that we rightly condemn in fundamentalism. We cannot hope to understand fundamentalism if we ourselves approach it in a fundamentalist spirit.[2]

In this paper I am concerned to explore the nature, the internal logic, the historical specificity and the origins of fundamentalism, and to highlight its ambiguities and contradictions. One of the most difficult questions raised by such an inquiry relates to where one starts. We intend to study the phenomenon of fundamentalism. But how do we recognize it? A stipulative definition will not do, for if it is arbitrary it misleads us, and if it is not, it must have a rational basis. Since we are not the first to investigate the phenomenon and since there is a well-established popular and academic discourse on it, we have good reasons to start with it. However, as we saw, the usage of the term fundamentalism has become inflated and vague and covers a disparate range of phenomena. What is more, it is suffused with understandable biases and prejudices and, as fundamentalism deeply threatens our way of life and interests, also with deep fears and crude political considerations. To remain confined to the current usage is therefore to be both trapped within these biases and to be subject to subtle political manipulations. Although we cannot avoid the current usage, we cannot uncritically accept it either. How then do we decide which of the current usages of the term offers the most neutral or the least biased and manipulative starting point?

Since these large questions are not directly relevant to my inquiry, I shall briefly state how I intend to proceed in this essay. By common consent, reinforced by my own intellectual intuitions, a unique phenomenon has been occurring for the past few decades in several Muslim countries. It is relatively new even to Islam, and has not occurred in quite this form in other societies. I shall therefore start with it, explore its internal structure and identify its specificity, later asking if, after making due allowances for the differences in their religions, history and stages of development, it occurs in other societies as well. Since the phenomenon in question is often called fundamentalism, I shall follow the usage and argue that, *if* we use the term in that way, then other similar-looking but logically different phenomena should be given another name. I thus begin with one of the current usages to guide my inquiry, and use my conclusions to evaluate and criticize its other usages, including the one I start with. If we were to find at the end of our inquiry that the phenomenon of fundamentalism is too incoherent, nebulous, contradictory or diverse to merit a single name, then we would need to drop not only the usage we started with but also the term fundamentalism itself.

---

[2] For a fascinating study of fundamentalism, see the three massive volumes of Martin E. Marty and R. Scott Appleby (eds), *Fundamentalisms Observed* (Chicago, The University of Chicago Press, 1991–3). Even here fundamentalism is treated as a universal phenomenon occurring in all religions. See also Lionel Caplan (ed.), *Studies in Religious Fundamentalism* (London, Macmillan, 1987). In

To anticipate, I shall argue in this paper that fundamentalism is a distinctly modern phenomenon which has historical analogues but no parallels. It arises in a society widely believed to be degenerate and devoid of a sense of direction, identity and the means of its self-regeneration. Fundamentalism represents an attempt to regenerate it by comprehensively reconstituting it on a religious foundation. It rejects the tradition, offers a 'dynamic' and activist reading of the scriptures, abstracts what it calls their essence or fundamentals, builds a moral and political programme around them, and uses the institutions of the state to enforce the programme. It is reactive but not at all reactionary, intensely moralistic, and represents an ingenious blend of rationalism and irrationalism. Since fundamentalism reduces religion to ideology and charters it to an alien purpose, it inevitably distorts and destroys it. I shall conclude by arguing that fundamentalism is characteristic of some religions but not of others, and quite different from conservative, traditionalist, orthodox, ultra-orthodox and other religious dispositions.

Context

Religions are of many different kinds. Some, such as the tribal, rest on orally transmitted beliefs and practices and have no sacred written texts. Some such as Hinduism, Buddhism and Jainism possess several texts, but are not centred on them and are largely non-credal in nature. Their texts are basically the transcripts of the experiences and practices of the communities concerned and do not form the sources of their beliefs. Some other religions, the so-called *religions of the book*, centre on specific texts believed to represent the exhaustive revelations of the will of God. Islam, Christianity and Judaism fall within this category. Although the sacred text has a very different status and authority and plays a very different role in each of these religions, it enjoys a kind of centrality not to be found in other religions. All major religions have sacred books, but only some of them are religions of the book.

Every religion is a joint creation of God and man. Its origin and inspiration are divine, but only the human beings can determine its meaning and give it a worldly reality. How to conceptualize and define God, who to accept as a prophet, a son of God or a recipient of transcendental accreditation, what kind of authority to ascribe to him, and how to institutionalize and transmit his charisma are all a matter of conscious and unconscious, individual and collective, free and coerced human decisions. Furthermore the prophet's life, deeds and utterances are capable of different interpretations, and his followers need to agree on one of these. They also need to read his life and the sacred text in the light of each other, resolve their inevitable discrepancies, and to arrive at a coherent interpretation of both. The sacred text, further, is dense and complex. Since the profoundest truths about human nature and destiny cannot be easily stated in a propositional language and are generally communicated in parables, allegories, images and cryptic aphorisms, these have to be patiently decoded and explained in simple terms. The moral principles laid down in the sacred text are often abstract and general, and need to be interpreted and explained. A broad consensus also has to be developed on what beliefs and practices are central to the religion, the permissible diversity of views, the manner of debating and

this otherwise excellent collection the term fundamentalism is used by the contributors to cover all religions and all kinds of conservative movements.

resolving the differences, and on who is entitled to take and enforce collectively binding decisions. In short, every religion requires a consensus on what it means to belong to it and how its authority is to be enforced.

The consensus evolves over time and is a product of tradition. The tradition defines the identity of the religion and shapes its structure of authority. Without a tradition the sacred text or whatever else is taken to reveal the will of God remains transcendental and unrelated to the human world. The tradition humanizes it and relates God to man. No religion is or can be a matter 'between man and his maker'. Man needs to know *who* his maker is, *what* He wants him to do, *how* He is related to him and so on, and these questions cannot be answered outside of a religious tradition. Every religion is a community of men and women bound together by a shared body of beliefs concerning their relation to a transcendental referent. They are related to God as members of a specific religious community, and to the community in terms of their relationship to God. Being at once both transcendental and social, the religious identity is necessarily two-dimensional. To be a Christian or a Muslim or a Jew is necessarily to be related both to God and to other human beings in a specific manner.

As a worldly reality existing among and for human beings, a religious tradition is subject to several constraints. It needs the support and loyalty of its adherents and cannot ignore their interests and needs. Some of them might make their religion the basis of their lives, others might assign it only a limited place, yet others might find it a painful burden which they seek to lighten at every available opportunity. Every religious tradition must find spaces for all of them and strike a balance between their conflicting demands and pressures. Since all human societies are divided along gender, age, economic, occupational and other lines, no religion can afford to alienate any of them. It must carry the rich and the powerful as well as the poor and the powerless, men as well as women, the old as well as the young, and cannot remain indifferent to their unavoidable tensions and conflicts. As new groups emerge it must also take account of their interests, views and sensibilities. A religion cannot ignore the cultural, technological and other changes taking place in the wider society either, and must come to terms with them. The beliefs that appeared self-evident to an earlier generation might strain the credulity of another and need to be restated and even revised. As the dominant intellectual idioms change, old ideas and principles risk losing their meaning and appeal unless they are recast and defended in the language of the time. Some of the finest minds of a religious community might develop new spiritual insights, and these too need to be accommodated and used to deepen and enrich the reading of the text. Thanks to these and other inescapable requirements of human existence, no religion can for long resist change. If it does not change, it becomes fossilized and irrelevant and commands no respect. But whatever changes it makes must be, or at least shown to be, consistent with the tradition of discourse woven around the text, its historical starting point and constant frame of reference. In other words the changes require and must be shown to be entailed by a new and more adequate reading of the text and the tradition.

Like the changes in other areas of life, religious changes inevitably provoke disagreements. The members of a religious community might disagree about the pace of change and divide into reactionaries, gradualists and revolutionaries, or about what beliefs and practices are open to change and divide into orthodox, ultra-orthodox and reformers. They might quarrel about the ideological biases and implications of the changes and divide into conservatives and radicals. The importance assigned to the text might also become a subject of debate, and the believers might divide into scripturalists, for whom the text is far more important than the tradition, and traditionalists for whom the text is constructed by and has no identity independently of the tradition. The manner of reading the text too might become controversial, the literalists asserting that every word in it is sacred and inerrant, and the liberals insisting on reading it in the context of its or their own time.

Being differently structured, different religions give rise to different kinds of disagreement and react to and resolve them differently. However no religious tradition ever can be or, as a historical fact, ever is free from some or all of these disputes. It is by its nature an ongoing conversation, sometimes friendly and sometimes bitter, between its constituent groups and points of view. Every religion has its share of orthodox, ultra-orthodox, revivalist, reformist and radical groups. And although each group claims to be its sole authentic spokesman, they generally know how to coexist in a climate of mutual respect. Acute tensions do sometimes arise and threaten to split the religious community. Those in charge of the religious tradition, be they the Catholic church, the established state churches, the *Ulema*, the Rabbis, the *gurus*, or the *pandits*, generally have enough political skill and moral and theological flexibility to contain or resolve these tensions. When their resources prove inadequate or the followers' demands are impossible to meet, the community concerned splits. The rise of Protestantism, Calvinism, Buddhism, Jainism, the Bohras, the Ahmadiyyas, and so on tell the story of how and why different religious communities break up. In some cases the dissidents rejected many of the beliefs and practices of their religion and established another religion; in some others they were outraged by the moral corruption of the religious establishment and set up separate homes within the shared religious tradition; in some others they interpreted the central theological doctrines differently and formed independent sects; in yet others the tradition was unable to accommodate the new 'prophets' claiming unusual insights into the religious text, and their followers built up an ambiguous relationship with it.

A wholly new situation arises when a religious community faces not just shallow or deep disagreements about specific beliefs and practices but what I shall call a *crisis of identity and authority*. In normal circumstances a religious tradition provides its adherents with a reasonably clear conception of who they are and what is expected of them, and uses such sanctions as it has to ensure compliance. The crisis of *identity* occurs when the consensus breaks down, and the believers are no longer clear about what is involved in belonging to their religious tradition. They do not know what beliefs they should hold, what values should guide their conduct, how they should relate to others, and the kind of life they should aspire to lead. The crisis of *authority* occurs when those in charge of a religion are unable or unwilling to secure compliance with its norms by imposing such sanctions as they possess on those found guilty of violating the norms. This may happen because there is no consensus on the norms, or because the religious establishment is for some reason unwilling or afraid to take action, or because it has become morally corrupt or politically compromised and lost its moral authority. The crises of identity and authority are dialectically related. The crisis of identity occurs partly because the religious establishment lacks the authority to evolve a consensus. But part of the reason why it lacks that authority has to do with the absence of consensus and the related crisis of identity. Each of the two crises causes and intensifies and is in turn caused and intensified by the other. They are part of the same larger process, which we shall call a religious crisis.

The religious crisis occurs for a variety of related reasons, some internal to a religion, others derived from outside it. As we saw it may occur because the religious tradition has become rigid, insensitive, unimaginative, and lacks the skill to reconcile and evolve a consensus from the disagreements endemic in every religion. A corrupt religious establishment or one in league with the vested interests is also a contributing factor. Another important factor is the pace and depth of changes in the society at large. When, for such reasons as industrialization and foreign conquest, a society undergoes a profound transformation, its dominant religion needs to keep pace with the changes and to redefine its central beliefs and values. If it does not, it loses its capacity to guide its adherents. Unable either to live by their increasingly irrelevant traditional values and beliefs or to abandon them for fear of a moral vacuum, they suffer profound disorientation.

Another factor that intensifies the religious crisis has to do with the presence of the hostile other. However corrupt or unimaginative a religious tradition might have become, it generally has *some* capacity to contain and perhaps even to resolve the crisis. But that needs time, self-confidence and a sense of security, all of which are denied it if it feels surrounded by what it regards as deeply threatening forces. The religion concerned then fears for its very survival and panics. The threat to a religion might come from another religion or from secularism. Which of the two is seen as a greater threat depends on the historical context and the nature of the religion concerned. The Hindus, for example, felt far more threatened by Islam and Christianity, especially when the two were in power, than by secularism. Since Hinduism is immanentist rather than transcendental and is more concerned with conduct than with belief, the Hindus well know how to contain and accommodate secularism but have great difficulty coming to terms with the two organized religions. Besides, since Hinduism is primarily concerned to maintain the caste-based social structure, it is more worried about religious conversion, especially of the volatile lower castes, than about the loss of religious belief. By contrast Islam and Christianity have long felt, and continue to feel, far more threatened by secularism than by each other or by other religions. They have enough religious self-confidence and institutional strength to counter the influence of other religions. But since they are credal in nature, they cannot survive the loss of religious belief and deeply fear the subtle and stealthy influence of secularism.

In a situation of religious crisis there are no agreed and effective norms to regulate belief and conduct, leaving the believers free to interpret their religion as they please. Almost everything is permissible and almost everybody can claim to be a true believer. There is no restraint on the familiar human tendencies towards greed, dishonesty, hypocrisy, lying, frivolity, corruption, misuse of power, and so on, and those able to do so take full advantage of the moral confusion. No one knows what to expect of others, what they can count on others to do or not to do, who to trust, and how therefore to plan their lives. The religion concerned loses its wholeness and integrity and is unable to perform the central function of guiding and holding its adherents together. Since morality is a vital part of every religion, the crisis of religious identity leads to a crisis of moral identity and affects the very basis of personal and social life. The entire realm of personal and social morality, which generally depends on religion for its articulation and enforcement, becomes problematic, leading to a widespread feeling of anomie, disorientation and rootlessness.

The religious crisis takes different forms and has different consequences in different societies. It is muted and has a limited impact in modern Western societies because they derive their world-views and values from several sources of which religion is only one, and because they have built up powerful economic, political, educational, cultural and other institutions that can resist and limit the disturbing effects of a religious crisis. The fact that they are prosperous, have gone through centuries of religious wars, and have built up an autonomous moral life are also of considerable help. However even in the West the impact of a religious crisis ought not to be underestimated. Although Western societies are largely indifferent to God and to religious dogmas and rituals, they rely on Christianity as one of the major sources of their values and are constantly nurtured and sustained by a deep religious undercurrent. The religious crisis does therefore have unsettling consequences for them. In Britain, the Thatcherite government, faced with the decline in moral standards, attacked the churches for failing to define and enforce Christian values, interfered with their senior appointments and even the doctrines, and sought to bully them into taking a conservative stand on important moral issues. In the United States, which has 'the soul of church' and in which religion plays an important cultural and moral role, the religious crisis has often dominated the political agenda and caused a moral panic during the past 150 years. Since the nonreligious strands of its culture are reasonably strong, and since the state and the civil society are fairly vigorous, its religious crisis has not generally got out of control.

The situation is quite different in those societies in which religion is the sole or major source of their world-views and moral values, and which have not yet had the time, the opportunity or the skill to develop vigorous institutions of the state and civil society. As they lack alternative sources of vitality and moral regeneration, their religious crisis leads to a deep spiritual and moral crisis and threatens the very viability of the prevailing moral order. Since their political, economic, educational and other institutions are relatively undeveloped and often lack popular legitimacy, they are unable to deflect, challenge or even participate in the articulation and resolution of the religious crisis. The religious crisis therefore is not only unusually acute but is left almost entirely in the care of religious leaders. If these societies happen to be subject to sustained Western or Westernizing influences, as they almost invariably are, they fear its secularism and the likely loss of their religion and cultural autonomy. The religious crisis then becomes politically charged and causes a veritable moral and political panic. Many a third-world country belongs to this category.

In such religiously confused and insecure societies, different social groups experience the religious crisis differently and seek to resolve it in their own distinct ways. Although not wholly immune to it, the professional classes are generally the least affected by it largely because religion plays a limited role in their lives. Their training gives them an access to secular culture and offers an alternative basis of social identity. It also cultivates a habit of independent and critical thinking and develops both a sense of status and professional ethos, all three of which are vital sources of self-discipline. Furthermore, their professional life, which generally constitutes an important part of their way of life, requires them to disregard many a religious belief and practice and exposes them to national and international contacts and currents of opinion. By contrast the petty bourgeoisie, that is, such groups as the lower middle classes, the shopkeepers, the traders, the merchants, the artisans and the clerical workers are generally *most* deeply affected by their society's religious crisis.[3] They enjoy some power and status in society, which they seek to preserve, but they are also economically and politically most vulnerable. They are atomized and fragmented, and when their interests are threatened religion is often their only or at any rate the most effective means of mobilization. They build up their limited savings by means of hard work, thrift and an austere lifestyle, and feel threatened by a moral climate of self-indulgence. Furthermore, the institution of the family plays a very important role in their lives. They rely on the willing co-operation, support and pooling of the resources of their wives, children, parents and brothers, and heavily depend on conventional morality to sustain their relations with each other, with their customers, and with those subject to their authority. More than almost any other section of society, the petty bourgeoisie therefore cherish and endeavour to live by conventional morality, define their self-respect and moral integrity in terms of it, and expect their religion to emphasize and enforce it. When conventional morality collapses, their personal and social world collapses. Since a religious crisis affects their vital moral and material interests and causes a veritable moral havoc among them, they generally clamour the loudest against the 'permissiveness' of the 'decadent' society and demand an unambiguous definition and a strict enforcement of their religious identity.

Another group making similar demands consists of the first and sometimes even the second generation migrants to the city. The traditional values, modes of interdependence and self-understandings upon which they generally rely in the villages no longer make much sense in their new environment. As a result, their lives lack rootedness, coherence and moral anchorage, and their sense of identity and continuity is subjected to an intolerable pressure. They are also deeply disturbed by the life-styles of their urban fellow-religionists and by the liberties they take with their religious beliefs and values. They find that these life-styles intrude into their own families, influence their wives, children, brothers and sisters, and undermine the traditional pattern of intra- and inter-familial relationships. All this threatens to destroy their social world and causes a moral panic. Although their moral requirements and demands are not exactly the same as those of the petty bourgeoisie, they share enough in common with them to join them in demanding a resolution of the prevailing moral crisis.

When a society is widely perceived to be corrupt, degenerate, lacking integrity and a sense of direction, its deeply troubled members wonder how it can be regenerated. Various alternatives are canvassed. The traditionalist argues that the corrupt and fractured tradition can be revitalized. The secularist argues that the society should be reconstituted on a rationalist foundation, which may take a liberal, socialist or any one of the other familiar forms. Yet others argue that the society is beyond redemption and should be left to God to set right in fullness of time, or that it is not as degenerate as is made out and will eventually sort itself out. It is in this context that fundamentalism arises. It offers a distinct explanation of why the society has become degenerate and how it can be

---

[3] Students of fundamentalism in different parts of the world are all agreed that it derives its greatest support from these groups. See, for example, Caplan, *Studies in Religious Fundamentalism*.

revitalized. The fundamentalist discourse is at bottom a moral and cultural discourse. It expresses the widespread feelings of confusion, disorientation and anger at the pervasive corruption and cynicism and articulates the society's search for a moral order and cultural coherence. It also gives it the hope and confidence that it can turn the corner, and seeks to mobilize those unconvinced by the traditionalist, secularist and other answers.

The Nature of Fundamentalism[4]

The fundamentalist argues that his society has become degenerate because it has lost its moral values, and that this is due to the corrosive climate of nihilism and doubt created by the pervasive spirit of moral relativism and scepticism. The society cannot be regenerated unless it is based on the solid and unshakable moral foundations provided by religion. In the fundamentalist view religion ought to be the basis of both personal and collective life and guide all areas of human conduct. Secularism or humanism is his greatest enemy and constant target of attack. The fundamentalist rejects the separation between politics and religion. For him, every religion necessarily seeks political articulation, and all sound politics is religiously grounded. The soul matters infinitely more than the body, and the true purpose of political power is not just to maintain law and order but to establish and nurture a way of life based on moral and spiritual values. Politics is a 'holy' activity, a messianic medium of serving God by bringing society in harmony with His will. As Khomeini put it in his will, 'Politics is religion'. For the fundamentalist, politics is not just a means of realizing God's will but also a mode of comprehending the 'secrets' of the universe. Only in the course of fighting against evil does one get to know its nature, the way it operates, the masks it wears, and the manner in which it organizes itself. Political struggle thus uncovers the 'secret rhythm of the universe', and both executes and offers glimpses into God's reason and will. It is a form of divine worship as well as a mode of participation in the divine self-revelation, and has both an ontological and an epistemological significance.

Since the state plays such an important role in the fundamentalist's view of the world, he aims to capture and use it to impose his regenerative programme. Where the state is strong and secular, he adopts the next best alternative of influencing it either by putting his sympathizers in power or by mobilizing public opinion or by creating chaos. The fundamentalist takes an entirely instrumental view of political power and judges its exercise in terms of its objectives. He has no interest in limiting, regulating or dispersing it. And since everything that furthers the cause of God is in his view fully justified, he takes a cynical view of political morality. Evil is too powerful to be easily defeated, especially in a world that has become rotten and degenerate. Good therefore cannot afford to be restrained by finicky moral considerations.

The fundamentalist takes his stand on the 'pure Word of God', and rejects the traditionalist view that the sacred text is inseparable from, and ought to be read in the light of, the tradition. In his view the tradition is human and therefore fallible. It also becomes corrupt over time and dilutes the Word of God by

---

⁴ For Islamic fundamentalism, see Hamid Algar (translator and ed.), *Imam Khomeini: Islam and Revolution* (London, Routledge, 1985); Youssef M. Choueiri, *Islamic Fundamentalism* (London, Pinter, 1990); James P. Piscatori (ed.), *Islam in the Political Process* (Cambridge, Cambridge

making all manner of compromises. By contrast, the sacred text is inerrant, perfect, uncontaminated by human touch, and a source of infallible guidance. By uncoupling and contrasting the text and the tradition, the fundamentalist creates the conceptual space he needs both to challenge the latter and to interpret the former freely. He is thus a scripturalist in the twofold sense that the scripture is for him not just the basis but the whole of religion, and can and must be read without reference to either its context or its tradition.

The fundamentalist approaches the sacred text with two closely related purposes in mind. First, to extract a moral and political programme that can form the basis of social regeneration and around which the faithful can be mobilized, that is, he looks for the religious equivalent of a secular political ideology. Second, he aims to provide a neat, unambiguous, exclusive and easily intelligible definition of the identity of his religion. As we saw, the religious crisis arises because, among other things, the consensus on what it is to belong to a specific religion has broken down and because the religious community feels deeply threatened by the presence of the hostile other. The fundamentalist responds to the crisis by so defining his religion that it is clearly marked off from others, leaves no room for doubt, provides a kind of checklist against which the believers can judge their own and others' religious commitment, and serves as the basis of mass mobilization.

The sacred text is incapable of serving either purpose. It is articulated at metaphysical, ontological, eschatological, moral, social and several other levels and cannot be read unidimensionally. It is full of deep and subtle allegories and images, and lays down a highly complex way of life that cannot be reduced to a neat ideological programme. Its moral principles are absolute and uncompromising and cannot be easily accommodated to the shifting demands and interests of various social groups especially the petty bourgeoisie. Faced with these and other difficulties, the fundamentalist has only one alternative, to simplify the scripture by extracting its so-called fundamentals, that is, those beliefs and values that are supposed to be central to and underpin the rest of the sacred text.[5]

Although he thinks otherwise, the fundamentalist's choice of the so-called fundamentals is inescapably influenced by the circumstances of his society, his diagnosis of the causes of its degeneration, the sources of threat to its identity and survival, the limits of what is likely to be acceptable to his followers, and so on. He cannot therefore avoid imposing his personal preferences and biases on and corrupting the sacred text. Not that he crudely reads his political project into the text, but nor is it the case that the project is logically entailed by the text as he claims. The relationship is necessarily much more complex and dialectical. His reading of the sacred text shapes and is in turn shaped by his political concerns. The two flow into each other so subtly and surreptitiously that he is often a victim of unconscious self-deception.

The fundamentalists's theo-political project runs into an obvious difficulty. He seeks to construct a political programme on the basis of the scripture. But the latter is not that kind of book and resists attempts to reduce religion to an

University Press, 1984); Edward Mortimer, *Faith and Power* (London, Faber and Faber, 1982); Dilip Hiro, *Islamic Fundamentalism* (London, Paladin, 1988).

[5] The term fundamentalism appears to have been derived from a series of booklets entitled *The Fundamentals* published in America between 1910 and 1915. In them the term 'fundamentals' referred to the 'central' doctrines of Christianity.

ideology. The fundamentalist resolves the difficulty by introducing the dubious concept of 'dynamic interpretation'.[6] Although he thinks that the sacred text is inerrant and every word in it literally true, a position to which his scripturalism commits him, he argues that the Word of God is too profound to be read in the ordinary way. Its 'true' meaning is discovered not by constant meditation on or a close reading of the text as the scriptural literalist argues, but only by means of a 'dynamic' reading of it. As he understands it, the dynamic reading involves two things. First, since the sacred text is meant for all times including ours, it must be read in the light of the prevailing needs, problems and challenges. Second, the text is meant not merely to be read and contemplated but to be acted upon, for God has revealed Himself in history in order that His word should become a worldly reality. The true meaning of the sacred text therefore unfolds and becomes evident only in the course of a *struggle against evil*, and is disclosed not to a contemplative scholar but only to God's humble soldier. For Khomeini, Maulana Maudoodi's theological commentaries on the Koran had an air of unreality about them because they 'have not been written in the process of a revolutionary struggle'. For him a scholar not 'actively involved' in political struggle can 'never' fully understand the word of God. The fundamentalist's activist epistemology, the philosophical basis of his claim to read the scripture in a dynamic manner, gives him a rare hermeneutic freedom.

The activist epistemology also solves one of his most important problems. The fundamentalist offers one interpretation of the sacred text, but there are also several others. And he needs to show why his must be accepted in preference to them. The traditionalist legitimizes his reading of the text in terms of the tradition whereas the liberal appeals to his detailed knowledge of its historical context and language and the current state of scriptural scholarship. Neither mode of legitimization suits the fundamentalist, and hence he skilfully undermines them. Since he abstracts the scripture from the tradition and rejects the latter's authority, he is released from the usual obligation to show that his reading of it accords with that of the tradition. And since he insists on the necessity of a dynamic interpretation of the scripture, he has also freed himself from the usual obligation to show that it is supported by a close and careful reading of it.

Since he cannot and does not wish to provide objective criteria for assessing the validity of an interpretation, the fundamentalist takes the more convenient path of laying down *who* is best equipped to offer a 'true' and authoritative reading of the sacred text. He insists that such a person must possess at least two qualifications. First, he must be a man of deep faith, morally upright, leading a life required by the scripture, and so on, and not a 'mere scholar' full of learning but devoid of faith and piety and reading the sacred text as if it were just another book. Only a man of faith is tuned in to the spirit of the text and likely to receive God's hermeneutic guidance. Secondly and more importantly, only an activist rigorously fighting for the realization of the Word of God on Earth is spiritually equipped to grasp the deepest meaning of the sacred text. His activism is not only an earnest of his faith but also a source of epistemological insights. For Khomeini the clergymen who prefer fasting to fighting and a prayerful reading of the Koran to political struggle 'will never know their true religion'.[7] His

---

⁶ See Choueiri, *Islamic Fundamentalism*, pp. 9f, 129 f, and 150 f.

⁷ Kohmeini used the derogatory word *akhund*, meaning hidebound and confused clergymen, to describe them. See James P. Piscatori, *Islam in the Political Process*, p. 170.

words are echoed by many a member of the Muslim Brotherhood, the Gama'at al-Islamiya and other organizations. Of the two hermeneutic qualifications, the first is designed to undermine the liberal, and the second to discredit both the liberal and especially the traditionalist. The fundamentalist claims or, if he is modest, lets others claim on his behalf that he possesses these qualifications in plenty. Khomeini himself only claimed to be a *faquih*, a learned jurist, but did not discourage his followers from believing and saying that he regularly received guidance from and was indeed none other than the hidden twelfth Imam. His *imamat* was widely proclaimed by the state-controlled media, and his followers declared, 'we believe in Allah and Khomeini, Allah's representative on earth'.[8] Khomeini is not known to have condemned such utterances as a grotesque piece of blasphemy.

Unlike the conservatives and the traditionalists who endeavour to live by their religious principles as faithfully as they can and either leave the corrupt world alone or hope to change it by the power of their example, the fundamentalist seeks to challenge and remake the world. Since he thinks that the evil is all-pervasive and unlikely to collapse of its own weight, and since he is confident of his ability to defeat it, he declares a war on the degenerate world and throws himself into a fight-to-finish battle against it. Unlike most other religious movements, fundamentalism is essentially a revolutionary movement. Not surprisingly it sees religion as a revolutionary ideology and the believers as revolutionary soldiers in God's army. For Maudoodi Islam is an 'ideological movement', a 'revolutionary ideology', very like Nazism, Fascism and communism and differing from them 'only in its aims'.[9] He politicizes and interprets the Islamic concept of *jihad* as a 'revolutionary struggle' and urges Muslims to form an 'international revolutionary part'. Syed Qutb thinks of the true Muslims as *talia* (vanguard) fighting a 'revolutionary theological programme'. For Khomeini the faithfuls are *hezbollahis*, members of the Party of God. Since fundamentalism competes with the secular ideologies on their terrain, it cannot avoid taking over their vocabulary, methods of action, and modes of organization.

Contrary to the widespread view that the fundamentalist is a fossilized relic of the past and oblivious of the demands of the contemporary world, he is really a modernist attempting to recreate religion within the limits of modernity. The ideas that religion is God's 'project' for man, that it requires a revolutionary struggle, that the scripture is an ideological text providing a social and political programme, that the right to interpret it has to be earned by acquiring appropriate religious qualifications, that the faithful must be mobilized for action and form the party or army of God, that religion can and should be rationalized and restructured into a simplified system of beliefs, and so forth are all *modern* ideas. Even Islam, which rejects the Christian separation of the state and religion, has never before been seen in quite this way. Fundamentalism does, no doubt, revolt against parts of modernity, but it does so with modernist weapons, in a modernist spirit, and in the interest of a modernist view of religion. It is at bottom an illegitimate child of modernity and inconceivable outside of it. Its modernist character marks it off from the pre-modern revivalist and millenarian

---

[8] Ramy Nima, *The Wrath of Allah: Islamic Revolution and Reaction in Iran*, (London, Pluto, 1983).

[9] Choueiri, *Islamic Fundamentalism*, pp. 120f.

movements, and makes it a new form of faith that did not exist until the modern times.[10]

Since fundamentalism is suffused with the spirit of modernity, it has little difficulty coming to terms with the modern world. It accepts the modern state and the ideology of nationalism. It accepts and exploits to the full the scientific, technological, organizational and moral resources of the modern age. The Islamic fundamentalists have proved extremely skilful at manipulating religious rituals and the media including the television, which is incompatible with the Islamic embargo on visual representation and which the conservative Saudis were able to domesticate only after much theological sophistry. Contrary to the general impression, the fundamentalists have increasingly come to terms with the modern science as well. Khomeini rarely referred to miracles and subtly marginalized the hidden twelfth Imam believed to be in occultation for the past few centuries. Having initially insisted that the universities should teach only the 'Islamic sciences', he later retreated saying they should concentrate on 'secular knowledge', albeit in a spirit of 'Islamic independence'.[11] Strange as it may seem, fundamentalism has a deep *secular* and rationalist core.[12] It simply cannot enter and seek to dominate the secular world without imbibing the latter's spirit and ethos and conforming to its imperatives. In order to reconstruct the society and the state on religious foundations, it must also suitably politicize and secularize religion.

All this is evident in the way the fundamentalist reconstructs the scripture. He simplifies its theology and reduces it to a cluster of highly formalized doctrines drained of their religious imagery. He expunges the element of mystery, explains away miracles, and reduces scriptural ethics to a set of bland moral injunctions. The rationalist spirit so deeply permeates his thought that he is incapable of simple and unquestioning faith and advocates it on largely utilitarian grounds. We must have faith in Allah *because* otherwise we will die in sin and go to hell! We must accept the Koran because otherwise we will flounder in *jahiliyya* and suffer both in this world and the next! We must return to religion *because* otherwise society will fall apart and lack true morality!

Even as the fundamentalist's religion consists of little more than a few simple beliefs abstracted from a highly complex theological system, the moral content of his programme does not and cannot rise above the conventional morality. This is so because fundamentalism is primarily concerned to preserve the traditional pattern of social relations and reflects the anxieties and demands of such social groups as the petty bourgeoisie and the urban migrants. Not surprisingly personal and social morality receives the greatest attention and is given a conservative content. The fundamentalist stresses the patriarchal family and the virtues of self-discipline, hard work, thrift, obedience, clean living, humility,

[10] A careful study of the pre-modern movements led by John of Leyden, Thomas Münzer, the Ranters, George Winstanley, the Anabaptists and others would show how radically they differed from the fundamentalist movements of today. Nearly all of them accepted their religion on faith, turned away from the 'unredeemed' world, set up their own communities, accepted persecution, rejected most of contemporary science and technology, shunned the state and political offices, modelled themselves after the early church, were guided by the ideal of brotherly love, and left it to God to punish the wicked. The practice of rebaptism, from which Anabaptism gets is name, was a means of symbolically expressing voluntary separation from the 'wicked' world. See Norman Cohn, *The Pursuit of the Millennium* (London, Mercury, 1962).

[11] Hamir Algar, *Imam Khomeini* pp. 292f and 298f.

[12] Caplan observes, 'rationalism is a crucial characteristic of fundamentalism', *Studies in Religious Fundamentalism*, p. 13.

piety, and so on. And he condemns gambling, adultery, premarital sex, prostitution, homosexuality, lesbianism, sexual promiscuity, drunkenness, pornography, divorce, illegitimate children, abortion, sex education, parental permissiveness, luxury and dependence on the state. Although Khomeini's ideas were more advanced, he gave in to the Mullahs' opposition to land redistribution and welfare programmes.

The fundamentalist needs to explain why his religion has failed to halt the apparently relentless decline of his community and why the Word of God has proved ineffective. Although he blames the corrupt religious establishment, he knows that is not enough. He needs to explain why the religious leaders remained corrupt for so long, why there was no movement against them, and why the ordinary believers acquiesced in this. For the most part he takes the easy option of blaming human sinfulness, by which he generally means the alleged human propensity to rebel against God and to prefer the world. The fundamentalist takes a dark and pessimistic view of human nature, has little faith in his fellow-humans and exaggerates the power of evil. He sees human existence as a relentless battle between good and evil. And although he is convinced that God will *eventually* ensure the triumph of good over evil, he is deeply pessimistic about the ability of good to withstand the enormous power of evil in the short run. For Khomeini 'true Islam lasted for only a brief period after its inception', in fact barely 100 years. The age of apostasy and *jahiliyya* set in with the advent of the Umayyad dynasty in the year 661 of the Christian era and has persisted for well over a 1000 years. Although the fundamentalist has faith in God's omnipotence, he thinks that God needs human help. And since most humans are believed to have only a weak and intermittent religious commitment, he argues that God relies heavily on a small group of thoroughly committed individuals.

Although the fundamentalist talks a great deal about sin and evil, his views of both are contradictory and shallow. In order to explain why his society has long remained decadent and in order to justify his own harsh measures, he needs a strong conception of human sinfulness. However as an activist aiming at a comprehensive social transformation, he needs to convince himself and his followers that they can win and successfully establish a society in harmony with God's will. And he cannot do so without presenting sinfulness as a weak and remediable human propensity rather than a deeply ingrained ontological trait. The fundamentalist needs both the strong and the weak conceptions of sin and is unable to reconcile them. If he sticks to the former, he has to admit that every society is bound to contain deep imperfections. This means that the society he seeks to establish cannot be qualitatively better than the existing one and justify the enormous sacrifices its creation demands. If he takes a weak view of human sinfulness, he can neither explain his society's and religion's relentless decline nor show why they cannot be trusted to regenerate themselves over time without his drastic regenerative remedy.

The fundamentalist's conception of evil is no better than his conception of sin. When he wants to explain the decline of a religion, he treats evil as a positive principle, a force in its own right, and attributes to it a power great enough to defeat God for centuries. When he engages in the task of reversing the decline and radically regenerating his society, the fundamentalist sees evil as a negative principle thriving in the absence of good and weak enough to be defeated by human efforts. In neither case does he have a clear understanding of the nature and power of either good or evil and their complex relationship. He either psychologizes evil and equates it with the superficially defined sinfulness, or politicizes it and traces it to such hostile social forces as communism and secular humanism.

As we have argued, the fundamentalist seeks to reconstruct society on a religious foundation. While he cannot avoid acknowledging that the individual is a bearer of multiple identities, he insists that the religious identity is the basis of them all and the only one that ultimately matters. One is first and foremost a Christian or a Muslim or a Sikh, and only secondarily an American or an Iranian or an Indian. For Khomeini Bakhtiar's greatest sin consisted in thinking that 'he was an Iranian first and a Muslim afterwards'. Such a view of personal identity has several consequences. First, religion becomes the governing principle of all areas of life, and leads to the demands for an Islamic or Christian economy, mode of governance, education and so on. Since each of these areas of life has its own distinct structure, psychological basis and logic, a fundamentalist society is necessarily incoherent and constantly at war with itself. Second, those not belonging to the dominant religion, atheists and others are turned into second class citizens, enjoying perhaps equal civil rights but denied the opportunity to participate in and shape the collective life of the community. And third, the fellow-religionists outside the borders of the state are drawn into some kind of international community and vested with rights and obligations. Such internationalism sits ill at ease with the statism inherent in fundamentalism and is a source of constant tension.

As we saw fundamentalism arises when a fractured, corrupt and nervous religious tradition fears for its survival. One way to respond to this situation is to repair and recompose or even invent a tradition and reassert its authority. But this is not as easy as it seems. Traditions do not exist in a vacuum. They are socially embedded and presuppose a substantial measure of continuity and coherence in the daily lives of those whose conduct they regulate. In the kind of situation we are talking about, such a continuity is either missing or tenuous in the lives of the vocal and volatile sections of society. Their lives and modes of thought are fragmented, wrenched or in the process of being wrenched from their social roots, and rendered abstract. Such abstract individuals cannot sustain a tradition and clamour for an abstract definition of their religious identity, namely one that is simple, narrow, rigid, exclusive and cleansed of all alien influences. The anti-traditionalist fundamentalist, thoroughly at home in the world of abstractions, is ideally equipped to furnish such a definition and to meet the needs of abstract men.

For the fundamentalist there is only one true way of being a Muslim. Whoever deviates from it or borrows elements from other religions and especially from secularism corrupts his faith, loses his identity, and becomes an apostate, a false brother, an enemy both of God and of his own religious community. As we saw, the fundamentalist defines religious identity in both doctrinal and actional terms. The true believer both holds specific beliefs, however bizarre and irrelevant they might appear to him, and zealously participates in the cause of God irrespective of the cost to himself and to others. The fundamentalist furnishes his followers with a checklist of beliefs they must hold and a model of behaviour they must earnestly emulate. The checklist and the model serve both as a measuring rod of their degrees of religiosity and as a means of identifying 'false' brothers.

In the fundamentalist view the preservation of the community's religious identity is the collective responsibility of all its members. The backsliding or apostasy by any one of them affects the rest, both because it is a possible source of general corruption and because its violation of the official norm lowers the level of collective discipline and ethos. Every true believer therefore has a dual obligation, to conform to the requirements of his religious identity himself and to ensure that others do so too. He is his brother's keeper, that is, a custodian of his religious identity and a guardian of his soul, and must make sure that the latter does not waver or backslide. Both his own spiritual self-interest and his religious duty to his brother require this. Every believer is an unofficial representative of his religious community and has the concommitant right and a duty to act in its name. This involves informing on others, reporting them to the appropriate authorities, and under certain circumstances to administer them instant justice.

As we saw, the fundamentalist is concerned to reconstitute his society on the basis of his definition of its religious identity. Such a revolutionary task necessarily entails considerable violence. The fundamentalist not only accepts the 'holy' violence with a clear conscience, but even welcomes it as the test of his commitment to the cause of God. It is God's will that His enemies should be chastized and, if necessary, exterminated. After all God Himself engages in the most horrendous forms of violence as the traditional descriptions of hell make abundantly clear. This means that God either sees nothing wrong with violence or has not been able to find better ways of coping with human frailties. In either case the believer need not feel too finicky about the use of violence and 'Islamic terror'. Khomeini pointed to the 'terror and fire of hell' and asked the likely waverers, 'What provision have you made against these overwhelming terrors and punishments?'

Since God Himself is supposed to practise holy violence, His faithful servants are freed from all inhibitions and restraints in executing His task on Earth. The fundamentalist sees himself as engaged in a just war or a *jihad* against God's enemies, and justifies such violence as his religious duty. His cause is just; he is guided by the highest of motives not by the considerations of personal gain or even hatred and vengeance; and he is only using violence against such 'proven' or self-confessed enemies as the apostates and humanists. He sees his violence as at once both a legitimate punishment and a military necessity, the former because it is an exercise of the authority inherent in a religious community, the latter because it is designed to protect the community against its enemies. As Khomeini calmly reassured those with a troubled conscience, 'The glorious Imam [the first Shi'ite Imam] killed in one day 4000 of his enemies to protect the faith'. Khomeini sent thousands of poorly trained youth to fight in a horrendous war against the 'infidel' Saddam Hussein, sanctioned murders of thousands of Iranian Muslims suspected of weak religious commitments, and encouraged the zealous *hazbollahis* to 'execute' hundreds on their own authority. In the fundamentalist view all such holy violence is amply justified and only an enemy of God would baulk at it.

To sum up, I have argued in this section that fundamentalism is a distinct and historically specific movement. As I have analysed it, it arises in a deeply troubled society, represents a powerful moral protest against the prevailing hypocrisy and corruption, and uses the institutions of the state to regenerate an allegedly degenerate society by reconstructing it on a religious foundation. It abstracts the sacred text from the tradition, offers an activist reading of it, and extracts from it a politically relevant ideological programme. It is revolutionary in its aspirations, authoritarian in its structure, conventional in its ethics, and represents an unstable but ingenious combination of morality and cynicism and of rationalism and irrationalism. Fundamentalism is militant, puritanical, aggressive and violent, and offers an extremely narrow and exclusive view of the identity of the religion concerned. Although it revolts against some aspects of the modern world, it is an essentially modern phenomenon competing with secular ideologies on *their* terrain and in *their* terms. It reconstitutes religion within the limits of modernity, even as it copes with modernity within the limits of religion.[13]

Fundamentalism and Other Religious Dispositions

In the light of our characterization of fundamentalism we may turn to the two questions raised at the start of this essay, namely how it differs from the other religious attitudes with which it is often confused, and whether it occurs in all religions.

If our analysis is correct, it is easy to see why fundamentalism is quite different from conservatism, traditionalism, revivalism and ultra-orthodoxy. They do, of course, share several features in common with it, but these are minor compared to their differences. Like the fundamentalist, the conservative cherishes traditional values, respects the past and stresses the social and political value of religion. But beyond that the two part company. Unlike the fundamentalist, the conservative respects the prevailing religious institutions and practices, believes that such reforms as are needed can be made within their framework, and is hostile to a radical reconstitution of his religion and society and to utopian thinking. Unlike him, again, the conservative deeply distrusts religious passions and enthusiasm, is averse to mass mobilization, rejects the fusion of religion and politics, and condemns all attempts to reduce religion to a neat ideological package.

Fundamentalism should not be confused with traditionalism either. For the traditionalist the sacred text is integrally bound up with the religious tradition, and the two together constitute the religion. The text must be read in the light of the tradition that has grown up around it, and the tradition derives its specificity from and is periodically enriched and revitalized by new ways of reading the text. For the traditionalist, further, the past is not a collection of dead and discrete units of time or 'periods' of which one might be privileged over the others or revived. Rather it has a wholeness and integrity which is preserved in and nurtured by the tradition. The tradition has a moral and epistemological authority not merely because of its age but because it has been vitalized by many minds and different kinds of historical experiences. If it is an accumulation of adjustments and compromises, it is also a storehouse of wisdom and insights.

As we saw fundamentalism is, among other things, a reaction against traditionalism. The fundamentalist rejects the tradition, seeks an unmediated access to the scripture and subjects it to the 'dynamic' and unconstrained reading of a charismatic leader. Unlike the traditionalist, he idealizes a specific historical 'period', usually the earliest, and leaps over centuries in a vain attempt to restore

---

[13] For a good discussion of how little Islamic fundamentalism reflects the spirit and thrust of Islam, see Seyyed Hussein Nasr (ed.), *Islamic Spirituality: Foundations* (London, SCM, 1985).

it in a suitably modernized form. He has an acute sense of the past but no sense of either history or tradition. His sense of the past is thus incoherent and inauthentic. Again, the traditionalist cherishes and stresses the importance of allegories, mysteries, symbolisms and the deliberately half-articulated utterances and stories in which all religions abound, whereas the fundamentalist simplifies his religion and reduces it to simple and easily intelligible beliefs and values. For the traditionalist religion is a highly complex form of life of which morality is a small though important part. The fundamentalist is above all a moralist, for whom religion is little more than a set of values topped up by a cluster of beliefs. Such other features as his revolutionary aspirations, activist epistemology, mass mobilization and a rigid definition of religious identity also separate him from the traditionalist.

As for revivalism, fundamentalism shares several common features with it. Both are anti-traditionalist, both blame the tradition for the degeneration of their religion, both are enthusiastic about a past golden period, both mobilize the masses, and so on. However, large and deep differences separate the two. Unlike the fundamentalist, the revivalist is concerned to revitalize his religion and not the society at large, his concerns are primarily religious and non-political, and he does not often share the fundamentalist's statism and uninhibited use of political power to regenerate his religion. Again, although both share an enthusiasm for a past golden period, their attitudes to it are different. While the revivalist aims to revive it or at least to use it as a model, the fundamentalist has his own blueprint, which is no doubt inspired by the golden period but also contains many radical innovations. While the revivalist basically wants to go back to the past in all its simplicity out of a profound discontent with modernity, the fundamentalist wants to master modernity and to create a new future suited to his times. He has no objection to and is in fact enchanted by many aspects of modernity such as the state, the nuclear weapons and the material prosperity in which the revivalist has limited if any interest.

Fundamentalism is often equated with ultra-orthodoxy scriptural literalism. The latter holds that every word in the sacred text is literally true and that every injunction in it must be scrupulously carried out down to its minutest detail. Ultra-orthodoxy has little in common with fundamentalism; indeed no two religious attitudes could be more different. Since the ultra-orthodox is a scriptural literalist, he considers it blasphemous to offer a 'dynamic' reading of the sacred text. He scrupulously adheres to the text and rejects all attempts to introduce innovations into it, whereas the fundamentalist reads the text in the light of his politico-religious project and grossly distorts it. The ultra-orthodox generally wants to be left alone, fighting back only when provoked, and has no wish to challenge and reconstruct his society, whereas the fundamentalist is an activist who has declared a war on his society. The ultra-orthodox is indifferent and sometimes even hostile to the technological and other offerings of the modern world; the fundamentalist is adept at exploiting them. The ultra-orthodox trusts God to set the world right in fullness of time and leaves it to Him to punish the wicked; the fundamentalist takes over the task of piloting history himself. Ultra-orthodoxy has a deep non-modernist and anti-secular core; fundamentalism is a profoundly modernist doctrine seeking to recast religion in a modernist mould. The ultra-orthodox is acutely aware of human limitations and displays deep humility; the fundamentalist is self-righteous and has only a superficial sense of sin. The religion of the ultra-orthodox has an organic unity and exudes quiet self-confidence; the fundamentalist's religion is man-made and nervous. It is striking that the Hasidims, an ultra-orthodox Jewish group, deny the legitimacy of the state of Israel and insist that a 'true' Israel at peace with herself and her neighbours will only be established by a Messiah in the fullness of time. Not surprisingly, they have repeatedly attacked the *Gush Emunim*, called 'Israeli Khomeinism' by its domestic critics, for politicizing and undermining the integrity of their religion, pursuing an aggressive security and foreign policy, relying on force rather than on the power of the spirit, taking an amoral view of violence and for 'provoking' the wrath of other nations and groups. Several ultra-orthodox Muslim groups in Iran and elsewhere attacked Khomeini, the Muslim Brotherhood and the Gama'at al-Islamiya, and many ultra-orthodox Christians have attacked the Christian fundamentalists, along similar lines.

Ultra-orthodoxy and fundamentalism then are very different religious dispositions. It is true that the former is sometimes called fundamentalism. I suggest that the term should be reserved for the kind of movement I have described and analysed above. The term was invented around 1909 to describe such a movement in the USA; its adherents even now use the term to describe themselves; others too use it to refer to them; and in so far as the term implies a preoccupation with both the fundamentals of a religion and the fundamental or radical reconstitution of religion and society, it captures a crucial feature of the movement I have called fundamentalism. However, it does not matter how we use the term so long as we appreciate that ultra-orthodoxy and the kind of movement I call fundamentalism are radically different phenomena, and that if we decide to call one of them fundamentalism, we should call the other something else. It might be argued that we should call one passive and the other active fundamentalism, but that would be most misleading. Such a usage blurs their qualitative differences and leaves unexplained why one kind of fundamentalism and not the other is driven towards activism.

Non-universality of Fundamentalism

The question whether fundamentalism, as I have defined it, is confined to modern Islam or also occurs in other religions is not easy to answer. In an interdependent world religions constantly impinge on each other and imbibe each other's good and bad features. Since fundamentalism is often a source of considerable political strength, religions that are structurally inhospitable to, and have no history of, political activism sometimes tend to mimic it in order to unite and activate their followers. If its adherents are so minded or are passing through particularly bad times, every religious tradition may throw up fundamentalist movements. The question however is whether such a fundamentalist propensity comes easily and naturally to a religious tradition, whether it provokes strong resistance, and whether it succeeds in securing a popular following. It seems to me that fundamentalism is largely limited to Islam and Protestant Christianity. This is not to say that other religions cannot be perverse, only that the kinds of perversity they throw up usually do not include fundamentalism.

As I have argued, fundamentalism seeks to regenerate an allegedly degenerate society by reconstituting it on a religious foundation and has a distinct character. As such it rests on several presuppositions, of which I shall briefly mention a few by way of examples. First, it presupposes a separation between religion and society. A society can be attacked and reconstituted on religious grounds only if the two are separate or at least separable. If a religion is deeply embedded in and has no existence independently of a specific social structure, as is the case with such ethnic religions as Hinduism and to some extent Judaism, it lacks the conceptual resources to transcend, evaluate and transform the society concerned.

Second, fundamentalism presupposes a sacred text. A religion without a text, such as a tribal religion, is nothing more than its traditions, and its adherents lack the means to judge, challenge and rebel against their traditions. They can of course mount an internal critique of them, but the critique cannot be radical and comprehensive.

Third, fundamentalism presupposes that a religion must have a *single* sacred text or, if it has several, it must have a clearly established hierarchy among them. If it has several texts of equal status as in the case of Hinduism and to a lesser extent Buddhism, its adherents are at liberty to choose any one of them. They do not then share a common identity and cannot be easily defined, distinguished and organized on the basis of a shared body of beliefs.

Fourth, fundamentalism presupposes that a religion should grant the believer a direct access to the sacred text. If only its officially accredited representatives are permitted to read or to interpret it, or if they alone are widely accepted as its true custodians, or if no new interpretation of it is allowed, the person challenging them is unable to legitimize himself and to reach out to and mobilize the religiously unavailable believers. This is why Protestant Christianity is more vulnerable to fundamentalism than Roman Catholicism, and those Islamic schools who permit *ijtihad* (interpretation of the Koran) are more vulnerable than those who have 'closed the door' to it.

Fifth, fundamentalism uses the state to enforce a uniform religious identity on its members and presupposes that a religion permits such a use of the state. If a religion is inherently anti-political or even apolitical, or so defines the religious identity that it cannot be enforced, or totally disapproves of the use of violence, it cannot be chartered in the fundamentalist cause.

No religion satisfies all these and related preconditions, and hence no religion even throws up fundamentalist movements in their purest form. However the more of these preconditions a religion satisfies, the greater is its propensity to throw up and sustain such movements in situations of religious and social crisis. Islam meets most of them and represents one end of the spectrum.[14] Tribal religions meet almost none of them, and represent the other. All other religions fall in between, and are closer to one or the other end of the spectrum. Since we cannot discuss them all, one example should suffice.

Unlike the religions of the book, Hinduism rejects an exhaustive and one-off divine revelation in favour of periodic revelations suited to the requirements of different *yugas* or historical epochs. Even in each *yuga* there are a number of sacred texts from which a Hindu is free to choose one that best suits his temperament and spiritual needs. Hinduism is almost entirely concerned with conduct, and leaves its adherents free to believe whatever they please so long as they conform to the socially prescribed mores of their *jati* or caste. It has therefore no doctrinal unity, and there is not one belief to which all Hindus are required to subscribe. Unlike Christianity and Islam, but like Judaism, Hinduism is an ethnic or communal religion grounded in the life and history of the

[14] See Thomas Hodgkin, 'The revolutionary tradition in Islam', *Race and Class*, xxi (1980).

Hindus. This is why it rules out proselytization and has no machinery for conversion. Since the religious identity of a Hindu is tied up with his social identity, it cannot be defined independently of the latter. As for the Hindu social identity, it is not easy to define. The Hindu social structure has undergone profound changes during its long history, and no institution and practice has remained constant. Initially it was divided into two, then three, and then four major *varnas* (groups). The *varnas* split into hundreds of *jatis* (or castes) to which were later added the 'caste' of outcasts. The Hindu society also left space for such men as the world-renouncers and the *yogis* who transcended the caste-system altogether and were expected to use their unique position to reflect on and periodically revitalize their social order.

All this means that a 'true' Hindu cannot be defined. Is he one who believes in castes? But the castes do not go back very far in the past, have varied over time, do not in their current form conform to their scriptural idealization, and do not encompass those falling outside them at either end. What is more, almost all Hindus are deeply embarrassed by the practice of untouchability which is a product of the caste system, and even the so-called Hindu fundamentalists are anxious to abolish it. One might say that a Hindu is one who subscribes to certain beliefs. But beliefs vary enormously with castes and regions. And in any case, since a Hindu is supposed to be free to choose his beliefs, he ceases to be one when required to subscribe to a specific body of them!

Not that the Hindu leaders have not tried to define a 'true' Hindu. Dayananda Saraswati tried to 'semitize' Hinduism and created the Arya Samaj. But he could neither give the *Vedas* the status of the Bible let alone the Koran, nor distil the basic Hindu beliefs. Later Savarkar tried to define *Hindutva*, the essence of a Hindu, but came up with nothing more than that a true Hindu was one who looked upon India as his *pitrubhumi* (fatherland) and *punyabhumi* (a sacred or holy land). He had to admit that on his definition even the Indian Christians, Buddhists and Muslims qualified as 'true' Hindus. The Bharatiya Janata Party (B.J.P.), widely referred to as a Hindu fundamentalist party, has run up against the same difficulty. After several unsuccessful attempts it recently concluded that a Hindu was one who had Hindu *bhavna* (Hindu disposition or goodwill towards the Hindus) and Hindu *manasikta* (Hindu attitude of mind or way of looking at the world). The B.J.P. was unable to give any meaning to these nebulous concepts, and was, like Savarkar, forced to admit that on its definition even the Indian Christians, Muslims and others could qualify as Hindus.

Our brief discussion of Hinduism indicates that it does not satisfy the first of the five preconditions of fundamentalism listed earlier. It satisfies the second, but not the third. Since it has no single sacred text, the fourth has no meaning for it. And as for the fifth, it expects the state to preserve and enforce the caste-based social order, but not to undertake a radical transformation of it. Hinduism therefore lacks the theoretical and practical resources necessary to throw up and, what is much more important, to sustain fundamentalist movements. Not that the Hindu leaders have not tried, rather that their attempts have provoked widespread unease and resistance as if the ordinary mass of Hindus instinctively felt that this was an alien and corrupting transplant. Given its structure and history, Hinduism's characteristic vices are orthodoxy, mindless ritualism, inertia, resistance to change, but not a radical collective adventure into the unknown.

If we closely examined other religions, we *might* find that although they can all be dogmatic, militant, murderous, fundamentalism is alien to some of them.[15] There is no obvious reason why all religions must be perverse in an identical manner. However, I do not wish to be dogmatic about this, and would only suggest that we owe each religion the moral obligation to study it in its own terms. Since all religions advance absolute truths and seek to realize God's will on earth, they all have a fundamentalist impulse. But they also have other impulses which point in different directions and check and regulate it. Every religion defines, balances and structures these impulses differently. When a religious and social crisis occurs they draw upon their resources and throw up different kinds of responses. We need to explore how and why their responses vary, why some spawn fundamentalism and others do not, and why the former succeed in channelling its enormous moral and spiritual energies in healthy and community-building directions under some circumstances but not under others. All this requires close attention to the specificity of each religion.

[15] In Lionel Caplan, *Studies in Religious Fundamentalism*, both Jonathan Webber and Angela Dietrich provide material that shows why Jewish and Sikh 'fundamentalism' are quite different from their Islamic and Christian counterparts. Surprisingly, they ignore the differences and keep talking about fundamentalism as if all militant movements had to be the same. In Martyn and Appleby, *Fundamentalisms Observed*, vol. 1, Daniel Gold's analysis shows that what he calls Hindu fundamentalism has little in common with its Islamic and Protestant counterparts. Donald Swearer is unable to go beyond showing that the Buddhists can be militant, and Manning Nash appears so keen to see fundamentalism in Islam that he cannot explain why Islam in Indonesia has no difficulty in accepting both its Hindu and indigenous heritage and living with an eclectic identity.

Nationalism: Ambiguous Legacies and Contingent Futures

Eugene Kamenka*

University of Sydney and the Australian National University

I

For at least one hundred years now, the death of nationalism has been predicted by good people confidently – and erroneously. Humanists and rationalists, liberals and utilitarians, socialists and internationalists agreed that the nation-state was becoming obsolete, that its tendencies toward aggression were dangerous and that moral concern, once need and ignorance had been banished, would encompass the whole of humankind. The Internationale shall be the human race.

Two terrible World Wars made those hopes less plausible but also more urgent. Yet, the arguments of the internationalists were not entirely misplaced. Neither was Marx's recognition, even more strongly emphasized by his followers, that economic activity, the world market and consequently Finance Ministers and the big bourgeoisie were becoming ever more international in outlook, scope and influence. Since World War II, ever more remarkable acceleration in the speed of communication and transport and ever-increasing population movements have helped further to internationalize the world. The formation of common markets, political unions, regional associations and the increasing authority of supranational laws, agreements and institutions have severely limited even the internal sovereignty of the nation-state. So has the increasing force of world public opinion expressed through various world-wide means of communication. Few countries can now seal their borders to the extent of keeping their own populations ignorant of developments and opportunities outside. These and other factors – the rise in standards of living, the spread of competence and skills, the growth of urban conglomerates – have lessened the gulf, for at least some of the world, between 'upper' and 'lower' classes to the point where both seem human. We have learnt, in the last two centuries, to see slaves, servants, the working classes, the 'coloured races' and indigenous peoples as moral subjects and, more gradually, as morally equally deserving subjects. Progress in these matters is unsteady and fitful but it is not an illusion.

* Dr Eugene Kamenka is Professor of History of Ideas at the Australian National University, Canberra.

Nevertheless, nationalisms – and among them some very nasty chauvinistic, xenophobic nationalisms – flourish. Population movements, economic internationalization, external pressure can increase friction even while they bring people more closely together. The revulsion from Nazism, the peace-oriented exhaustion that follows great wars, fade with time. Xenophobia re-emerges more nakedly, as it has done in Germany, especially east Germany, the Caucasus and parts of the old Austro-Hungarian and Ottoman Empires. Rationalists, or those who believe in the ultimate rationality and perfectibility of humankind, used to ascribe this to what Marxists call the law of uneven development. In the matter of progress, some nations were ahead and some behind; some parts of the world were secure enough to relax with their neighbours and see them as equally human and some were too deprived, poor, frightened, insecure or oppressed to do so. Only time could cure that. The truth is more complex and less comforting.

Nazi behaviour in Europe and especially the Holocaust seriously undermined the credentials of the 'civilized nations' to be the bearers of progress and to lead the world into one human community – though, in fact, it is still the democratic nations which have contributed most and stand in the forefront of the struggle for tolerance, human rights and willingness to set one's house in order. But ranged against them is not only the law of uneven development, or even the familiar revitalization or birth of nationalisms as empires collapse, but a partial or complete rejection from many quarters of rationality, individualism and pluralism as moral and political guidelines.

'It needs to be said', the late George Lichtheim wrote some twenty years ago, 'that – irrespective of political attitudes distributed over the entire ideological spectrum from Communism to Fascism – the Anglo-American world has for long appeared to Continental Europeans as a 'de-centred totality', to employ the currently fashionable jargon. It is to them a philistine culture with a void at the centre, lacking anything worth being called a philosophy, i.e., any kind of conceptual thinking that tries to make sense of life as a whole, or even of the social order in which culture is embedded'.[1] That criticism of the tolerant, democratic but individualistic societies that elevate technical rationality, social atomism and pluralism of values has long formed the substance of the Slavophile rejection of Western Europe, which contrasted the emotional solidarity of the *Gemeinschaft* with the conflict-ridden individualism and commercialism of the *Gesellschaft* well before Tönnies (honestly) or the Nazis (cynically) did so. It is today widely echoed, for better or for worse, in Africa and Asia, especially by the semi-educated and the fanatically religious. It is also echoed by many allegedly 'alienated' intellectuals in the West, seeking inspiration anywhere but in the liberal democratic tradition, admiring (selectively) the nationalisms of other peoples, uncomfortable with national or cultural achievements and traditions of their own, unless they can be shown to stem from deprived groups or to come 'from below'.

There are many philosophies, religions and ideologies that have sought or claimed, in one way or another, to fill this void, to make sense of life, of culture and of social existence. In the modern world, none has been more significant historically or ultimately more pervasive geographically than the ideology of nationalism. This is so even if 500 years from now the democratic, populist and socialist themes in modern life may have proved themselves to have been ultimately more significant and as in any case providing much of the content of

---

[1] George Lichtheim, *George Lukács* (New York, Viking Press, 1970), p. 13.

nationalism. Certainly, the intellectual substance of nationalism may seem thin when compared with such ideologies as democratic radicalism, socialism and conservatism, on which it has at different times been largely parasitic intellectually. Its theoretical grasp of the dynamics of modern societies, as opposed to its opportunistic use of them, has not been great. In pitting emotion against reason, it has created an ambiguous legacy we go on to discuss: it has elevated a side of human life and human action ignored by the nineteenth-century rationalist to the detriment of social and psychological understanding. At the same time, it has substituted campfires for learning, demagoguery for argument, and thus fallen into increasing cynicism – for emotional truth is no truth at all.

Nevertheless, nationalism came to dominate Europe in the nineteenth century and dominates much of the world in the twentieth. It helps to make those two centuries and what were previously comparatively distinct areas of the world part of one history. For a period, it was indeed a principal vehicle for a Vichian historicization of culture, politics and social enquiry generally. The Jews as a people, though not as individuals, or as a 'reformed' religious cult, have entered modern history through Zionist nationalism. So, in their own way, have Latvians, Finns, Estonians, and many other 'ethnic' groups denied independent statehood in the past, whether in Europe, Asia, the Americas, parts of Africa and Oceania. For many of the cultured and semi-cultured everywhere, nationalism has given meaning to life. It has provided a fundamental assessment of (a particular) human community and a total critique of culture. Among what Marx and Engels called the historic nations (which included more than they admitted) it elevated a concept of great traditions, of abiding problems and of their interaction with overpowering events. Nationalism at its cultural best can provide a concept of classical periods, of cultures and civilizations, of the human predicament and of world historical forces and demands essential to cosmopolitan understanding. It can give a sense of centre and periphery, foreground and background, as well as an appreciation of that which is, at various times, overpoweringly *novel* or different in human affairs. Through its concentration on history, it can in fact transcend both temporal and regional provincialism and *atemporal* utopianism. Through its elevation of literature, history and philosophy as part of one story, it can promote a literary-historico-philosophical capacity for understanding often lacking in more comfortably tolerant and unself-conscious nations. Like Marxism, it could be – for a period? – a stepping-stone to universal understanding and like Marxism it could also destroy it, make the mind narrow and prejudiced, or keep it in the past. It depends, in the end, on whether we see nationalism as a means to intellectual development and practical understanding and control or as the end to which the latter are subordinate. Nationalism has educated 'the people', popularized history and culture, but it has also vulgarized them.

Nationalism has stood, and perhaps still stands, at the centre of modern history. Nationalist thinkers do not. The spread of nationalist ideology in Europe and Latin America in the first half of the nineteenth century depended, largely, on second-rate thinkers and even more on dramas, festivals, romantic historiography and political calls to action. Rousseau had already advocated public cults as increasing human virtue and deepening love of the fatherland. The French Revolution had put these cults into practice, though seeing them as Cults of Reason. 'Germans who advocated such festivals', George Mosse has reminded us,[2] 'changed their thrust in an important manner; history and democracy must

---

[2] George Mosse, 'Mass politics and the political liturgy of nationalism' in Eugene Kamenka

inform their ritual'. Friedrich Ludwig Jahn, for example [1810], advocated the celebration of the past deeds of the people themselves and thought the battle of Merseburg in the early Middle Ages a particularly suitable memorial occasion, for here the peasants had defeated kings and bishops. Ernst Moritz Arndt's *German Society*[1814] had as its special task the celebration of 'holy festivals', partly pagan, such as the summer solstice, and partly recent, like the victory over Napoleon at the battle of Leipzig. He thought a festival to commemorate the noble dead in Germany's wars would be especially effective, for here 'history enters life and life itself becomes part of history'.

The German students who attended the Wartburg Festival in 1817, consciously taking part in a nationalist festival, were asked to come with oak leaves in their caps; by 1837 32,000 German men and women were marching in procession up to Hambach Castle, wearing the black, red and gold and celebrating a 'German May'. Monuments like the famous Hermannsdenkmal [1836–75], built to commemorate the victory of Hermann or Arminius over the Roman legions, were erected in natural surroundings filled with memories and relics of ancient German civilization. Huge Germanias began to dot the landscape. The Tannenbergdenkmal of 1925, erected to celebrate the German victory over the Russians in World War I, created a sacred space surrounded by walls and eight towers in which nearly a hundred thousand people could be turned from a crowd into a congregation. The contrast with the typical Australian war memorial – which shows a life-size statue of a single Australian soldier, head bowed, rifle reversed, mourning his fallen comrades with not a bayonet or symbol of victory in sight, or even a national flag, is most striking and, to me, most reassuring. But Australia, too, in a search for Australian identity and Australian pride, is changing the symbols, if not really its outlook.

All this, outside the 'continuing' nations and the newly self-governing and then independent 'white' British dominions, as Mosse has sensitively reminded us[3] put nationalism at the centre of the new age of mass politics – disciplining the crowd, giving it unity, coherence and purpose through ritual, the use of space, discipline and theatre, uniforms, chants and processions. As mild-mannered a liberal, indeed socialist, nationalist as Mazzini, through his Young Italy, already linked nationalism with the elevation of youth and of violence. The cult of blood and soil, of race and place, became readily Maurice Barrès's *culte de la terre et des morts*, though Barrès himself finally turned to working for Franco-German reconciliation. Even Michelet had sung a paean of praise to the armies of France, always sacrificing themselves for the good of Europe and of humanity. *B'dam v'esh Yudah nafla, b'dam v'esh Yudah takum* (In blood and fire Judea fell, in blood and fire Judea will arise) has been sung, with the appropriate change of place, by more than one nationalist. Nor will the Zionist cult of the Maccabees strike the historian of other nationalisms as at all surprising. To him or her, the uniform and liturgy of the Jewish nationalist youth movement Betar in the 1920s and 1930s will seem much more familiar and much less specifically Jewish or at least born of Jewish experience than the attempt of Labour Zionists to link their ideology with the Passover as the festival of freedom (liberation from slavery in Egypt) and the universalistic message of the Jewish prophets. Labour Zionists insisted that practical work in the end is more important than chants and rituals,

(ed.), *Nationalism: The Nature and Evolution of an Idea*, (Canberra, A.N.U. Press, 1973; London, Edward Arnold, 1976), p. 40.
[3] George Mosse, *The Nationalization of the Masses* (New York, Howard Fertig, 1975), *passim*.

that visiting Massada (the ruined fortress site of Judea's last stand against the Romans, ending in mass suicide) is a *tiyul* (an outing) and not a sacred space. Yad va Shem – the memorial in Jerusalem to the Holocaust – is a totally different matter. Just as the truly great writers of any nation from Sophocles to Shakespeare, from the authors of the story of King David and the Book of Ruth to Goethe and Tolstoy, do not fit well into nationalist concepts of culture and nationalist philosophy, so Yad va Shem does not take its place beside Massada and the Tannenbergdenkmal. The horror of the Holocaust was too great to be of merely national significance; it belongs to the history of humanity.[4]

Despite these Jewish and other memories or revivals, most writers agree that nationalism is indeed a modern phenomenon. It emerged in northwestern Europe and northern America in the eighteenth century. To say that, we have to distinguish between nationalism as a political or social ideology, as a central unifying concern, taking up other characteristically modern trends and *idées-forces*, and national consciousness or even in-group and out-group sentiment, loyalty to tribe, region or empire. There is now, too, a derivative modern, *post factum* search for a national identity (in Australia, New Zealand, Singapore, and other political units that became independent states first and nations after. Has that no precedents in the past?) As all historians of nationalism recognize, there was a remarkable flowering of national consciousness and national prejudice in Europe in the twelfth and thirteenth centuries, which saw the beginnings of national or even nationalist historiographies in Britain, France, Denmark, Poland and Spain and strong national feeling in Italy and Sicily. Those interested in the history of the idea of nationalism have not, I think, studied this phenomenon and compared it with the style and content of later nationalisms carefully enough. Nor do we have, as far as I know, adequate consideration of 'nationalist' (or 'proto-nationalist'?) themes in certain countries and nations, where they developed much earlier and more powerfully in reaction against the pressures of great empires – among the people (or peoples?) of Israel and Judea in the Middle Eastern world and the people of Vietnam and Korea at opposing ends of the Middle Kingdom. All three had a remarkable history, for small peoples, of resistance and conquest. Did they also have an early 'nationalism' – and, if so, in what sense? Were there other peoples that created something that was more than tribal loyalty and yet not just dynastic allegiance? A fascinating under-explored subject in which the temptation to read modern ideologies into the past has to be firmly resisted, but where comparative conclusions do need to be drawn with conceptual clarity. This postulation of the problem is rejected by proponents of the writing of 'history from below' and by those anxious to bestow the 'honorific' title of being ideologists, implicit political theorists and having a nationalist political ideology on substate groups and indigenous peoples at any time of their history. For them, the distinction between communal and national sentiment and 'true' nationalism as ideology disappears.

The story of the growth of national consciousness into true nationalism by way of an extraordinary complex of economic, political, social and intellectual developments has often been told. The decline in the pull of the Roman Empire as an historical ideal, the invention and spread of printing, the rise of national vernaculars as literary languages, the development of transport, the revolutionary growth of capitalism and the middle classes and the creation of

⁴ See Eugene Kamenka, 'The Holocaust: explaining the inexplicable?' in John Milfull (ed.) *Why Germany?* (Providence, Oxford, Berg, 1993), pp. 1–6.

national as opposed to local markets, the role of aggressive divine-right monarchs in suppressing feudalism and consolidating and secularizing their realms on a national basis, the religious upheavals and reforms that ended in the establishment of state churches, have all been given their place. So has industrial society's need for an increasingly literate labour force, sharing one language and common cultural style. The modern ideology of nationalism has rightly been seen as dependent upon and presupposing the emergence of the nation-state and as standing in fundamental contradiction with the aspirations of rulers – from the Habsburgs to the Teutonic knights, the Prussian military and administrative state and the Viceroys and their British-oriented elite in the Indian Civil Service – that saw themselves as fitted to rule any nation and any people, because they saw people as subjects and not as citizens. More recently, especially since the First World War, nationalism has also acquired a strong populist and demotic edge turned against middle classes of a different or wider culture and outlook.

Modern nationalism, I have argued elsewhere,[5] is best understood as deriving its political charge and social bite, and much of its content, from the change-over, within large territorial states, from the concept of subject to that of citizen. The American and French Revolutions had proclaimed a new sovereign – the People, which conceptually and practically lacked the unity and coherence provided by a person, a monarch. In the United States and in France the change-over was less problematic because history or geography had already created a nation or the obvious foundation for it. Elsewhere, it was otherwise. As Rousseau saw, and emphasized to the Poles, a democracy required a political community, a common language, culture and set of customs within which political debate could be conducted. In those countries where the change-over from subject to citizen had been preceded by the successful formation of a comparatively homogeneous community and nation-state, nationalism emerged only fitfully as a reaction to real or fancied threat. This is why Rousseau and the Abbé Sieyès were not nationalists – they saw nations as administrative units. In those countries where unity was lacking or provided only by the monarch – as in the Austro-Hungarian Empire, in the German Confederation, Italy, the Indian sub-continent, the Russian and then the Bolshevik empires – nationalism was the first item on the democratic agenda. Their nationalism emphasized language, culture, the unity of the *Volk* as much as or more than it emphasized the state. In China, which is both state and empire in its pretension, the same now applies to Tibet (an annexed colony) and Muslim-Turkish Xinjiang (Chinese Turkestan).

The first creators of cultural nationalism, indeed, such as Herder, were not political nationalists at all – they distrusted the state as something external, mechanical, not emerging spontaneously from the life of the people.

'Nationalism' Ernest Gellner argues at the outset of his *Nations and Nationalism,*[6] 'is primarily a political principle, which holds that the political and the national unit should be congruent'. It is thus parasitic on two concepts, that of the state and that of the nation, and it is through the concept of the nation that Gellner makes room for the cultural element that has been so strong in much modern nationalism, but which has distinguished those nationalisms from classical liberal Western nationalism.

So far, the theoretician of nationalism willing to follow me along the broad highway I have charted has no difficulty with Zionism, to take what some have

    [5] Eugene Kamenka, 'Political nationalism – the evolution of an idea', in E. Kamenka (ed.), *Nationalism*, pp. 3ff.
    [6] Ernest Gellner, *Nations and Nationalism* (Oxford, Blackwell, 1983), p. 1.

seen as an anomalous or theoretically troublesome nationalism. It fits into the ideology of modern nationalism quite naturally and bears, in my view, no distinctive features that place it in any way outside the history of modern nationalism. It constituted a secularization of the notion of 'Jew'. It recognized and related itself to the change-over from subject to citizen and made a sharp distinction between the Jew as subject in the Diaspora and as citizen in his own country – a distinction strengthened by the Zionist belief that it is not possible or safe for a Jew as a self-determined and conscious Jew to be a citizen in a country dominated by others except by assimilating or converting Judaism into a religious sect. This accounts, incidentally, for the difficulty Zionist historiography feels about King Solomon and his Empire as opposed to King David and his nation-state. As Gellner's argument reminds us, the Zionist needs both a state and a nation. (The PLO, whether cynically or not, made a similar shift from a Pan-Arabism ultimately rooted in the Islamic mission to a modern secularizing nationalism – though the Islamic tradition of elevating the military function of the Commander of the Faithful was not excised until Palestinians actually living in Israel came to greater prominence.)

Under somewhat greater difficulties than most national movements, Zionists have had to create both *nation and state* – emphasizing political independence as well as cultural renewal and re-education, virtually creating or re-creating a language as some other nationalists have also done, seeing, as twentieth-century nationalists increasingly do, the state and national institutions, including for a period the kibbutz, as playing central roles in cultural, educational and ideological life as well as in economic and political life. Nevertheless, Zionism has been able to rely on a very important precondition. This is the fact that the Jewish nation had been defined and given shape in that surprisingly early piece of national historiography that we call the Old Testament, especially the Five Books of Moses and in the rabbinic tradition; that the Jews who survived the assimilatory pressures in Babylon, the Roman Empire, Europe, Asia and Africa took this seriously; and that the sentiment of belonging to a Jewish people was significantly re-enforced by the external pressures of the non-Jewish, especially the Christian, world. All this was not enough to make Zionism the unquestioned life-path of the majority of Jews in a secular age. But it was enough to save Zionists from the cultural hysteria or excesses of peoples who have to create their national existence out of cultural myths. The incapacity of many Arabs to understand that there are natural bounds to the territorial claims of Zionism is linked with the weakly defined concept of an Arab nation as opposed to an Arab culture in their own new nationalism. Their nationalism has elevated Islam and still hovers uncertainly between an Islamic empire and a local national group. It recognizes the Syrian Arab nation, the Lebanese Arab nation, the Egyptian Arab nation, the Palestinian Arab nation, in an attempt not blatantly to suppress Arab Christians, who have been of great importance in the modern nationalist movement. But it is still not at home with, or has simply rejected, the concept of a Syrian nation, an Egyptian nation, a Palestinian nation as such. There has been an Arab world, connected but not coterminous with the Islamic world. There has not been and there perhaps still is not an Arab nation, though most Arab nationalists would feel that something essential is missing if they did not add Arab to the name of the country they profess to be citizens of. So strong is the Islamic influence that even Iran has proved not to be simply an Iranian nation. That problem of hovering between *Reich* and locality or *Volk* is not a Jewish one, even if Jews, like most nations, but with more hanging on it, can argue about where their vital historic boundaries should end. Jews now too have their 'Khomeiniacs', though they do not, thank god, rule them; but even their Khomeiniites have a clear and limited conception of the Jewish people and Jewish territory – the territory of a nation-state, perhaps one of the early ones in history, and not of an empire. God, in a piece of perhaps unusual wisdom for him, did not set the Jews up to rule over others. But like the Armenians, Jews have not been improved by the manners and customs of those they are forced to fight against.

II

Nationalism, it is widely recognized, has a positive side and a negative side: it can be democratic or authoritarian, backward-looking or forward-looking, socialist or conservative, secular or religious, generous or chauvinist. Some great students of nationalism, including Hans Kohn, have believed that Western European nationalism began at least as predominantly liberal and democratic, while the Eastern nationalism of the Slavs had and has what Kohn saw as fundamental and pervasive tendencies toward illiberalism. Certainly, nationalism, for most of the nineteenth and twentieth centuries, has been seen both as the precondition for and main carrier of democracy and as its main enemy. Certainly, the romantic nationalism of the end of the eighteenth and the first half of the nineteenth centuries – the nationalism of Herder, Michelet, Mickiewicz, Palácky, Mazzini – for all the undertones of national chauvinism and self-glorification displayed in it, was both democratic, elevating the people, and universalist, believing that each people had something to contribute to the development of humanity. For Michelet, Mickiewicz, Palácky and Mazzini, the special mission of their nations, their messianic, or in Czech lands mediating, role, was in each case on behalf of humanity as a whole.

Of course, other notes were struck in the work of these thinkers and in the work of less liberal, chauvinist and often racist and anti-semitic thinkers that flourished even in the first half of the nineteenth century. Fichte, addressing the German nation, found it to be the best and perhaps the only real nation. He called in the name of human perfection, of freedom and equality, for a holy war and a sacred hate against the Napoleonic invaders. Schelling, too, saw holy universal law in wrath, hate and war and called for a truly divine leader, a messenger from heaven – a leader to whom Novalis, too, was ready to ascribe the attributes of Christ. For Adam Müller, it was the state itself that was divine, while Ernst Moritz Arndt and *Turnvater* Jahn called for a moral regeneration of Germany that was, above all, a call against the alien, against humanitarianism and cosmopolitanism, against what Arndt called 'Jewish one-worldism' and for an undefiled pure language and a pure race. By the second half of the nineteenth century, as nationalisms came increasingly to compete within one area, as multi-ethnic societies came to the forefront of world attention, and as new groups sought to become part of the middle classes and to attack existing allegedly alien commercial elites, nationalism became in many respects predominantly illiberal – a fact that accounts for the increasing and continuing ambivalence of socialists and democrats in the modern world when confronted with the claims and phenomena of nationalism.

Karl Marx, the greatest of all nineteenth-century European internationalists, spent more time attending meetings to support or commemorate Polish and Irish struggles for independence than he spent organizing or supporting strikes. The creation of the nation-state as a precondition for, or part of, the creation of a democratic polity – the struggle for national independence and for the fragmentation of supranational autocracies – had his support and that of most socialists. Socialists and liberals admired Mazzini, but they hated Bismarck, much as socialists and liberals later admired Nasser and Kenyatta while hating Franco and Vorster. Nationalism, for them, had a dark side and a light side, a reactionary one and a progressive one. Thus the Jewish liberal nationalist Simon Dubnow insisted, early in this century, that the sentiments that were progressive nationalism in the Jew were reactionary chauvinism in the Great Russian. The distinction had to be made in terms of the objective historical situation of the nation concerned. For nations whose national territory was secure and whose state had long been created, nationalism was a reactionary reversion to primitive hates: for nations that politically were not yet nations, that were oppressed or fragmented, for men and women whose nationhood still lay in the future, nationalism was a necessary step on the path to progress. In the eyes of such socialists and liberals, then, nationalism was never an end in itself: it was a means toward human development. Some nations had been fortunate and had gained their territorial and political status before the demand grew for popular sovereignty; they could settle down, needing little more than a modest glow of pride in their history and culture, to the task of economic and political progress and to friendly co-operation with other nations. Nationalism was for the deprived, for the unfortunate, for those who still had to find or create the conditions for their own dignity. As Dubnow put it in his discussion of Solovyev:

> Solovyev, the representative of the Russian people, is right in rejecting the 'fanatical concern for one's own nation'. He is right from the point of his nationality, since the ruling Russian nationality does not need such concern; it is useful only to the fanatics who have adopted the slogan of 'Russia for the Russians'. But Solovyev would be entirely wrong were he to extend his condemnation also to the national minorities in Russia, who can only maintain themselves if they are 'concerned for their own national individuality'. In the case of a nationality which is persecuted or which lacks political liberty it is perfectly reasonable to encourage a group of nationalists, because such a nationality must fight for its national character and its autonomy against the ruling nationality which seeks to weaken it or to swallow it up. When the ruling nationality in the state, however, sets up groups of 'nationalists' of its own, it is bent not on defence but on attack, and it seeks to strengthen its rule by crushing the freedom of the subject nationalities; it wants to turn its national minorities into Germans, Russians, Poles, etc. and to force them to adopt its language, its educational system, its political aspirations . . . We are all in the habit of associating this kind of nationalism and patriotism with violence and oppression and with political despotism, and we understand perfectly well why our liberal friends among the ruling nationality emphatically declare: 'We are not nationalists and we are not "patriots"!' The word 'patriots' is put in quotation marks to indicate that there is also a reputable kind of patriotism . . . It would be advisable to use quotation marks also for the extreme nationalism of aggressive groups.[7]

[7] Simon Dubnow, 'The ethics of nationalism', being Letter III in Koppel S. Pinson (ed.), *Letters on Old and New Judaism* (1897–1907), trans. in Simon Dubnow, *Nationalism and History* (New York, World Publishing, 1961), pp. 125–6.

III

Nationalism has been seen by such protagonists as Fichte, Michelet and Mazzini, by such political sympathizers as Presidents Wilson and F.D.R. Roosevelt and by such critics as the late Elie Kedourie as arising from and implied by the Kantian elevation of self-determination. Gellner protests that Kant was not a nationalist, which is true but in my view irrelevant. The Kantian elevation of autonomy over heteronomy, shorn of many Kantian complexities and practical modifications, is perhaps the central abiding theme in the ideological development of the modern world. The American Revolution, the French Revolution and the French revolutionary wars, the demands of 1848 and movements of colonial independence from South America in the 1820s to the Pacific in the 1970s and 80s were all launched in the name of self-determination, fusing the self as individual and the self as nation in the slogan Liberty, Equality, Fraternity. Despite the strength of nationalist ideology, the fundamental shift in the governance of men inaugurated by the eighteenth-century Enlightenment was a shift from an authority of origins to an authority of ends. Neither descent, custom nor divine right and tradition now lay at the base of government but the promise to deliver the goods, to guarantee and promote life, liberty and the pursuit of happiness, to ensure progress and further development, economic, social and moral. From guarantor, the state turned active agent and beneath the backward-looking rhetoric of nationalism in the twentieth century and in much of the nineteenth has lain conscious and unconscious commitment to 'modernization' – development, industrialization, the elevation of youth, the imaginative use of new technology (often in the worst of causes), the development of propaganda, mass education and mass participation. Gellner may be right in arguing that tendencies toward uniformity and increasing mass involvement were implicit in and furthered by the development of industrial society, but I do not believe that nationalism as an ideology can be separated out and treated as epiphenomenal to that development. It is part and parcel of it. Nor have modern ideologies, except in times of contingent crises, favoured the continuing elevation of the state and nation as ends in themselves rather than as means to human autonomy and development in advanced industrial and rational societies – much as the world may also be threatened by the fear of freedom and of progress, by retreats into the mysticism of the German forest or by the fundamentalism of the Islamic *Gemeinschaft* of believers.

The UN in many regards has not been a respectable organization, principally because the majority of its members have been neither honest nor respectable and because large parts of its civil service have felt the need to please them and defend them. Nevertheless, at the ideological level, the United Nations in its human rights activities has both encapsulated major ideological trends characterizing the modern world and helped to further these trends. It provided in the Preamble and Articles 1 and 2 of its Universal Declaration of Human Rights, proclaimed in 1948, that all human beings were born free and equal in dignity and rights, that they should act toward one another in a spirit of brotherhood and that they were entitled to the (rather traditional Common Law civil and political) rights set forth in the Declaration 'without distinction of race, colour, sex, language, religion, political or other opinion, national or social origin, property, birth or other status'. A principal difference between the United Nations and the League of Nations was that League of Nations Mandates were granted without term on the assumption that some peoples would need to be in tutelage for very extensive periods; United Nations Trusteeships were granted as limited trusteeships charged with the task of preparing a people for independence. As the UN proceeded to spell out the specific implications of the Declaration of Human Rights in the International Covenants on Civil and Political Rights and on Economic, Social and Cultural Rights, it provided in Article 1, para.1 of both Covenants that 'All peoples have the right of self-determination. By virtue of that right they freely determine their political status and freely pursue their economic, social and cultural development.'

Philosophers and other serious persons have rightly been critical of many aspects of the UN proclamations, emphasizing their selectivity in focusing on particular problems or rights and not others, their failure to explore or admit the intrinsic conflict between the rights proclaimed in each Covenant as well as the fundamental conflict between civil and political rights (rights as immunities) and economic, social and cultural rights (a large part of which are claims to benefits acting as demands or justifications for state interference rather than immunities). The tolerated distinction between those UN members who sign these Covenants and intend to observe them and those who sign but do not is, of course, scandalous when both are given equal status in drafting them. UN support groups in various countries, abstractly and stridently proclaiming a selective list of rights to an even more selective list of addresses have done much harm and would have helped in some countries to destroy what rights there were rather than to further them. Nevertheless, there is a real sense in which the existence and work of the United Nations has made international law, for those who choose to observe it, more than a set of pious proclamations or a statement limited to sketching what is desirable rather than what is.

The United Nations later turned to what it saw as the elaboration of the third generation of rights implicit in the Universal Declaration, which has become in the last twenty years or so a document of international law elaborated by the Covenants and interpreted by the International Court of Justice and the UN Human Rights Commission rather than a statement of aspirations. The first generation of rights consisted of the civil and political rights proclaimed in the Covenant devoted to them, which had been ratified by thirty-five member states and thus brought into effect by 1976. Those rights were seen and are still seen as the rights that constituted political autonomy or emancipation, the political self-determination of the individual and his or her equality before the law. The second generation of rights, strongly emphasized by socialists and many Afro-Asian states that see political and civil liberties as secondary or derivative and not urgent in their own situation, are the rights proclaimed in the Covenant on Economic, Social and Cultural Rights, also in force since 1976. These are said to constitute the path to social and economic and not merely legal and political emancipation and equality. More recently, under pressure from its Afro-Asian members, including an Arab bloc seeking to promote the cause of the 'Palestinians' or the P.L.O. and with support from the then Soviet bloc, the UN turned to discussion of a 'third generation' of rights connected with solidarity, with the emancipation and self-determination of groups. These rights, the theory ran, are vested not in individuals or in states but in peoples. The difficulty of defining peoples, of deciding who are and who are not peoples, was recognized in the discussions and is one of the reasons – another is the end of the Cold War – why both enthusiasm and discussion have waned, except in relation to 'indigenous' peoples, most of whom do not seek independent statehood. Nevertheless, the notion that rights under international law can be vested in groups of individuals or in individuals as such, implicit in recent UN activities, is a major revolution in the theory of international law, which was previously seen as the law governing the conduct and relations of states. It was insufficiently emphasized to a wider public in western democracies, however, that all communist-governed countries accepted the innovation only to the most limited extent, even in theory, and that most United Nations members do not and will not accept it in respect of any individuals or groups within their own territories. Something like widespread backing for the 'rights of peoples' and the right of 'self-determination' was being reached in the United Nations only by interpreting self-determination not to mean democratic government, but only the rejection of former colonial rule and (Western) economic imperialism or 'neo-colonialism'. In the rhetoric of the General Assembly, all this became identified with racism and Western European domination; economic, military and political hegemony on the part of socialist, African or Asian states was passed over in silence. An eminent international lawyer, Antonio Cassese, summarized the totally different conceptions of self-determination and the rights of peoples represented in the United Nations. He wrote:

> Socialist countries understand self-determination essentially as the liberation of non-self-governing peoples from colonial domination. They have broadened the concept – under pressure from African and Arab countries – to include liberation from racist domination (South Africa and Southern Rhodesia) and from foreign occupation (Arab territories occupied by Israel). Moreover, with the support of Afro-Asian countries (which are worried lest the collapse of colonialism should involve the breaking up of colonial territories), the socialist countries deny that self-determination can legitimate secession. Thus, to socialist countries, self-determination means only 'external' self-determination and only for peoples subject to colonial or racist rule or to foreign occupation. The achievement of independent status by peoples living in non-racist sovereign States entails the implementation of self-determination. This applies in particular to socialist States: 'only in socialist States and through the sovereignty achieved by them can self-determination be completely realized'. Ultimately, for sovereign and independent States self-determination becomes tantamount to the right to non-intervention. This point is very important and deserves to be particularly stressed. According to socialist countries, self-determination, considered as the right to non-intervention, means the right that foreign States shall not interfere in the life of the community *against the will of the government*. It does not include the right that a foreign State shall not interfere in the life of the community *against the interests of the population* but at the request or at any rate with the tacit approval of the government.

> Western countries have, on many occasions, attacked this outlook for being too restrictive and one-sided. They maintain that the right of the peoples oppressed by totalitarian regimes must be recognized and that in any case self-determination must include respect for fundamental freedoms and the basic rights of individuals. The close link between self-determination and individual human rights is one of the main features of the Western doctrine. As was stated in 1972 by the US delegate to the Third Committee of the General Assembly: 'Freedom of choice is indispensable to the exercise of the right of self-determination. For this freedom of choice to be meaningful, there must be corresponding freedom of thought, conscience, expression,

movement and association. Self-determination entails legitimate, lively dissent and testing at the ballot box with frequent regularity.'[8]

Much of this – together with Soviet totalitarianism and Bolshevik but not Chinese statecraft – has collapsed and passed into history. The American and general liberal democratic view of things now has more power in the UN and in the conflict of world ideologies than any Communist view. East Timor is still governed by its occupiers and treated as part of the occupying state by the government that invaded and annexed it, so is Tibet. But even China has now conceded implicitly that human rights may be a matter of international concern and not a mere pretext for meddling in the internal affairs of a country. However, we can still say that neither economic, social and cultural rights nor rights of peoples are well treated as ends in themselves, divorcible from a conception of human autonomy, development and the plurality of moral values. Talk of generations of rights means, or should mean, what it says – that the second and third generations are extensions of and to be seen through the conception of human beings implicit in the first generation. The trend of treating the second and third generation as deriving from distinct and separate ideologies, as representing the claims of socialism, communitarianism, 'republicanism' in the American radical's sense of the term and nationalism versus those of liberal democracy is part of a deliberate attempt to destroy the latter. It must be resisted, above all by those who rightly recognize that the very concept of abstract human rights is valuable only as an expression of the concern for human autonomy and development, as part of a wider moral sensitivity that involves the recognition that other people, no matter how different, are in crucial respects ourselves once more. Even claims like national independence and national autonomy are ultimately means to be assessed and pursued in a wider moral context.[9]

IV

Today, the ambiguous legacy of nationalism is even more multi-faceted. There are, in many parts of Europe especially, traditional, backward-looking, sometimes chauvinist or xenophobic nationalisms that have derived new strengths from internal and external threats to the somewhat romanticized cohesion and placidity of a community that looks back on better times. The collapse of Communism, like the collapse of the Ottoman and Austro-Hungarian Empires, has only brought out that suppression of nationalistic movements can intensify, rather than weaken, their influence and their demands once the regime loses power and authority. The Caucasus is now the cauldron it was when Russia conquered it. Yugoslavia or the nations that were forced into it now relive its unhappy history. Asian nationalisms – in Malaysia, in Cambodia, in Vietnam, in Korea and in Japan – have been tempered by economically rising standards of

---

[8] A. Cassesse, 'Political self-determination – old concepts and new developments', in A. Cassesse (ed.), *U.N. Law/Fundamental Rights: Two Topics in International Law* (Alphen aan den Rijn, Sijthoff and Noordhoff, 1979), p. 137ff. at pp. 154–5.

[9] See on this E. Kamenka, 'Human rights – peoples' rights', in James Crawford (ed.), *The Rights of Peoples* (Oxford, Clarendon Press, 1988), pp. 127–39, and with slight alterations as 'Law and man in a changing society: the problem of human rights', in S. Panou, G. Bozonis, D. Georgas and P. Trappe (eds.), *Human Being and the Cultural Values*, ARSP Supplementum for Vol. IV (Stuttgart, Steiner, 1988), pp. 93–103.

living or the hope of such. In much of the world, including much of Western Europe, Singapore and Malaysia, statesmanship has guided modern nations, with less nationalistic and racist reactions than one might have expected, through major changes in ethnic and racial mix. To some extent, Singapore, Malaysia, Australia and Canada – all seeking a sense of national identity after gaining political independence – have had reasonable success in basing their nationhood on a willingness to work together for the future rather than on deep-rooted sentiment from the past. So, earlier, did the United States. Where all this takes place in the context of a genuinely democratic structure of government, recognizing pluralism of parties and interests, the prospects are encouraging.

They are least encouraging where the recognition of the importance and pluralism of civil society as distinguished from the state or the church has no deep historical roots or where the concepts of religion and of nationhood have become deeply intertwined. Here, reversions to fascism or the continued or renewed elevation of authoritarian government are perfectly possible. But there are authoritarians and authoritarians. Pilsudski was a shining beacon of humanity compared with Admiral Horthy and Horthy was not Hitler. To explain those differences and the likely progress of different countries as they move through a new or renewed nationalist phase, one needs not only economics and sociology, but also a sense of history and culture. Humanity has always known bad times, at least in some parts of the world and often in many parts of the world. I see no reason to believe that that will change. But the long term trend, it seems to me, lies in the direction of a demotic society, overpopulated, full of problems, pretending to the populism of the supermarket while encouraging managerial manners among its governments, but not elevating nationalism as an end, rather than a means, in the long term. Every country, its government and its citizens, now has too much to gain from the rest of the world and too much to lose by alienating it or treating it as necessarily hostile. In the middle term, the still non-tolerant religions, from Islamic fundamentalism to Russian and Serb Orthodoxy and Croat Catholicism, may prove the basic energizing charge in vicious nationalism or in the communal tensions that plague India and Sri Lanka. Religion and nationalism are a frightening mixture indeed, though in religion as in nationalism, one has to be backward-looking to be really terrifying.

What is even more encouraging is the fact that alleged scientific and racial foundations for nationalism are, and in the foreseeable future will surely remain, in ill repute. They smack of Nazism whose power of repulsion, though gradually diminishing and not preventing some nationalists from claiming that their respective nations are founded on a common ethnic past in which certain groups do not have and do not deserve a share, is still overwhelmingly strong. Most nationalisms are turning today instead to seeing nationhood as founded on a common desire of sharing with other nations a free future. This does not bode well for the revival of or formation of new nationalist authoritarian coalitions, analogous to those formed by the fascist leaders of the 1930s. There is very little doubt that nationalists now in power, when acting on the international scene, are anything more than sheer opportunists. Totalitarianism required and wanted a world in its own image, and before such a world was created, it lived under completely sealed borders. The authoritarian nationalists of the present do not have either the power or the strength of conviction to pursue such a course. And it seems that the present conditions, when projected into the future, indicate that the creation of stable coalitions of them or their like, to say nothing about the emergence of a new world ideology, will become increasingly difficult.

It is possible to say what I have said – and many strive to do so – with an air of doing solid, serious predictive social science that tells us what the future of nationalism is and sets out the conditions under which it will take this form or that. To promote such claims and that air is to foster illusions. To know a country is to understand its history, to feel its language and cultural heritage, to note its constantly changing situation. Despite the claims of nationalism, a country has not one history but many histories, not one future but many futures. Some may seem unlikely; more of them will be unpredictably contingent.

The People, the Intelligentsia and Russian Political Culture

MARC RAEFF*

Columbia University, New York

'Il est incroyable combien de systèmes de morale et de politique ont été successivement trouvés, oubliés, retrouvés, oubliés encore pour réparaître un peu plus tard, toujours charmant ou surprenant le monde comme s'ils étaient nouveaux, et attestant l'ignorance des hommes, et non la fécondité de l'esprit humain. / . . . / C'est, ainsi que la plupart de ces faiseurs de théories sociales, que nous voyons de nos jours, et qui nous semblent, avec raison, si dangereux, nous paraîtraient de plus fort ennuyeux, si nous avions plus d'érudition et plus de mémoire'.†

About a century ago, the first foreign scholarly 'expert' on Russia, Anatole Leroy-Beaulieu, stressed that in comparing Russian society and history with Western Europe's, it is necessary to bear in mind a chronological discrepancy (*décalage*). Nineteenth century Russia should be compared with Western Europe in the 16th or 17th, or the Russian 18th century with the Western 15th, and so forth. Without developing or illustrating this observation, I would merely urge that it be kept in mind while writing and talking about Russian history; in particular we should remember that more than anywhere in Europe the élites and the common people seem to have followed different paths.

Ever since the reign of Peter the Great there has been a perception, both in Russia and outside of it in the West, that the first emperor's reign had indeed marked a caesura in what seemed the organic, 'natural', course of events on the plains of European Russia. Perhaps his reign might be compared with those upheavals in West and Central Europe that we subsume under the headings of Renaissance and Reformation. The latter should remind us, I think, that the almost equally dramatic upheaval in Muscovite history, the church schism, *raskol*, barely a generation before the accession of Peter I, 'softened up' the soil for the transformation wrought by the last tsar and first emperor. We have to start with this watershed if we wish to understand the dynamics of modern Russia's social, cultural, and political history and its legacy to the late twentieth century.

* Dr Marc Raeff is Bakhmeteff Professor Emeritus of Russian Studies at Columbia University, New York, USA.
† Alexis de Tocqueville, Discours d'ouverture, 25 Octobre 1851, Séance publique annuelle des cinq Académies. (*Oeuvres Complètes*, tome XVI, pp. 236–7.)

In order to characterize the main features of pre-Petrine, muscovite or 'pre-modern', Russian culture we may begin with Edward L. Keenan's challenging interpretation of the political culture of the Great Russian peasant: a culture, we should stress, that *mutatis mutandis* was also shared by the élite classes – the tsar's servitors, the clergy, and the big merchants (*gosti*).[1] It is Keenan's thesis that the harsh climate and unfavourable geographic conditions of Central European Russia (i.e. the headwaters of Oka, Volga, Western and Northern Dvinas, the cradle of the Muscovite state) made for an extremely fragile economy: the growing season was short and the small yields were at the mercy of unpredictable, small climatic irregularities. In addition, the exposed nature of the great Russian plain made for military insecurity and social instability that gave rise to the burdensome and costly Muscovite military and government apparatus. All these factors generated among the Great Russian population, as they had done in Western Europe at the dawn of the Middle Ages, an acute sense of physical insecurity and fear of innovation and change. Without sharing Keenan's geographic determinism one has to agree that his analysis provides a key to one important dimension of the Great Russian's mentality in the pre-modern, i.e. pre-scientific and pre-industrial, era. He quite rightly emphasizes the socio-psychological consequences that made the Great Russian fear anything that might threaten the delicate equilibrium he believed essential to his survival. Any innovation was viewed with suspicion as potentially destabilizing; anything foreign, under whatever guise, was rejected in favour of long acquired customs and traditional beliefs. The world that God had created was full of dangers and served to test man's obedience to divine will and commands; to oppose God's (and His vicars' on earth) commandments inevitably brought about His wrath and punishment.

As had been true of Western men in the Middle Ages, the Muscovites believed that the universe was defined once and for all and its potential delimited forever by the act of creation. It thus would be hubris on man's part to even fathom the workings of this once-created universe, let alone to mould it for his selfish advantage. Man had to accept the world as it was, he was its passive member and obedience to the world's order was, therefore, his most essential duty. Ritualized acts and traditional beliefs ensured stability, and whatever degree of predictability man could expect to guide his activities. This is the explanation for the Muscovites' frequently noted strict adherence to the minutiae of ritual behaviour, whether in church or at official and family occasions. Strict ritualistic behaviour, of course, is common to all so-called pre-modern societies, but the Muscovites struck the European observers as carrying it to extremes. Such a pattern implied a strong consensus concerning religious beliefs, moral values, and the formal manifestations of socio-political organization.

Crucial to the Muscovite consensus was the total and uncritical acceptance of Orthodox Christian faith, rites, and precepts. Unquestioning obedience of tradition, rejection of any innovation such were the mainstays of Muscovite culture – and it was something all foreign observers noted and stressed. It explains, among other things, Moscow's anxious response to the last ditch effort made by Byzantium to secure Western help by agreeing to union with the Roman Catholic church at the Council of Florence (1438). The fall of Constantinople to the Ottoman Turks soon thereafter served to confirm the Muscovites in the righteousness of their refusal to recognize the union. As the only independent

---

[1] Edward L. Keenan, 'Muscovite political folkways', *Russian Review*, 45, 2 (1986), 115–181.

Orthodox power left, Moscow became more than ever convinced of its God-chosen task to preserve intact the 'true faith' (which Byzantium had deserted at the last moment) – that is, abide literally by all its rituals, commandments, and dogmas. This was the meaning of the theory of Moscow the Third Rome (Two Romes – Rome and Constantinople – have fallen, the third – Moscow – is standing, and there will be no fourth) formulated at about the time of Basile III (1505–33), the father of Ivan IV the Terrible;[2] it was essentially a conservative and defensive theory: Moscow's historic fate is to keep intact the dogmas and rites of true Orthodoxy as received from Byzantium in the tenth century, and to maintain them until the Second coming – any departure from them is the work of Antichrist and a first step to eternal damnation. Contrary to commonly held belief (formulated in the 19th century), the theory of Moscow the Third Rome did not function as an aggressive or expansionist (imperialist) ideology of the Russian state; it was not even an element of Russian public opinion, once the latter made its appearance in the late St. Petersburg period. As an ideology of defence and isolation from the West it appealed in the mid-17th century to the Old Believers and their predecessors.

The Old Believers were indeed those who refused to accept the reforms introduced by Patriarch Nikon into the church ritual, reforms based on contemporary Greek practices and elaborated and promoted by Ukrainian clergy that flocked to Muscovite service.[3] The tsar's government supported the Nikonian reforms and considered those refusing to accept them as schismatics and dangerous 'dissidents' (or traitors), prosecuting and persecuting them with great energy and still greater cruelty. The Nikonian reforms thus brought about a collapse of the hallowed religious consensus which in Muscovite terms meant all non-material culture. The large minority of Old Believers (about 25% of the population) stubbornly clung to literal ritualism in fear of any change in the traditional system of values and social comportment; they felt confirmed in their unquestioning belief that the Russian land alone had preserved the true faith and the God-ordered ways, and that it was man's last chance of salvation.

Far from being an exclusive characteristic of Old Believer mentality, its essentially conservative, isolationist, and passive stance was also shared by the peasants of 'Great Russia', as well as by a good part of the urban élites (merchants, artisans), way past the reign of Peter the Great. The peasantry retained their traditional psychology and culture into the second half of the 19th century when, only gradually and hesitatingly, they began adapting to the new conditions brought about by the emancipation of the serfs.[4] If Keenan is correct in his analysis, and in some basic ways, I think, he is, there was nothing until the end of the 19th century to alleviate the Russian peasants' sense of instability and insecurity, for nothing in the technological and economic circumstances of his life had appreciably changed since the 17th century. Of course, by and in itself the situation was not basically different from that of large sectors of the peasantry in

[2] D. Strémooukhoff, 'Moscow the Third Rome: sources of the doctrine', *Speculum*, Jan. (1953), 84–101 (reprinted in M. Cherniavsky (ed.), *The Structure of Russian History* (New York, 1970); Hildegard Schaeder, *Moskau das Dritte Rom – Studien zur Geschichte der Politischen Theorien in der slawischen Welt* (Darmstadt, 2nd ed., 1957).

[3] M. Cherniavsky, 'The Old Believers and the New Religion', *Slavic Review*, XXV (1966), 1–39 (reprinted in *The Structure of Russian History*, (New York, 1970); Robert O. Crummey, *The Old Believers and the World of Antichrist*, (Madison, University of Wisconsin Press, 1970).

[4] Cf. P. I. Mel'nikov-Pecherskii, 'The "anthropological novel" ' *V lesakh* (many editions, most recent in *Sobranie sochinenii v shesti tomakh* (Moscow, 1963), vol. 2.

the West before the 19th century. Here, too, much of the Middle Ages lived on in the countryside; except for the fact that the rural world in Western Europe was much more tightly connected with society at large (towns and political establishment) than was the case in Russia. The peculiarity of Russia's situation was due, above all, to the Petrine revolution of the first quarter of the 18th century.

No need to rehearse the changes wrought by Peter the Great, nor to debate the perennial question of whether these changes were revolutionary or rooted in the past of Muscovy. It was, I believe, the loss of religious and cultural consensus, as a consequence of the *raskol*, that made Peter's programme at all possible. But the people's passive opposition to the Petrine measures was to split Russian society in two: those – a minority – that were touched by and accepted the innovations, and those – the overwhelming majority until mid-19th century – who did not. Peter's ruthless introduction of institutional and cultural innovations was like a hurricane that suddenly irrupted into the traditional pattern of the Great Russians' norms and ways, and violently bent them to let in contemporary West European ideas, values, and practices. The process has been often described and its nature and impact analysed and debated: my focus will be somewhat different.[5]

The basis of Muscovite political culture – i.e. set of ideas and practices that inform political behaviour – had been Eastern Christian Orthodoxy as interpreted and practiced by the Establishment, and as it was anchored in the social beliefs and practices of the population. The new conceptions Peter introduced consisted of the following foreign Western elements: the 17th century belief in rationalism and science that the laws of nature could be known and applied to the benefit of man; a secularized conception of natural law that provided the underpinnings of social morality; the administrative practices and regulations of centralized government to take the lead in economic 'modernization' and productivity; a pattern of civility and interpersonal conduct that respected an individual's dignity and worth, and promoted personal security and social peace.[6] Church and religion remained major instruments of social control, but lost their monopoly of intellectual and creative endeavour. The functions of the state, on the other hand, were expanded: they had been of a negative (preservative) kind – keep law and order, dispense justice, defend from foreign attack; Peter endowed government institutions with the task of actively furthering the maximization of the country's potential resources and society's creative energy, in order to enhance the state's military and political power and the population's prosperity – naturally, first that of the élites, but eventually also that of all classes of society.

In the West the 'modern' norms of political and economic action had developed slowly; at the same time the development had gradually drawn into its orbit representatives of all sectors of society. In this way there developed a 'third estate' (or a bourgeoisie, in later parlance) drawing on the rich strata of the peasantry while sending its more successful members to swell the ranks of the nobility of office, the church hierarchy or the professional-intellectual leadership.

    [5] V. Klyuchevski, *Peter the Great*, (New York, 1958); R. Wittram, *Peter I, Osar und Kaiser*, (Göttingen, 1964, 2 vols); for a handy overview of most important aspects, see James Cracraft (ed.), *Peter the Great Transforms Russia*, (Lexington, MA., D. C. Heath, 3rd ed., 1991).
    [6] M. Raeff, *The Well Ordered Police State: Social and Institutional Change through Law in the Germanies and Russia 1600–1800*, (Yale University Press, 1983).

In Petrine Russia (and long thereafter), on the other hand, the Western innovations affected only the noble service class. Neither the peasantry, of course, nor the other non-noble classes of society – clergy, merchantry and artisans (there were no professional classes) – associated themselves to the new ways of life and culture (naturally there were a few individual exceptions). Moreover in Russia an important, nay crucial, aspect of modern Western culture – namely the endeavour to be *'maître et possesseur de la Nature'* did not find common acceptance. The service nobility, relying primarily on the rewards of their service, similar in this respect to the *noblesse d'épée* in *Ancien régime* France, was not overly concerned with matters economic; anyway, their cultural influence on the serf peasantry, whose labour provided most of their regular income, was limited in any case. As far as these nobles were concerned, whether in service, at court, or at leisure on their estates, the elements of contemporary Western European civilization Peter had imported served to enhance not so much their material condition as their social status; and give them a sense of individual worth and dignity by surrounding themselves with foreign objects of luxury, and made possible stimulating social intercourse and entertainment. Of course, the degree of sophistication among Westernized nobles varied a great deal; many poor provincial nobles retained much of the traditional boorish ways and superstitious beliefs of their ancestors and neighbouring peasants. The effect of the Westernism acquired by the élites in the 18th century was primarily 'paedagogic' in character: it served to bring into being a 'civilized' (in the sense of *'honnête homme'*) worthy individual, capable of participating in cultural endeavours, as well as to serve the state and society. We may call it an *'Ersatzideologie'* for the ruling élites and the imperial establishment.

I call it an *Ersatzideologie*, for it was never stated in terms of specific philosophic concepts and did not provide a comprehensive system of ideas and values that determined explicitly formulated and goal-directed social and political action by the officials of the imperial Establishment. It was, rather, a cento of Western-inspired norms of social and cultural (i.e. intellectual) behaviour; norms that were to be acclimatized among the common people as well. Hence the *Kulturträger* role of those élite members that had acquired a European-style education. The *Ersatzideologie* also served as guideline for the government's efforts at modernizing the country. To this end it was also used (subconsciously perhaps) in bringing Russia into direct contact with 'Europe' by extending the borders westward ('Peter the Great cutting a window to Europe' in Pushkin's memorable phrase) and acquiring a 'cultural glacis' with the Baltic provinces, Poland, and Ukraine.[7]

In the process there developed an 'imperial ideology': first, complete the traditional 'gathering' of the inheritance of Kiev and the Golden Horde initiated by Moscow in the 14th century, and preserve it from foreign threats and, second, create and assert a new image of Russia as that of a great European power, whose élites led a civilized (that is European) way of life and also contributed to the progress of civilization.[8]

Another aspect of the Petrine state's *Ersatzideologie*, of great domestic importance, can be put briefly by saying that it was the application of the conception and practices of the well-ordered *Policeystaat* of German cameralism. As alluded to earlier, it meant that the state, through its institutions and

[7] M. Raeff, 'Un empire comme les autres?', *Cahiers du monde russe et soviétique*, XXX (1989), 321–8.
[8] Wm. C. Fuller Jr, *Strategy and Power in Russia 1600–1914*, (New York, 1992).

officials, led in the country's 'modernization', that is maximizing its economic productive potential while at the same time educating the élites to be more European. Thus the government took the lead and strained at overcoming the opposition of tradition and existing social arrangements in order to introduce those forms of economic organization and social relationships that prevailed in the West, although lagging far behind them in fact, especially with respect to the agrarian sector (where serfdom prevailed until 1861). It is essential to stress in this context that such a leadership role of the state implied the continuing existence and dominant role of the autocracy and its officials. The unfettering of civil society and promoting its progress was not part of the state's programme, though it was a necessary consequence of its goals of Europeanization and modernization. The contradiction existing between the exclusive leadership role claimed by the state (i.e. the autocratic establishment), and the inevitable emergence of an autonomous civil society was at the root of a fundamental polarity in Russia's political culture throughout the 19th and early 20th centuries, and in different form under the Soviet system as well.

The polarity stemmed from the obstacles autocracy put in the path of the formation of a genuinely free civil society, and the consequent development of that peculiarly Russian social formation – the *intelligentsia*.[9] By a curious paradox the intelligentsia was a direct consequence of the innovations Peter the Great introduced into the nature and practice of the service élite, as it was also the child of Western ideas and norms.[10] The intelligentsia's moral assessment of, and response to, Russian reality was a heritage of 17th century German pietism 'peppered' with a strong dose of norms about human nature and a just social order borrowed from the writings of radical enlightenment *philosophes* (e.g. J. J. Rousseau, Mably, Raynal) and their post-revolutionary pupils (Young Germany). The moralistic approach was complemented by an emotional commitment to absolutes, especially social ones, that became the intelligentsia's hallmark in the 19th century and gradually turned it into a revolutionary movement of liberation from autocratic political authority and social injustice (i.e. serfdom, peasant backwardness, plight of the urban proletariat). But the intelligentsia also owed its self-appointed role of social critic and of commitment to the welfare of the people to the heritage of the Petrine concept of service – service to the state, service to the people, and *in fine* service to that total community called Russia. Members of the intelligentsia saw it as their special task to prepare for and shape the Russian people's future by developing – or

---

[9] The *intelligentsia* should not be confused (as is done nowadays by following the Soviet redefinition of the term) with intellectuals as a group. The members of the Russian social group called intelligentsia shared the following characteristics:

They possessed a certain level (which varied in the course of time) of a *Western* education; on moral grounds they were critical of the existing socio-political system and advocated its radical transformation. This entailed working for the overthrow of the imperial regime and in so doing fulfill their moral commitment to serve the common people (i.e. the peasants and later also the proletariat). On the basis of this *Gesinnung* or *mentalité* (the concrete ideologies and programmes of action took numerous forms) individuals joined the ranks of the 'knightly order of the intelligentsia' (G. P. Fedotov) by an act of personal self-identification, regardless of their social origins and occupation. Quite naturally the first members of the intelligentsia came from the ranks of the service nobility, while towards the end of the imperial regime they were joined by representatives of the professions and sundry urban classes.

R. Pipes, (ed.), *The Russian Intelligentsia* (New York, 1961); T. Szamuely, *The Russian Tradition* (London, 1974).

[10] M. Raeff, *Origins of the Russian Intelligentsia – The Eighteenth-Century Nobility* (New York, 1966).

borrowing from the West – new types of institutions and cultural norms. As moral critics of society they felt it their duty to denounce the inadequacies of the existing system of social, economic, and political relationships, and as *Kultur-träger* instil in the masses those principles that would make for the ideal organization of national life. Most fundamentally, the intelligentsia was at the very opposite of the traditional presuppositions of Muscovite culture (obedience and passivity in the face of a finite physical and social world created and commanded by an all powerful God) – a culture that still dominated the thoughts and actions of the peasantry and all commoners associated with it. As heir and pupil of Peter the Great, the intelligentsia wanted to bring to this tradition-bound people the 'benefits' of the European cultural sphere (even though it was critical of some of its manifestations) with its reliance on individualism, activism, productivity, and secular science. Moreover the intelligentsia took most of the specific ingredients of the alternative ideology it offered in opposition to that of the imperial establishment from Western sources; that is from mental sets and socio-philosophic ideas totally foreign to the people's traditional values. Little wonder if the intelligentsia had but a faint, if any, genuine spiritual affinity or even contact with the Russian people – although both slavophiles and populists in the 19th century made some efforts at a *rapprochement*. In the final analysis, the members of the intelligentsia found themselves isolated and alienated, both from the establishment that had brought them into being and from the people that was their self-appointed object of service and political-cultural transformation. It is hard, at this point, to resist applying to the intelligentsia Jean-Jacques Rousseau's prophetic analysis of Peter the Great's reforms:

> 'Il est pour les Nations comme pour les hommes un temps de maturité qu'il faut attendre avant de les soumettre à des loix; mais la maturité d'un peuple n'est pas toujours facile à connaître, et si on la prévient l'ouvrage est manqué .... Les Russes ne seront jamais vraiment policés, parcequ'ils l'ont été trop tôt. Pierre avoit le génie imitatif; il n'avoit pas le vrai génie, celui qui crée et fait tout de rien ... Il a vu que son peuple étoit barbare, il n'a point vu qu'il n'étoit pas mûr pour la police; il l'a voulu civiliser quand il ne faloit que l'aguerrir. Il a d'abord voulu faire des Allemands, des Anglais, quand il faloit commencer par faire des Russes; il a empêché ses sujets à jamais devenir ce qu'ils pourroient être, en leur persuadant qu'ils étaient ce qu'ils ne sont pas .... L'empire de Russie voudra subjuguer l'Europe et sera subjugué lui-même ...'
> (*Du Contrat social*, Livre II, ch. IX)

This is not the place to rehearse the major ideologies that have inspired the intelligentsia, from its inception in the 18th century (by common consent A. Radishchev's book denouncing the moral evils of serfdom, *Journey from St. Petersburg to Moscow*, 1790, was the opening shot), to the attainment of its first goal, namely the overthrow of autocracy (in 1905, if we take its first breach, or in 1917 if we select the date of the dénouement). All the intelligentsia's ideological presuppositions, as well as its concrete programmes for far-going socio-political transformation, were drawn from Western sources, most were also quite radical in nature. At the very end of the imperial regime, and only hesitatingly at that, can we speak of the appearance of an intelligentsia that put the development of a civil society at the top of its agenda, and that advocated genuinely liberal programmes and tactics. This new intelligentsia (whose most important manifesto was the collection of essays *Vekhi* [Signposts], 1909)[11] which showed signs of breaking with the uncompromisingly radical stance of its progenitors, owed its existence to the growth of a class of professionals (doctors, lawyers, economists, teachers, scientists, engineers, etc.), as well as to a realization of the spiritual and social dangers inherent in social transformations by fiat and violence.

By some of its aspects the new intelligentsia – or should we not rather speak now of liberal intellectuals? – illustrated a return to religious spirituality and the desire to rediscover the path leading to Russian 'popular' (i.e. pre-Petrine) tradition and culture (e.g. popularity and imitation of pre-Petrine artistic creation in such fields as icon painting, church music, folk decorative motifs and song, etc.). Even then, however, a genuine coming together of intelligentsia and people did not take place. The concrete political and social institutional forms advocated by liberal or progressive intellectuals were predicated on the values of individualism, political rights and freedoms; but these did not offer solutions to problems created by the modernization of Russia's socio-economic structures, and they flew into the face of the peasantry's communal ways and values.

We do not know, of course, whether the emergence of a genuine civil society of enterprising and creative individuals on the one hand, and the 'modernization' of a people rapidly drawn into a capitalist-industrial economy, on the other, would not have led to the convergence of interests and values. The process, whatever its transitional results, was abruptly cut short by the events of 1917. We should note, however, that the urban masses of shopkeepers, clerks, blue collar workers (in contrast to industrial labour) remained refractory to ideology, but they were imbued with an intensely emotional sense of insecurity, fear of the foreign and a dislike, nay hatred, of the intelligentsia and of all intellectuals (especially of non-Russian background), as demonstrated by proto-fascist riots against students and the educated that swept the major cities of European Russia in the last decades of the imperial regime. They proved to be a rehearsal for the much more bloody and anarchic violence in 1917–8 directed at all representatives of 'European' culture, their way of life and education – quite reminiscent of Pugachev's destruction of all examples of Western civilization.

It is my opinion that 1917 and the experiences of the civil war radically changed Russia's historical evolution. On the intellectual level we witness the triumph of an intelligentsia-carried ideology imported from the West – an ideology that had as its goal the total remaking of society and of human nature itself (Stalin's 'engineering of the human soul'), in complete disregard of Russian popular tradition and experience. In the name of this ideology the Soviet regime destroyed both social 'classes' that had constituted the two opposite poles of 19th century Russian society: first, the intelligentsia that was replaced by the so-called 'Soviet intelligentsia' which is nothing else but the class of professionals and intellectuals. Whether the dissidents of the Brezhnev era have turned into the traditional intelligentsia remains to be seen; since Yeltsin's coming to power they seem to have lost their function altogether. Second, by means of the collect-ivization of agriculture, the peasantry was destroyed as a socio-economic entity and living social organism. To what extent the collective farmers may have preserved, or may be in the process of recapturing, traditional peasant culture and values, I do not know. It is a subject noticeably absent from practically all reports on current happenings in Russia.

[11] Marshall S. Shatz and Judith E. Zimmerman (trans. and ed.), *Signposts: A Collection of Articles on the Russian Intelligentsia*, (Irvine CA, 1986).

On the other hand, in the course of World War II and since, the *Ersatzideologie* of imperial Russia has been revived in the form of Stalin's and Brezhnev's policies on nationalities and promotion of a Great Russian national-chauvinism. It doubtlessly appeals to many – especially when it means preservation of a Slavic, or more specifically Russian, great power status. However, it is equally worthy of note how easily Russian society (and the present establishment) appears to reconcile itself to the abandonment of non-Russian lands and imperial ideological claims.

From the perspective of my observations on Russia's historical process, 'what is the future of *isms* in the former RSFSR?' Significantly, the major socio-political notions that are opposed to the rejected ideology of the Soviet system – an ideology rooted in a perverted form of Marxist socialism – constitute a set of moral-political values that, under the label of democracy, posit free election of political organs, the guarantees of individual rights, and the basic freedoms of expression and belief. Their counterpart in the economic domain – market economy – appears rather vague, a mere stating of the right to individual enterprise and action, within an institutional framework that provides for legal guarantees of the security of property and person. The Leninist-Stalinist system, in the name of an ideology, destroyed most traditional and historically formed social and economic relationships; it is therefore unlikely that radical ideologies will have any attraction or appeal – as we may observe in the well-nigh universal condemnation of the very word 'socialism'. The Soviet experiment exacted too high a price in human lives and in the destruction of cultural objects and values to offer much enticement to any 'rational constructivist' (F. von Hayek's terms) approach to society. I would suspect that there is a profound distrust, if not outright hatred, of the kind of pedagogic Westernism and modernization that have been advocated (in a variety of guises) by both the imperial bureaucracy and the intelligentsia before 1917. On the other hand, the moral criticism of certain contemporary forms of Western culture made by older intellectuals (e.g. D. S. Likhachev) fall on deaf ears in the case of the younger generation, that is thirsting for novelty, lack of constraints, genuineness and honesty, regardless of their moral and aesthetic implications. To what extent this trend represents the hopes and values of the Russian people at large remains an open question, for the Soviet system has destroyed all the elements that make for a civil society of social classes and communities capable of expressing their views. So far, it would seem, the urban masses have not yet created a full gamut of institutions that might provide channels for the expression of their needs, desires, and expectations; although there are hopeful signs that new civic and cultural organizations are emerging slowly. If this is the case, Russia may now be following the time-honoured Western patterns of associations for the sake of concrete practical goals that precede the formulation of ideological statements and the constitution of political parties.

Given the distrust of rational ideologies displayed in the former USSR, emotionally laden bundles of beliefs and ideas have come into prominence. Most noticeable and vociferous are manifestations of isolationist nationalism, strongly tinged with nostalgia for the lost past, advocating a return to a kind of retrospective utopia that had never existed. Such a nationalism represented for example by V. Rasputin, V. Astaflev and V. Belov[12] (mixed with 'love of the land'

[12] J. -U. Peters, '*Nationalistische Tendenzen innerhalb der Literatur der Perestrojka*' and John B. Dunlop, '*Russischer Nationalismus heute: Organisationen und Zielsetzungen*' in Andreas Kappeler (ed.), *Die Russen: Ihr Nationalbewinsstsein in Geschichte und Gegenwart*, (Köln, 1990).

– *pochvenichestvo* – and village ways – '*derevenshchina*' – on the model of a
M. Barrès or E. Wiechert) reminds one strongly of 19th century Slavophilism,
equally vague and equally unreal in its distorted view of Russian history. A
related, equally prominent form of return to tradition is the revival of a dynamic
religious life. Given the nature of Russian orthodoxy, and perhaps also the
surfacing of Old Belief with its traditional passive resistance to 'modern' ways,
the religious revival emphasizes the emotional, cultural and philanthropic sides
of church activities (cf. Fathers Mein, Iakunin). Will the organized church play a
practical role in the political process? It did during the *putsch*, but it remains to be
seen whether as an institution it will be a strong, organized political force. It may,
of course, provide moral support and ecclesiastic blessing to specific political
associations and activities, but its tradition of obedience and accommodation to
the powers that be make it more likely that its political role will remain a
subordinate one.

But has the emigration, free from Soviet oppression and isolation, and in direct
contact with the West for over a generation not produced anything that might
serve for developing a new political discourse in Russia today? This question
should also be asked because of the great interest in Silver Age and *émigré*
cultures displayed in the homeland. The rediscovery of the spiritual-religious
dimensions of the Silver Age only reinforces today's significance of *émigré*
writing and thinking, for the latter carried on when the Soviet government cut
short that important phenomenon of modern Russian cultural history.[13] It is,
however, unlikely that this tradition can offer more than a moral validation to
social and philosophical analysis; it can hardly constitute the underpinning of a
programme of political action. Yet the spiritual thirst may also bring about the
revival of what we may call *raskol* mentality, especially in view of the criticism
directed at the institutional church for its meek acquiescence to the Soviet regime
(e.g. Letter of Solzhenitsyn, the church alliance with Gorbachev, etc.). What such
a revival on a large scale would mean under present circumstances is hard to
imagine, but it seems doubtful that the Old Believers could come up with
alternative ideological programmes or become the organizing nexus of political
movements.

Understandably, under the historical circumstances of its formation, the
emigration has recognized the importance of religious and historical traditions,
and of their specifically national traits, in shaping the country's culture. An early
manifestation of this concern was the doctrine of Eurasianism (propounded in
1921 by the linguists N. Trubetskoi and R. Jakobson, the musicologist
P. Suvchinskii, the geographer P. Savitskii, the theologian G. Florovsky).[14] Its
interpretation of Russian history was based on the notion of a perennial struggle
between steppe and forest, that, in turn, was rooted in the specific climatic

[13] Most scholarly work on the Silver Age deals with its literary and artistic manifestations – for the
most recent collaborative effort see E. Etkind, G. Nivat, I. Serman and V. Strada (eds), *Histoire de la
littérature russe – Le XXe siècle: L'Âge d'Argent*, (Paris, 1987). For its philosophic manifestations, V.
V. Zenkovsky, (translated by George L. Kline), *A History of Russian Philosophy*, vol. 2 (New York,
1953). On the religious scene Nikolai P. Poltoratzky (ed.), *Russian Religious-Philosophical Thought of
the 20th Century*, (University of Pittsburgh Press, 1975); Bernice G. Rosenthal and Martha
Bohachevsky-Chomiak, (eds), *A Revolution of the Spirit: Crisis of Value in Russia 1890–1924*
(Fordham University Press, 1990). An original interpretative synthesis is Karl Schlögel, *Jenseits des
Grossen Oktober: Das Laboratorium der Moderne-Petersburg 1909–1921* (Berlin, 1988).
[14] Otto Böss, *Die Lehre der Eurasier – Ein Beitrag zur russischen Ideengeschichte des 20.
Jahrhunderts* (Wiesbaden, 1961); Nicholas V. Riasanovsky, 'The emergence of Eurasianism',
California Slavic Studies 4 (1967), 39–72.

conditions of the Eurasian land mass. (There are no doubt echoes of this conception in Keenan's characterization of the Great Russian peasants' political culture mentioned at the beginning of this paper.) In addition to their geographic determinism, the Eurasians strongly stressed the formative influence of Eastern Christianity on Russian culture and national psychology. Implicit in the Eurasian doctrine was also an affirmation of a Russian *empire*, under Slavic domination, encompassing the steppe lands and their peoples. These features might make Eurasianism attractive to many in Russia today who wish the revival of an organic connection between state and religion, and for whom the spiritual particularism of Russia's cultural tradition constitutes the ground for isolating themselves from the many pernicious manifestations of Western culture that are threatening traditional Russian values. The geographic and climatic determinants of Eurasianism might also give support to those primarily concerned with the ecological state of the former Soviet Union. The attractiveness of Eurasianism suffers, however, from the fact that the Eurasian movement, that arose in the mid-1920s was much compromised by its acceptance of the Bolshevik revolution as a positive and necessary event, and especially by its shady connections with the Soviet intelligence apparatus (e.g. S. Efron's participation in the Reiss murder). Nor is its implicit xenophobia – and cultural chauvinism – to the taste of genuine liberals and democrats.

Related to Eurasianism, but unburdened by its historiosophical presuppositions, was a variety of political groupings and movements whose political programmes had at least two characteristics in common: first, a virulent nationalism that insisted on a strong central government and on a great Russian *state*; and, second, they acquiesced not only to the revolution as a historical fact, but also as a positive contribution made by the Bolshevik regime to Russia's power and greatness. To this group belonged first of all the National Bolsheviks whose influence, however, was greater in Weimar Germany than among the emigration.[15] The movement displayed a nationalism that came close to chauvinism, extolled the power of state authority, and endorsed the Bolshevik policies of nationalization of industry and central economic planning. At the same time National Bolshevism strongly denounced finance capitalism (and its 'Jewish' character), individualism, and materialism. Another group, the *Smena vekh*, whose members presented themselves as contrite intellectuals, provocatively applauded the revolution and the Soviet regime for having rebuilt Russia's national power and prestige.[16] The '*smenovekhovtsy*' acted as if they were self-appointed agents of the Soviet government (which some indeed became) and subsequently returned to the Soviet Union. The movement petered out in the mid-1920s, rejected by practically the entire emigration.

The younger generation of *émigrés*, those who had emigrated in their late teens before completing their studies, had a particularly hard time in finding employment and a meaningful role in the countries of asylum; they also felt very much alienated from the older *émigrés* who occupied all recognized literary, intellectual, and political positions in 'Russia Abroad'.[17] In developing their

[15] The main Russian theorist was Nikolai Ustrialov. The study of M. Agurskii, *Ideologiia natsional- bol'shevisma*, Paris 1980 concentrates on the Soviet participants and dimension. For the German side, cf. Abraham Ascher and Guenter Lewy, 'National Bolshevism in Weimar Germany – alliance of political extremes against democracy', *Social Research*, Winter (1956), 450–80.

[16] Hilde Hardeman, *Coming to Terms with the Soviet Regime – The 'Smenovekhovstvo' Movement among Russian Emigrés in the Early 1920s*, Leuven, Ph.D. Thesis, February 1992.

[17] B. Prianishnikov, *Novopokolentsy*, (Silver Spring MD, 1986); V. S. Varshavskii,

political ideas, this young generation owed a great intellectual debt to European corporatist ideologies of the 1920s, a fact that brought some of them dangerously near to fascism and Nazism. Among these 'post-revolutionary' (as they labelled themselves) movements were first the *Mladorossy* (Young Russians):[18] young monarchists who dreamt of re-establishing a modernized monarchy on the basis of socio-political institutions representing corporate entities and interests (labour, management, peasantry, professionals, businessmen). They proclaimed the primacy of the community over that of the individual, but did not reject individual enterprise, initiative and rights. Without completely rejecting political democracy the *Mladorossy* relied also on a kind of *Führerprinzip*, so that their local and youth organizations were quite authoritarian in imposing discipline and group solidarity on their members. They flirted with Italian fascism and German Nazism (the latter took over what was left of the *émigré* movement in France after the latter's occupation by Germany), but during World War II many made display of Soviet patriotism. Not surprisingly the Mladorossy were suspect in the eyes of most *émigrés* (as well as Western police authorities) and their appeal remained quite limited. It is doubtful that their confused amalgam of fascism and soviet bolshevism, with a very sketchy socio-economic programme, can be of much use or attraction in Russia today. But who knows if 'an emperor with soviets' may not attract remnants of the communist *apparat* and the chauvinist fringe of disgruntled nationalists and imperialists?

Another movement that originated among the young generation of the first emigration in the late 1920s and early 1930s was the National Labor Union (*Natsional'nyi trudovoi soiuz*, or NTS – it changed its name a few times, but this simple title and abbreviation clung to it).[19] Its programme was also a mixture of corporatist, socialist and nationalist elements. The Union tried to establish itself as a political force under the slogan 'neither Hitler nor Stalin' in the areas of the USSR under German occupation during World War II, and in General Vlasov's army when the latter was organized in the very last days of Nazi rule. This uncomfortable (and misguided) association with the Nazi war machine (its main support came from the Wehrmacht and the Foreign Office) precluded success. After the Second World War the NTS has been able to make and maintain some contacts in the Soviet Union. Since the war, too, the NTS has professed genuine belief in, and adherence to, the democratic process, insisting on the rule of law and the guarantee of individual rights and freedoms. In its most recent efforts at formulating a viable political platform the NTS has argued for a liberal constitutional framework and a moderate welfare capitalism. This reorientation in favour of Western inspired democratic and liberal values might make the NTS attractive to professionals and thus become the heir to *Vekhi* and Silver Age liberalism and welfare state corporatism. But its activities in Russia today do not seem to elicit a significant response.

The seizure of power by the Bolsheviks and their victory in the civil war drove the leaders of all pre-1917 parties into emigration. Most reconstituted rump party

Nezamechennoe pokolenie, (New York, 1956).

[18] N. Hayes, 'Kazem Bek and the Young Russian Revolution', *Slavic Review*, 39 (1980), 255–68; P. Petrovich, *Mladorossy* (London Ont., 1973). Cf. also the not entirely satisfactory J. J- Stephan, *The Russian Fascists* (London, 1978).

[19] S. A. Levitsky, 'The ideology of the NTS', *Russian Review*, 31 (1972), 398–405; A. P. Stolypin, *Na sluzhbe Rossii – Ocherki istorii NTS* (Frankfurt/Main, 1986); Catherine Andreyev, *Vlasov and the Russian Liberation Movement – Soviet Reality and* Émigré *Theories*, (Cambridge, Cambridge University Press, 1987).

organizations abroad and reaffirmed their old ideals and programmes. There was but little adjustment to changed circumstances, and not much effort was made to draw the lessons from the revolution and civil war.[20] With the death of the old leaders their parties and programmes disappeared also, and we find practically no traces of them in today's publications. An exception to this generalization, however, may be the Trotskyites and the Mensheviks, although none of their active members lived to see the disintegration of the Soviet system. I have no idea whether Trotskyism has any appeal in Russia today. I would doubt it, as it is too much bound up with Bolshevism and many of the policies of the Soviet regime. As to Menshevism, since it is a form of Western-style Social Democracy, it may prove attractive to those who reject full capitalism and the market economy on moral and cultural grounds, as well as to those who retain faith in some form of collectivism provided it is on a voluntary democratic basis, and respectful of individual rights and freedoms. Menshevism has been traditionally oriented towards the industrial proletariat, it has been quite blind and deaf to the village and the peasantry; one can only speculate about its possible popularity today.[21] Socialism – in the soviet definition – has become a bad word for most citizens of the new Russia, but its moral and economic values should still be very much alive, the more so that they can be connected – in the way populism tried to do in the 19th century – with the traditional communal values of the Russian peasantry.

One form, however, of the social democratic tradition may prove of value and appeal in Russia today. This is a form of Christian socialism that combines the spiritual contents of religion with a distributive approach to justice, equality, and the satisfaction of basic needs. Such a combination also stresses respect for the individual and the person's right to creative freedom and spiritual autonomy, in opposition to the depersonalization of contemporary mass society, the anonymity of urban existence, and the dissolution of creative individuality and expression in mass entertainment and mass media. Its critical view of modern society and civilization has roots in the Russian Silver Age (e.g. the philosophical and critical writings of N. Lossky, N. Berdiaev, S. Bulgakov and S. Frank), as well as in Western Europe's intellectual orientations represented by C. Péguy, E. Mounier, the circles around *Die Tat* and *L'Esprit*. The philosophic-religious premises and values of this trend were formulated in the 1930s in Paris by a group gathered around the journal *Novyi grad* (most particularly G. P. Fedotov, I. I. Fondaminskii, F. A. Stepun, Mother Maria Skobtsova and K. V. Mochulskii).[22] There are many signs that their ideas arouse much interest in Russia – for example the reprinting of Fedotov's writings, the canonization of Mother Maria Skobtsova, and numerous laudatory references to *Novyi grad*'s philanthropic efforts in pre-war France and under German occupation. *Novyi grad* was also uncompromising in its opposition to Stalinism and all excessive manifestations of nationalism and imperialism. On the other hand, it always stressed its patriotic loyalty and commitment to the welfare of Russia and of its peoples. It drew its

[20] Robert C. Williams, *Culture in Exile – Russian émigrés in Germany 1881–1941* (Cornell University Press, 1972); Robert H. Johnston, *New Mecca, New Babylon: Paris and the Russian Exiles 1920–1945* (McGill-Queen's University Press, 1988).

[21] André Liebich, 'Mensheviks, then and now', *Russian Review*, 48 (1989), 67–79; André Liebich, 'Diverging paths: Menshevik itineraries in the aftermath of revolution', *Revolutionary Russia*, IV-1 (1991), 28–37.

[22] M. Raeff, 'L'émigration et la "Cité Nouvelle"' *Cahiers du monde russe et soviétique*, XXIX (1988), 543–52, and more generally, M. Raeff, *Russia Abroad – A Cultural History of the Russian Emigration 1919–1939* (New York, 1990).

inspiration from Russian orthodox spiritual tradition and from the Russian church's role in the Middle Ages in protecting and succouring the people, denouncing injustice, and guarding national culture and independence. It may play now a significant part in fighting crass materialism and cultural vulgarity, primitive collectivism, and callous disregard of social justice and equitable distribution of the national wealth. The ideas of *Novyi grad* hardly constituted a comprehensive political system: their main feature, and to my mind advantage, was their open-endedness, their flexibility in adapting to various political and socio-economic circumstances, while steadfastly preserving fundamental personalistic ethical values. It should appeal to a nation whose traditional social structures have been destroyed, and where the people are searching for new principles to restructure society within a broad traditional framework of values, under a political system that will guarantee individual rights and social harmony.

Are there any conclusions to our survey and discussion? Only two observations perhaps: first, the history of modern Russia has been characterized by a powerful and profound cleavage between, on the one hand, the people who continued to live within the framework inherited from the traditions of Muscovite culture, and, on the other, the intelligentsia, a creation of the process of modernization initiated by Peter the Great. The latter, effectively cut off from the former, endeavoured to impose cultural values and socio-political forms of organization derived from Western European intellectual sources that were totally new to Russia. The victory, in 1917, of one highly ideologized radical segment of the intelligentsia initiated the rule of an ideocracy bent upon 'transfiguring' society and man and, in the process, destroyed both the old intelligentsia and the pre-revolutionary social classes, in particular the peasantry. What emerges from this process will determine the future. We do not know this future, of course, but it suggests my second banal observation. Since the future will be made by social formations whose very shape and essence are still in flux and poorly known and understood, whose ability to give themselves a structure has not been put to the test, and whose cultural (i.e. philosophic, moral, socio-psychological) preferences are as yet undetermined, the future is very open indeed. Yet it is also fair to say, and it is but another aspect of my banal observation, the ideologies elaborated by the pre-1917 intelligentsia, and wellnigh all those doctrines and programmes formulated by the emigration, hardly will have great appeal. We are thus left with the emotional appeals of nationalism and religious faith – but these are only emotions. Important as an element in any viable political and social organization, they do not represent concrete goals and principles for social and political action. Is the veneration that Andrei Sakharaov enjoys posthumously today the harbinger of a politically active pluralist liberalism whose specifics will be worked out in the course of the political debate? We do not know. Not before the dust raised by the great upheaval we are witnessing settles shall we be able to discern the intellectual and political configuration of Russia's future – '*l'homme n'écrit pas sur le sable à l'heure où passe l'aquilon*'.

The United States: Liberals, Conservatives, and the Challenge of Liberation

ROBERT K. FAULKNER*

Boston College, Massachusetts

The old American division of political-intellectual movements into liberal and conservative has had to be supplemented at least since the 1960s, obviously on the Left but also on the Right. Such political causes as multi-culturalism, women's liberation, and environmentalism may tempt liberals, but they are not exactly liberal. There are radical and Marxist feminists as well as liberal feminists, deep ecologists as well as liberal environmentalists, etc. There is also an Old Right and a New Right that are discontented with a conservatism which would conserve the New Deal or even liberal democracy in an earlier sense. One segment would return to the liberalism of the founders (which in the United States has been called conservative since the spread of the progressive liberalism derivative from Mill or Kant), others, to one or another pre-modern tradition.[1]

The present state of these movements, which is the topic of this article, still has much to do with the vast plan for constitutionalism and capitalism that governed the country's founding. It has most to do with those twentieth century reforming imprints, F. D. Roosevelt's New Deal and the liberationism (as we call it) that has found its way into the Supreme Court, many Great Society programmes, and the educational and cultural establishment. The present situation might be very loosely described as a struggle over whether and how far to go back or farther forward. The liberals in 1992 reassembled their divided forces and sects under Presidents Clinton's ambiguous call for 'change' that was not to be simply a return to the liberal call for change. The conservatives, whose rise to power since the fifties culminated in Ronald Reagan's efforts to restore middle class morality, freedom of enterprise and limited government, are licking their wounds and confronting their own divisions. And such movements as those for gay rights and multi-culturalism press a criticism of the repressive and hierarchical rationality of 'Western culture' in ways that would overthrow much of both the original plan and the New Deal's revisions. Liberationism had much to do with the radicalizing, the splits and the defections that have beset liberals since the 60s and 70s, and the efforts of liberals to contain the radicals, and of conservatives to stress growth, defence, patriotism, morality and religion, remain a big part of the present scene.

* Dr. Robert Faulkner is Professor of Political Science at Boston College, Massachusetts, USA.
[1] The author wishes to acknowledge instructive help from friends of various political persuasions, especially from Marc Landy, Daniel J. Mahoney, David Manwaring, and Susan Shell. Jennifer Lacy gave forthright suggestions as well as other assistance.

We will not, then, see an 'end of ideology' while the United States remains the liberal democracy that we know or, for that matter, while human rights, industrialism and power-politics in whatever form continue to expand around the globe. Philosophic doubts about modernity may seep world-wide, but their effect in the United States has been to aggravate the strife over modern political-intellectual creeds, not to allay it. Post-modernism itself proves to be a creed for worldly reform, even if one principally 'critical' or negative. It is also a creed more modern even in substance than is commonly admitted, since it is tied to individualism, albeit as pallid 'autonomy', and to scientific rationality, albeit as historicist 'genealogy' of ideas. Nor will the implosion of Marxist socialism defuse these ideological conflicts. The demise of the Soviet empire removes the leading force behind Marxism, a very great event. But when taken with the defeat of the fascists forty-five years before, this extraordinary collapse leaves the liberal democratic project in its American embodiment the definitive super-power and thus visibly authoritative in the world. No one can say how long such a political situation will last. But it is the situation within which the political question of the demise of modern projects, as opposed to the philosophic question of their truth, has to be now discussed.

The liberal movement just now is an uneasy mixture of two imprints. There is a civil libertarian concern for freedom of expression and for legal protection of the weak, which began in the New Deal and became somewhat radicalized by a liberated attention to 'privacy' and the 'disadvantaged'. There is also the welfare-oriented social planning of the New Deal which became somewhat more redistributive with the Great Society. At the centre of the movement remains a shared concern for increasing equality. Social liberalism looks to an equality in satisfaction of basic needs, the civil libertarian, to equality in safety under the law and now in social respect or dignity irrespective of life-style. At the periphery of this somewhat divided movement are sympathetic little groupings nonetheless critical of one side or another. 'Neo-liberals' (Senator Paul Tsongas is best known) have doubts about the service state. 'Communitarians', mostly professors, have doubts not only about the old individualism of private rights and self-interest, but also about liberals' conversion to the causes of privacy and autonomy.

It was the inability of liberals to draw a line against a liberationism contemptuous of middle-class America that as much as anything led to the unexpected rise of modern conservatism. In the late 1960s and the '70s a certain segment of the liberal intelligentsia either did not move or moved right; they came to be called 'neo-conservatives'. In the '70s a large populist movement, the New Right, was organized for political influence under the leadership of evangelical and fundamentalist Christian preachers. These groupings were potent additions to an unhyphenated conservatism newly rejuvenated during the '50s and '60s. Actually, that too deserved a hyphen or two. For contemporary conservatism has contained since its revival both a somewhat anti-modern traditionalism, itself divided among Burkean, Aristotelian and Catholic tendencies, and a much more powerful impulse, continuing a reaction to the New Deal, to restore the country's original modern plan.

The Conservatives

No doubt the defeat of the Republicans in 1992 was due in good part to the curiously passive and tongue-tied managerialism of President Bush and his advisors. Yet it also exhibited on a broad canvas some characteristic weaknesses of the conservative movement. Bush had constantly to defend himself against the charge that he had neglected domestic hardships of the middle class, especially the recession of 1990–92, and the Bushites's market-oriented theories fostered a pragmatic passivity in domestic affairs. They muffled perceptions about voters' concerns and they hindered imaginative responses, not only to the short-term economic downturn and to questions of fairness in the distribution of income and taxes, but also to the long term problems of the deficit and of the country's competitiveness with the rival economies of Japan and Germany. Also the New Right and the Old Right caused problems. The Christian movement strongly influenced the Republican platform, which recommended a constitutional amendment that would in effect proscribe abortions. The paleo-conservative Patrick Buchanan's speech at the Republican convention, with its language of 'religious war' on behalf of patriotism and against the cultural liberationists, followed upon his primary campaign that had savaged the Bush administration (in the name of 'America First') for devotion to free trade and patronage of Israel. In 1992 the Republicans lost millions of voters that had supported them for three elections before, notably among blue collar Reagan Democrats, socially liberal Republicans (especially women), Jews (including some inclined toward neo-conservatism), and the young who had gravitated toward Reaganite buoyancy.

Ronald Reagan had put together in practice a coalition that had much to divide it in principle. Conservatism had been in the United States ever since Edmund Burke's attacks on the French 'doctors of the rights of man', which influenced Hamilton, John Adams, John Randolph, and many others. It appeared among apologists for Southern gentry, sceptics about the ethos of the self-made man, patriots, isolationists and opposers of the New Deal. Still, the revival of conservatism after the Second War and amidst the consolidation of the New Deal comes not from one father and not chiefly from the South, nor from businessmen as such. George H. Nash told the tale authoritatively.[2] A powerful revival of the theory of free enterprise followed upon Friedrich Hayek's *The Road to Serfdom*, which was a frontal attack on socialism (not just on Marxism). There were also important revulsions from Baconian progress and modern mass society (not just from the socialist versions), notably by Richard Weaver in the name of 'distinction and hierarchy' and pre-Occamite 'transcendental values', and by Leo Strauss in the name of classical philosophy and its accounts of virtue, the philosophic life, and a free republic.[3] In 1953 Russell Kirk's rather Burkean and aristocratic *The Conservative Mind* made the first big public splash. Kirk attacked modern rational planning, egalitarianism and the squalid 'cheapness' of a 'consumption society'; he went on to chronicle the thinkers about England and the United States who 'stood by tradition and old establishments'. Kirk would reverse Sir Henry Maine's dictum and return 'from contract to status'. In a spirit of 'sound prejudice' he defended 'orders and classes', inequality of property, 'suspicion of change', the mystery and variety of 'traditional society' and faith in a 'divine intent' for society.

---

[2] G. H. Nash, *The Conservative Intellectual Movement in America since 1945* (New York, Basic Books, 1976).
[3] R. Weaver, *Ideas Have Consequences* (Chicago, University of Chicago Press, 1948). Of Strauss's many books, those of most general influence are *Natural Right and History* (Chicago, University of Chicago Press, 1953) and *What is Political Philosophy?* (Glencoe, The Free Press, 1959).

But it was William F. Buckley's journal *National Review*, founded in 1955, that provided a megaphone for the newly awakened voices on the right. It provided above all a spirit of 'fusion'. In his first issue Buckley worried about 'the inroads that relativism was making on the American soul', and about the 'ideologues' of 'Social Engineer(ing)' who had won over the 'intellectual class' and the 'Fabian operators' in both parties. His *Review* exhibited a certain scent of traditional and Catholic concern for the soul and its character, a devotion to a 'market economy' and to limited government (limited to providing for the rights of life, liberty, and property), and opposition to 'coexistence' with communism and to the fashionable concepts of internationalism. Buckley could support both Young Americans for Freedom and Alexander Solzhenitsyn. His journal provided a forum for diverse voices to dispute and reconsider, and to work together in practice even if radical libertarians dropped off one side and single-mindedly devout Catholics the other.

Senator Goldwater's presidential campaign of 1964 was a turning point for the movement, despite the crushing defeat. It marked the first nomination of a true devotee (Goldwater had published a book called *The Conscience of a Conservative* that sold 3,500,000 copies by 1964), and in the effort many of the streams joined and took the message to middle America. Four years later Richard M. Nixon was elected by appealing to a 'silent majority' and running not least against the Warren Court and the revolutionaries who disrupted universities, the cities and the Democratic convention. But by that time a variety of formerly liberal intellectuals were becoming alienated by the failure of liberals to stand up to students on campuses and to black mobs in the cities, and to stand up for American policies and allies abroad (not least in Israel). Daniel Patrick Moynihan, Irving Kristol, Nathan Glazer and others had begun the march in once-liberal magazines such as *Commentary* and the *New Republic*, and in new journals such as *The Public Interest*. A sceptical questioning of liberal and liberated nostrums thus became a part of the middle among intellectuals as well. There arose the American Enterprise Institute and the Heritage Foundation to challenge the policy intellectuals at the Brookings Institution. Conservative writers and pundits such as George Will, while distinctly a minority, entered visibly on the public stage. Then, in the late 1970s, in a manner hardly visible to secular and policy-oriented intellectuals, a powerful electoral force grew – or, rather, was organized. Leaders such as Paul Weyrich, Rev. Jerry Falwell and Richard Viguerie mixed religion, media, and mass mailings to rouse a populist and religious New Right. It reached out to tens of millions concerned with the new 'social issues', especially to evangelical Christians opposed to the Warren Court's establishment of a constitutional right to abortion and prohibition of prayer in public schools. There followed in 1980 the mother of all victories for modern conservatives. An explicitly conservative Reagan won the Presidency by defeating the best representative of New Deal liberalism, Carter's Vice-President Walter Mondale, and Republicans won control of the Senate by defeating the most left-liberal Senators, notably George McGovern and Frank Church.

What then is the situation and what are the prospects for the conservative movement after the Reagan attempt at a revolution and the defeat of President Bush? There is no doubt that in foreign affairs the conservatives helped the country succeed beyond their fondest dreams. Castro's Cuba and the other tentacles of Soviet empire are now independent states or barely noticeable irritations. The very Soviet Union is gone. Americans again take public pride in their military forces, the 'Vietnam syndrome' being vigorously attacked, and the arms tested in petty interventions in Grenada and Panama proved to be ingeniously potent and correspondingly popular in Desert Storm. But the conservatives' influence in domestic affairs was and remains inconclusive. Nothing like FDR's consolidation of his New Deal occurred. The Republicans never succeeded in winning the House and by 1986 they had lost the Senate. True, the almost 600 appointments to the judiciary were a conservative triumph, and the five new Supreme Court justices during the Reagan-Bush years moved a Court that had been dominated by Justices William Brennan, Thurgood Marshall, and the rest. Under Chief Justice William Rehnquist, the new majority moved away from some Warren Court activism on behalf of the disadvantaged, away especially from its special solicitude for defendants in criminal cases, and turned somewhat toward the old fixed constitutionalism of separate powers. Still, even this victory was limited. The Rehnquist Court has not reverted in important ways to the pre-New Deal limits on the government's reach over the economy. While it has limited some liberal doctrines concerning privacy, expression and protections for criminals, it extended the liberal interpretation of the First Amendment's protection of speech to include flag-burning, extended the secularist separation of religion from the public order and reaffirmed the right to an abortion according to a right of privacy.[4] The champion of conservative jurisprudence, Robert Bork, was kept off the Court by the Democratic Senate and by a powerful and unprecedented campaign of liberal lobbying, a campaign whose success was nearly repeated during the unprecedently uproarious confirmation hearings of Justice Clarence Thomas.

In other domestic matters the effects of conservative policies were even less conclusive. It is no doubt true that the spending reductions and tax cuts in 1981 were planned by 'supply-side ideologues', as David Stockman's regretful memoir attests,[5] and that the resulting deficit limited social spending somewhat and produced a long boom without the return of the 13% inflation that the chastened Stockman predicted. But it is also true that the welfare state more than survived. If indeed the plan for a 'minimalist government' combined with free markets was the 'central idea' of the Reagan Revolution, as Stockman the erstwhile supply-sider maintained, then the reluctance of people and Congress to cut spending meant the triumph of the enemy. The supply-siders in fact produced a 'free-lunch economics' and the ominous deficit that Stockman accurately foresaw. Similarly, the plans to reduce the centre by turning powers and policies over to the states did not get very far, and the Justice Department's efforts to attack affirmative action were not successful in the courts or in the major institutions of government, business or the academy. Perhaps the greatest effect of the Reagan-Bush presidencies was on morality and morale, restoring the middle class's pride in their country's ways and in particular in the old ways of self-reliance and free government, and this in face of the liberal and liberated orthodoxies. There are now many conservatives on the airwaves and in the political magazines, despite the predominantly liberal tone of both. Nevertheless, the most prominent universities, colleges and law schools have during these years lost much more of the instinct for toleration that graced New Deal liberalism, being increasingly

---

[4] See David Bryden, 'Is the Rehnquist Court conservative?,' and 'A conservative case for judicial activism,' in *The Public Interest* no. 109 (1991), 73–88; No. 111, (1993), 72–85, and Richard E. Morgan, 'Conservative Constitutionalism: The Counter-Revolution That Couldn't' (unpubl. ms.). But see Michael W. McConnell's comprehensive 'The Counter-Revolution in Legal Thought' in *Policy Review* (Summer, 1987) 18–25.

[5] D. Stockman, *The Triumph of Politics* (New York, Harper & Row, 1986), p. 8, p. 406.

possessed of the liberated orthodoxy that was directed against the ruling liberals in the 1960s and '70s and is now militantly hostile to conservatives.

The conservative movement that was in its origins so suspicious of generalization and rational planning is above all an intellectual movement, as James F. Pontuso has remarked,[6] and it has now a settled presence and power in its politicians, journals, and pundits and its publishers, professors and writers. But it has been a coalition of diverse views, diverging as to what part of the American tradition should be conserved. The coalition is now cracked. The most obvious internal conflict is between 'paleo-conservatives' such as Russell Kirk and the late M. E. Bradford (an anti-Lincoln, pro-Confederate lover of the old South), who in the Republican primary of 1992 supported Patrick J. Buchanan, and the free traders and neo-Conservatives. In their antagonism to the neo-cons especially, the paleo-cons have now joined forces in the John Randolph Club with extreme libertarians – 'paleo-libertarians', as they inevitably have been called. The libertarian Murray Rothbard is president of the Club and he has announced that with the new alliance and the political prominence of Buchanan, 'the Old Right is suddenly back'. He means by this 'the Original Right' as it existed from 1933–55, and he defines it as wishing, at a minimum, the 'total abolition of the New Deal'. Others of the Old Right would get rid of Woodrow Wilson's Federal Reserve System and 'that mighty instrument of tyranny, the income tax and the Internal Revenue Service'; Rothbard himself would continue on to repeal the authority of the federal judiciary over state courts (which dates to 1789) and maybe even 'restore the good old Articles of Confederation'.[7] This is conservatism as 'the radical Right'. The 'word "conservative" is unsatisfactory', according to Rothbard, for it conserves what 'left-liberals have accomplished'. Rothbard attacks expressly the fusion that the *National Review* promoted, for that fusion subordinated the Old Right to the neo-cons. But 'we' want to 'uproot the status quo, not conserve it', we old 'individualists, or "true liberals", or Rightists'. It may be that the two schools in the Old Right share an animosity towards the neo-con patronage of interventions abroad and of welfare programmes and public support for the arts at home, and toward a federal government occupied with leveling. But it is hard to believe that the radical rationalism of the libertarians, and their animosity toward all but minimal government, will not clash with the aristocratic, Christian and agrarian traditions powerful among the Southerners and those influenced by Burke.[8]

As a columnist Patrick Buchanan had inveighed against pet projects of the neo-conservatives. He criticized the war against Iraq, suggested that American policy tilted in favour of Israel and its 'amen-corner', and rejected any internationalist crusade for democracy as 'messianic globaloney'. By 1991 he was also attacking the free-marketeers, especially their devotion to free trade, and advocating a 'protectionist' strategy. His campaign in the Republican primary wounded an already weak Bush. He attacked the President for violating his no-tax pledge, advocated tariffs and other protectionist measures in dealing with the Japanese, and attacked the National Endowment for the Arts for funding an artist who produced a cross hung in urine. This, like Buchanan's gibes at gays and

    [6] Mark J. Rozell and James F. Pontuso (eds), *Conservatism After Reagan* (Boulder, San Francisco; London, Westview Press, 1990), p. 4.
    [7] From a speech to the John Randolph Club, January, 1992, quoted in *National Review*, March 16, 1992, S-28ff.
    [8] Here I rely considerably on Judis's 'The conservative crack-up,' in *The American Prospect*, Fall (1990), 30–42.

his proclamation at the Republican Convention of a religious war over culture, caused a series of storms. In particular, columnists including Norman Podhoretz, the editor of *Commentary*, called Buchanan anti-Semitic and demanded that Buckley and the *National Review* repudiate him. Although the magazine (now under the editorship of John O'Sullivan) endorsed Buchanan's candidacy as a tactical move to push Bush from the middle, Buckley in an enormous article reviewed the whole problem of anti-Semitism on the right and eventually acknowledged that what Buchanan had said and done 'amounted to anti-Semitism'. In a moving open letter Podhoretz acknowledged himself 'relieved' (if not fully satisfied) and went on to acknowledge Buckley's 'very honourable record', even his 'high statesmanship', in leading with *National Review* the struggle 'to cleanse the conservative movement of anti-Semitism' for which it had before provided a 'rather comfortable home'.[9] Another kind of attack on Buchanan's version of the Old Right was made during the primary campaign by William J. Bennett, a prominent Catholic neo-conservative who had been Reagan's Secretary of Education. True Reaganism, he said, involved an 'active internationalism', 'free and open trade', a rather open immigration policy, and concern for 'problems in the inner city'. It involved not least 'a spirit of optimism and cheerfulness, good-spiritedness' and 'pluckiness', which had reversed the angry, brooding, and 'anti'-mood typical of conservatism prior to Reagan.[10] Still, there is a growing sentiment that conservatives must make a stand against the waves of immigrants, legal and illegal, pouring into the country.

Divisions exist not only between the Old Right and the rest, but also between the neo-conservatives and the 'supply-siders'. The neo-conservatives were sceptical of ideology, from their experience with the liberation movements, and not least of laissez-faire ideology, as children of the New Deal and democratic socialism. They were not unsympathetic with social policy. But free enterprise economists such as Milton Friedman and George Gilder are perhaps the most influential strand within modern conservatism, if only by virtue of mutual affinities with powers in the world of business. These economists may not be libertarian, but in cases such as Friedman's they are touched by contemporary libertarianism: they would leave things moral, intellectual and political, as well as economic, to the presumed harmony of markets. Friedman would decriminalize drug use. The old-time political economy, of an Adam Smith or an Alexander Hamilton, attended to the moral and political prerequisites of a free economy. It was not, as Friedman declared himself in *Capitalism and Freedom*, in principle 'against coercion in any form' or against regulation of monopoly, or, as he also declared himself, for 'complete free trade in goods and services' or for leaving the existence of parks to the forces of supply and demand.[11] Gilder, on the other hand, is no such libertarian. He has urged against the economic libertarians 'the moral and familial values on which all capitalist systems rely for their success'. He has urged against the feminists the necessity of facing up to natural differences between the sexes and to the importance for the happiness of both women and men, and for the sound upbringing of children, of men in marriage.[12]

[9] *National Review*, March 16 (1993), S-12.
[10] See also Bennett's *Our Children and Our Country* (New York, Simon & Shuster, 1988), pp. 217–34.
[11] M. Friedman, *Capitalism and Freedom* (Chicago and London, The University of Chicago Press, 1962), pp. 29, 31.
[12] G. Gilder, *Men and Marriage* (Graestra, Pelican, 1986), p. 196; Gilder's best known book is *Wealth and Poverty* (Toronto, Bantam Books, 1982).

Neo-conservatives such as Kristol, Nathan Glazer and the jurisprudes Alex Bickel and Robert Bork had been sceptical of apparently simple moral principles. They were certainly sceptical of an orientation by rights, which reflected an order that they inclined to think historically obsolete, or which had been expanded into a panoply of claims to self-expression, 'privacy' and welfare. Kristol had at least recurred to earlier models of capitalism, praising repeatedly the moral and political richness of Adam Smith's political economy. Yet he expressed doubts even as to the original, fearing especially that bourgeois capitalism corroded the moral capital on which it depended. While indeed as American as apple pie, capitalism had become corporate and removed for the most part from individual enterprises. Executives and workers warmed to the security thus provided, the acquisitive instinct itself waning in affluent society. Kristol gave only 'two cheers for capitalism', and he defended it on grounds political rather than economic: in the age of the increasingly centralized democratic state, corporate capitalism diffuses power and thus gives 'space' for individual liberties.[13] But it does not or cannot inspire its adherents. Its functionaries are not very 'heroic' or attractive, and it somehow corrodes even the work ethic on which it depends. Gilder's arguments as to the virtues required by capitalism were in part directed to this criticism, and Kristol's views have changed somewhat. Under his influence *The Public Interest* had printed in the 1970s essays by the supply-siders Arthur Laffer and Jude Waniski. In 1981 Kristol himself defended supply-side economics, as a 'humanistic' account of the entrepreneurial ambitions and economic arrangements that promote growth, against the established 'mathematical-mechanical' economics, which merely relates by equations various economic aggregates.[14]

The tensions between free-marketeers and neo-conservatives are especially visible in the realm of constitutional jurisprudence. A variety of professors have urged a return to the 'original intent' or 'original understanding' of the Constitution. But only a few, led by Bernard Siegan, Richard Posner and Richard Epstein, would recur to the priority of property rights and free markets in such a way as to overturn the supposedly unauthorized judicial constructions of two hundred years, especially the constructions of the New Deal and Warren Courts. Epstein, for example, finds the very cornerstone of the Constitution to be the 'takings clause' of the Fifth Amendment – 'nor shall private property be taken for public use without just compensation', – contends that Locke's understanding of the priority of property rights is the spirit of the Constitution, and advocates a 'level of judicial intervention far greater than we now have, and indeed far greater than we have had'. Because of disproportionate levies that amount to 'takings' the Court should strike down the minimum wage, the progressive income tax, the National Labor Relations Act, and even 'the ultimate citadel', welfare programs.[15] In an orientation by Constitution and original understanding, the property rights school is similar to some of the neo-conservatives, to those influenced by Herbert Storing, Martin Diamond and Robert Bork, for example. But Storing and Diamond attended to the strong if limited government that was the Constitution's primary concern, dwelling on a

[13] I. Kristol, 'On corporate capitalism in America,' *The Public Interest*, no. 41 (1975) 139–40.
[14] I. Kristol, 'Ideology and supply-side economics,' *Commentary*, 71, (1981), 48–54.
[15] R. Epstein, *Takings: Private Property and the Power of Eminent Domain* (1983). See Lane V. Sunderland, 'Contemporary Constitutional Commentators and the Philosophy of the Constitution: *Public Interest Law Review* (1991), 121–146. See also Michael McConnell's account of the "law and economics" schools, in "The Counter-Revolution in Legal Thought", 23–24.

Hamiltonian mixture of effectual institutions with popular representation and understanding the protection of individual rights as merely a guiding spirit. Bork, on the other hand, while an originalist, was wary of any importation of rights from without. He tended to hold that judges should be guided by what was explicit in the Constitution, or at most by 'core values' there indicated and not to be extended in generality beyond the original understanding.[16] Fearful like his influential friend Alexander Bickel of the egalitarian and libertarian rights talk of the 60s and 70s, Bork turned to the Constitution without much attending to the constitutionalism of the original constitutionalists. He like Bickel emphasized instead a rather formal deference to political bodies and democratic majorities. Bickel, a law professor at Yale and perhaps the most influential of neo-conservative constitutionalists before his death at 49 in 1974, himself had turned against Warren Court constitutionalism. But he disdained originalism because of his belief in evolving law and society and struggled unsuccessfully to provide some better guidance for the modern judge. He had been a believer in evolving idealism judicially imposed, and he remained a supporter of *Brown v. Board*. But he was repelled by the general egalitarianism of the Warren Court, especially its redistricting of legislatures according to one man-one vote, and its life-style libertarianism, especially the new priority it gave to privacy, self-expression, and the exclusion of morals and religion from public schools. He moved toward social conservatism and away from legalism altogether. In his last little book Bickel praised Burke's attention to virtue, hierarchy, and the small platoon, and he sought to develop a 'morality of consent' that would foster tolerance and respect for democratic institutions.[17] Where that left the Constitution was unclear.

This emphasis upon society and mores (rather than economy and law) is not unusual among the neo-conservatives, perhaps because many were once socialists or sociologists. Robert Nisbet, a sociologist, has with others revived the authority of Tocqueville and in particular the famous warning that democracies breed a despotic and centralized government mixed with an atomized society of soft and needy individuals. There has been a loss of community in modern times, and this, coupled with the pre-eminence of the modern state, breeds a dangerous readiness for new despotisms. Nisbet would cultivate 'intermediate institutions' such as family, firm, church, province, and city.[18] One should also notice James Q. Wilson's turn to reconsider the importance of moral character and the family, and the broad political-constitutional thinking that was displayed in two numbers of *The Public Interest*, the first celebrating the Revolution and the extraordinary second, the Constitution.[19] This journal of the neo-conservatives had been founded in their first sceptical impulse, sceptical especially of ideology; it was infused with what might be called public policy incrementalism. These two numbers, led by Martin Diamond's 'The Declaration and the Constitution: Liberty, Democracy, and the Founders', showed an awakening respect for the

[16] See R. Bork, *The Tempting of America, The Political Seduction of the Law* (New York and London, The Free Press/Collier Macmillan, 1990).

[17] A. Bickel, *The Morality of Consent* (New Haven, Yale University Press, 1975); see Faulkner, 'Bickel's constitution: the problem of moderate liberalism,' *American Political Science Review* 72 (1978), 925.

[18] See J. David Hoeveler, Jr., *Watch on the Right, Conservative Intellectuals in the Reagan Era* (Madison, University of Wisconsin Press, 1991), pp. 177–206: R. Nisbet, *The Quest for Community* (New York, Oxford University Press, 1953).

[19] J. Q. Wilson, *On Character* (Washington, AEI Press, 1991); 'The American Commonwealth, 1976,' *The Public Interest*, no. 41 Fall (1975); 'The Constitutional Order', *The Public Interest* no. 86, Winter (1987).

comprehensive political ideas and plans behind the original American institutions of government and economy. The essays also showed doubts about the activism of the recent Supreme Court, the dominance of a sluggish Congress, the effects on mores and citizenship of a preoccupation with self-interest and work, and the contemporary disintegration of the family.

In general, the neo-conservatives are like the old traditionalist Right and the new evangelical Right, but not most free enterprisers, in their concern with a moral-political crisis. They too are involved in the 'culture wars'. Both Kirk's Burkean traditionalism and Buckley's fusion of religion, tradition and free enterprise arose in protest against contemporary equalizing and collectivizing, and yet both, in their respect for Christianity, aristocratic ways and the liberal arts, show some longing for a pre-modern tradition altogether. The neo-Conservatives arise especially in reaction to the liberationists' egalitarianism and libertarianism and to their critique of 'Western civilization' generally. Some, such as Hilton Kramer (founder of the critical journal of the arts, *New Criterion*), would restore the best of modern art and culture. Others, such as Diamond and Thomas Pangle, would revive the comprehensive political thought of the founders of the American nation, but in the prudential spirit of Aristotelian or Platonic political philosophy. And others, especially Irving Kristol, the most influential neo-conservative, 'believe the secular era is fading', oppose especially the relentless attempts at secularization by liberals in the American Civil Liberties Union, regret the turn of the mainstream churches to modernity just as modernity itself is undergoing a 'spiritual collapse', and would have American conservatives lead in restoring a tactful toleration that is able to respect the spiritual dimension of life.[20]

The Liberals

Clinton ran in '92 as a new kind of Democrat, but not exactly as a liberal. Part of the novelty of the 'change' he advocated lay in appearing not as a tax and spend Democrat and not in the pocket of 'special interests', especially of labour unions and of blacks of the Jesse Jackson type. Still, he was to some extent of the liberated mold. He sent signals of favour to gays, even if he barely mentioned them, and he was open about his ties to the woman's movement. His strategy was miles better than Dukakis's in '88. Dukakis had said the issue was competence, not ideology, and the Republicans had ridiculed the unutterable as the 'L-word' and ridiculed him and his Massachusetts liberalism as weak on crime (tacitly on black urban crime), patriotism, and defence; hence the powerful TV ads about Willie Horton, the flag, and the tank ride. Liberals and liberalism have remained on the defensive throughout the Reagan-Bush years, but both are out of the closet with the Clinton presidency. They have been attacked from the Right and the Left, for taxing and spending and being too soft on the counter-culture and on defence, and for being 'cold war' or unliberated liberals, who retain something of the sexism, racism and repression associated with western civilization and American imperialism. While some liberals of the 60s moved Right to become

      [20] I. Kristol, 'Christmas, Christians, and Jews,' *National Review*, December 30 (1988), 27; Kristol, *Reflections of a Neoconservative* (New York, Basic Books, 1983), p. 326; Hoeveler, *Watch on the Right*, pp. 81–142; Pangle, *The Spirit of Modern Republicanism* (Chicago and London, The University of Chicago Press, 1988), *The Ennobling of Democracy, The Challenge of the Postmodern Era* (Baltimore and London, The Johns Hopkins University Press, 1992).

neo-conservatives, and a number returned to the Democrats when a new kind of Democrat ran, most moved to the Left to become advocates for women, blacks, Hispanics, gays, and others who claimed to be victims of the dominant culture. When Theodore White went to the Democratic Convention in 1980 he found the party offices at the Statler in Detroit a rabbit warren of disparate offices for 'cause lobbies and political action committees'. This was not by pluralistic accident but in accord with an idealism of 'participation', an idea that benefited chiefly minorities and was inevitably offensive to the majority. White called the Democrats a 'party that had lost its way'. He called his wonderful account of the election of Reagan, and of the crack-up over 25 years of the Democratic party, *America in Search of Itself.* 'By the time of the 1980 election, the pursuit of equality had created a system of interlocking dependencies, and the American people were persuaded that the cost of equality had come to crush the promise of opportunity.'[21] Liberals were in danger of ceding the defence of the country, the Constitution, and the economy to modern conservatives and of finding themselves so devoted to the alienated as to be partisans of the country's adversaries and an adversary culture. It was perhaps with this in mind that President Clinton's inaugural address in 1993 placed his plans within the country's long effort to provide for 'life, liberty, and the pursuit of happiness'. He is supposed to be an admirer of Lincoln, and Lincoln's calling of the Union to the old cause of the Declaration is not a bad model for a Democratic President in Clinton's situation.

Liberalism has been undergoing attempts at corrective surgery. The President had himself become chairman in 1990 of the Democratic Leadership Council, an association founded in 1984 of moderate or conservative Democrats, many Southern. According to its affiliated research body, the Progressive Policy Institute, the DLC's programme involves 'opportunity', 'reciprocal responsibility' and 'entrepreneurial government'. Such an outlook reflects two movements connected with modern liberalism as more or less friendly critics, the neo-liberals and the communitarians. The neo-liberals revolve about the *Washington Monthly* and its editor Charles Peters. The communitarians are a rather more academic and struggling grouping led by professors such as Amitai Ezioni, William Galston, and Mary Ann Glendon (all among the editors of a house journal, *The Responsive Community,* which first appeared in the winter of 1990–1). Both of these schools share much of the modern liberal concern for equality (hence they are not neo-conservatives although the neo-liberals sometimes come close), but doubt some traditional liberal means.

We have to 'retain our goals', Peters said in a 'A Neoliberal's Manifesto', 'but to abandon some of our prejudices'.[22] No longer should liberals *automatically* favour public school teachers, civil servants, unions, big government and larger programmes while opposing big business and the military, or believe that all the poor are deserving, or bleed for the criminal, or prefer government by administrators and courts to government by politics. The neo-liberal thus questions in contemporary circumstances the old New Deal priority of administration and programmes, especially programmes ministering to those

[21] Theodore H. White, *America in Search of Itself* (New York, Warner Books, 1983), pp. 419, 333.
[22] C. Peters, 'A neo-liberal's manifesto', *The Washington Monthly,* May (1983), 9–18; see also Peters' 'The second coming of neo-liberalism,' *New York Times Sunday Magazine,* January 17 (1993), and the last two chapters of his *Tilting at Windmills, An Autobiography* (Reading, Addison-Wesley, 1988).

supposed to be socially disadvantaged. He takes seriously problems that New Deal liberals typically did not: low productivity, the rise of a querulous and expensive adversarial culture, the rise of a staid and soft society fixed on seniority and credentials, 'indifference to performance'. He also takes seriously problems that did occupy the old liberals, such as the excessive disparity between executive salaries and worker wages. Peters advocates worker ownership of firms where possible, suggests that half of civil service jobs be opened to political appointment, and can say that 'our hero is the risk-taking entrepreneur' and even that 'risk is the essence of the movement'. The neo-liberals seem young Turks amidst dullards and sclerotic bureaucracies and remind us of the vigour and ambition (but not of the confidence in social planning) of the young Turks of the '30s.

A recent book by Mickey Kaus, a protégé of Peters, exemplifies their eclecticism. In *The End of Equality* Kaus suggests that economic inequalities are inevitable and that the very programme that liberals favour will increase it. Both 'skills-based' training and increasing opportunities for able women themselves foster meritocracy.[23] Liberals should at least acquiesce in the inevitable. They must also give up their faith in social conditioning and face up to ineradicable and often inherited differences in ability and intelligence. They must also give up their faith in redistributing and face up to the fact that a focus on equalizing incomes neglects the incentives needed for growth and may not make society as a whole better off. It is almost surprising after this that Kaus remains devoted to equality, but it is rather diluted stuff, a 'social equality' with incomes off limits. Not economic equality but equality of dignity should be the priority, and thus steps such as the draft or compulsory national service, which encourage everyday association among those of different social status. Kaus actually limits even these tendencies. For the public interest or common good is perhaps more important than individual rights, and character, not programmes alone, is needed for the underclass. The work ethic is particularly important. Here Kaus explicitly refers to the neo-conservative Charles Murray, whose *Losing Ground* (1984) held that the big Great Society programmes, especially aid to single mothers, made things worse. Kaus concludes: neither welfare, nor work 'incentives', nor work 'requirements', nor work 'experience', nor workfare, work. Eliminate Aid to Families with Dependent Children. 'Only work works'.[24]

While neo-liberals look toward individual initiative and the market, albeit sometimes with averted eyes, the communitarians criticize the individualism of both the free enterpriser's self-interest and the contemporary liberal's autonomy. In the name of democratic community they attack 'the whole idea of the unencumbered self'.[25] If the neo-liberal would reinvent government, the communitarian would rejuvenate social cooperation and citizenship. William Galston was an issues advisor to Mondale in '84 and to the Clinton campaign as well, and much of that campaign's language of 'family', 'community' and 'hard work' came from the communitarians. So also did proposals for voluntary national service, workfare, replacement of the welfare system as we know it, reduction of the place of special interest groups, and 'fairness': an expectation

[23] M. Kaus, *The End of Equality* (New York, New Republic/Basic Books, 1992).

[24] M. Kaus, 'The work ethic state,' *The New Republic*, July 7 (1986), 22–33. I have benefited from James Q. Wilson's 'Redefining equality: The liberalism of Mickey Kaus,' *The Public Interest*, no. 109, (1992), 101–8.

[25] Michael Sandel, *Liberalism and the Limits of Justice* (Cambridge, Cambridge University Press 1982); cf. 'Morality and the liberal ideal,' *New Republic*, May 7 (1984), 17–19.

that the fortunate will, as Galston put it delicately, participate in the 'task of national renewal'.[26] The purport for taxes and politics is democratic and non-hierarchical, and reminds us most of Rousseau's democratic citizenship (despite some talk of Aristotle). The point is a 'more participatory, more cooperative, and less competitive democratic governance'. If the neo-liberal's animus is chiefly against a creaking welfare state, the communitarian's is against the privacy-oriented liberalism of, say, the American Civil Liberties Union. In early issues of *The Responsive Community* Galston makes a 'liberal-democratic case for the two-parent family'. Marc Landy would foster democratic citizenship by devolving political administration to the lowest level of government and encouraging senior officials to be 'civic educators'. In her book *Rights Talk* Mary Ann Glendon attacks the 'absolute' priority given rights by attacking the contemporary 'dialect of rights' that focuses on the 'lone rights-bearer'. Glendon's effort is to recover older 'languages', notably the several 'indigenous languages of relationship and responsibility' that within the family, for example, can 'refine' an imperialistic but corrosive individualism. This like other efforts of the communitarians is less about government, to say nothing of ruling, than about moral suasion for civic responsibility. According to Sarah Ferguson of the *Nation*, the word 'responsibility' occurred more than 20 times in the address with which candidate Clinton accepted the Democratic nomination. Indeed, the communitarians seem to shrink from governing, and this keeps them from insisting that responsibilities be performed and that only responsible communities be fostered and upheld. 'The responsive community is not coercive'. Policies are to be accepted because they are 'legitimate', not because they are 'enforced'.[27]

Galston is a professor of political philosophy and it is important to see that he (and Michael Sandel) have challenged the peculiarly rights-based and redistributive liberalism that has dominated debate among academic liberals since John Rawls' *A Theory of Justice*. Rawls had maintained that inequalities might be justified only if they were used to overcome the disadvantages of less equal selves, understood as equally possessed of rights. Sandel and Galston argue that people are to some extent constituted by social or civic roles such as that of son or citizen, and that responsibilities as well as rights are coeval with selves. Rights do not trump all ideas of the good. Human beings (as Aristotle said) are to be understood as social and as citizens and not as merely unencumbered selves. Galston addresses also Rawls' attempt to 'bracket' the question of liberalism's truth in the face of relativism and historicism; Rawls' later articles depart from the foundationalism of *A Theory of Justice*. Is such a move faithful to the 'specific public culture' that Rawls' thinking is now committed to defend, the old liberal tradition of self-evident and universal rights, or even to the human wish for the truly good and thus the truth?[28]

Whatever be the intellectual penetration of the neo-liberals and the communitarians, their penetration into the liberal establishment is by no means assured. It is quite unlikely. As the Clinton presidency proceeds, there are complaints from new Democrats that after the campaign Clinton has reverted to 'shibboleths', such as affirmative action to achieve diversity, and is snubbing his old allies from the DLC.[29]

[26] W. Galston, *The Chronicle of Higher Education*, December 2 (1992), A52.
[27] *The Responsive Community, Rights and Responsibilities*, Winter (1990/91), 3.
[28] W. Galston, 'Pluralism and social unity', *Ethics*, July (1989), 711–26.
[29] John Judis, 'The Old Democrat,' *The New Republic*, February 22 (1993).

What is certain is that much of the liberal movement wants to begin again where it left off, to 'reclaim liberalism,' as Robert Kuttner put it while attacking neoliberalism in *The American Prospect*, 'without prefixes, qualifiers, or apologies'.[30] The liberals of the old school incline to press for economic equality through control and regulation (with an animus against economic individualism), and to press for social equality by law and consciousness-raising (with an animus against middle class morals). A problem for liberalism is the conflict between these two, between the old New Deal or Great Society types and the newer 'life-style' liberals, and another problem is the difficulties intrinsic to each, not least the difficulty that both are inclined to replace liberal democracy as we have known it.

To start where Great Society liberals left off, according to Kuttner, means returning to 'egalitarian goals and interventionist means', with a fundamental suspicion of private concentrations of wealth and power and the market organization of the economy. True, a bad press continues for the old liberal era, questioning its guilt-ridden foreign policy, failed social programmes, and automatic deference to those claiming the status of victims. Kuttner attacks the press and contends: (1) that the liberal travail over Vietnam was basically a spontaneous reaction to a now discredited war; (2) that the universality of Medicare and Social Security ('bribes' for the middle class according to some neoliberals) provides the political support needed for subsidies to the poor; (3) that Galston's 'demonizing' of 'liberal fundamentalists' such as civil rights groups and feminists plays into the hands of conservatives; and (4) that the major flaws in civil rights, Medicare, and anti-poverty programmes resulted from doing too little and compromising too much. There is no good reason to question liberal egalitarianism, in short, and democratizing of society requires more equalizing and regulating of what has hitherto been the private sector.

In Kuttner's thrust and parry one sees the zeal within real liberals and also a tendency beyond liberalism. Present day liberalism seems an unstable mixture in process of transformation by its advocates. They are for progress beyond it or to a new vision of it, be that Kuttner's rather socialist hope for democratic society or the civil libertarian's hope for liberated society. One may find the occasional effort to restore the old liberal tradition that focused on liberty or equal rights of the individual, the tradition of Locke, Jefferson, Lincoln, John Stuart Mill.[31] To one such attempt Kuttner replied in a not atypical way, even if his socialism is atypically thorough-going: liberalism is not an 'ideal type' but an evolving system, and the evolution into the liberalism of social insurance, social policy and union power owed a lot to democratic socialism. One must go forward, for to go back is to go the way of Mickey Kaus, i.e., to become a 'convert to conservative fantasies of market meritocracy or ungrounded genetic theories of intelligence'.[32] Liberals must avoid falling back with the neo-conservatives into inequalities and a government too limited to promote real equality. They must understand that 'capitalism is a system' and has to be reduced wholesale.

---

[30] R. Kuttner,'The poverty of neoliberalism,' *The American Prospect*, Summer (1991), 6–10. This new journal is meant to aid in the revival of liberalism. In its inaugural issue co-editor Paul Starr (the other editor is Kuttner) quoted Walter Lippmann on the need for 'vision' and said that *The American Prospect* will expound the ways to 'national renewal' by public means, especially by 'creative government' as opposed to 'private virtues', 'conservative policies', and the 'casino capitalism' of the eighties (Winter, 1990, 7).

[31] See Stephen Holmes' 'The liberal idea,' *The American Prospect*, Fall (1991), 81–96.

[32] Quoted by Wilson, 'Redefining equality', 104.

Liberalism must reject the liberalism of free markets and of opportunity – while avoiding the 'command economies' and 'dictatorship' of the Marxist versions of socialism. According to Kuttner, progressive taxation and the welfare state cannot make a liberal democracy equal enough. 'A bigger dose of social democracy would enrich liberalism, not confuse it'.

Among the civil libertarians, on the other flank, a similar development occurs: the scope and content of liberty and law are to be revised with a view to 'moral progress'. Former Supreme Court Justice William Brennan was for three decades the most influential liberal of this kind. According to Brennan, the United States and in particular its Constitution should be understood in the light of 'the sparkling vision of the human dignity of every individual'.[33] This means that individuals should above all be freed from repressive stereotypes or other badges of unequal status, and that federal judges should enforce this spirit in their protections of due process, equal rights and other relevant provisions of the Constitution. Only during the last few decades, we observe, have the courts treated as presumptively unconstitutional a state's discrimination, say, between male and female on pay or ability to act as parent, illegitimate and legitimate children with respect to a right to inherit, married and unmarried on the availability of contraceptives, residents and non-residents on eligibility for welfare, and voters of more or less voting power with respect to apportionment by district. Rights of a new sort appeared: a right to be free of the stigma of inferiority that causes psychological suffering, rights of 'privacy', 'self-expression', and even satisfaction of 'basic needs'. One can speak of entitlements, rights not merely to the opportunities of civil society or to some minimal relief, but to be treated as if possessing equal dignity as a human being. And one can speak of a focus especially on a right to things intimate, such as abortion, pornography and contraceptives, without any qualification from notions of 'social worth' or of 'a worthy person', or, in general, from 'moral prejudice'. The judge's preferences should be with the disadvantaged and in particular with all who are despised or victims before custom and morals. Even as to criminals, according to Brennan, 'there is no better test of a society than how it treats those accused of transgressing against it'. Liberty and equality are radicalized into what Brennan himself calls libertarianism and egalitarianism. They reflect a counter-culture at war with traditional creeds and morals, not least religious creeds, sexual morals and moral judgements (which tend to be disdained as 'majority' judgements).

It is true that Brennan holds this to be the authentic vision of the Constitution, but it is also true that he regards a 'ratification' by 'contemporary' views as the proof of this. He attacked the conservatives' efforts to revert to the 'original intent' of the Constitution, helped enlarge the old 'political question' doctrine that had limited judicial action, focused on the historical development of a moral consensus, and evinced a burning animus against the 'moral prejudice of bygone centuries' (which looked more favourably on legitimates than illegitimates), or 'the long and unfortunate history of sex discrimination' in America (which kept women 'not on a pedestal, but in a cage'). Rights-oriented liberalism as Justice Brennan practised it was to get the country beyond the old moral hierarchies, the old fixed understandings of the Constitution and the amendments, and the old authority of governments to regulate and enforce mores and morals.

---

[33] The discussion of Brennan's views draws on Faulkner, 'Difficulties of equal dignity: the court and the family,' in Robert A. Goldwin and William A. Schambra (eds), *The Constitution, the Courts, and the Quest for Justice* (Washington, American Enterprise Institute, 1989), pp. 93–115.

Such a jurisprudence now predominates in prominent law schools and law journals and is likely to be influential for generations to come. Among writers on constitutional law such as Lawrence Tribe, Michael Perry, Bruce Ackerman and a host of other professors, the older task of social reform is taken for granted and now surpassed by the contemporary task of providing new rights. Perry's work provides an example. He simply supposes unconstitutional the limits put by the pre-New Deal judiciary on Congress's powers over the economy (the limitation, for example, of the commerce power fundamentally to regulations of and for commerce). He is chiefly concerned to justify a 'non-interpretive' power for judges with respect to 'human rights', and this 'extra-constitutional' authority is where the stakes are high. The justification has to do with the 'moral evolution' of the 'American people's understanding of themselves', which is a 'vision', a source of 'meaning in the sense of existential orientation or rootedness'. What is striking is both the hazy supposition of moral progress (the Court is to look not simply to 'the sediment of old moralities' but ahead 'to emergent principles' of 'a new moral order') and the 'religious' significance given to creed and Supreme Court (the Americans are a modern 'chosen people' that needs 'to be called to judgment' and this task, the Court's, is 'the task of prophecy').[34]

However Perry's formulations might strike a Jefferson, a Hamilton, or an FDR, they illustrate how in our time the old foundations of liberalism in natural rights and self-interest have been replaced by something analogous to religious devotion and sectarian moralism. Almost any smoker in middle class surroundings can feel this, as can anyone who maintains publicly an argument for the superiority of men or the inferiority of gays. The phenomenon goes deep, and the depth of the problem is visible in those occupied with the foundations of liberalism, the professors of liberal philosophy.

For twenty years the most famous liberal philosopher in the United States has been John Rawls, rivaled only recently by Richard Rorty, and both Rawls and Rorty now reject the possibility of any philosophic foundations for liberal democracy. Both confront thematically the difficulties posed by value relativism and by historicism. It is a question, as Rorty puts it, whether 'liberal institutions and culture' can 'survive the collapse of the philosophic justification that the Enlightenment provided for them'.[35] But both then turn to support democracy by resting it on 'judgments' or 'moral intuitions' that are merely relative and parochial. Such perceptions result from our 'specific public culture' (Rawls), or 'the moral intuitions of a particular historical community' that has created our institutions (Rorty). Out of loyalty to democracy these professors of philosophy turn from inquiry to rest upon, indeed to insist upon, mere belief. One of Rorty's telling arguments on the subject is called 'The Priority of Democracy to Philosophy'. Both he and Rawls defend democracy neither as best nor as reasonable in the circumstances, for either argument would make democracy depend upon argument or a reason. 'We' are liberal democrats because of our contingent and historical attachment to a certain culture or community.

This strange mixture of rational scepticism and insistence on historically given traditions recalls Burke, and Rawls and Rorty can be found defending a kind of

---

[34] M. Perry, *The Constitution, the Courts, and Human Rights* (New Haven and London, Yale University Press, 1982); I have drawn on the description of Perry's jurisprudence in Sunderland, 'Contemporary Constitutional Commentators.'

[35] R. Rorty, 'The priority of democracy to philosophy,' in Merrill D. Peterson and Robert C. Vaughan, (eds), *The Virginia Statute for Religious Freedom* (Cambridge, Cambridge University Press, 1988), p. 259.

practical prudence ('a reflective equilibrium') or quoting Michael Oakeshott as to the value of 'theoretical muddle for the health of the state'. But, as Rorty's explicit deference to the eclectic social democrat John Dewey illustrates, neither returns to Burkean politics. There is nothing in their thought much like Burke's defence of religion, gentlemanly virtue, free enterprise, constitutionalism and hierarchy. On the contrary, both Rorty and Rawls are peculiarly principled or moral in defending the 'justice', the 'democratic liberty', the 'moral progress', of the American tradition as they understand it. The core of the tradition proves to be the social provision of equal rights for all. In Rawls' work, for example, the first principle of justice has to do with equal rights to political and social goods, of which not a mere formal opportunity but some 'fair value' must be provided, and the most important of the 'primary goods' to which all citizens are entitled is the 'social basis of self respect'.[36] Rawls proceeds to reformulate constitutionalism into a means of promoting such rights and promotes the judicial branch as the leading authority in applying the constitution – and even in defining the constitution. 'Where rights are trumps, it is judges who take the tricks', as Clifford Orwin and James R. Stoner, Jr, put it, at least until the well-ordered society and its well-disposed representatives have arrived.[37] Since such legislators are to legislate very idealistically, without regard for their ambition or interests or even for the interests of their constituents, governance by judges may be with us for some time if Rawls' theories are followed. Where the rights are rather egalitarian in tenor, and especially egalitarian as to status, judges are decisively patrons of equality and especially of those hitherto looked down upon – the 'disadvantaged', 'marginalized' or 'other', to use terms now current.

For his part, Rorty argues that precisely our liberation from rational 'foundationalism' can lead to 'the end of ideology' and thus to a pragmatic liberal statesmanship. It can lead to Deweyite 'experiments in social cooperation' with the help of a knowingly 'instrumental' philosophy and science. But a sectarian political creed, one unusually ideological in the everyday sense, seems more likely. Rorty holds the central philosophic problem to be 'what serves democracy', attacks the distinction between 'reason' and 'preference' and suggests that commitment to enlightenment is not very different from faith in divinity. He also maintains that arguments from a 'vocabulary' foreign to liberal democracy should be disdained, not 'met'; they should be dismissed as from someone 'mad' or 'insane'. One should show 'contempt for the spirit of accommodation and tolerance' especially when someone questions the 'kind of human being' that liberal democracy produces. Questions about human quality are most to be disdained. What applies to a philosophic attentiveness to opinions and to concern for what is good, applies also to this liberal's attitude to truth. An attitude of laughter, of 'light-minded' carelessness, should be directed to anyone who objects that Rorty's system rests on what it denies, that is, on foundational philosophy. But Rorty does in fact presuppose as true a certain philosophic

---

[36] J. Rawls' *A Theory of Justice* (Cambridge, MA, Harvard University Press, 1971), has been followed by a long series of articles that explain and revise, including 'Justice as fairness: political not metaphysical' (*Philosophy and Public Affairs*, 14, 23–251), 'The idea of an overlapping consensus' (*Oxford Journal of Legal Studies* 7, 1–25), 'The priority of right and ideas of the good' (*Philosophy and Public Affairs*, 17, 251–76). Rawls has now published his revised thinking in *Political Liberalism* (New York, Columbia University Press, 1993).

[37] 'Neoconstitutionalism: Rawls, Dworkin, and Nozick,' in Allan Bloom (ed.), *Confronting the Constitution* (Washington, D.C., AEI Press, 1990), pp. 456, 447–52. I rely extensively on this excellent account.

critique of Enlightenment rationalism by Heidegger, Derrida and the other authorities to whom he explicitly and repeatedly defers. He presupposes also 'moral progress', that is, that his special version of liberalism is the result of a historical development toward true morals.

It is not easy to see why Rorty's own fundamental position, despite his quick stepping, is not made arbitrary by the arbitrariness of his non-fundamentals. His very understanding of democracy becomes arbitrary. Is the American public culture about democracy or about republicanism; about popular power or about economic growth; about equality of respect or about equality of opportunity? These have been politically controversial. To preserve a tradition, one has to select what is important to preserve, and it is impossible to select considerately if one cannot do it for a reason, that is, by thinking out the kind of equality (for example) that is better for people. Evading a statesmanlike consideration of the obvious political alternatives, Rorty insists upon his particular beliefs, that is, the beliefs he chances to have concerning social progress, democracy and European historical and critical philosophy. The result makes the philosopher in politics into a sectarian and partisan, less politically judicious than a politican, to say nothing of a statesman. It also takes Rorty's interpretation, *contra* definition, some way from the American tradition as understood by all but a few liberated professors of historicist bent. It is removed enough from the tradition of individual rights, for example, to deny the very existence of individuals: they are really but 'centerless networks of beliefs and desires determined by historical circumstances'.

The Cause of Liberation

While movements such as women's liberation and multiculturalism have penetrated contemporary liberalism, they are essentially foreign to the old liberalism of the New Dealers. One can certainly speak of a 'Left' beyond liberalism, but the 'New Left' in the United States (and in Europe) differs from the old socialist Left, even if often allied in revolt from bourgeois society and in devotion to 'autonomy'. The new Left is 'committed', anti-bureaucratic, anti-careerist, and environmental. It means to be liberated from Western systems statist as well as capitalist, from science and technology, from morality and socialist morality as well as 'self-interest', and in general from all 'Western' rationalisms including socialism. Also, one finds now and again in the United States a liberated Right (the novelist Ayn Rand, the 'Republican reptile' P. J. O'Rourke) and a liberated Camille Paglia who disavows both liberals and conservatives. However ensconced in the language of rights, in short, the liberated movements lack the social planning and the constitutionalism that Rawls and Rorty attempt to salvage, even if there remains an eviscerated Kantianism, 'autonomy' without reason and without morality, that marks a disguised dependence on liberal individualism.

'Hey, hey, ho, ho – Western culture has got to go,' chanted a crowd of Stanford students about (of all matters) a core course requirement. The loose phrasing, and the politicizing of an alleged literary canon, show the comprehensiveness of the attack and also a certain puerility of aim. But there is nevertheless a serious political target. For it must be said that the modern sciences had been intended as not only comprehensive but authoritative. They contained, that is, both epistemological critique and constructed systems, and the mixture of critique and construction had indeed been designed for effectual control. The design was for 'useful knowledge', in the words of Bacon, of Locke, and of that formative American child of Bacon and his heirs, Benjamin Franklin. Locke's critique of any natural or religious morality, in the *Essay Concerning Human Understanding*, cleared the ground for his foundationalism, for his foundation of rights in self-interest, and thus for his construction of acquisitive society and representative government in the *Two Treatises*. The critical thinking of Heidegger and Michel Foucault (and Rorty) can be understood as a radicalizing or historicizing of the critical side of modern rationalism, but with an animus directed precisely against empiricist foundationalism and its constructions. It misunderstands this foundationalism as emblematic of all rationalism, of not only modern philosophers such as Locke but also and especially of the tradition of philosophy that originates with Socrates.

The thought at the core of the many movements of liberation is then both critical of all rationalism – and a modern rationalism. It is both bitterly disillusioned with progress and confident that history culminates in its critical knowing and in the possibility of autonomy. There is a mixture of openness and zeal. Those devoted to liberation prefer to be 'non-judgmental', call for 'ambiguity' and 'sensitivity', and are less for mere toleration of other cultures than for whole-hearted openness to other cultures. But not quite whole-hearted. For they are unambiguous in condemning the disciplinary culture of modernism and in seeking 'empowerment' for the cultural minorities judged to be its victims. Hence the rise of such designations as 'politically correct', 'adversary culture', 'oppression studies' and the 'culture of victimhood'. Hence also the movement's attacks, as 'hegemonic', upon virtually every modern teaching or therapeutic authority. A conference on teaching writing is dominated by speeches attacking remedial writing as imperialist, colonialist and generally racist; the real enemy is 'good writing' and 'standards' for writing. A powerful faction among advocates for the deaf defends 'deaf culture' and attacks those who promote hearing aids, encourage speaking rather than signing and uphold hearing as the norm. At a conference at Yale a distinguished professor of literature suggests that limiting the humanities to the study of humankind is a form of 'speciesism'. A much ridiculed brochure from an office at Smith College warns against discrimination not only as to sexism, racism, or sexual orientation, but also as to lookism and ableism.

The political effects of the movement go far beyond squirrelly professors and zealous deans to 'culture wars' over the very definition of family and of education. Are art and media for exposing 'authentic' violence and domination? Is science a rape of the earth? Are courts for protecting minorities of all sorts from the oppression of the past?[38] As in all such movements there is a flabby body and a hard core. At the core is a very radical understanding indeed. Some radical feminists urge lesbianism as the only way for women to be liberated from dependence and condemn altogether male hegemony and God the Father. 'Deep ecologists' urge war against exploiters of the earth and prefer to mankind the other species not burdened with exploitative reason. Multi-culturalists regard precisely 'standards' or 'excellence' as a sign of obsolete 'white male' hegemony. To illustrate the radical bite we will rely on samples from the feminist movement in particular: first, the radical feminism of Catherine Mackinnon, second, the problems caused by radical doctrine for the liberal feminism of Betty Friedan.

[38] See James Davison Hunter, *Culture Wars, The Struggle to Define America* (New York, Basic Books, 1991).

Catherine Mackinnon is probably the most prominent radical feminist of the 80s. She is a much publicized law professor at the University of Michigan, a public figure profiled in the *New York Times Magazine*, an occasional TV commentator who has appeared on the MacNeill-Lehrer news hour. According to a key article of Mackinnon's, the task at hand is to make feminism not merely a common attitude but a comprehensive outlook, i.e., 'a theory'.[39] Marxism had shown the way in exploitation theory but it is insufficiently feminist. Women have indeed been used labour and unpaid labour at that, as a Marxist analysis shows, but Marxism's scientific bent, and its historical determinism, abstract from the special exploitation of women. The Marxist misses in particular the social construction of sexuality, and thus of femininity, according to male power. 'Love' and 'beauty' are but invented images and thus tools of male domination, according to Mackinnon, and it is the service and the task of self-consciously feminist theory to 'unmask attitudes'. 'Consciousness-raising' is then the distinctive expression of feminism and this means especially an attack on the notion that woman's qualities are all sexual or are defined by her femininity. The definition of woman is not by biology but by politics, and although the constructions hitherto have been by men, henceforth they are to be by women for themselves. 'The personal is political'. But it is also true, according to Mackinnon, that women's personhood may give her a special insight compared to the 'objectifications' and universals of men. 'Our politics begin with our feelings', and this can serve humanity through a 'strategy of deconstructing' modern systems and especially the state. There is a contradiction here. Has not the nature booted out the back door been welcomed through the front? The turn from person, to a female persona of feelings, brings back something similar to 'biologism'. The notion of a contribution to humanity brings back, if not 'objectivity', then some truth common to the sexes. Be that as it may, feminism as Mackinnon interprets it will turn against the political state – 'male in its objectivity' – and revolutionize politics by criticizing 'all as domination'. One might wonder what can be left of the state after this political war between the sexes – and what a feminism that would deconstruct all politics can retain of politics or of authority of any kind.

Betty Friedan had long disputed with the radicals, and in 1981, a year before Mackinnon's article, she announced troubled second thoughts about even what she had encouraged in *The Feminine Mystique* (1963). That book more than any other set off the feminist movement in the United States. Appealing to the bored housewife of some education and leisure, Friedan indicted a sentimental preoccupation with being the perfect American sweetheart, housewife and mother. The pampered suburban house, that 'comfortable concentration camp', was the mystique Friedan attacked in the name of interesting careers somewhere in the economy. Even in *The Feminine Mystique* Friedan was far from contemptuous of love, marriage and family, warning against the lesbian movement and the radicals, but she did not think out the strains and tensions involved in being super-woman and super-mom, and her primary agenda was the fostering of careers. In *The Second Stage*,[40] published eighteen years later, Friedan's aim was to help women break free precisely from 'the mystique' of feminism 'that I helped create'. While appreciative of the new opportunities, and

---

[39] C. Mackinnon, 'Feminism, Marxism, method, and the state: an agenda for theory,' *Signs: Journal of Women in Culture and Society*, 7 (1982), 515–44.

[40] Betty Friedan, *The Second Stage* (New York, Summit Books, 1981).

emphasizing a woman's freedom 'to choose', she very self-consciously (and courageously) encouraged frank talk about 'feminist denial of the importance of family, of women's own needs to give and get love and nurture'. The blind spot of the old feminists was 'our own extreme of reaction against that wife-mother role'. *The Second Stage* moved away from mere reaction, and Friedan would move women away from necessarily aiming to be like men and to join the mainstream workforce. 'The equality we fought for isn't livable, isn't workable, isn't comfortable in the terms that structured our battle'. Still, equality remains the aim for the liberal Friedan. The means to equality of women, then, must be a certain change in men, in fact what must be called a feminization of men. The old hierarchical, competitive and quantitative rationality is becoming obsolete, Friedan tells us. It is being replaced by a 'contextual' and relational power style. The polarization of masculine and feminine roles can end. While defending certain compromises of equality involved in the family, Friedan confidently expounds a vast revolution in which West Point warriors lose their machismo and become 'strong enough to be sensitive and tender to the evolving needs and values of human life'. Men in general can turn to home-making, and people in general cluster in new kinds of housing that is communal and accommodates expanded 'families of choice'.

Confronting Liberation, Especially in the Universities

Thus far in the United States the response among conservatives to the rise of liberationism has been far more confident and vigorous than among liberals, as Friedan the liberal feminist herself noted with chagrin. The old New Deal liberals took for granted new rights (such as Roosevelt's Four Freedoms), an 'evolving' constitutionalism, a movement toward more equality, and, in general, an historical progress toward social democracy. For these and other reasons women's lib, gay rights, community participation and the attacks on capitalism and hierarchy could seem like a continuation of democratic reform by new means. Rawls and Rorty exemplify liberal assimilation of the politics of the civilizationally disadvantaged. The few who stood out eventually accepted the label of neo-conservative and were attacked as turncoats. It took a long time, and defeats in five out of six Presidential elections, including three defeats by a free enterprise conservatism that liberals supposed historically obsolete, for a Democrat to run clearly as a new kind of Democrat. But it is also true that the tone of the country and its media has changed to accept much of the liberated agenda. The affair about candidate Clinton's affair eventually showed a considerable public tolerance bordering on the temper of sexual liberation. President Clinton has emphasized from the start diversity of gender and ethnicity in his appointments, the right of a woman to choose abortions, public admission of gays to the military forces and the right of privacy as a litmus test for a Supreme Court nominee.

Two impressive recent books by E. J. Dionne, Jr, and Arthur S. Schlesinger show liberals attempting to free liberalism from the fundamentals of the liberation movement – and also show some of the difficulties. Dionne is a liberal who would get beyond ideology.[41] He is an unusual liberal who takes seriously the conservatives – but only for the past. Now, he says, the conservatives are tired

---

[41] E. J. Dionne, Jr, *Why Americans Hate Politics* (New York, Simon & Schuster, 1991).

and hopelessly divided between free marketeers and right-to-lifers, and no more relevant than the life-style liberationists whose assaults so wounded liberalism and the Democrats. It was indeed the New Left that broke the Democrats but its time is also past; now the Democrats should be able to discard ideology and agree on 'a new coalition for social reform'. There must be a return to majority politics, a 'politics of remedy' for the middle class. 'The people' themselves are correctly concerned with mixing work and welfare, with intact families as well as personal choice, with good schools as well as integration, with roads and jobs as well as subsidies and free markets. They need not a politics of liberation but a 'civic politics' that includes national service, greater tax benefits for the family, universal health care, aid to education and more jobs. Dionne thus turns refreshingly to a certain pluralistic statesmanship like FDR's and away from 'profound' critiques and commitments. But there are difficulties. First and foremost, the New Deal's pragmatic politics itself involved a certain theory, that is, an account of rights such as the 'Four Freedoms' and of society, powers of government, and above all of the progress through history from laissez-faire to social planning and public administration. Even American 'pragmatism', after all, is a theory. Dionne leaves all this unarticulated, undefended and uncorrected. Second, Dionne neglects the people's wishful thinking, that is, the contradictions between, say, their belief in both the family virtues preached by Reagan and the personal liberation preached by the Left, or between their wish for security and their reluctance to pay for it. And third, he slights the divisions within the people, especially the profound challenge from the liberating movement among professors and those influenced by professors in law schools and universities. He wishes for sensible unity but does not face up to the problems of doctrine, the doctrines that might unify or those that divide and mislead.

Schlesinger's *The Disuniting of America*[42] does address the political-intellectual crisis. That the old patron saint of New Deal liberalism should think it necessary to step forth, and show quietly some alliance with neo-conservative critics of the public schools such as Diane Ravitch and with conservative critics of the universities such as Dinesh D'Souza and Allan Bloom, is significant. Still, Schlesinger confines himself to the situation in the secondary schools, which he thinks most important and endangered, and to the issues raised by 'multi-culturalism'. He does not himself address the universities, saying that the silent majority of professors will eventually turn the tide, nor treat of feminism, gay rights, etc. Still, he sees big implications. If the history of America continues to be addressed through the 'compulsive skepticism of the modern mind', we will stop being America. One is reminded of Theodore White's gloomy comparison of the United States in 1980 to Rome near the republic's fall, but Schlesinger the believer in cycles thinks that the United States will stand. Still, he stands up to make a political defence and a political attack on the attackers. There is no reason for a 'guilt trip about America', which has brought individual liberty, political democracy and the rule of law, and certainly no reason for shame besides the 'sun people' of Africa now so celebrated. The tradition of America is not of oppression. The Western tradition of Locke, Marx and Nietzsche is a tradition neither of oppression nor of the *status quo*, and any tradition that encompasses both St. Francis and Machiavelli is not even one tradition. Despite these telling observations Schlesinger's articulation of liberal democracy and of the West is half-relativistic and rudimentary at best. His defence is chiefly an attack on the

---

[42] A. S. Schlesinger, *The Disuniting of America* (New York, London, W. W. Norton, 1992).

alternative. He attacks especially the claims for an ethnic education and especially for an education in Africanism for African-Americans. There are arguments out there for the relevance and superiority of Africa that are sweeping educators and curricula before them, and they generally rest on lies, lies as to the influence and superiority of African culture and as to the real Africa. The beauty and the influence of black civilizations are being much exaggerated. There is a wilful slighting of the squalid politics of slave-trading and slavery, of African war, imperialism, tyranny and barbarism. The lies are only part of the harm. These teachings are an opium of false hope for the really needy. They discourage useful training for American life and are thus a fundamental misdirection for life. If the 'Ku Klux Klan' had wanted to mislead and marginalize American blacks, Schlesinger says in one moving passage, it could not have dreamed up a better device than the multi-cultural curriculum that is now making its way, city by city and state by state, into the American schools.

The most extensive confrontations of these nostrums have come from conservatives, in particular from the diagnoses by D'Souza and Bloom of the situation in higher education. D'Souza's *Illiberal Education*[43] enters into the immense controversy over sex and gender. There is a comprehensive 'victim's revolution on campus' and it lowers standards so as to be 'inclusive' and it ideologizes content. The result is many poorly qualified students and many crude and partisan orthodoxies. Campuses are balkanized. There is an increase in racial and ethnic incidents. A righteous 'empowerment of minorities and women' leads commonly to intimidation in the classroom, and this at the most distinguished universities, especially at Harvard and Stanford. The intimidation is by administrative indication and action as well as by chants, sit-ins, and newspapers, and the occasion is more inference from allegedly insensitive language than confrontation of real bias or of genuinely dissenting arguments. A teacher's language must now be gender- and ethnic-sensitive, and his or her books must be properly diverse. Plato, Shakespeare or Locke are treated as part of a hoary and now discredited Western 'canon' devised by Dead White Males. Quite generally one finds students fed on a few second rate books by authors of approved revolutionary bent (Franz Fanon), colour (Alice Walker), or of a third world background and an ersatz 'third-world' outlook (Rigoberta Manchu). If the books happen to be promising, the mode of treatment is often not. D'Souza suggests that a great book of Shakespeare or Aristotle might be involved with politics and yet be above our political partisanship, because it weighs various opinions in the light of the promise of human life. It can be liberal in liberating the reader from prejudice. It is therefore in the political senses neither liberal, liberationist nor conservative. But the very suggestion that some books are 'great' is disdained by those filled with the teachings of sensitivity and empowerment, according to D'Souza. It is seen as merely a partisan statement and an elitist one at that.

'Fancy German philosophic thought fascinates us and takes the place of the really serious things. This will not be the last attempt of its kind coming from the dispossessed humanities in their search for an imaginary empire, one that flatters popular democratic tastes.' The words are from the conclusion of *The Closing of the American Mind*,[44] Allan Bloom's diagnosis of the universities that sold over a

[43] D. D'Souza, *Iliberal Education, The Politics of Sex, Race, and Gender on Campus* (New York, The Free Press, 1991).

[44] A. Bloom, *The Closing of the American Mind* (New York, Simon & Shuster, 1987).

million copies despite its topics and tenor. Bloom disavows conservatism, indicts academy and democracy alike, appeals to Plato, advertizes his book as a teacher's 'meditation on the state of our souls, in particular of the young, and of their education', describes in detail the genesis of modern philosophy, and reminds the young of their dependence on the achievements of the founders of American institutions. There is a problem with good American students, according to Bloom, but it is not zealous politicization. Few students believe the strange preaching. The problem is instead an openness so open that it is complacently undiscriminating. Taught relativism, the belief that no values can be proved better than any other, the promising student's natural love of the best and the true withers within. This relativism is not a necessary condition; it is 'nihilism, American style'. It is but a complacent and egalitarian variation on nihilistic late Germanic philosophy, on one or another version of the breakdown of the modern project for humane progress. But there is a true kind of education as old as the Socratic way. It remains possible alike for faculty and students, contrary to the opinions of progressive professors. Taught to enter expectantly but considerately into the promising alternatives, into books like Locke's *Second Treatise* and Plato's *Symposium*, a serious student might become wise about the merits and difficulties and thus rise above conventional platitudes. He or she would not be conventional and thus not be 'ideological'.[45] Bloom's outlook reflects something of the endeavour of Leo Strauss to revive political philosophy and philosophy itself and there is no doubt that this endeavour has influenced a small number of academics and the occasional neo-conservative. But on the whole Bloom's argument was trashed by the professors. It is hard to foresee what if any large effects such thoughts will have upon the universities that are pushed by very different impulses and that to some extent were and are the intellectual citadel of American politics.

Conclusion

It is not hard to foresee the effect of the Soviet Empire's collapse on the general political-intellectual struggle within the United States: it will weaken the conservatives. It was forcefulness in foreign affairs that especially helped conservative Republicans to win elections during the past two decades. It was an unequivocal anti-communism that did the most to bind together a conservative movement that might seem an impossible combination of free-marketeers, traditionalist Catholic and traditionalist aristocratic intellectuals, rather Jewish and half New-Dealer neo-conservatives, and the populist New Right of fundamentalist preachers and flocks of pro-family moralists. Accordingly, the collapse of communism is likely to strengthen contemporary liberals (although certainly not to the extent that the defeat of Hitler allowed the British democracy to turn to Labour in 1945). One might think that it would strengthen the rights-oriented, redistributionist, and socially compassionate portions of the liberal movement at the expense of the more conservative or 'neo-liberal' revisionists. The removal of the Soviet military threat may also weaken some of the barriers to gay rights, women's rights, multi-culturalism, environmentalism, and other

[45] 'Ideology', as Bloom takes care to explain, is an artificial term derived from certain positivistic and historical philosophies of the nineteenth century. It implies an invented idea or ideal, and one that is baseless and a rationalization to boot. The term as now used participates in the contemporary crisis of liberalism.

aspects of the 'counter-culture'. But precisely the strengthening of left and liberating segments is likely to weaken the electoral appeal of the liberal movement as a whole.

These effects will be indirect because the state of political creeds in the United States is largely independent of the fall of Marxism. There is truth in the famous explanation: the country retains much of its belief in natural rights, constitutional government and free enterprise, the creed that socialism came to bury and that returned the antipathy in spades. It is true that liberalism has changed considerably. Progressive liberals of the New Deal and then of the Great Society favoured compassionate, redistributive and energetic social planning and regarded the old constitutionalism of equality of opportunity and limited government as but an out-of-date eighteenth century shibboleth. But FDR, LBJ, and Justice Brennan led the way to a progressive and socially conscious liberalism and a right to privacy, not to social democracy or to a progressivism (like Henry Wallace's) that flirted with communism. Even this progressive liberalism of the last fifty or sixty years has been sharply rebuffed, prior to the collapse of Communist power, by the victories of Ronald Reagan and his conservative movement.

The situation in 1992 after Clinton's victory and Bush's defeat is a certain demoralization and splintering of the conservatives, a politic reuniting and moderation of a long-splintered liberal movement, and a continuing penetration into the educated classes of the post-modernism of critique and liberation. Although the modern conservative creed has only been a political force since the Republican nomination of Barry Goldwater for President in 1964, and progressive liberalism in power goes back to Wilson's New Freedom and Roosevelt's New Deal, the present resurgence of the liberals will not necessarily issue in a substantial victory, that is, a decisive redirection of the country on the order of the New Deal. An opportunity is there and it is perceived. The 'change' promised by candidate Clinton included taxing the rich more, providing universal health care and stimulating the economy to produce more jobs. But he accompanied these traditional New Deal proposals with promises to cut taxes on the middle class, to mix workfare with welfare and to cap the time that a recipient might receive benefits, to face up to the defects of American economic competitiveness by 'investing' in education and transportation, and, most notably, to face up to the federal deficit by cutting spending, including such benefits as Medicare. It is doubtful whether a Democratic coalition can survive such innovations. This is not only because of its constituencies among the poor, the minorities and the elderly but also because of the differences on such matters among liberals themselves. Also, liberals continue to find it hard to separate themselves from the proclivities of their liberationist step-siblings. But it is certainly also a question whether and how the conservatives can themselves unite about an alternative that can win a popular majority.

Ideological Politics and the Contemporary World: Have We Seen the Last of " 'Isms"?

ALEKSANDRAS SHTROMAS*
Hillsdale College

I. Problems of Definition

What do we mean when considering the fate of "'isms"? Professor Kenneth Minogue, in initiating the discussion of that problem for this book, has no doubt that its topic is ideology which he defines as 'the project of creating social perfection by managing society' (p. 19). One could infer from this that for Minogue an ideology is what it is only if it claims universality, that is the capacity to serve as a valid blueprint for bringing perfection through management to any society on Earth, whatever particular – national, religious, cultural, economic or geopolitical – characteristics that society may bear. It logically follows from this, as Minogue unambiguously himself states, that Marxism is truly paradigmatic of ideology or, in his own words, 'the archetypal ideology' (p. 5). Minogue also explicitly attacks those scholars who regard any political doctrine as ideology and include into the definition of ideology even 'some bodies of ideas, like democracy, which were not political doctrines . . . at all'. (p. 6)[1]

Dr. Alex Callinicos, on the other hand, finds Minogue's use of the term ideology eccentric, although he does not deny him the right to stick to his own definition, as the term ideology today 'has acquired so many meanings, some mutually incompatible' (p. 60), that it lost any definitional meaningfulness altogether. Callinicos is clearly not in the business of discussing ideologies, anyway; his task is to prove that classical Marxism is not an ideology in any sense of the word (and least of in the Marxist sense, according to which ideology is 'false consciousness') and that its standing as the best developed objective social theory has not been even in the slightest affected by the collapse of communism in the former USSR and elsewhere in the world.

*Dr. Aleksandras Shtromas is Professor of Political Science at Hillsdale College, Hillsdale, Michigan, U.S.A.

[1] He cites to that effect Lyman Tower Sargent, an American, and Andrew Vincent, a Briton, as representative exponents of such views. For these scholars, and they are the great majority in the field, any value or belief system accepted by some group as fact or truth qualifies, without any further discrimination, as ideology.

I agree with Callinicos that arguments about the meaning of the term ideology and its definition are futile. What may, however, be possible is for a restricted group of people involved in a discussion of a topic to agree upon a meaning and definition of the topic under their discussion. Without such an agreement their sensible interaction on it would hardly be possible. In this sense I fully agree with Minogue that the term ideology as defined by Sargent, Vincent and scores of other scholars dealing with the subject, is practically unusable in any discussion because its literally limitless broadness blurs the distinctions between ideology and a number of related concepts, such, for example, as religion, philosophy, ideal, value, policy, prejudice, etc. This is to say that Minogue's attempt at defining ideology in a narrower and more precise sense is both necessary and highly commendable.

For this purpose the original concept of ideology given by the man who introduced it to the world, Antoine Louis Claude, Comte Destutt de Tracy (1754–1836), seems to be quite useful. In Destutt de Tracy's terms, *idéologie* is a science of ideas. Any ideas, if analyzed by Destutt de Tracy's methodology, could be either validated as based on experience and thus true or, if they are not lending themselves to such verification, should be discarded. In his four volume work *Elements d'idéologie*, published between 1801–13, Destutt de Tracy arrives at a system of such, in his opinion, true ideas (very liberal ones by the way) and then focuses his attention on how to translate these 'true' ideas into socio-political reality by conceiving appropriate programmes of political action. Hence, according to Destutt de Tracy, an ideology: (1) is based on a verified cognitive general theory of universal and comprehensive nature explaining human beings and their relationship with the external world, including also other human beings; (2) expresses itself in a programme of social and political organization of human beings; (3) entails the necessity of struggle for the realization of this programme; (4) demands proselyting and commitment; (5) addresses the public at large but confers special role of leadership to properly qualified groups of intellectuals (*les idéologues* or, one could say, the enlightened 'vanguard' of society).[2]

Destutt de Tracy excludes religion from ideology altogether, because he considers religion to be irrational and fictitious; and thus to him any sets of religious ideas are the ones destined to be discarded in the first place. For those, however, who do not share Destutt de Tracy's belief in the possibility of evolving a scientifically true ideology (and I am one of those myself, taking on this issue, unlike many others, a truly Popperian view), religion is as good a basis for formulating an ideology [in the sense of Destutt de Tracy's point (1) above], as is any secular theory claiming to be scientifically or otherwise true. In order to serve as a viable foundation for an ideology, a theory, it seems to me, should be able to present a claim to universal validity and comprehensive scope, sufficiently credible at least to some group (in addition, of course, to claiming to be the expression of ultimate truth); and religion based theories are on the whole even more effective at presenting such claims than the secular ones.

The inclusion of religion into the category of possible foundations for elaborating an ideology brings into the concept of ideology yet another element which

---

[2] For Destutt de Tracy's relevant and relatively easily accessible text in English, see Count Destutt de Tracy, 'A treatise on political economy to which is prefixed a supplement to a preceeding work on the understanding, or elements of ideology; with an analytical table and an introduction on the

Destutt de Tracy was naturally unable even to consider – that of ethical values – which entails an ardent belief of the adherents not merely in the correctness of the ideology they profess but also in its absolute moral goodness. This, in turn, dictates the necessity for these adherents to subscribe to a specific hierarchical structure of ethical values corresponding to the ideology and usually based on the conviction that any means advancing the ideology's proclaimed ultimate political goal (which also constitutes the ultimate good) are perfectly ethical, however much at variance with the commonly accepted moral standards these means may be. Lenin's formula about the advancement of the goals of proletarian class struggle forming the sole criterion of morality[3] expresses this attitude in a nutshell.

With these revisions and amendments added, Destutt de Tracy's original concept of ideology becomes, in my view, perfectly valid for the purposes of discussing "'isms" in this book. To sum it up, ideology – the concept subsuming these "'isms' – should be understood as an action oriented theoretical creed which: (1) has its foundation in a universal and comprehensive philosophy and/ or religion; (2) establishes a specific hierarchical structure of ethical values, usually subordinated to what is believed to be the ultimate political goal; (3) sets out a programme for the creation and operation of such a socio-political system which is uniquely suitable for implementing this goal; (4) entails the necessity of founding and running a closely-knit political organization devoted to the struggle for the practical realization of this programme; (5) demands this organization's engagement in a proselytizing effort addressed to the public at large and a full commitment to its work on the part of the converted proselytes who have joined that political organization as members; and (6) confers special role of political and theoretical leadership to the intellectually and morally advanced 'vanguard' endowed, among other leadership functions, with the most important one – the authority for authentic interpretation in given practical-political circumstances of the ideology itself.

The action-oriented nature of ideology is quite adequately reflected in Max Skidmore's 'brief definition' of it as 'a form of thought that presents a pattern of complex political ideas simply and in a manner that inspires action to achieve certain goals'.[4] Minogue's definition, being more specific than Skidmore's, has, in my view, the advantage of trying to disclose the contents of the action Skidmore merely refers to. But why is Minogue emphasizing so strongly only one, though a very important one, aspect of that action, namely the society's management for the sake of making it perfect? I think Minogue is so overwhelmed by the task of identifying welfare-statism as the new ideology vigorously succeeding Marxism and able to pose even a greater threat to liberty than Marxism itself ever did, that he unconsciously tailors his general definition to suit his particular purpose. But welfare-statism *per se* is not planning revol-

faculty of the will,' translated by Thomas Jefferson, in John M. Dorsey, *Psychology of Political Science* (Detroit, MI, Center for Health Education, 1973).

[3] In his speech to the 3rd Congress of the Russian Communist Youth Organization on October 2, 1920, Lenin said: 'We say that our morality is entirely subordinated to the interests of the proletariat's class struggle. . . Moral is what serves to destroy the old exploiting society and to unite all the working people around the proletariat, which is building up a new communist society. . . We do not believe in an eternal morality, and we expose the falseness of all the fables about morality' ('On the Tasks of the Youth Unions', in V. I. Lenin, *Collected Works*, Vol. 31 (London, Lawrence and Wishart, 1960–1970), pp. 291–4.

[4] Max J. Skidmore, *Ideologies: Politics in Action* (Fort Worth and New York, Harcourt Brace Jovanovich, 2nd ed., 1993), p. 7.

utionary action against the established system; on the contrary, it tries to use the same modern liberal-democratic state for the purposes of managing society in order to make it truly just. Nor does welfare-statism openly attack the free market and other liberal institutions; on the contrary, it tries to use the free market and other facets of the liberal order for implementing by management what it ideologically considers to be true equality and thus, again, true justice. Hence, Minogue excludes from his definition of ideologically motivated behaviour activities aimed at systematic subversion of the established political order; at planning for its replacement by an ideologically correct one and at executing such plans; at winning by propaganda and mobilization ever more adherents to the ideology in question; and at projecting its vision of change to the world at large. I do not think that such an approach is fully justified even by Minogue's own standards established by his profound analysis of ideology's substance. Welfare-statism to me is not a separate ideology but a constituent part of a larger socialist ideological vision outside of which it becomes a mere policy that in the context of continuity of the extant liberal-democratic system may represent a major nuisance, a deviation, but by no means a real challenge, let alone a dangerous threat, to the established liberal order. There are many variations of socialist ideology, starting with Marxism itself and stretching all the way down to what one could call the social-democratic vision of political change, and in all of them welfare-statism plays a substantial but not necessarily pivotal role. The pivotal role in all of them is still accorded to drastic political change, to the establishment of a new just political system and to all other typically ideologically motivated actions which I tried to encapsulate into my six-point definition based on Destutt de Tracy's original concept and given above. I will return to the problem of the ideological contents of welfare-statism and Minogue's view of it below. For now I would like just to stress that, in my view, Minogue's definition of ideology by no means warrants Callinicos's qualification of being excentric. I think that for the purposes of this book it is a perfectly good working definition, albeit, one which, may be, is a bit too narrow and thus requires a certain extension which I ventured to propose above.

II. Ideology vs Philosophy and Religion

What is in my view important to stress first is the difference between ideology, on the one hand, and philosophy and religion, on the other. To me at least, philosophy is in the business of explaining the world, and the man in it, as they are. It is using for this purpose the available knowledge on them and tries to sum it up in a theoretically sensible and methodologically viable way. The modern philosopher who first sought to transcend the epistemological confines of philosophical inquiry and conceive a philosophical theory of practical action was, perhaps, Johann Gottlieb Fichte whom Marx, in *The German Ideology*, not without reason, admiringly called the Napoleon of philosophy. When Marx, in his eleventh thesis on Feuerbach, said that 'up till now the philosophers have only interpreted the world in various ways; the point, however, is to change it',[5] he was in fact quoting Fichte and, at the same time, accomplished the great leap by which his own philosophy was to be transformed into an ideology *par*

[5] Karl Marx, 'Theses on Feuerbach', in Robert C. Tucker (ed.), *The Marx-Engels Reader* (New York, Norton, 2nd ed., 1978), p. 145.

excellence. [Not, of course, into an ideology in Marx's own terms, that is into 'false consciousness', but into what Marx thought was a truly scientific social theory capable of properly informing practical socio-political action (i.e., a scientific ideology as what, by the way, ideology was supposed to be in its original conception evisaged by Destutt de Tracy).]

Ideology is more akin to religion than to philosophy, as religions are also total and universal belief systems combining the questions of truth with those of human conduct by projecting for governing the latter a strict hierarchical structure of ethical values. Ideologies are, however, entirely 'this-worldly', while religions are usually concerned about 'things not of this world' and concentrate on personal virtues and modes of individual behaviour capable of winning for a particular human being favour with God and thus insuring peace and harmony for the eternal life of his or her immortal soul.

In his essay on Fundamentalism, included as a chapter in this book, Professor Bhikhu Parekh made a succinct distinction between religious fundamentalism, as a device by which religion is translated into 'this worldly' ideology, and religious revivalism or ultra-orthodoxy which represent different ways of expressing the faithfuls' concern about protecting the purity of religious faith and traditions from the severe challenges of modernity.

According to Parekh, 'fundamentalism. . . arises in a society widely believed to be degenerate and devoid of a sense of direction, identity and the means of its self-regeneration. . . [and] represents an attempt to regenerate [society] by comprehensively reconstituting it on a religious foundation'. In order to achieve this goal, fundamentalism 'rejects the tradition, offers a "dynamic" and activist reading of the scriptures, . . . weaves a moral and political programme around them, and uses the institution of the state to enforce the programme'. Parekh is absolutely right when he says that '[s]ince fundamentalism' – and, I would add, every religion based political ideology in general – 'reduces religion to ideology and charters it to an alien purpose, it inevitably distorts and destroys it'. (p. 4) Indeed, an ideology may be based on an interpretation of a certain religious tradition, but by its very nature it is alien to, and works across the purposes with, a God-centred religion. Differently from Parekh, I do not think, however, that religious ideology of the fundamentalist kind is typical exclusively to modernity. As religion in pre-modern times was the dominant form of human consciousness, all pre-modern ideologies were inevitably based on religion. In my view, Thomas Münzer and Jean Calvin were typcial religious ideologists, and so were also the Puritans, both those who initiated the English revolution of 1640–60 and those who sailed to north America to found a New England and with it to start from scratch a new way of life *in this world*, to found a new social and political system which would accord with their vision of religious virtue. One could say that they were the religious fundamentalists *avant la lettre*. The roots of religiously based ideologies conceived in the Christian tradition go, in my view, as far back as St. Augustin's *De Civitatis Dei*, and only since the 13th century Western Christianity, with and through St. Thomas Aquinas, learned thoroughly to distinguish between temporal matters and matters spiritual and eternal or, in other words, between the concerns of life in this world and the life with God *sub specie aeternitatis*.

Ideology should thus be treated as a concept distinct from the concepts of philosophy and religion. Using philosophies and/or religions as their basic source, ideologies *per se* represent, in fact, a bridge between them and practical political action. It is the programme and methods of such action which form the ideology's main core. And it is because of such an overwhelmingly practical-political orientation, that an ideology is bound to distort and, ultimately, to destroy, the very philosophy and/or religion on which it claims to be built.

One could argue that this latter conclusion does not apply to Marxism, for Marxism is supposed to be a consistent and complex system of philosophical and economic thought from which logically and coherently follows a pro-gramme for practical political action or, which is one and the same thing, an ideology. But is Marxism really a philosophy? It is doubtful, because Marx used a quite skilful amalgamation of philosophical systems propounded by others – first and foremost by Georg Wilhelm Friedrich Hegel, but also by Lüdwig Feuerbach, Henri de Saint Simon, Johann Gottlieb Fichte, Adam Smith, David Ricardo and a few others – in order to draw from it his own purely ideological conclusions expressed in the body of thought known as Marx's historical materialism. Marx's own claim to his role in the development of social thought is, by the way, not much different. In the letter to his friend Joseph Weydemeyer of 5 March 1852, Marx wrote, for example, that all he 'did that was new was to prove: (1) that the existence of classes is only bound up with *particular historical phases in the development of production,* (2) that the class struggle necessarily leads to the *dictatorship of the proletariat,* (3) that this dictatorship itself only constitutes the transition to the *abolition of all classes* and to *a classless society*'.[6]

In other words, according to Marx himself, the novelty of his thought consisted in projecting a vision of class struggle resulting in the future institu-tion of a workers' state (the dictatorship of the proletariat) which is going to work towards the creation of a classless, i.e. communist, society. The fact that he claimed this process to be objectively inevitable and unavoidable does not change the purely ideological nature of his self-defined original contribution to social thought, as such claims are usual for most ideologies trying to dress themselves up as the expressions of the ultimate truth. In the science-worship-ping 19th century such a dress up required to claim for the ideology in question the status of an objective, moreover scientific, social theory; and this was what Marx actually did claim. It is by so doing that Marx had virtually distorted and, utimately, destroyed the classical Hegelian-Fichtean philosophical premises on which he founded his ideology. It is exactly this distortion and destruction by Marx of the original philosophical foundations of his ideology that leads so many of us to believe that Marx has indeed created a novel philosophical system which is entirely consistent with his ideology. My point is that Marx has created a mere ideology but, by carefully trying to present it as a consistent scientific and philosophical theory, fooled himself and so many of us into believing that this was indeed the case.

III. What Systems of Ideas and Values Qualify as Ideologies?

So far we have identified two systems of thought and action that, in my analysis, qualify as full-fledged ideologies: religious fundamentalisms of any variety (and ancient or medieval ones, as much as modern; not to be confused, however, with

----

[6] See in, Tucker, *The Marx-Engels Reader,* p.220.

what, following Parekh's classification, qualifies as religious revivalism or ultra-orthodoxy) and Marxism. Let us now have a look at the others.

A. Socialism, Communism, Jacobinism

Pre- and non-Marxist varieties of socialism and communism qualify as ideologies, in my view, too, These, alongside the ideas of agrarian socialism (such as those of the Rusian *narodniks*) and the modern social-democratic tradition, include, in the first place, Anarchism, as conceived in the works of William Godwin, Pierre-Joseph Proudhon, Mikhail Bakunin and Petr Kropotkin, by now an over two centuries old ideological tradition on the basis of which a number of international political movements were established in the 19th century with some such movements continuing to function at the present time, too. Early communist ideologies were conceived in the 17th century by Gerard Winstanley who also created what one could call the first English communist party, The Diggers; and in the 18th century by François-Noël (called Gracchus) Babeuf who, in addition to having projected in his theoretical works a consistent communist world view, had also formed a clandestine political organization which plotted to established the 'Babeuvists' (the Party of the followers of Gracchus Babeuf) as a communist government in an already republican France, but was found out and destroyed even before having started to stage their coup d'état, known under the name of the Conspiracy of Equals.

In the revolutionary situations of 17th century England and 18th century France, the civil wars and interventions taking place then were dominated by opposing ideologies not only on the radical fringes represented by the extremists, such as the Diggers or John Lillburne's Levellers in England and the Babeuvists in France, but also in the mainstream forces which actually played the revolutionary processes out. The Parliamentarian Party (both the Presbyterians and the Independents) in 17th century England was, no doubt, inspired by its ideological (to a large extent religiously fundamentalist) vision of a good and just society, and so were the leaders of the Third Estate in 18th century France, although their ideological vision was purely secular and antithetical to any established religion. Faced with such an ideologically motivated challenge, the defenders of the old regimes in both countries had to respond by projecting their own traditionalist ideologies, based on such concepts as the divine rights of kings and the sanctity of the 'natural' hierarchical structures based on feudal rights and privileges. The radical Independents in England, who came to the fore with Pride's Purge – the ejection of the Presbyterian dominated Long Parliament and its replacement by the radical Rump executed by Colonel Thomas Pride – were as ideologically motivated in their actions as, over a century later, were the French Jacobines. If the former derived their ideology from religion, the latter, having rejected Christianity and the Church altogether, used as the foundation for their ideology the secular philosophies of the 18th century's French Enlightenment, mainly Jean-Jacque Rousseau's theory of the general will which the Jacobine leaders (especially, Maximilien Robespierre) managed to translate into a consistent programme of revolutionary political action meant not only for France but for the world at large. All the pragmatically motivated and 'feudalizing' adjustments notwithstanding, Napoleon's rule was in essence nothing else but a consistent continuation of the effort to entrench the Jacobine ideology in the politics of France and, at the same time, to propel the Napoleonic version of Jacobinism onto the rest of Europe, which at that time was tantamount to the entire world.

B. Fascism and National Socialism

Mussolini's Fascism and Hitler's National-Socialism were full-blooded universal ideologies, too. They were bound to be that, as they sought to provide an adequate counter-ideology to Marxist Communism on a global scale.

It is true that both these ideologies were to a large extent preoccupied with their own nations, the Italians and the Germans, respectively. For Mussolini, the task of Italy was to recreate and embody the former greatness of the Roman Empire and to provide for the rest of the world what *Pax Romana* has provided for the ancient universe. Italy, according to him, earned the right to be in the forefront of contemporary political developments, as it was the first nation to establish for itself the total and absolute fascist state, one that in the 20th century is uniquely able to propel a nation to a secure and bright future. The future will thus belong, according to the Fascist creed, to those nations that are going to establish for themselves in good time a fascist ideology-based totalitarian state; the nations whose decay went so far as to making them unable to create a totalitarian system of government, will have to subordinate themselves to the morally, culturally and politically superior totalitarian powers. Hence, Italy is to become in the future a prominent, if not (because of its initiating role and rich historical tradition) the leading, partner in a world alliance consisting of a few totalitarian empires dominating the rest of the world. In Mussolini's own words, '[i]n the doctrine of Fascism, Empire is not only a territorial, military or mercantile expression, but spiritual or moral. One can think of an empire, that is to say a nation that directly or indirectly leads other nations, without needing to conquer a single square kilometer of territory. For Fascism the tendency to Empire, that is to say, to the expansion of nations, is a manifestation of vitality; its opposite, staying at home, is a sign of decadence: peoples who rise or re-rise are imperialist, peoples who die are renunciatory'.[7] Thus much about the Italian fascist vision of the future world order and Italy's role and place in it.

Not less explicit was Mussolini about the universal nature of the Fascist doctrine itself. He squarely bases it on Hegel's philosophy of right and, more specifically, on his view about the state being the reality into which the absolute idea finally materializes itself. 'The keystone of Fascist doctrine', he writes, 'is the conception of the State. . . For Fascism the state is the absolute before which individuals and groups are relative.'[8] 'Therefore', he states in another passage of the essay, 'for the Fascist, everything is in the State, and nothing human or spiritual exists, much less has value, outside the State. In this sense Fascism is totalitarian, and the Fascist State, the synthesis and unity of all values, interprets, develops and gives a strength to the whole life of the people'.[9] To Mussolini, 'Fascism is a religious conception. . . besides being a system of government, [it] is also, and above all, a system of thought'.[10] 'If it is admitted',

---

[7] Quoted from Mussolini's Fascist ideology foundation-laying aritcle, 'The doctrine of Fascism', which he published in 1932 in the *Italian Encyclopedia*; see its abridged rendition in: Terence Ball and Richard Dagger (eds), *Ideals and Ideologies: a Reader* (New York, Harper Collins, 1991), p. 297.

[8] Mussolini, 'The doctrine of Fascism', p. 295.

[9] Mussolini, 'The doctrine of Fascism', p. 290.

[10] Mussolini, 'The doctrine of Fascism', pp. 289–290.

he continues, 'that the nineteenth century has been the century of Socialism, Liberalism and Democracy, it does not follow that the twentieth must also be the century of Liberalism, Socialism and Democracy. . . It is to be expected that this century may be that of authority, a century of the "Right", a Fascist century. If the nineteenth was the century of the individual (Liberalism means individualism), it may be expected that this one may be the century of "collectivism" and therefore of the State'.[11] And he concludes: 'If every age has its own doctrine, it is apparent from a thousand signs that the doctrine of the present age is Fascism. . . Fascism henceforward has in the world the universality of all those doctrines which, by fulfilling themselves, have significance in the history of the human spirit'.[12]

Fascism is commonly regarded as an extremist nationalist ideology. This is a profound misunderstanding of the very essence of Fascism. In fact, Fascism is a universal and globally conceived ideology, based on Hegelian philosophical premises and setting conditions for all nation-states to meet the challenge of the twentieth century and either grow into fascist-totalitarian states, or, alternatively, sink into subordination to those nations who have become such states, and, ultimately, into historical oblivion. The only truly nationalistic element in this doctrine is the praise of Italy for her being the first to initiate fascist-totalitarian statehood and for 'rising again after many centuries of abandonment or slavery to foreigners'.[13]

If Mussolini based his doctrine on the universal theory of the state, Hitler chose as a foundation for his ideological Weltanschauung the not less universal and global in its scope, theory of the race. For Hitler, the paramount political institution is not the state but the Volk, or a nation as such, bound into an integral entity and a naturally organized political body by racial ties of common blood and by a common soil (*Blut und Boden*). The state is just one of the institutions the Volk may use to serve its political purposes and interests, but the state is also prone of falling into the hands of the Volk's enemies, as do liberal or communist states which pervert the nation and contribute to its gradual disintegration and demise

Like Mussolini, Hitler also envisages a new European and, ultimately, world order that is bound to emerge from the millennia long racial struggle which, according to him, shaped the course of human history. The German nation is to Hilter not an end in itself, but rather a means to achieving that European and world order as an end, through the 'thousand years' Reich' that Hitler instituted in Germany for the latter to be in position to preserve, and continue with, the struggle for achieving that end after he had passed away. This is to say that the German Volk, in Hitler's view, is designated to become a sort of a 'fighting vanguard' of the Aryan race in its ceaseless (though, at most times, unconscious) struggle for becoming the globally dominant force. The Germans were destined to take upon themselves that vanguard role, because, being in Hitler's view, more than any other Aryan Volk exposed to miscegenation and racial degradation, they were the first among the Aryans to become conscious of the threat to their identity and continuous existence. That is why, under Hitler's leadership, they rose to the defence of their racial integrity, thus willy-nilly also taking upon themselves the championship of the Aryan cause generally and on

[11] Mussolini, 'The doctrine of Fascism', p. 295.
[12] Mussolini, 'The doctrine of Fascism', p. 297.
[13] Mussolini, 'The doctrine of Fascism', p. 297.

the global scale. Hitler never excluded the possibility of Germany perishing, virtually getting nationally extinct, in this long-lasting struggle, but Germany's sacrifice was supposed to insure victory in the battle for Aryan supremacy on this planet and for establishing the New Europe and the New World based on this supremacy – a cause, in Hitler's view, worth to perish for. If, however, the Germans survived all the battles they will have to fight for the Aryan cause, Germany will, no doubt, occupy in the New World which will emerge as result of these battles, an honourable place, but the purer national brands of the Aryans, those farther removed to the North and thus less spoiled by miscegenation (for example, the Scandinavian nations), will most certainly acquire a position superior to that of the Germans.

The first and most important task of the 20th century's racial struggle is, according to Hitler, the elimination from the life and the social fabrics of all Volks, to whatever race – Aryan or sub-Aryan – these Volks happen to belong, of the Jews, the alien inclusion into each Volk which undermines its integrity from within and thus tries to subordinate the Volk to itself. The enormity of this task is made clear by Hitler's definition of both the 'Demo-Plutocratic Liberalism' and Communism as special Jewish devices invented for the purpose of subverting each nation and putting it under the alien Jewish control. This is to say that, in Hitler's view, the task of eliminating the Jewish menace to the world implies the necessity of destroying the states organized as liberal democracies, as well as the states ruled by the communist parties, restoring all of them, bit by bit, to their original national-socialist integrity of organically structured and racially pure *Volkstums*. The alternative to the undertaking of this enormous task is, according to Hitler, the extinction of human species, including the Jews themselves, for this will be the inevitable result of Jewish rule over nations through the means of liberalism and communism. As he himself says, '[t]he end is not only the end of. . . the peoples oppressed by the Jew, but also the end of this parasite upon the nations. After the death of his victim, the vampire sooner or later dies too'.[14] Hence, National-Socialism is also a globally conveied universal ideology, a holistic world view aimed at remodelling the entire world in accordance with its own image. In this sense, National-Socialism cannot be classified as a nationalistic ideology, despite of the fact that it confers to the German nation a very special role in the process of the world's remodelling in accordance with Hitler's scriptures.

. . .

This is not to say that a national idea cannot in principle become a foundation for a universal ideology. But for a national idea to serve this purpose it has to posit a particular nation's superiority over all other nations and, by so doing, justify that particular nation's claim to rule the world. I, for one, am not aware of such an ideology having ever even been in existence and, because of its sheer impracticality in preaching nothing positive but a war against the rest of the world, doubt whether it could have ever been attempted to get formulated. There were of course warriors trying to conquer the world and put their own kin in charge of it, but even the most ferocious of them, Attila the Hun, apparently tried to do so not for the sake of establishing a Hun dominated world empire, but in order to realize his universal ideological commitment of relieving huma-

---

[14] Adolf Hitler (Ralph Manheim, transl.), *Mein Kampf*, (Boston, Houghton and Mifflin, 1971), p. 327.

nity from the bondage of a settled civilization, every vestige of which he set himself the task of destroying. As shown above, neither Mussolini and Hitler nor Lenin and Stalin sought their respective nation's undivided domination over the world. They were all pursuing the institution of a much more complex 'new world' based on a universal, not on a narrowly conceived purely national, ideology.

One could, perhaps, say that the practice and legacy of colonial rule created in Great Britain and other colony-possessing European nations an attitude of national superiority with regard to the nations of the colonies they used to rule. This phenomenon is impressively discussed in another chapter by Professor Bhikhu Parekh in this book, 'Decolonizing Liberalism', to which I have nothing much to add. What I would like to stress, however, is the fact that no colonial European nation ever made an ideological claim about its inherently constant superiority entitling it to a permanent rule over these 'second class' colonized nations, let alone over the entire world. Britain and other colonial masters claimed to exercise, with regard to their colonies, a civilizatory mission which, after having been successfully accomplished, would allow them to release their colonies into, first, autonomous and, later, independent existence. And this, as we know, had indeed become the case.

C. Millian (Militant) Liberalism

The above by no means challenges Parekh's extremely well presented and logically impeccable arguments about Western Liberalism's colonial arrogance, its spurious anti-traditionalism, its extremely narrow definition of, and accordance of exaggerated importance to, 'such values as autonomy, choice, individuality, liberty, rationality and progress' (p. 14); as well as Liberalism's unwarranted denial of communitarian and other collectivist institutions of the non-European nations under his discussion. But these arguments represent Parekh's critique of Western Liberalism as an universal ideology rather than of the non-extant Western ideological claims to rule the Third World, let alone the entire world. Actually, Parekh's critique of the Millian variation of Western Liberalism is valid in regard to all nations without exception, not only the ones which were colonized by Western powers and now form the Third World. A typical Millian liberal has no patience for or tolerance of communitarian collectivist beliefs and traditions wherever they continue to exist, be it distant India or nearby rural England. They had no understanding of or sympathy for the Irish national struggle and continue to wonder about the passionate attachment of some Welshmen to their 'antiquated and useless language', treating the struggle for its preservation as incomprehensible, irrational and thus reprehensible.

Millian Liberalism is, in fact, militant liberalism. By absolutizing individualism and, accordingly, treating every form of collectivism as a reactionary remnant of the 'dark ages', a relict of the feudal past and symbol of rural backwardness, it militantly opposes collectivist tendencies and traditions, puts itself into combat for their elimination from the life of contemporary society altogether and does so wherever such tendencies and traditions are to be found (and they are to be found everywhere, indeed). Millian liberalism treats any variety of traditional collectivism, including nationalism, as a phenomenon which, with the further progress of modernity, is bound to vanish into the records of the historic past, anyway, but every true Millian liberal nevertheless sees his task in pushing by all means in his power this process of progressive modernization (which to him is tantamount to the process of mankind's level-ing) forward and thus facilitating and hastening its happy conclusion – the universal predominance of the liberal-individualist uniformity. In this Millian liberalism closes ranks with socialism/communism – they both share the dream about a 'new man' who is fully devoid of any national or other traditional collective identity and lives exclusively by the universal values of his respective ideology.

D. The Problem of Conservative Ideology

So far we talked about ideologies which are pretty obviously universal and conceived for global application. Furthermore, these already evoked ideologies are militantly revolutionary ones, as they set the goal of remodelling and reshuffling the established socio-political order and demand of their adherents to do their utmost in the struggle for, and realization of, the new order the respective ideology envisions. What then about the counter-revolutionary, conservative ideas? Do they not have a potential of developing into fully blooded ideologies? It was actually these ideas to the sets of which Karl Mann-heim exclusively accorded the term ideology, while calling the revolutionary ones utopian – utopian, as long as they were inspired and driven by the vested interest in change rather than by objectivity and 'realistic thought' of which, Mannheim believed, only the relatively uncommitted intellectual class of society, the 'intelligentsia', is capable. The revolutionary theories conceived by the intelligentsia could therefore qualify, in Mannheim's view, as non-utopian and situationally correct – *situationsgerecht*.[15].

To me, however, conservatism is, as a rule, not ideological. It expresses itself mainly in the not necessarily uncritical acceptance of, and accommodation to, the given social-political reality usually accompanied by a certain nostalgia for that reality's original or past purity and a resentment of 'bastardizing changes' introduced into that reality by recent modernizing currents and trends. Tradi-tionalism, the instinctive attachment to familiar rituals and a routine way of life, that is, to what Max Weber so aptly called 'the eternal yesterday', is no ideology but a natural result of a successful process of socialization. It is only when this reality is disintegrating and becomes increasingly unable to secure a successful socialization into it of substantial numbers of oppressed and/or alienated people that the normally non-ideological conservative orientation may start growing into a set of ideas deserving the name, 'conservative ideology'. This usually happens when there is an urgent need for the conservatives to present an adequate response to the spread and menacingly increasing impact of revol-utionary ideologies.[16]

[15] 'The concept "ideology",' Mannheim writes, 'reflects the one discovery. . . that ruling groups can in their thinking become so intensely interest-bound to a situation that they are simply no longer able to see certain facts which would undermine their sense of domination. . . [I]n certain situations the collective unconscious of certain groups obscures the real conditions of society both to itself and to others and thereby stabilizes it. The concept of utopian thinking reflects the opposite discovery. . . that certain oppressed groups are intellectually so strongly interested in the destruction and transformation of a given condition of society that they unwittingly see only elements in the situation which tend to negate it.' Karl Mannheim, (Louis Wirth and Edward Shils, transls) *Ideology and Utopia: an Introduction to the Sociology of Knowledge*, (London, Routledge and Kegan Paul, 1936, reprint 1972), p. 36.

[16] This is what actually Mannheim also believed to be the case. In his brilliant analysis of the conservative idea (see *Ideology and Utopia...*, pp. 206–15) he even attributes to it in this 'accom-plished form' a utopian quality, thus blurring his own distinction between ideology and utopia to

Comte Joseph de Maistre (1753–1821) could be seen as, perhaps, a typical founder and exponent of such a full-blooded conservative ideology. Basing his ultramontanist doctrine on medieval Catholic theology, de Maistre indeed sought to destroy the republican political doctrines of the French Enlightenment and to build upon 'their ruins' a consistently all-round and universal ideology extolling royal absolutism. Paradoxically, one could define de Maistre's ideology as also a revolutionary one: his *Considerations sur la France*, the first attempt at a systematic presentation of his ultramontanist ideology, was written in 1796 and called, in fact, for a revolution against the already established by that time republican regime in France.

On the other hand, the Fascist and National-Socialist ideologies of the 20th century, though, no doubt, revolutionary, could also be defined as conservative, for they preached a revolution against the capitalist system which, in their view, in a revolutionary manner had itself devastated the natural foundations and organic structures of the traditional national societies which they sought to restore on a new, modernized foundation. In other words, their revolutionary anti-capitalist stance was presented as being actually a counter-revolutionary one, since, in their conception, capitalism itself was a perverse revolutionary imposition upon a nationally organic society threatening that society's very existence. Being born in response to the socialist-communist challenge, these ideologies thus positioned themselves to defend the conservative continuity of nations by combating not only the 'divisive and levelling' Marxist ideology, but also the whole tradition of 'splintering individualism', including the established bourgeois-liberal order based upon, and centred around, this tradition, which they considered the primary cause of that continuity's destruction.

Indeed, as these few examples show only too clearly, it is very difficult to tell a conservative ideology from a revolutionary one, which is to say that the cognitive value of Mannheim's attempted distinction between ideology and utopia is extremely relative and makes sense only in so far as we are prepared (and I have already admitted that I am not) – together with Destutt de Tracy, Marx and Mannheim himself – to recognize that systems of socio-political ideas could be fully objective, realistic and scientifically true. [This does not mean, however, that in my view all such systems of socio-political ideas are necessarily bound to be mere reflections of false consciousness (ideologies), rationalized wishful thinking (utopias) or a combination of both (the conservative ideas); these systems of ideas usually represent honest and firm, though usually rushed and not properly substantiated, convictions about the nature of society and politics, the possibility of an effective solution for all socio-political problems and, above all, about the proper realization of the ideal of absolute justice.]

. . .

Ideologies we have so far defined as such, in addition to being universal, conceived for global application and militant, are also holistic. They usually identify an enemy and believe that the defeat and elimination of that enemy (it may be a certain class, race or nation, but also a set of prejudices and irrational attitudes from which their human carriers should be freed) is the key to univer-

---

the point of unrecognizability. Where I differ with Mannheim is in his reduction of ideology to the instinctive, subsconsciously defensive attitude towards the socio-political status quo. Apparently, what to me is ideology, for Mannheim is either utopia or an entirely realistic, *situationsgerecht*, social theory.

sal salvation and the prerequisite for the creation of the ideal society a 'holistic' blueprint for which every such ideology has elaborated in advance. Although, as W. H. Dray by quoting May Brodbeck rightly stresses, the common opinion holds that '[c]ulturally, holism is intimately connected with hostility toward the liberal political individualism of the Western tradition',[17] militant Millian liberalism is, doubtlessly, a holistic creed, too. Liberals of this denomination know exactly what in society is backward and thus rejectable, and what is progressive and thus deserving support and enhancement; they scorn national bonds and patriotic attachments, traditional loyalties and irrational prejudices (e.g. religion) that are still a part and parcel of social fabric in all nations and dream of a time when religious, national, cultural, linguistic and other spurious differences dividing mankind will disappear and all men will become just human beings, equally rational and equally sharing the same individualistic liberal values. Believing that this 'higher unity of men' will inevitably, sooner or later, come about, such Liberals nevertheless do not shy away from social engineering and gladly resort to imposition of their 'correct' ideas almost in the same way (though, may be, not exactly as cruelly) in which non- and anti-liberal ideologues do. It is this propensity that, as mentioned above, creates a remarkable affinity between Millian liberalism and socialism/communism, a propensity that had been quite clearly expressed in the later works of John Stuart Mill himself and that had inspired Herbert Spencer to oppose the Millian variety of liberalism and present his own, much more libertarian version of it.

IV. The Problem of Nationalism

Alongside the universal and globally concerned ideologies, there exist hosts of specific sets of action oriented ideas conceived for limited application – limited to a specific group of people, a nation, a country or a certain ethno-geographic area of the world. The question is whether these latter sets of ideas also qualify as ideologies in terms of the definition given above. But before answering this question, I would follow the established tradition of calling them ideologies. Let us consider a few examples.

The ideology of *negritude* evolved by black French writers (Léopold Senghor, Aimé Césaire *et al.*) in order to assert the positive socio-cultural qualities of the blacks and expose the coldness and narrowminded bigotry of their white European masters, was originally meant to be more educational than political, although it served as a powerful argument in the Francophone black Africa's movement for termination of French colonial rule. A fully and exclusively political character this ideology acquired in its interpretation by Dr. François Duvalier in his quest for political power in Haiti. In its Duvalierian shape the ideology of *negritude* was completely 'Haitianized' by concentrating almost exclusively on a programme of taking power in Haiti from the hands of the ruling mulatto elite into the hands of the poor and 'purely black' majority of Haiti's population. Leaving aside the question of how true to his ideology Duvalier has remained when, as 'President For Life', he was the omnipotent dictator of his country, there is very little doubt that outside Haiti and the specific relationship between mulattos and blacks which historically formed

[17] W. H. Dray, 'Holism and individualism in history and social science', in Paul Edwards (ed.), *The Encyclopedia of Philosophy*, vol. 4 (New York and London, Macmillan, 1967), p. 53.

itself there, this ideology did not make any sense at all. In a way, this was not so much an ideology as an attempt at justifying a claim of a certain racially defined group to establish for itself a superior status in a particular society and state. The same could be said about the South African ideology of apartheid which, although based on the principle of separation of races, was not racist in the usual and globally applicable sense of the word. It had a strictly limited South African application and was much more a policy directed at securing local whites' exclusive sovereignty over their claimed parts of the country (that is over all of it with the formal exclusion of the so called bantustans) than an ideology in that sense of this word which has been defined above.

It is in the nature of man to try to prove to himself and others that his claims are his natural rights and the policies aimed at realizing these claims are those of attaining true justice. That is why in politics interests are always backed up by ideas presenting these interests as possessing absolute moral and legal value and as being undisputably just by absolute standards of justice. And that is also why every set of even the most practical-pragmatic, interest driven policies appear on the political surface as ideological causing, in turn, so much confusion between policy and ideology. This immutable relationship between pragmatic group interest based policies and the ideas of absolute justice has been already noticed by Aristotle who formulated it as the basic rule of political struggles and disputes. According to Aristotle, groups of people engage in factional conflict mainly in order to aggrandize themselves but they always portray their case in that conflict as that of true justice. He notes, however, that this is usually a perverse notion of justice, one that justifies the goals of a particular group, for '. . . while there is agreement that justice in an unqualified sense is according to merit, there are differences: . . . some (the socially inferior ones – A.S.) consider themselves to be equal generally if they are equal in some respect, while others (the socially privileged ones, usually the rich – A.S.) claim to merit all things unequally if they are unequal (superior – A.S.) in some respect.[18]

Of course, not all claims and policies aimed at attaining the realization of these claims are based exclusively on self-interest or self-promotion. In modernizing societies, for example, the need for an adequate response to the demands and challenges of modernity often create opposite reactions roughly definable as traditionalist and progressist. Both of them are based not so much on any particular group interest (although these certainly also play an important role in determining a group's position towards modernizing changes) as on a more general idea of 'common good' or the national interest as a whole. The Slavophiles and Westernizers in Russia's 19th century politics are here a typical case in point, but their ideas were also strictly policy bound and concerned about the future development of Russia only, not of the world at large. What the ideas were lacking in order to qualify as full-blooded ideologies was a comprehensive and universal programme for the creation of a new just society even in Russia, let alone on a global scale.

Even the extension of Slavophile views resulting in the supra-national idea of Panslavism, endowing the Russian Tsar with the function of the protector of all the Slavs and, more specifically, of their liberator from the alien Ottoman and Habsburg imperial yoke, formulated in Russia by the official historian Mikhail Pogodin (1800–75) but passionately supported by significant forces among

[18] Aristotle, (Carnes Lord, trans.) *Politics*, Book 5, Ch. 1, (13), (Chicago and London, University of Chicago Press, 1984), p. 148.

Southern Slavs, Czechs and, later, even by some groups of Poles (esp. Roman Dmowski and his Endeks, the People's Democrats), did not change its basically policy formulation directed nature, with the policy proposals being addressed to the extant but accordingly reorientated government. Only in its Panslavic shape this policy was proclaiming a major nation's (the Russian one's) duty to other kindred nations and the unification of all these nations into one 'brotherly' political entity. However imperialist, this policy (as well as the ideas behind its formulation) was limited by a precise boundary of the lands inhabited by Slavic nations in the Balkans and Central Europe and pursued a limited goal of their liberation from alien rule and incorporation into a 'natural union' with each other and under the auspices of the most powerful member, Russia. Furthermore, not only did the Panslavic idea not envisage any changes of the indigenous socio-political systems or of the traditional ways of life of the nations involved, but, on the contrary, it aimed at preserving and enhancing their true, conservatively defined identities and 'selfhood'.

Pangermanism was not much different. This was an idea born basically in response to Panslavism. It mirror-imaged the latter in so far as the unity of all Germanic (or rather German-speaking) nations was concerned, but outdid it by claiming to protect the Slavic nations of Central and Eastern Europe, as well as the nations (Slavic as well as non-Slavic) already incorporated into the Russian Empire, from 'Russian world-domineering objectives'. Of identical specific and regionally-limited nature were also the policy related ideas of Panturkism and Paniranism.

In a way, the ideologies of *negritude* and apartheid, Slavophilism and Panslavism, Pangermanism and Panturkism were no more than specific expressions or extensions of corresponding nationalist ideas, which by their very nature are not universal, but particularistic, and either entirely self-centred or, if even expansionist, envisioning that expansion on a strictly limited, regionally-bounded scope.

The 20th century saw, however, the virtual end of the 'limited expansionist' nationalist ideologies. Panslavism was demolished by the Bolshevik revolution in Russia. The new, ideologically communist, regime established in Russia was internationalist and explicitly condemned the reactionary, imperialist and backward looking ideas of Panslavism. Instead, it assumed a global, Marxist ideology inspired mission of promoting the world socialist revolution and establishing a world-wide communist society. Pangermanism, having, in its turn, suffered from Germany's defeat in World War I, was in the 1930s not really resurrected but drastically transformed by Hitler into a racially based new global ideology which perverted the very essence of the Pangermanic idea. With the fall of Hitler's Reich, that idea finally disappeared from the world's stage altogether. Panturkism was practically destroyed by Turkey's defeat in World War I but its definitive theoretical collapse was caused by the Kemalist revolution (1918–23) whose main goal has been Turkey's radical transformation into a modern, European-type nation-state which that revolution had effectively started and successive governments successfully accomplished by the end of 1960s.

The Panarabic idea, tossed with by a number of Arab leaders, starting with Gamal Abdel Nasser and then taken up by Michel Aflaq and his ideologically socialist Ba'th Party, only to crumble, together with that Party itself, as a result of the irreconcilable rivalries and disputes between its Iraqi and Syrian branches, never really took off ground. As for Paniranism, it has not been resurrected under the late Ayatollah Ruhollah Khomeini, as many believe, but was virtually replaced by a new version of the ideologically universalist Panis-lamism, claiming as its overall task the unification under its own Shi'ite auspices not only of all the already established Islamic nations (whether they were Suni or Shi'ite) but also of the entire world. When Ayatollah Khomeini wrote his notorious letter to Gorbachev, urging him to abandon 'pernicious communism', convert to Islam and, in alliance with him, combat the 'Great Satan' (which in his vocabulary meant the USA) in order to establish an ideologically unified Islamic world order, I am sure he was not joking but meant it in most serious and real terms, indeed. After Khomeini's death, however, the Panislamic (and by that also Paniranic) overtones in the Iranian leadership's political parlance have been dramatically muted, and today Iran acts on the international stage much more like a regular nation-state.

Much more attention than to these by now basically obsolete, semi-imperial-ist ideas should be certainly paid to the ideas of single nations' nationalisms — the ideas which have lately gained so much prominence and, after the collapse of communism, moved to the centre stage of world politics where, I believe, they will stay for most of the 21st century and, may be, even longer. These nation-alisms, being focused almost exclusively on a single nation, become increasingly directed not any more to the aggrandizement of these nations at the expense of others, but to the dismantlement of the remnants of old empires and the formally non-imperial multi-national states. This tendency is, of course, not entirely a one way street, as the old imperial reflexes are still noticeable in the behaviour of some governments of the former 'masters of the world' and linger on in the mass psychology of the nations used to ruling other nations and instinctively still treating this 'prerogative' as the way of their natural existence in the world. This sort of 'counter-tendency' is exemplified by Turkey's long and embittered struggle aginst Kurdish separatists or by Spain's reluctance to allow the Basques and the Catalans freely, by the way of a referendum, to decide whether they wish to continue to be a part of the Spanish state or, which is one and the same, to live under Castillian rule which many of them consider alien. It is also demonstrated by the Zhirinovsky phenomenon in Russia, which reflects the nostalgia some, though not numerous, sections of the Russian population feel for the former Soviet Union, or by the remnants of the 'Yugoslav syn-drome' in Serbia, although the leading national idea there today is not anymore the restoration of old Yugoslavia, but the creation of a 'mono-national' Great Serbia at the expense of the nation-states of Croatia and Bosnia-Herzogovina, both of which in a substantially diminished size Serbia would be prepared to tolerate.

The tendency of progressing differentiation of nations into separate nation states is in my analysis unbeatable and by that also unstoppable, however strong at the moment any 'counter-tendency' to it may be. As mentioned above, even the Serbs fight today for establishing on their own terms a separate Serbian nation-state rather than for preserving the position of a dominant force in such an artificial multinational entity as was former Yugoslavia, and this, in my judgment, is a very eloquent argument in favour of this thesis. The Rump Yugoslavia is maintained by the Serbs not for real but out of international convenience and the advantages of inheriting the former federal assets; it can be maintained without much trouble because 'for all their colorful traditions, the

Montenegrins' (the other, beside the Serbs, constituent nation of Rump Yugoslavia) 'are basically Serbs'. . . [19]

This unbeatable and unstoppable tendency of national differentiation in the modern world did not start with the collapse of the Soviet Union and Yugoslavia or even with the dismantlement of British, French and other European colonial empires after World War II. It goes back to the gradual collapse of the Ottoman Empire, started in the 18th century and followed by the end of Napoleon, Habsburg and Russian empires, and continues unabated, and on an ever increasing scale, ever since. The multinational entity which broke up in 1972, that is long before the end of the USSR but already after the end of the colonial era in Asia, was Pakistan whose eastern part became then a separate state for the Muslim Benghalis, Bangladesh. The 1966–70 determined, but at the time unsuccessful, attempt at creating out of Nigeria a separate state for the Ibo nation, Biafra, sent a powerful signal indicating the future 'splintering' developments in the still nationally undifferentiated states of black Africa. Ethiopia, a traditional empire on the African continent dominated for millennia by the Amharas, is already bursting at the seams with this process now clearly becoming irreversible. India, Myanmar (Burma), Shri Lanka, Afghanistan, Indonesia, Nigeria, Sudan, Burundi, Philippines, Iraq and dozens of other countries are increasingly turning into battlefields on which scores of, by now still stateless, nations incorporated into these political entities, posing as genuine nation-states, are fighting for their selfhood.

China is next in the row. The restless Tibetans are being gradually joined in the struggle for national self-assertion there by Mongols, Uygurs, Kazakhs and other non-Khan nations. The strength of a single identity of the Khans themselves is becoming increasingly doubtful in China, too. The peaceful appearance at present of the Iranian ethnic scene is also grossly misleading. The Kurds and the Azeris, the Baluchis and the Bakhtiaris just wait for the opportunity to activate their respective movements for national self-determination.

The globally-wide process of national differentiation is leading, however, not only to the fragmentation of the political structure of the world but is also getting simultaneously accompanied by a strong, though substantially modified, process of global integration – actually it is powerfully precipitating that process, because the new political nations, in order to establish for themselves a secure, independent of the previous master, and equal position in the world at large, try to get themselves associated with wider regional and global institutions much more actively and in a much closer fashion than do any firmly established political nations. The new world order projected by this tendency is supposed to be based not so much on the principle of unlimited sovereignty of the member states as on that of equal sovereignty for all nations without exception, including the ones not yet constituted as sovereign states, which would be in some ways limited by certain regional and global political institutions expressing the sovereignty of mankind and, at the same time, geared effectively to protect the equality of sovereign rights equally for all nations.

It is in this ever more rapid process of national differentiation accompanied by global and regional integration on a fair, firmly stable and optimally sustain-

---

[19] David Binder, 'Conversations: Milovan Djilas', in *The New York Times*, December 26, 1993, p. E 7. (The words in quotation marks are attributed by Binder verbatim to Djilas, himself a proud Montenegrin.)

able new foundation, that the nationalist ideologies of single nations acquire in the contemporary world such a major, indeed central, significance.

The topic of nationalism is dealt with in this book by Professor Eugene Kamenka. Basically, I agree with the main thrust of his argument that single nations' nationalisms are not real ideologies but rather natural forms of collective consciousness dictating certain common attitudes, preferences, values, orientations and goals. Indeed, a nation is a self-defined and unique organic entity bound together by what it deems to be its common origin and fate, but what in fact expresses itself in a specific set of values and goals shared exclusively by those who identify themselves and are reciprocally identified by others as members of that particular nation. According to Joseph Ernest Renan, the nation is an everyday's plebiscite, and I believe that such a subjective definition of the nation, first put forward by Johann Gottfried Herder and then accepted and put into wider philosophical circulation by Immanuel Kant, is the only one which makes sense. To this definition I would only add one qualification, that of territorial identity. A nation which is not identifying itself with a certain territory that it deems its sole and exclusive historical and existential homeland, is not a nation but a nationality which, by living in another nation's land without claiming for itself any different status, constitutes itself within that other nation's territorial realm as a national minority.

The ethnically determined values and goals form what Martin Heidegger called the specific mytho-poetical substance which, according to him, alone throws the nation into being. The landscape, the folklore, the accumulated linguistic variations, the way of working together and associating with one another, are all a part of this substance. But, in the formation of diverse ethnic values, even more important, I believe, is each nation's particular historical experience, the common fate of the people determined by that experience and uniting them by certain anxieties, suspicions, preset attitudes to others, ideas, aspirations, tasks. This fate is as unique as the mytho-poetical substance itself, and, in turn, it also uniquely shapes each nation and its specific system of values and goals.

In fact, insofar as each nation's attitude to its specific mytho-poetical substance is concerned, all of them share the same values. They all seek to preserve and protect that which makes up their specific substance. The contents of that substance in each nation's case may be different, but the nation's attitude to that substance is exactly the same for all of them. Indeed, all nations equally want to be free, safe, self-sufficient, and, if possible, influential and affluent, but since these are quite scarce commodities, only some nations, and to various degrees, realized these goals. It is the nation's successes and failures in its ability to attain and preserve these values which shape that nation's view of the world and of itself in it, relate that nation to other nations, and, ultimately, form that nation's hierarchical value structure. Hence, national self-righteousness varies from one nation to another in ways that more often than not may be mutually exclusive; expresses itself in various interethnic and other animosities and preferences; evolves contradictory concepts of primary virtues and, accordingly, contains concepts of the virtuousness/viciousness of other nations, etc.

Insofar as a nation tries to establish itself in the world as an entity independent from another nation's rule and recognizable as a separate and equal partner by other nations and the world at large, that nation's nationalism is jusified in the same way in which is justified the demand of the individual for the recognition and guarantee of his right not only to liberty but to life itself – for a nation is a kind of a collective personality which, differently from an individual human being, cannot survive without liberty even in sheer physical terms; it will, in the end, either get assimilated by the nation state's in which it lives main nation or is going to be otherwise annihilated. In all other respects the rights of nations as collective personalities are akin to the human rights of individuals, too. In today's world of nation-states, this translates itself, in the first place, into each nation's equal right to self-determination and sovereign statehood. Therefore, as long as nationalism is understood as 'primarily a political principle which holds that the political and the national unit should be congruent',[20] as long as it demands for each nation the equality of political condition, it is a healthy nationalism deserving in my view the wholehearted support of every fairminded person and every free and democratic nation.

It is wrong, in my view, to try to counteroppose, as many scholars do, the rights of nations to individual rights, claiming that the latter take precedence over the former. The rights of nations in principle do not contradict the rights of the individuals, for no nation is willingly submitting itself to rule by a regime oppressive of the individuals who make up the body of that nation. Repressive authoritarian or totalitarian regimes by violating human rights of their subjects violate at the same time the right of the nation freely to choose the form of rule under which it wishes to live and thus become abusive and oppressive of the nation they falsely claim to rule in that very nation's best interests. It seems to me that the scholars who consider the rights of nations antithetical to the rights of individuals are actually confusing the nation with the nation-state which indeed may submit itself either to an unpopular ideology or to a group pursuing through the state its vested interests at the expense of the interests of the nation and thus becoming oppressive of both the individual and the nation at large. On the other hand, the right of nations to self-determination and sovereignty on a par with other nations can become a real right only if it is rooted in individual human rights and is projected onto the political surface as a natural extension of these rights either exercised or claimed by a multitude of people as individuals in a simultaneous manner. For if the nation is an organic entity with which a great number of people freely identify themselves, no individual belonging to that nation can enjoy any rights accorded to him in an abstract and limited fashion ignoring or even suppressing his collective identity as member of a certain nation. As long as the individual has no right to be what he really is or wants to become – and this, in the first place, means being/becoming a member of what one considers to be one's own nation – he is not free and is thus deprived of his primary right to liberty. This is especially true of individuals who consider themselves members of one nation but are forced by another nation's state to assume that other nation's identity. It was, because of that, only fair for the 1948 Universal Declaration on Human Rights and its accompanying two later Covenants, as well as other international human rights' instruments approved by the UN and the majority of its member states, to proclaim the right of nations to self-determination and to freely choose their respective form of government as the primary source for all other human rights. Of course there is a great distance between the declarative recognition of these rights in a variety of internationally approved documents and their practical realization. The masters of the outmoded multinational states, opposing and actively resisting

---

[20] Ernest Gellner, *Nations and Nationalism* (Oxford, Blackwell, 1983), p. 1.

the realization of these rights by the now still stateless nations, represent a different kind of nationalism from the one described above – a nationalism that tries to preserve that particular nation's superiority over others in what it deems to be its own exclusive realm, and thus a chauvinistic brand of nationalism – although sometimes it reflects a merely defensive conservative idea of preserving the *status quo*.

Nationalism, as Kamenka rightly points out, can, however, acquire different shapes and forms in any of its many varieties. It can be defensive and aggressive, friendly to, or at least tolerant of, other nations and chauvinist or xenophobic, democratic and authoritarian; all these shapes and forms of expression can be found within the context of the, on the whole, benign nationalisms of stateless nations as much as within that of nations possessing their own nation-states and more often than not unjustifiably opposing the former kind of nationalism. I think that Aristotelian ethical theory provides perhaps the best available guide for determining the moral quality of every variety and aspect of nationalism and also for defining which elements in any nationalism are evil and reprehensible and which ones are benign and commendable.

According to Aristotle, good and evil are quantitative rather than qualitative categories. This is to say that excess or defect of a certain orientation or attitude are what makes it evil, but if this orientation or attitude expresses itself as the mean between these two extremes, then it is good. In this sense courage is the good and virtuous mean between the two bad extremes of rushness and cowardice, the virtue of generosity is the mean between the two blamable extremes of extravagance and stinginess, etc. Nationalism *per se* should be then also understood as the virtuous mean between the two immoral extremes of chauvinism and abstract (anational or even anti-national) catholicity, the former being the excessive and the latter the defective expression of an individual's or a group's sense of collectivist national identity. Xenophobia, though less excessive than chauvinism, will find its place in the quantitative continuum between good and evil in a space closer to the excessive extreme than to the virtuous mean. Hence, chauvinism and xenophobia, as excessive expressions of nationalism, are reprehensible and should be ethically evaluated as evil, but not less so is catholicity which fully ignores or even actively negates national identity and usually tries to substitute for it a universal ideology based and artificially construed collective identity, such as, for example, a certain world religion, a certain world wide social class or, ultimately, the mankind as a whole.

Racism would lend itself to the same quantitative distinctions with regard to one's own race, but insofar as it proclaims the inferiority of other races, and this is what it usually is all about, it falls into the category of racist excesses, equal to those which in the case of nationalism we have defined as chauvinism and/or xenophobia.

The defective nationalism is, on the whole, a passing phenomenon, although the Millian liberals are still trying to stick to it. Other universal creeds, in order to survive, had to arrive at a compromise with the national idea and sometimes even concede some priority ground to it. The Roman Catholic Church, for example, successfully survived throughout the two millennia of its quite turbulent history only because it learned how to adjust to the national idea and work in the form of multiplicity of national churches much before Vatican II, although it was only Vatican II which, finally, fully recognized the nation as a collective personality and, alongside the family, a natural form for the realization of the universal brotherhood of men – in fact, a further extension of the family onto the next step, after which comes already the unity of all men under God. The communists, who tried but did not know how organically to square their catholic internationalism with the national idea, have failed in this endeavour and, accordingly, went by the board. I have no doubt that if the Millian liberals do not revise soon enough their uncompromizingly anti-nationalist and indiscriminately universalist stance, they are going to go the same way too. I am not sure, however, whether, after having revised that stance, they could still be identified as Millian liberals.

Now let us have a closer look at the forms nationalism takes in nations which have already established for themselves sovereign nation-states and have to deal with their own minorities and outside nation-states. The nationalisms of nation-states express themselves, first, in the way a nation-state positions itself in the world and, especially, vis-à-vis its neighbours. Most eloquently such nation-alisms are, perhaps, revealed in the cases in which one nation-state has some irredentist claims against other nation-states. The problem in today's world is that it still lacks any firmly established singular principles of international justice by which such claims could be legitimately and authoritatively resolved by an international court of law. Historically based claims to possession of a territory often clash with the demographically based ones and, since there are no universally agreed criteria on the respective moral and legal validity of such claims, nation-states are usually judged only by the means they employ when trying to realize their respective claims. If, for example, a nation-state under-takes a unilateral armed invasion against another nation-state to get from the latter the claimed piece of territory, its nationalism will be qualified as lawless (disregarding the established norms of international law), aggressive and, thus, also excessive in the Aristotelian sense, irrespective of the substantive legitimacy of the claim for which it undertook such an invasion. In this sense Argentina's invasion of the Falkland Islands (or Malvinas) with the view of incorporating them into Argentina was clearly illegitimate, however justified its claim of historical right to possession of these islands may have been. And the same applies to Iraqi invasion of Kuwait, regardless whether this country is the 19th vilayat of Iraq or not.

As for the universally applicable moral and legal criteria for assessing the legitimacy of various irredenta, there are different proposals on what they should be like,[21] but, even before any of them are agreed upon, one could state with full assurance that if a nation-state applies such criteria arbitrarily and in a self-contradictory manner, choosing either one or another or both, as long as the chosen ones work to that particular nation-state's advantage, then this nation-state's nationalism should be assessed as excessive (that is, in Aristote-lian terms, immoral), unequivocally aggressive with regard to other nations and, subsequently, illegitimate and also in direct breech of extant international law. Such arbitrary and inconsistent use of mutually exclusive principles of interna-tional justice is again best exemplified by Serbia which, with regard to its territorial claims to Croatia and Bosnia-Herzegovina, uses the demographic criterion while, when trying to justify the continuation of its rule over Kosovo-

---

[21] For one such proposal and a more detailed discussion of this problem generally, see: Alexander Shtromas, 'The future world order and the right of nations to self-determination and sovereignty', *International Journal on World Peace*, VII, No. 1 (1990) as well as, Alexander Shtromas, 'Religion and ethnicity in world order', *International Journal on World Peace*, IX, No 2 (1992).

Metohia (where the Serbs are only about ten percent strong), uses the historical criterion.[22].

Secondly, the nationalisms of the nation-states established in multinational societies express themselves in their treatment of other nations incorporated into that state. France, for example, considers all its national French, whether they are Kanaks in New Caledonia or Corsicans in Corsica or Bretons, Catalans and Basques in metropolitan France. Only recently, after some serious disturbances, has France made a few concessions regarding the recognition of separate national identities of some overseas Frenchmen (e.g., the Kanaks and the Corsicans). Spain, on the other hand, allows qualified political autonomy to its seventeen regions which include some that are populated by non-Castillians (e.g., the Basques and the Catalans) but jealously guards its territorial integrity. Perhaps, only Great Britain and Canada have instituted a system whereby territorial peoples who consider themselves different from the rest of the country's population could secede from, respectively, the United Kingdom (Northern Ireland and Scotland already held referenda on that question which the secessionists lost) or the Canadian union state (the Quebequois are going to hold a referendum on that issue this year).

In a way, democratic France shares the excessiveness of its nationalism in regard to the 'non-French Frenchmen' with such authoritarian countries as Indonesia which fiercely fights the East Timorans and every other Indonesian nation daring to claim a separate identity. The mean is here best represented by the Anglo-Saxons, although they perhaps have the most difficulties in properly appreciating the nature and validity of smaller nations' nationalisms.

Thirdly, the nationalisms of all nation-states express themselves in the way they treat their national minorities. On that issue all liberal-democratic states adopted an almost identical attitude: members of national minorities are enjoying in these states equal citizenship rights and are accorded the specific rights of national-cultural and religious self-expression and development; national or racial discrimination is in all such states explicitly prohibited by law. This aspect of the democratic nation-states' policies is creating, however, some controversies, especially with the view to immigration laws and treatment of the immigrants. The other controversy, as indicated above, concerns the treatment by some nation-states, even the most democratic ones, of the territorial nations incorporated into these states as if they were mere national minorities or, even worse, members of the same dominant nation (as the Turks until recently

[22] A prominent Yugoslav journalist Goran Milic described his conversations with Serbian nationalists justifying their wars of aggression in the following, most telling passage: "Their arguments were really idiotic. 'Kosovo is Serbian historically.' I said then, 'but Vojvodina is not Serbian 'historically.' Their answer, 'But Serbians are there in majority.' Logical answer. 'But they are not in Sandzak.' The answer is, 'Sandzak is a part of Serbia.' We continue the dialogue: 'So, you are recognizing republics' borders. Then why is Knin Serbian, when it is in Croatia?' Answer: 'Because Croatia's borders are administrative. We don't recognize them. They were drawn by Tito.' 'But do you recognize those of 1918, drawn by French generals?' 'Yes. They were internationally recognized.' 'Perhaps those recognized in 1992 are more important than those recognized in 1918?' 'Croatia and Bosnia-Herzegovina should not have been recognized.' 'But that is not the opinion of 178 countries in the world. That is only the opinion of the authorities in Serbia trying to justify their conquests.' 'Then that is the problem of those countries.' 'Well, what is the right of Serbs to possess 70% of the land of Bosnia, when they make up 31% of the population? Bosnia is not Serbian historically and you are not a majority there. . .' 'According to land-registry, from 1920 Serbs owned 65% of the land in Bosnia.' 'But in Slavonia you are not a majority, nor is Slavonia Serbian historically, nor would the argument about land-registry work there. . .' 'Well, we are militarily stronger there.'" (Goran Milic, 'The letter from Zagreb', *Politika*, February 1 (1993)

treated their Kurds as 'Mountain Turks'). It goes without saying that some non-democratic nation-states are directly pursuing the policy of their minorities' assimilation or openly discriminate against them in both the citizenship rights and minority rights aspects.

Every single nation, being the form of social cohesion for a large number of individuals divided into various social strata, is in itself inevitably a heterogenous entity which stays nevertheless united because the national idea is capable of subsuming to itself all other ideas and interests, however contradictory and conflict-ridden the latter may be. These ideas, usually related to socio-political issues affecting the country as a whole, produce diverse and sometimes mutually exclusive policy proposals and plans, but in all of them the national idea and the overall nationalist orientation remain dominant and are used as means of justification and substantiation of every such proposed policy and plan.

In Britain, for example, all main political parties, despite their acute ideological differences, could be easily defined as equally nationalistic, because all of them share the same basic commitment to the defence of the British sovereign realm, to the enhancement of the country's security and its influential position in the world, as well, of course, as to the betterment of the welfare of the British people. What they differ about are not these basic national interest directed orientations but the ways they think are best for improving their country's and its people's lot. The many socialists in the Labour Party believe that their ideas provide the best answers to the country's problems, while the Thatcherite Conservatives are sure that these ideas can only ruin Britain and are putting forward their own ideas, such as 'People's Capitalism', believing that they are the ones which would serve British national interests best.

On the other hand, the National Front accuses the three main national parties of overlooking the real threat Britain and its indigenous people face from the increase in numbers and in influence on the British way of life of the 'alien elements' within British society. For this reason the National Front alone earned the title of a nationalistic party. But since all other parties are, as explained above, nationalistic parties, too, it would be more appropriate in my view to call this party chauvinistic or xenophobic, which the other parties are clearly not. Some would argue that these other parties are patriotic rather than nationalistic and that nationalism is inevitably becoming chauvinist or xenophobic. I would, however, strongly disagree with that view, as to me patriotism is a concept related to the country's territorial integrity and inviolability of its borders, as well as to the automatic support of the current government's policies towards the external world. Actually, an unqualified patriot is therefore prone to turning into a jingoist whose slogan is: 'my country, right or wrong'.

Differently from patriotism, nationalism is a concept related to the nation and to identification with the support of the interests of the people who constitute that nation, which can be in direct opposition to the country's current political regime and its policies. Many German nationalists during World War II fought Hitler's Germany with us, as they were convinced that their pronounced anti-patriotism serves in this case the interests of their nation best. And so did many Russian nationalists who, during the Cold War, were on our side of the front line and 'anti-patriotically' tried to undermine the Soviet regime hoping to relieve their nation of communist oppression and save it from degradation under Soviet rule.

The conclusion I would like to draw from this extensive review is that nationalism, even in its ugliest xenophobic forms, is basically non-ideological, although some sentiments, that in the more extreme cases it usually evokes, may be used by an ideology to capitalize upon and draw its support from. For example, the sentiments of xenophobic anti-Semitism present to a certain degree in every nation were used by Hitler for spreading and popularizing his racist ideological message in which anti-Semitism played a pivotal role. On their own, however, anti-Semitism and xenophobia generally, do not have the capacity to develop into an ideology, as they are exclusively concerned with the alleged threat or danger an alien nation or nationality can present to one's own nation and does not care about that alien nation or nationality or, actually, anything else outside its own nation's realm, as long as the presumed threat or danger is evacuated from it or otherwise dissipated. Xenophobia is a nervously, or even hysterically, defensive attitude towards the 'mysterious aliens', usually based on its bearers' profound national inferiority complex and on irrational suspicions fed by that complex. Usually it operates under the slogans: 'Britain for the Brits', 'France for the French', 'Germany for the Germans' or 'Russia for the Russians', without giving even the slightest consideration to the fate of the non-Brits, non-French, non-Germans or non-Russians outside the realms of, respectively, Britain, France, Germany or Russia.

Just to reiterate what has been already said above, an ideology, like that of Hitler's National-Socialism, can benefit and draw a lot of its strength from the spontaneous xenophobic sentiments in every nation but, on their own, these sentiments could only inspire certain policies, not ideologies. In this sense neither the British or Jean-Marie Le Pen's French National Fronts nor the German Republican and Vladimir Zhirinovsky's Russian Liberal Democratic Parties are ideological entities. Their exclusive concern is with policies which, in their view, would be able to preserve the integrity of their respective nations from what they perceive to be destructive 'alien inclusions' into them. It seems to me that the most extreme and entirely open proponent of such xenophobic policies is the leader of the Bulgarian Renewal Party (*Vazrazhdane*) Father Gelemenov who proclaimed to have abandoned traditional nationalism as toothless and ineffective, embracing instead the combative Nazi ideology of Adolf Hitler. Following the prescriptions of this ideology, Father Gelemenov stated, he and his Party are from now on going to fight for the adoption of a law, according to which Bulgarian Turks and Roma Gypsies will be deprived of the rights of Bulgarian citizenship, made into Bulgarian subjects and thus 'subordinated to the Bulgarian nation'.[23] This, he said, is necessary because the policies of forceful assimilation and expulsion of the non-assimilable ones practised by the communist regime proved ineffective and would not yield the desirable results of building up Bulgaria as one nation's state, even if the current or a future regime would consider recurring to the application of these policies. This, despite Gelemenov's claims to the contrary, is by no means, however, an exact rendition of the Nazi ideology either in full or even in its substantial parts (Father Gelemenov, by the way, has never even mentioned the Jews), but a direct reference to the infamous 1935 Nuremberg Laws which were at the time, indeed, designed for the purpose of implementing the 'transitional policy' of 'squeezing out' the Jews from Germany – not yet, however, for the ideological purpose of accomplishing 'the final solution' of the Jewish problem.

[23] See his interview in *Trud* of December 29, 1993.

As mentioned above, chauvinism in the extreme form of the belief that one's nation is superior to all others is, perhaps, the only variety of nationalism that has the potential of developing into an ideology, that is into a view about instituting a world order system in which this particular nation will rule the rest of mankind. But, as also noticed above, this is an impractical ideology that, at best, could be professed as a sort of a mere pipe-dream. Much better suited for this purpose, as Hitler had proved quite convincingly, are racist, not nationalist, ideas, and in the discussion of ideology the former are the ones which are much more relevant than the latter, although the latter in its excessively xenophobic forms provide a fertile breeding ground for the former.

The excesses, as well as the defects, of nationalism that so often lead to conflicts, wars and other protracted political disasters, remain a problem that people are increasingly getting concerned about and ever more intensively try to find solutions for. They ask themselves whether imperialism, aggressive assimilationism, chauvinism and xenophobia could be effectively controlled and, finally, eliminated, and try to arrive at a positive answer to this question. Politicians and political thinkers have always pondered about the possibilities for instituting a peaceful world order. And, in terms of arranging for a peaceful and cooperative co-existence of nations, they sought such a world order ever since the 16th century, when the nation firmly entered and, later, in the 17th–19th centuries, established itself as the paramount force on the European political arena.[24] And not only the excesses or defects of nationalism were in this respect calling their attention – knowing that even benign nationalism, when two or more of such nationalisms clash, may present humanity with enormous pain and ruin, they could not avoid also addressing the problem of how to accommodate competing nationalisms generally, creating out of this accommodation a humane and politically viable new world.

All ideologies, as was briefly shown above, have elaborated ready-made recipes to achieve such a state of the world. But, alongside the ideological solutions, the philosophical ones which were formulating certain desirable ideals and, then, elaborating conditions for practical realizations of these ideals, were gaining increasing prominence and application.[25] To clarify this point, I would suggest that Plato's ideal state, contrary to what Karl Popper had to say about it, was not an ideological projection of a totalitarian order he liked or preferred to other kinds of order, but an objective philosophical analysis of the conditions necessary for preservation of the original 'best state' which to him was kingship and which he posited as the common political ideal agreeable by everyone. What Plato tells us is that, in order to arrest the natural and otherwise unstoppable process of the state's decay and deterioration from the original 'best state' of kingship through timocracy, oligarchy and democracy into tyranny and then nothingness, one must institute in that 'best' or 'ideal' state such a kind of socio-political organization which involves the suppression of some

---

[24] For a detailed and thorough treatment of the problem of formation of nations and nationalisms in Europe, see: Liah Greenfield, *Nationalism: Five Roads to Modernity* (Cambridge, MA and London, Harvard University Press, 1992), esp. 'Introduction', pp. 1–26.

[25] I am grateful to Professor Aron Katsenelinboigen of the Wharton School at the University of Pennsylvania for pointing out to me the difference between ideology and ideal: if ideology formulates one-dimensional, universalist and absolute solutions to all socio-political problems, an ideal rejects such solutions in principle and tries to project instead a situation desirable or at least optimally acceptable to all shades of public opinion and then to assess the sacrifices which would have to be made in order to implement such an ideal into practical political life.

basic instincts inherent in human nature, especially among the political elite, and thus amounts to what we could call totalitarianism, but which, nevertheless, is the only one available to live up to this task and has to be recognized as such, whether one likes it or not. In effect, Plato leaves to us the choice to decide whether the ideal he projects is worth the price we would have to pay for its secure institution and preservation, implicitly emphasizing that the refusal to pay that price would be tantamount to our acceptance of, and reconciliation with, inescapable political decay and deterioration.

Similarly, there is nothing ideological in Kant's vision of perpetual peace. The six preliminary and three definitive articles of the Treaty on Perpetual Peace he envisaged, simply point out the prerequisites and mutual obligations that the parties involved in that Treaty have to take upon themselves in order to avoid ever slipping back into a war against each other. In other words, Kant takes the ideal of a peaceful world as, at a certain stage in humanity's evolution, a commonly agreeable one and shows what it takes to secure its implementation and preservation.

Kant is impeccably consistent in according the pivotal role in the world to the nations of which it consists. According to his Preliminary Article 2, peace could not be achieved as long as there remains in the world a nation ruled by another nation without that former (ruled) nation's explicit consent. Nor should there ever be instituted a world government – an institution superior in its sovereign rights to the national governments. The federation of free states forming the League of Peace (*foedus pacificum*) the creation of which is foreseen by Kant's Definitive Article 2, 'would be a federation of *nations*, but it must not be a nation consisting of nations'. 'The latter', he explains, 'would be contradictory, for in every nation there exists the relation of *ruler* (legislator) to *subject* (those who obey, the people); however, many nations in a single nation would consti-tute only a single nation, which contradicts our assumption (since we are. . . weighing the rights of *nations* in relation to one another, rather than fusing them into a single nation)'.[26] What Kant really projects in his *foedus pacificum* is a multitude of fully sovereign nation-states voluntarily submitting themselves to a single body of laws in accordance with which conflicts and disputes between them could be properly adjudicated and authoritatively resolved. For such an agreement on subordination to the same single body of law to become possible, all nations entering his projected *foedus pacificum* should, according to Kant, undertake the obligation under the Definitive Article 1 to be and remain republics, that is to live under a consitution which, 'first, . . .accords with the principles of the *freedom* of the members of society (as men), second, . . .accords with the principles of the *dependence* of everyone on a single, common . . . legislation (as subjects), and third, . . .accords with the law of the equality of them all (as citizens).[27] In other words, equal freedom of nations under the law in the *foedus pacificum* should, to Kant, be based on equal freedom of indi-viduals under the law within the nation joining the *foedus pacificum*.

This plan is to me typical of one projecting an ideal and totally antithetical to one basing itself on, or embracing, an ideology. Unlike the ideologues, Kant does not even try to establish a single set of universal principles to which

[26] Immanuel Kant, 'To perpetual peace: a philosophical sketch', in Immanuel Kant (Ted Humphry, transl.), *Perpetual Peace and Other Essays on Politics, History and Morals* (Indianapolis, IN, Hackett, 1983), p. 115.
[27] Kant, 'To perpetual peace', p. 112

people's existence would have, first, to be uniformly adjusted and, then, firmly subordinated. On the contrary, his whole endeavour is aimed at maximizing people's freedom to be what they are or want to become as individuals and nations, which is inevitably enhancing variety rather than uniformity. Kant's main task is to find a formula for such a pluralist political system which would allow for an optimal accommodation of that liberty enhanced variety of different, and sometimes clashing, identities, interests, ideals, values and goals, as well as for a peaceful handling and solution of contradictions and conflicts which are bound to flare up among them.

James Madison, when writing the American Constitution and defending its principles in *Federalist Papers*, also sought not to eliminate factions and factional conflict, as that would be tantamount to the elimination of liberty, but to create institutional arrangements able to control their effects. Neither Kant nor Madison had any illusions about human nature. They knew pretty well how 'strong is this propensity of mankind to fall into mutual animosities' – so strong, as Madison says, 'that where no substantial occasion presents itself, the most frivolous and fanciful distinctions have been sufficient to kindle their unfriendly passions, and excite their most violent conflicts.'[28] But they also knew that this propensity is not limitless and that it can be organically subordinated to the commonly agreed concept of right. 'Given the depravity of human nature,' Kant wrote, '. . .one must wonder why the word *right* has not been completely discarded. . . as pedantic, or why no nation has openly ventured to declare that it should be. . . The homage that every nation pays (at least in words) to the concept of rights proves, nonetheless, that there is in man a still greater, though presently dormant, moral aptitude to master the evil principle in himself (a principle he cannot deny) and to hope that others will also overcome it. For otherwise the word *right* would never leave the mouths of those nations that want to make war on one another. . .'[29]

I think, here we have finally touched upon the basic difference between an ideology and an ideal. Ideology strives for the elimination of factional conflicts and, accordingly, projects formulae under which this goal can be achieved and universal harmony in human society established. An ideal, recognizing the 'basic depravity of human nature', seeks to accommodate the freedom of engaging into factional conflict within a pluralist political system based on a commonly agreed concept of right. An ideal always seeks a balance between maximum liberty and preservation of order under the law, while an ideology seeks order by eliminating in one way or another those forms of liberty which sustain social divisiveness and foster factional (national, class or other) conflicts. In this sense, Millian liberalism remains an ideology, while Kantian or Madisonian – and, by that same token, Spencerian – liberalism is absolutely non-ideological, as it concentrates on the elaboration of certain social techniques, of specific legal and political instruments and procedures allowing for simultaneous side-by-side existence and free competition of various ideologies and political doctrines, distinct material and ideal interests, diverse and even alternate values and goals. Differently from Millian liberalism, Kantian, Madisonian or Spencerian liberalism allows for, and encourages, not only the expression of a person's individual nature and preferences, but also equally caters for

[28] Alexander Hamilton, James Madison and John Jay, *The Federalist Papers* (New York, New American Library, 1961), p. 79. (The quotation is from Madison's No. 10.)

[29] I. Kant, 'To perpetual peace', p. 116.

that person's ability freely to express and foster his collective identity. It treats man not simply as an individual but, quoting Emile Durkheim's famous formula, as *homo duplex* or man possessing a dual, individualist and collectivist, nature. And, together with Emile Durkheim, such a liberal assesses the quality of a society by that society's ability to accommodate and protect in a balanced manner both the individualist and the collectivist natures of man.

Of course, one could say that Kantian, Madisonian or Spencerian liberalism is also an ideology, and some people, indeed, do say so. It all depends, no doubt, on the usage of the term ideology, on how one agrees to interpret it. For example, the great Russian dissident human rights' campaigner, Nobel Laureate Andrey Sakharov, proclaimed himself and his associates and counterparts in the country and around the world 'rightdefenders' or partisans and advocates of what he defined as 'the ideology of human rights' which he sharply counter-opposed to 'ideologies based on dogmas and various metaphysical beliefs aimed at the reconstruction of the world'.[30] 'The ideology of human rights', Sakharov explains, 'is by nature pluralistic, it is the one and sole ideology allowing for the liberty of various forms of social associations and for the co-existence of these various forms, which endows man with the maximum liberty of personal choice.'[31] In Sakharov's portrayal, this 'ideology' is actually non-ideological almost by definition. As he himself has put it, 'the ideology of. . . human rights is perhaps the only one which has the potential to accommodate within itself such otherwise incompatible ideologies as the communist, the social-democratic, the religious, the technocratic, the nationalistic; it can also serve as the foundation for [socio-political] positioning of those men who do not want to tie themselves to any theoretical finesses and dogmas and who are sick and tired of the multitude of ideologies none of which has brought people any, even the most elementary, human happiness'.[32]

I do not mind Andrey Sakharov and those who phrase their ideas likewise to call Kantian, Madisonian or Spencerian liberalism a 'human rights' ideology'. I am only sure that this kind of ideology is not the one which we are discussing as "'isms" in this book.

V. Any " 'Isms" for the Future?

A. Marxist or Non-Marxist Socialism?

Among the authors of this book, only Alex Callinicos predicts a healthy future for Marxism. 'The variant of Marxism most likely to have a future is', in his view, 'what Isaak Deutscher called "classical Marxism" – the tradition as it was first developed by Marx and Engels, which prevailed in the Russian revolutionary movement in 1917, and which Trotsky and the Left Opposition sought to defend against the emerging Stalinist *nomenklatura*', (p. 64). Focal to him in this respect is Marx's own, rather vague, formula of 'the self-emancipation of the working class'. Callinicos translates it for today's use as the 'process of self-liberation, driven from below by the mass of working people's aspiration to take

---

[30] Andrey Sakharov 'Dvizhenie za prava cheloveka v SSSR i Vostochnoy Evrope – Tseli, znachenie, trudnosti' (The movement for human rights in the USSR and Eastern Europe – goals, significance, difficulties). *Kontinent* (Paris), No. 19 (1979), p. 171.

[31] Sakharov, 'The movement of human rights in the USSR and Eastern Europe', p. 172

[32] Sakharov, 'The movement of human rights in the USSR and Eastern Europe', p. 188

control of their lives' (*ibid.*). What he does not explain, however, is who in his view are in today's developed industrial and post-industrial societies the 'working people' and who, respectively, are the 'non-working people' depriving the working ones of control of their lives. In his 1991 book. Callinicos says that workers' self-liberation is to be realized through the 'democratic socialism of workers' councils', but he does not provide there an answer to the above question either. According to Callinicos's idea of self-liberation, the collectives of workers in each enterprise will form themselves into councils democratically deciding on all important issues the enterprise faces and electing administrators to fulfil these decisions. It still remains unclear whether these collectives of workers will include all employees or only some specific categories of them, and whether the 'old capitalist administrators' will be eligible to act as either members of the workers' council or candidates for election to administrative positions. In other words, one does not notice in Callinicos's works the division between antagonistic classes, the front lines of class struggle in contemporary capitalist society, although class analysis is supposed to form the core of any study conducted in accordance with the principles of classical Marxism.

In Callinicos's vision workers' self-liberation also entails the necessity of such a democratic 'workers' managed' enterprise becoming the foundation of the society's overall political organization. He writes: 'The most distinctive feature of the soviet [workers council] as a political institution is that it is based not on any particular geographical unit, but on the workplace'.[33]

What we encounter in this concept is a combination of the Yugoslav experiment in workers' self-management within the enterprise and of the early Soviet attempts – started in 1918 and formally retained in operation till 1936 – at building up the entire structure of their socialist state on what they called 'workplace democracy', that is on the principle of forming the basic network of local authorities as representatives of the enterprises workers' collectives, and central authorities – as those of the thus step-by-step formed local authorities. As we now know, both of these endeavours failed without having enriched mankind with anything positive or worth retaining and following up. The Yugoslav experience proved that the workers' councils have never been really concerned with their enterprises' commercial success and that they mainly acted (when meaningfully acting at all) as enhanced trade unions, whose ruinous impact on the enterprises' economic performance could be, and with mixed success usually was, offset only by the strict system of the state's administrative management of the economy, starting on the level of the enterprises' administration itself and permeating the whole structure of the Titoist Yugoslav Party State. On the other hand, the Soviets' tossing with workplace democracy turned out to be, from its very outset, just a meaningless façade for the unbridled exercise of the 'leading role of the Party', the Bolsheviks, or, in real terms, of that Party's blatant dictatorship over the workers, each and every single workplace and the whole state system which was supposed formally to emanate from the workplaces.

In essence, the idea of management by workers' councils is meant to turn enterprises from institutions serving the market into practically self-serving institutions which, when organized into the state, are supposed to be serving the overall interests of the working people of these enterprises as a whole. Enter-

---

[33] Alex Callinicos, *The Revenge of History* (University Park, PA, Pennsylvania State University Press, 1991), p. 110.

prises, however, by their very nature and function cannot be self-serving entities. If they stopped serving the market, they are going to be bound to end up
serving the market's only possible substitute – the totalitarian managerial state.
Nor can the enterprises, as producing and trading institutions, constitute or
'emanate' the state. For that they would have to be supplemented and permeated by a specifically political body – the ruling Party or any other analogous
political institution – which will thus become the state allegedly in the name and
on behalf of the enterprises but actually by and for itself. This was what had
actually become of the Yugoslav experiment with workers' councils, to say
nothing of their early Soviet prototypes.

The ideological artificiality of 'council socialism' is best demonstrated by the
fact that in the contemporary political and economic battles there is not much
demand on the part of the workers for instituting this kind of democratic
socialism. The experience of Yugoslavia shows that the workers were not
interested in spending their free time in meetings deciding on managerial
problems and, as long as the administration did not infringe on their working
conditions and pay, left it alone to do the job, although legally they could
exercise on the way their enterprises were managed much more influence. The
famous workers' *Mitbestimmungsrecht* in Germany is also mainly exercised for
insuring workers' welfare and job security. The 'council socialists' usually
explain it by saying that this is the case because the workers do not own the
enterprises in which they are entitled to form their councils; if, however, the
workers were owners, they add, this situation would drastically change. But,
again, there were many cases of workers' cooperatives taking over the ownership of the enterprises in which they worked but very few of such cooperatives
were economically successful and, as a consequence, either went bankrupt or
have returned to private ownership (by selling their shares). Professor Richard
H. Hudelson, himself a person sympathetic to the socialist idea, in his recent
study very succinctly proved that in a market situation this is an entirely logical
development and that the only alternative to it is the introduction of state
planning and management of the economy.[34]

There is, however, no traceable demand among the workers of capitalist
countries for changing the market system to the system of state planning either.
Although that latter system might allow them secure ⋎ to continue in their jobs
as long as they obediently fulfilled the state's ordͤ ϩ, the workers somehow
know that the managerial state is a much more ferocious and even a much less
generous master than the market in a liberal democracy could ever afford to be.
As we see, the idea of 'council socialism' remains unrequested, whatever the
intellectual proponents of that idea may think about it.

As for the creation of a comprehensive network of workers cooperatives
maintaining a market system, this is, first of all, not a Marxist but, in fact, an
Anarchist idea, totally antithetical to the basic principles of classical Marxist
thought which was largely built upon the critical assessment and rejection of
that idea in its classical representation by Pierre-Joseph Proudhon.[35] Secondly,

[34] See, Richard H. Hudelson, *The Rise and Fall of Communism* (Boulder, CO and Oxford,
Westview, 1993), esp, pp. 154–9. Hudelson unambiguously states that in their theoretical constructions '[c]ouncil socialists . . . have [in fact] returned to a system of central planning, one of the evils of
"bureaucratic state socialism" for which council socialism was supposed to provide an alternative'
(p. 156).

[35] Marx's smashing critique of Proudhon's idea of workers' cooperatives (mutualism) is detailed
in his *Poverty of Philosophy* (1847). There Marx unequivocally shows that socialism has to negate

this idea, in the conditions of liberal democracy, lost its revolutionary or even visionary meaning. As long as in such a democracy the rights of private ownership are universal and properly protected by law, nobody could prevent the workers' cooperatives from being created and becoming owners of enterprises without any revolutionary changes as prerequisites for the realization of such a possibility taking place; furthermore, if in those conditions the workers' cooperatives would prove to be the most successful operators in the market place, they would in due course inevitably become the dominant form of the economic organization of society, anyway. The problem is that they proved to be less economically effective than private enterprises and thus, at least for now, cannot expect much proliferation.

The only way to make such workers' cooperatives what their proponents want them to be, is by imposing them upon society in a forceful, ideologically motivated revolutionary manner. This is, however, not a very likely perspective for, as long as the free market is maintained, it will reject any unproductive forms of economic activity imposed upon it. Hence, again there would be a necessity to substitute the market by state planning and management which by now has been fully discredited even in the view of the proponents of workers' self-management and council socialism, including Callinicos himself.

Another abortive attempt at implementing a practically identical idea was the total corporate state which Mussolini tried to build in Italy. Although any objective observer would have to admit that Mussolini's corporations, in their efforts to introduce a more reasonable balance between the productive and commercial interest of the enterprise, on the one hand, and the interest of the enterprise's employees, on the other, were much more sophisticated than the workers' councils of the council socialists, they were as dysfunctional as the latter and either operated as covered private enterprises or had to be managed by the Fascist Party backed by the full strength of that Party's state. Thus, so far the ideas of council socialism, wherever they have been tried and whatever their ideological origins – Marxist, Anarchist or Fascist – may have been, proved to be defective and failed to take root. On the other hand, if they were productive and ethically desirable, they could, and certainly would, be practically instituted without much ado within the extant system of the 'bourgeois-liberal democracy', which, alas, they were not.

All this is to say that Callinicos's ideas of council socialism neither save Marxism for the future, as these ideas are basically non-Marxist (and some of their basic aspects even anti-Marxist), nor do they on their own provide a viable tool for shaping the future world. As a matter of fact, these ideas prove the death of Marxism better than the burial marches enthusiastically incanted for, and critical assaults directed against, Marxism by the non- and anti-Marxists. Indeed, to take out from the complex and sophisticated legacy of Marx one single phrase on the self-emancipation of the working class in order to prove that Marxism remains a productive and viable social theory, is in itself a self-defeating enterprise, and especially so when even the notion of the working class remains blatantly undefined (and, in present circumstances, is for Callinicos's purposes obviously undefinable). Equally flawed is Callinicos's attempt to justify Marxism's present day viability by its having taken original shape as a

capitalism in its entirety, as a system, and that therefore Proudhon's attempts at incorporating into socialism the so called positive features of capitalism, i.e. the free market, are undialectical and thus totally fallacious.

critique of capitalism. First, capitalism which was the subject of Marx's critique no longer exists, and Callinicos did not bother to explain how he relates present day capitalism with the system witnessed and presumably effectively criticized by Marx. But, even more importantly, a critique of an 'unjust and destructive path' on which capitalism, according to Callinicos, still continues (p. 65), is by no means an exclusive prerogative of Marxism. The democratic theory, the ideas of individual and national liberty, the practice of defence of human rights and pursuit of justice in conditions of political freedom, are in this respect much more effective than Marxism; and, in combating injustice and social destruction in whatever socio-political system these phenomena took place (and each such system, including capitalism, produced more than its fair share of them), they – the liberal democratic ideals – achieved much better practical results than had Marxism at any time and in any of its varieties or forms.

To a large extent the demise of Marxism is the result of the general decline of scientism, of the by now almost universal healthy scepticism with regard to the absoluteness of scientific knowledge and the omnipotence of science as method of inquiry into man and society. As Professor Noël O'Sullivan has convincingly shown in his chapter of this book, ideologies claiming their infallability on the basis of their allegedly scientific veracity do not cut ground anymore today, in what is fashionable to call the post-modern era, even with the most rationally minded people. Therefore if socialism can at all survive in our post-scientistic and post-holistic times, it can do so only as an ethical idea, as a specific variety of the idea of justice or as a part of a religiously based morality. Marxist socialism obviously does not enter into any of these categories.

Ethical, non-Marxist socialism can, however, also develop into an ideology and, as such, should be assessed from the point of view of its viability in the capacity of an '"ism" for the future. Professor David Marquand in his chapter of this book argues that out of the five dimensions of socialism that have made it into a powerful ideology, the pivotal four – namely, the socialist economic theory, a general social science, a platform for the advancement of social interests of the working class and the secular substitute for a religion (the basic ideological dimension) have been eliminated by the demise of Marxism and its impact on the socialist idea generally. What in his view will remain of socialism for the future is its ethic extolling the values of community and fellowship. On that basis Marquand comes to the conclusion that socialism – may be under a different name – is going to survive the test of time and will be prominently figuring in the battle of ideas in the future. I share this conclusion and clearly said so in the previous paragraph. I only do not think that ideas promoting community and fellowship are specifically socialist and that they could ever on their own make socialism survive as a full-blooded ideology. The difference between Marquand and me on this score consists, I believe, in our different assessments of the potential of the free market system to provide for, and co-exist with, adequate social justice and effective work of charitable institutions. In the debate between Marquand and Ebeling on the potential of the free market to provide for these values, I am afraid, I tend to take Ebeling's side rather than Marquand's. Marquand's sceptical view of the free market, his disbelief in its humanistic potential, indeed imply the necessity of the resurrection of socialism as an economic and social theory and even as religious creed – that is, as a full-blooded ideology – because the present rise to dominant prominence of the liberal free market ideas and policies may in his view undermine '[r]eformed, welfare capitalism' which, according to Marquand, 'is a gift of history, as fragile as it is precious' (p. 49). In other words, capitalism, in Marquand's opinion, may now revert to its unbridled, unreformed, pre-Keynesian shape – the shape that made socialist critique of it valid and viable – and, subsequently, revive socialism as an ideology on its original scale and intensity.

I do not think that this logic of Marquand is correct. First, nothing can be resurrected in an identical form, especially phenomena that were tried in historical practice and did not prove a success. Second, policies in a democratic state depend on decisions made by the majority of that state's electorate. As long as this is the case – and today it is true for Russia and East Europe as much as to the proper West – tensions between liberty and justice, which Minogue has so convincingly discussed in his chapter (see pp. 15 ff) and which inevitably exist in every society, will each time be resolved in a fluctuatingly flexible manner – more restrictions of liberty for the sake of increasing justice at one stage, followed by relative liberalization on another stage, and then, by the introduction of some corrections and adjustments of liberal policies, inspired by the sense of justice and charity, on yet the next stage, etc. These fluctuating policies will for the foreseeable future most probably continue unabated, but they will hardly acquire an explicit ideological dimension. In a democratic polity explicitly ideological policies are the ones no political party, however ideologically inspired and committed it may be, can afford to put in an undiluted form to the electorate without losing the support of its mainstream sections. That is why even Margaret Thatcher had to stress every so often that the National Health Service is safe with the Tories and the Labour Party had never dared to include its Clause 4 (on nationalization of the means of production) in its pre-election manifestos.

It follows from the above, thirdly, that as long as the old- or new-style ideologically committed socialists are going to subordinate themselves to the democratic political process, their policies will willy-nilly drastically differ from their overall ideology. Only the revolutionary socialists of the Marxist-Leninist variety – those who defy parliamentarism and, in my view rightly, believe, as did Lenin, that socialists who value democracy above socialism betray the latter and by abdicating from ever implementing it in reality become in fact the labour lieutenants of the capitalist class – are the ones who remain and will continue to be in the future truly ideological socialists. But this is exactly that kind of socialism which has been thoroughly and irreversibly defeated by the demise of Marxism. Marxist or any other kind of revolutionary socialism cannot be resurrected in the foreseeable future due largely to the fact that its collapse in the former USSR and East Europe has immensely fortified the foundations of the liberal-democratic order which could be reversed to an authoritarian one not anymore by the pursuit of socialist or other abstract ideological goals but only by national emergencies and nationalistically (that is by definition non-ideologically) inspired extraordinary tasks.

Finally, the values of community and fellowship are much better served and strengthened by religious, local, corporate and other similar voluntary communities than by socialism in whatever shape it is going to exist. For, in contrast with these public sentiments and bonds which draw on natural instincts of fellowship in men, socialism is inevitably trying to involve into everything it deems just and charitable the coercive machinery of the state and law, thus expressing its profound disbelief in the natural goodness and the cooperative and charitable spirit of man. I believe with Durkheim that social history consists of the unending search for such a socio-political system that could best accommodate the dual – individualist and collectivist – nature of man, which implies the necessity of socio-political promotion of organic human partnerships based on communalism and fellowship. But also, together with Durkheim, I believe that socialism is the least suitable, in fact a fake form for such a promotion. Only in Durkheim's time this was not yet a socially proven fact which, I believe, at this juncture in time it certainly is.

All this is to say that, in my view, not only Marxism but every other variety of socialist or communist ideology is by now fully bankrupt and thus must be excluded from consideration as candidates or an '"ism" for the future.

Thus, Socialism and Communism, as viable and powerful ideological creeds, followed in 1991, after the Soviet collapse, the way to oblivion Fascism and National Socialism went in 1945, after having been not only militarily but also morally thoroughly defeated in World War II. This does not mean that there will be no socialist or communist ideologues left in the world at all; one glance at the academic communities of the West would obviously belie such a conclusion. But, as the neo-Fascists and neo-Nazis, the neo-Marxists and other neo-socialist or neo-communist revolutionaries have been doubtlessly relegated now to the position of excentric political groupings acting on the marginal flanks of national and world politics and will have to reconcile themselves to remaining in that position at least for the foreseeable future.

B. Religious fundamentalism?

I am convinced that no different destiny awaits religious fundamentalism, despite of its recent expansion and prominence. To me the enhanced role religious fundamentalism started to play in the last few decades of the 20th century is the natural result of rapid proliferation of the processes of modernization (or, which is one and the same, of westernization) and subsequent secularization to all, even the remotest parts of our globe. Strongly affected by these sweeping processes, traditional societies and communities reacted to them by partly joyfully and thoughtlessly embracing them (mainly the Millian liberals, but also the socialists and communists), partly by trying to adjust to them without losing their traditional identity (the liberal nationalists) and, partly, by totally rejecting, and trying to mount a vigorous defence against, them. The very appearance in traditional societies and communities of the former two groups was by itself a strong incentive for the latter one to actively start combating modernization and considering to take extraordinary measures baring it from deeper penetration into their realm and otherwise enforcing the traditional, premodern way of life in their respective societies and/or communities. As Professor Fouad Ajami has put it, 'traditions are often most insistent and loud when they rupture, when people no longer really believe and when age-old customs lose their ability to keep men and women at home'.[36]

On the whole, the vigorous resistance of conservative traditionalism to the extremes of modernization and moral relativism that it tends, especially during

---

[36] Fouad Adjami, 'The Summoning', in *Foreign Affairs* collection of articles, *Agenda 1994; Critical Issues in Foreign Policy* (New York, Foreign Affairs, 1994), p. 150; the article originally appeared in the September/October 1993 issue of *Foreign Affairs* as a response to Samuel P. Huntington's provocative piece on the presumably forthcoming clash of various civilizations into which after the end of Cold War the world, according to Huntington, is getting rapidly divided.

the transition, to encourage, is a healthy phenomenon. Being by no means able to stop this process, such resistance makes it more moderate, more steady, and thus also compatible with the continuity of people's specific religious, cultural and ethnic identities, with the moral principles and spiritual values which, having been established long before the modern times, remain nevertheless a reliable guiding light for the people to take a lead from in the modern and post-modern times, too.

Religious fundamentalism, in its more extreme and radical forms, is, however, capable of strongly overreacting to the challenges of modernity and, as it was shown above and more explicitly elaborated by Parekh in his chapter on Fundamentalism contributed to this book, turn into entirely modern and 'this-worldly political ideology capitalizing on people's modernization related anxieties and strong conservative instincts. Founded on a universal religion, such an ideology also tends to preach not to one particular nation or religious community but to the world at large, trying to convert it to that ideology's particular eschatological vision. In all this, religious fundamentalism is but an inverse expression of revolutionary socialism/communism; and, vice versa, because revolutionary socialism/communism espouses the ideal of a rigidly organized, strictly regimented, closed – and by that supposedly also harmonious – society, it is itself nothing more but a specific form of fundamentalism seeing itself as destined to confront and prevail over the unstable, overflexible and thus decadent society of the Western type – or, in other words, the open society.[37]

In my view, these fundamentalist ideologies – as well as the socialist/communist ones – are fighting hopeless rearguard battles against the unstoppable advancement of modernity which, by taking ever deeper root on a global scale, is rendering them increasingly marginal and, finally, is going to make them almost totally irrelevant. I fully agree with Professor Mark Juergensmeyer's analysis according to which religious fundamentalism, after having grudgingly developed a tolerant attitude to secular nationalism, will have to merge in the end with the overall nationalist movement of the nation within which it operates, occupying in that movement a section which, however distinct, is going to form an organic constituent part of that movement.[38] Such an evolution of religious fundamentalism will substantively cut its ideological edge. The fundamentalists' universalist claims within the framework of a non-ideological nationalist movement will inevitably have to take the back seat and get subordinated to current, mainly pragmatically determined national-religious concerns and actions.

The other problem with religious fundamentalism (also pointed out by Professor Juergensmeyer) is its inherent inability of reaching across religious-denominational and even national divides to unite people for concerted political action on a scale larger than the one determined by these inherently very stubborn divisions. It is to a large extent because of this limitation that religious

[37] I share this idea with the contemporary leading Russian philosopher, Grigory Pomerants; see, for example, his "Fundamentalism i XX vek" (Fundamentalism and the 20th Century), in *Literaturnaya Gazeta* (The Literary Gazette), No. 7 (5487) of February 16, 1994, p. 11.

[38] See, Mark Juergensmeyer, *The New Cold War: Religious Nationalism Confronts the Secular State*. (Berkeley, CA, University of California Press, 1993). I do not think, however, that this analysis could be applied to the socialist/communist ideologies which have been proved unable to merge with nationalism without hopelessly compromising their basic foundations. Their destiny, at least in the West, is more likely to take them ever closer to joining forces, however grudgingly, with Millian liberalism.

fundamentalism is destined to degenerate into becoming a part of a nationalist movement, as only within such a movement it could be adequately accommodated and continue to exert a constant and relatively significant influence on politics.

Very few religious fundamentalist ideologies have ever acquired a transnational dimension, anyway. Perhaps the sole example of a transnational influence is the Islamic Shiite ideology of the late Ayatollah Khomeini which is commanding allegiance among some of the rather geographically distant Lebanese Shiite Muslims (the Hezbollah movement), but, as the Iranian-Iraqi war had demonstrated, not among the geographically adjacent Iraqi-Shiites who were pretty much afraid of Khomeini and did not rush into embracing him in preference to their arch-enemy Saddam Hussein, the Suni (by origin, but secularly-socialist by his proper ideological identity) leader of Iraq.

In his recent study, Professor Bernard Lewis has very convincingly revealed how, in fact, weak and divided Islamic fundamentalism is.[39] According to him, only two Muslim countries – Iran and Sudan – fell victim to the fundamentalists' revolutionary endeavours, and only in Iran have the fundamentalists realized some of their ideological prescriptions, while in Sudan the Islamic fundamentalists' ideological plan was fully consumed by the ceaseless civil war Sudanese fundamentalist rulers chose to wage against the non-Islamic and non-Arabic population of the country's Southern provinces in a murderous but vain endeavour to get it forcefully Islamicized, too. In all the other Islamic states Muslim fundamentalism is kept under strict, though uneasy, restraint and, when daring to raise its head, getting ruthlessly suppressed, as is the case in Anwar el-Sadat's and Hosney Mubarak's Egypt and revolutionary Algeria, where the Islamic fundamentalist movement closely associates itself, by the way, with the pro-Western and anti-socialist liberals opposing the current socialistically oriented Algerian military dictatorship. As we see, the so called "Great Green Peril of Islamic Fundamentalism" is not so much a reflection of political reality as the product of Western imagination anxiously looking after the defeat of Communism for yet another global ideological enemy and falsely identifying as such an enemy the 'imaginary Muslim monsters', as Leon T. Hadar puts it.[40] Even people who believe that Islamic fundamentalism is the great new threat for the West to cope with, recognize that 'militant Islam is as diverse as the Arabs themselves and the countries in which it is taking hold, ... that Islam is not inherently at odds with modernity' and that there are no serious grounds to believe that a 'new "Khomeintern" – a vast conspiracy led by Iran and Sudan' – is about to emerge.[41]

All this is to say that in my opinion religious fundamentalism generally and Islamic fundamentalism, in particular, are not the glimmers of the future, as so many believe them to be, but rather the last desperate and therefore remarkably intransigent defence lines of the passing pre-modern past; the fundamentalist ideological exponents of that past are determined to oppose the invincible challenges of modernity and, by so doing, turn them, as much as it is at all possible, to their own political advantage. What they really seek is to put

[39] See, Bernard Lewis, *Islam and the West* (New York and Oxford, Oxford University Press, 1993).

[40] Leon T. Hadar, 'What Green Peril?', in *Agenda 1994* ... p. 171 (originally, this article was published in the Spring 1993 issue of *Foreign Affairs*).

[41] Judith Miller, 'The challenge of radical Islam', in *Agenda 1994* ... p. 176 (originally, this article was published in the Spring 1993 issue of *Foreign Affairs*).

themselves in charge of the traditional societies and/or communities in which they function and use their thus acquired political power for controlling the processes of modernization taking place in these societies and/or communities in such a way that would subordinate the processes of modernization to their particular ideological preferences and the enhancement of their power and influence in their respective countries and the world at large.

There is no way religious fundamentalisms can continue to claim in this overall context the role of universally valid "'isms" for the future; nor will they by any means be able to provide consistent ideological foundations for building upon them a number of separate and mutually hostile civilizations, as Harvard's Professor Samuel P. Huntington curiously wants us to believe.[42] Professor Fouad Ajami in his reply to Huntington,[43] has convincingly shown how wrong Huntington is in equating 'indigenization' with 'de-Westernization' of societies and how he mistook for 'civilizational duels' mere national struggles for self-determination and for settling old-standing irredenta which, after being for so long suppressed by the oppressive discipline of the Cold War, with that war gone, have liberated themselves to powerfully burst out onto the surface of world politics and to occupy in it the primary place which previously was held by the Cold War itself.

The struggle of nations for the preservation of their identity and for what they regard to be their justly deserved decent place in the post-Cold War structure of the world's system of nation-states is indeed neither ideological nor civilizational. It does not seek either ideological pre-eminence over, or 'civilizational isolation' from, the rest of the world. Quite the contrary, it is the struggle for accomplishing their transition to westernized modernity and for organic integration into the global system dominated by the West and Western liberal-democratic principles without having to renounce or compromise their unique historical and cultural heritage, that is to say, for getting integrated into that system on a par with the originally Western nations which a few centuries ago were themselves neither so much economically advanced nor yet so rich in liberal-democratic traditions. Thus, contrary to Huntington's vision, in today's world the nations are fighting not for 'civilizational integration' with culturally similar nations in order viably to oppose and, eventually, defeat other similarly multi-national 'civilizational entities', but for their separate full-blooded nationhood that has to be asserted by clearly pronounced separation from other nations and, in the first place, curiously, from the ones belonging to their own civilizational realm. And, in order to accomplish this task, nations have to seek to become fully sovereign states, equal in this respect to every other previously established or more powerful sovereign nation-state, and be recognized by them as such. This is today's true *Zeitgeist* which evolves within the overall undisturbed process of each nation's modernizing westernization and of the common for them all integration into the global system dominated by Western principles and values. To put it simply, nations are reluctant to join the world without having insured first their unassailable integrity and identity within it. To conclude, I would like to quote again from Fouad Ajami's recent piece: 'We have been delivered into a new world, to be sure. But it is not a world where the writ

---

[42] See, Samuel P. Huntington, 'The clash of civilizations?', in *Agenda 1994* . . . (originally, this article was published in the Summer 1993 issue of *Foreign Affairs*).
[43] See footnote 36.

of civilizations runs. Civilizations and civilizational fidelities remain . . . But let us be clear: civilizations do not control states, states control civilizations'.[44]

The struggle of nations for equal sovereignty allowing them to get integrated into the global (Western-dominated) system on their own, non-discriminatory terms, is willy-nilly going, in the end, to absorb and subordinate to its tasks the various extant religious fundamentalisms which, accordingly, will have to mute their universalist or 'civilizationist' ideological claims and be driven to enhance those elements in their respective doctrines which pertain to the strengthening of their particular nation's separate identity and the definition of that nation's place and role in the world.

C. Millian Liberalism?

The dominance in present-day's world politics of the non-ideological national-ist issues is as mentioned above equally undermining the strength and influence of the Millian kind of liberal ideology. Liberalism is becoming today increas-ingly inconceivable without due and proper recognition of collective human rights which include not only the rights of nations, religious denominations and minorities, but also the rights of various other communities forming themselves in concordance with their freely chosen specific moral and cultural traditions and values to be what they are or wish to become. The ubiquitous and irrever-sible progress of modernization leading to global westernization is thus pro-ceeding not in the way of creating a uniform liberal world society the Millian liberals always predicted and never ceased promoting (and Huntington is, no doubt, one of such liberals; it is because of his Millian liberalism that Hunt-ington sees the ongoing natural processes of the world's peoples' collectivist self-assertion in such an erroneously dramatic and falsely alarming light), but by opposing the levelling liberal uniformity and promoting tradition and variety which are being thus incorporated into, and accommodated within, the pattern of modern (and even post-modern) world. And this is exactly what makes Millian liberalism with its intolerance to even the most natural and organic forms of collectivism, as well as to variety in general, as obsolete and unquali-fied for the role of an "'ism" for the future, as the other ideologies discussed above are. The identity of the emerging new world order remains, no doubt, liberal, but its liberalism is certainly not Millian but rather Kantian-Madis-onian-Spencerian.

D. Anything Else? What about Welfare-Statism?

Does this really mean that mankind has had enough of ideological delusions and that, with the collapse of communism, it has indeed firmly entered not only into the post-communist, but also into the altogether post-ideological era? Professor Noël O'Sullivan believes that this is indeed the case. In his chapter for this book, he practically equates the transition from modernity to post-modernity with transcendence from the ideological to the post-ideological stage in mankind's development. Professor Kenneth Minogue, however, disagrees. What for O'Sullivan represents '[t]he new politics of inclusion and [recognition of] differences' that makes for 'a world in which the "'isms" could be mutually accommodated' (p. 42), is for Minogue a situation in which new ideologies,

[44] 'The Summoning', *Agenda 1994* . . . p. 157.

based on 'the morality of egalitarian humanism' (p. 18), proliferate. Although, according to Minogue, 'the end of communism might be taken as the final proof of the end of ideology', this is unfortunately not the case. 'Instead,' he says, '. . . ideologies of one kind and another seem to be thriving' (p. 5). Marxist social-ism's 'decline', he continues, 'has seen a most remarkable revival: that of utopian socialism' (p. 16). In today's world, this 'ideology generates an ever expanding set of rights which it is the duty of the state to implement'. What Minogue, actually, talks about is welfare-statism which, in his view, treats 'man as a bundle of needs, utilities, satisfactions and preferences. In a sense, this is the natural man of civil society, for political man as an independent citizen has lost his place at the centre of political philosophy'. The utilitarian ideology of welfare-statism has thus 'converted human beings into organisms suitable for [state] management in terms of their happiness'. (p. 19).

In this controversy I am inclined to take O'Sullivan's side rather than Min-ogue's. As I said above, welfare-statism may be a constituent part of an overall socialist ideology, but separately, within the context of the retention of the liberal democratic state and of a market economy,[45] it amounts to no more than a pragmatically conceived policy which, when, or if, it proves to be unable to deliver the desired benefits, can be, without much of a hassle, revised or altogether discarded in the same way in which it was introduced in the first place. Without a socialist ideological context, welfare-statism loses its sanctity – the status of the untouchable foundation-laying principle for the just society's organization, the symbol of true justice and of the truth of the ideology itself – and therefore rather easily lends itself to pragmatic re-evaluation and revision. This being the basic trait distinguishing a policy from an ideology, effectively deprives welfare-statism as such from the qualifications necessary to pronounce it an ideology and relegates it to the realm of mere policy.

Minogue treats allocation of welfare rights and benefits exclusively in terms of a new statist ideology, while for O'Sullivan it could come in both statist and non-statist, that is civil society bound, forms. He is as negative about the former as is Minogue,[46] but remains hopeful 'that the formal or civil model of post-modernity is adopted' (p. 41). On that I beg to differ with O'Sullivan, as to me such a dilemma is rather spurious and entirely academic. In a democratic polity, as long as the majority of the electorate will be willing to lend its support to the welfare state in its administrative form, that type of the welfare-state will continue to exist, whether one likes it or not. But as soon as the state will, for all to see, prove to be unable to maintain its welfare services on the level to which

[45] Minogue clearly states in his essay that these new, welfare state oriented ideologies are neither dependent upon nor are at all envisaging 'a revolutionary seizure of power by a knowledge possessing elite who would use their power first to smash the state and then to guide humanity towards the forms of communal life. That classic version seems now to be dead' (p. 16), which is to say that the liberal-democratic state is here to stay and continue delivering the goods. In another passage, he unequivocally says that '[t]he old ambition of ideologies . . . to replace the market by a system of administrative allocation of goods and duties' is also discarded by '[t]he new ideology' which 'is enthusiastic about the market – but insistent that the market must be thoroughly regulated so as to guarantee a set of desired outcomes' (p. 19).

[46] O'Sullivan writes that only the adoption of the non-statist civil perspective can preserve the link between human welfare and human dignity. If, however, 'the new politics of inclusion and differ-ence' is 'accommodated . . . within an administrative rather than a civil framework . . . this would mean . . . the final replacement of the Western tradition of limited politics – the politics of dignity – by a post-modern politics of security', effectively ending 'the dream of a more genuine and more open democracy which inspires the optimistic version of post-modern politics . . . ' (p. 42).

the recipients of welfare are used, as soon as the natural diminution of wealth produced and available for redistribution will render these services clearly ineffective, the majority of the people will start supporting policies rolling the welfare-state back and energetically encouraging production of wealth. Even if this majority consisted of welfare recipients,[47] which, fortunately, is so far not the case, it would be reluctant to kill the goose laying the golden eggs and would thus most likely opt for such policies, too.

It seems to me that the time for the implementation of policies rolling the welfare state back has already come. Even the socialist parties of Western Europe, wishing to increase their electoral support, were forced since the latter part of the 1980s to adopt monetarism and public spending cuts as prominent, and even tone-setting, points of their economic policies. Furthermore, I believe that the welfare-state has passed its apex and is now in the stage of slow but sure decline. On this point I am not at all in two minds, as O'Sullivan seems to be, and am prepared to state in absolutely unambiguous terms that, according to my analysis, the welfare state is gradually approaching today its natural end. It becomes, for example, increasingly apparent to the users of the National Health Service that this Service is unable to provide anymore adequate health care, and the same could be also said about other state-run welfare institutions. These plain facts are inevitably going to motivate the people to start looking for better alternatives to the present, state-based welfare system; and I am sure, in due course, the political market will have to respond to the people's – that is that market's customers' – rising demand for a new commodity, that is for ideas on how to replace the present welfare system by a more humane and effective one which, whatever it is, will have to be, I am sure, non-statist. Before that, however, any premature attempts at doing away with the welfare state will come to nothing and will result in sending those who undertake them, as Margaret Thatcher's example eloquently shows, into the political wilderness. It was the socialism of the social-democrats which I have 'condemned to death' above; not, so far, their democratically accepted policies of social justice. I am afraid, however, that if the social-democrats insist on continuing to stick to their traditional welfare-statism, they may find themselves in as antiquated and irrelevant political situation as it was (and to some extent, or in some part, still is) the case with their socialism.

E. Feminism? Environmentalism?

Are there any other candidates for an '"ism" for the future? In his chapter Minogue says: 'Marxism and syndicalism have fallen on evil days, while feminism and environmental forms of salvation have in recent decades flourished mightily' (p. 11). Feminism, in my frame of reference, does not by itself qualify as an ideology. It could only serve, within a broader anti-capitalist ideological context, as an argument for stating that the capitalist system is inherently unable to provide for women a decent place and role in society and thus needs to be replaced by an alternative, ideologically conceived system which would, among other things, bring patriarchate to an end and ensure true equality of women with men. Without such a context, feminism turns into yet another policy item on the agenda of affirmative action which could be handled in either a more or a less radical way.

---

[47] I consider people eligible for preferential treatment under the policies of affirmative action recipients of welfare benefits, too.

'Environmental forms of salvation' are, however, different from all the other items encompassed by Minogue under the umbrella of 'the morality of egalitarian humanism', as they are equally applicable to all categories of human beings and deal with the problem of sheer physical survival of the human race as a whole. Nevertheless, Minogue in his chapter does not pay to environmentalism any special attention and neither does O'Sullivan, who simply lists ecological issues, along with sexual and racial ones, as those which were 'hitherto excluded' and which 'the "new politics" . . . postmodernism represents' seeks to 'include'. I think, however, that if one looks for a truly potent candidate to fill the ideological void the demise of Marxism produced in the contemporary world, environmentalism is the one to be singled out and identified as fully qualified to be such a candidate.

Apart from being an issue equally affecting all mankind and claiming to represent the only reliable remedy for its assured survival on this planet, environmentalism has solid philosophical roots going all way back to Jean Jacques Rousseau and his call, 'back to nature'. The Rousseauist philosophical tradition of reasoning about the relationship between nature and man, by having been extended to Edmund Husserl's phenomenology outlining the periodical conflicts between man's intentionality and the constants (and/or constraints) of the natural world, has firmly established itself in the academe as a methodological discipline covering both natural and social sciences. Husserl's disciple, the greatest German existentialist philosopher Martin Heidegger, introduced phenomenological ideas on the relationship of man and nature into every variety of modern existentialist philosophy; and Heidegger's disciple, Jean Paul Sartre, by having constructed the 'Practico-Inert' concept of the world, provided quite solid philosophical foundation for practically every environmentalist movement or organization under the sun. On the other hand, a special academic discipline, ecology, was created in order to investigate the natural environment and the damage man is inflicting on it. The best known and most influential offshoot of this rapidly expanding discipline was the Club of Rome. Created in the 1960s, it still manages to coordinate the efforts of the ecologists and other academics concerned with the environment which are directed at promoting zero economic growth and other similarly radical measures and which, they claim, are the only ones able to save mankind from self-destruction. As we see, the philosophical and academic foundations and credentials of environmentalism are as, if not more, solid as those of Marxism.

Environmentalism has the potential of becoming a full-fledged ideology not only because of this, but also because it appeals as to the highest ethical value to mankind's survival – a value, that is, to which all other values should be naturally subordinated – and is also capable of elaborating a comprehensive programme for the creation of such a new socio-political system which will be uniquely suitable effectively to protect the environment and through it mankind itself. It goes without saying that environmentalism also entails the necessity of building-up a closely knit political organization struggling for its goals and actively engaging into propaganda and other forms of proselytism; environmentalism naturally confers a special role of leadership to its 'vanguard' represented by the professional experts on ecology, too.

Environmentalist ideology is incompatible not only with capitalism, but also with every other socio-political system promoting economic growth and technological progress. In this respect it is much more radical than socialism which, as

Friedrich Nietzsche had aptly observed, differs from capitalism only in so far as it wants more of it. Turning all the way back from its modern philosophical foundations in phenomenology and existentialism to the classical primary source in Rousseau, environmentalist ideology would indeed acquire the potential to force all of us to go 'back to nature' in the very literal sense of this phrase, branding those who are likely to resist, dissent or simply manifest reluctance to follow that road not simply enemies but killers of mankind.

One should not underestimate the appeal of this ideology and its potential popularity either. Some religious groups may lend it their support and some underdeveloped countries may see in it their only chance to catch up with the more developed ones. I do not infer by so saying that this ideology will indeed become the next big menace threatening the survival of the free world. I hope it never does. But in a time of social crisis and dire stress, when people will start hungrily looking again for a simplistic, ideological-type solution to their complex and difficult problems, the environmentalist ideology will surely be standing ready for some desperate people to jump on its bandwagon and, paraphrasing Francis Fukuyama, bring us back to history again.

Index